Our New Location
309 W. Mountain Ave.

A NEW
CONVENIENT,
COMFORTABLE and
PRACTICAL STORE
We Hope You Like It

USDA Choice, trimmed just right
T-Bone Steaks 95¢ Lb.

USDA Choice, trimmed just right
Short Cut Steaks 95¢ Lb.

Bar-S or Sigman's
Wieners Lb. Pkg. **49¢**

Lean, Tender
Pork Steak Lb. **39¢**

Sigman's Best Grade, Mile Hi
Bacon Lb. **49¢**

Fancy, Quick Frozen, 5 to 7 lbs.
Roasting Chickens Lb. **39¢**

Lean, Fresh
Ground Beef 3 Lbs. $1.00

Colorado
Delicious APPLES Lb. 10¢

Colo. Jonathan, Med. Size
Apples Lb. **10¢**

California
Carrots 1 Lb. Bag **8¢**

Buttercup, Home Grown
Squash Lb. **4¢**

Colo. Red, Utility Grade
Potatoes 25 lb. Bag **59¢**

The Meat Department

re's an inside look at the spacious and modern walk in meat refrigerator while
ager, Harold Steiner, second from left, examines one of the USDA Choice sides
they'll be cutting for opening day. The three assistant professional butchers
m are Dean Toner, Wayne Ball and John P. Hill, who many folks will recognize
friend in the meat department from the Oak Street store.

SALAD DRESSING Bluhill Quart Jar 33¢

PictSweet Frozen Vegetables

mpbell's Tomato Soup ½ oz.	**10c**	Sara Lee Frozen Chocolate Cakes 14 oz. **77c**
orr up Mixes	**37c**	Sara Lee Frozen Pound Cakes, 14 oz. **77c**
lsbury cuits, Pkg.	**9c**	Morton Chocolate Cream Pies, 14 oz. **47c**
adowlake argarine	**17c**	Morton Lemon Cream Pies, 14 oz. **47c**

Northern Tissue, 4 for	**32c**
Kaiser Foil, 25 feet	**22c**
DuPont Medium Size Sponges, 2 for	**22c**
Simonize Floor Wax, ½ Gal.	**1¹⁵**

**PEAS
CUT CORN
CUT BROCCOLI
MIXED
VEGETABLES**

10-oz. Pkg. **15¢**

Secret Recipes
from the
Corner Market

recipes by **Carol Ann Kates**
the "Authority" on Ingredient Shopping

"Thanks to the many distributors and manufacturers
I had the pleasure of working with over the years.
While my use of specific brand names constitutes
an endorsement of the quality of certain products,
substitutions should not result
in a significantly different outcome."
—CAROL ANN KATES

PUBLISHED BY:
Penny Lane Press of Colorado
1518 Brentford Lane
Fort Collins, CO 80525-4703
katescarol@aol.com

COPYRIGHT: 2007 © Carol Ann Kates
DESIGN BY: F + P Graphic Design, Inc., Fort Collins, CO

ALL RIGHTS RESERVED
ISBN: 0-9773485-0-4
LIBRARY OF CONGRESS CONTROL NUMBER 2005908584
Second edition
Printed in China by Favorite Recipes Press

Dedication

This book is dedicated in loving memory of:

My father, *Merrill Seth Steele,* a simple, hard-working grocer, who taught me the importance of using only the freshest ingredients in the meals I prepare.

My mother, *Ellen Pauline Allen Steele,* an accomplished cook, who taught me the satisfaction of perfecting simple recipes.

My aunt, *Beryl Mae Allen Henry,* a woman with class and style, who taught me to nurture the food I prepare with tender loving care.

My uncle, *Edgar Parkins Henry,* an expert butcher, who taught me to appreciate a good steak and cook prime rib to perfection.

My grandmother, *Olive Amelia McNary Steele,* a consummate hostess, who taught me the joy of having special treats tucked away to share with company.

My grandmother, *Gladys Loveall Finch,* whose playful spirit, taught me the fun of having secret ingredients.

and in loving devotion to: My husband, *Russell Keith Kates,* who has always been a pleasure to cook for.

This recipe collection and bits of food wisdom are gifted to my children and grandchildren: Jennifer Ellen Kates, Brian Merrill Kates, Alisa Anne (Leelee) Kates, and Aliyah Jordan Kates-Kirkes.

Acknowledgements

With gratitude to my sponsors:

Chelsea Milling Co., Mr. Howdy Holmes

Eggceptional Concepts, Inc., Rayno and Patty Seaser

Gulley Greenhouse & Garden Center, Jan and Jim Gulley

Inteccorp, Inc., Ms. Karen Deitesfeld

Sharon and David Neenan

With thanks to the team:

Ron Jackson, former advertising director for Steele's Markets, suggested I include recipes in our weekly advertisement in the Fort Collins *Coloradoan* in the early 1990s. Had it not been for his encouragement, this recipe collection would not have been created. Thanks also go to Donna Visocky who took Ron's position when he retired and continued to assist me with this project. To the numerous talented chefs from Carol Ann's Deli, I am proud of the secret recipes you so lovingly created, and I am delighted to share them with your fans.

I owe a special debt of gratitude to Susan Stuessie whose professional expertise saw value in the publication of this collection and to Nancy Hansford who has encouraged me for many years to write.

Special thanks to Harleen Alexander who agreed early on to create artwork for this book, but whose untimely accident led her on another journey. My best wishes to her as she recovers. I am ever so grateful to Christie Martell, who stepped in for Harleen and produced the perfect cover for this book in an amazingly short period of time.

I extend my heartfelt appreciation to Rebecca Finkel, my book designer, whose patience and perseverance helped me see this project to completion. Although tempted, she never threw "in a small bowl" back at me.

To my editors for their countless hours of reading and scrutinizing my text, I extend my appreciation to Kathy Willard, Pamela Wyman, Teresa McElroy, Karen Boehler, Pam Fellers, Mary Jo Faith Morgan, and Helen Collela. Thank you for your eagle eyes.

And, last but not least, my family. All my recipes are "kid tested and father approved." Thank you for making the creation of this recipe collection such a pleasure and for your undying support through the thick and thin of compiling my endeavors into a book.

Project Self-Sufficiency

A portion of the proceeds from the sale of this book benefit Project Self-Sufficiency.

Project Self-Sufficiency (PS-S) is a community-based organization that assists single parent families in Larimer County, Colorado. Program participants are guided by professional staff in creating and implementing a Self-Sufficiency Action Plan that becomes their road map for success. At the heart of the program is a caring atmosphere that promotes healthy family functioning and living wage employment. Expert career planning and job search assistance are offered.

Single parents who are enrolled in Project Self-Sufficiency face many barriers, both practical and personal, as they move toward goal accomplishment. In order to assist participants in addressing barriers, the following creative programs have been established by the organization: volunteer car repair, the "Cars for Families" donation program, a special scholarship fund with some dollars set aside for child care, an emergency fund, a career closet, donated computers, a printer loan pool, sponsorship of mental health evaluations and treatment, self-esteem classes, parenting classes designed just for single parents, and housing for twenty families.

The children of single parents are given a positive start in life through a number of programs that encourage their healthy development, safety, positive attitudes toward school, and happy holidays in December. These programs include the Boundless Children's Fund to assist with gymnastics, music lessons, and other classes; the "Cool Kids" back-to-school clothing program; "Kid Power" abuse prevention; and holiday sponsorships and parties.

We would like to share a success story with you. Everyone at Project Self-Sufficiency is truly proud of Katie. When she came to PS-S she had many years of experience as a waitress and assistant manager for a restaurant. When she became a mother, she was concerned about her ability to support her son on her own. With help from her PS-S advisor,

Katie chose a career in radiology technology. She endured many years of hard work to complete prerequisite classes, demanding radiology tech course work, and long hours of clinical experience. Katie graduated with honors in May, 2005, from the Aims Community College Radiology Technology Program. Her young son, mother, sister, brother, and other family members where there with her to celebrate.

Katie earned a President's Medallion with her 4.0. She was also "Student of the Year" for the Radiology Department at Aims. Even better, Katie was hired by a local medical center as a Radiology Technologist and started work just a few days after graduation.

For more information about Project Self-Sufficiency visit www.ps-s.org or call 970.635.5901.

Table of Contents

Introduction iv

History of Markets. vi

Appetizers 1

Salads. 17

Soups 43

Sandwiches and Pizza 69

Chicken and Poultry 89

Turkey 117

Pork 127

Beef and Lamb. 151

Fish and Seafood. 183

Side Dishes 217

Pasta 239

Mexican 264

One Dish Meals 261

Desserts 285

Selecting Superior Produce . . . 297

From Carol Ann's Deli 349

Index 391

Bibliography 396

Order Form 397

Merrill Steele (center), Longley's Market,
Eaton, Colorado, circa 1935

Robert, Merrill, Pauline
and Carol Ann Steele,
circa 1955

Introduction

Born the daughter of a simple grocer, I grew up in the corner market environment, living and breathing the grocery business. Over the years, I learned how to select superior products much like other children learn the alphabet. My father taught me my most valuable lesson about cooking. Great food begins with shopping. The quality of the ingredients used when preparing a meal is just as important as the recipe.

I spent the majority of my adult life owning and operating supermarkets and delis in Northern Colorado. This cookbook contains a collection of the recipes I created, adapted, and perfected for the Steele's Market weekly ad in the Fort Collins *Coloradoan*. These recipes provided our customers with creative ways to use items that were on special. Brand names used in the recipes are the result of items included in the ad. I also revived and included our customer's favorite secret recipes from Carol Ann's Deli.

Russell and Carol Kates, Robert Steele, 1992

A major focus of this collection is the proper selection and storing of ingredients. Only when the ingredients are exceptional will the meal be truly superb. The proper storage of food not only enhances its quality but also ensures its safety. In *Secret Recipes from the Corner Market* I give readers very personal advice about shopping—the same advice I used to give the customers patronizing our market.

Packed full of anecdotes about the history of food and the corner market, this cookbook is a celebration of the life and times of Steele's Markets and its founder, my father, Merrill Steele, and a tribute to the dwindling presence of corner markets all across America.

❦ From Carol Ann's Kitchen ❦
Carol Ann's Broccoli Souffle

1/2 pound fresh broccoli
1 teaspoon minced garlic
2 tablespoons butter
2 tablespoons flour
1 cup milk

Preheat oven to 350 degrees. Wash broccoli... medium-sized pan with just enough water... boil broccoli about 7 minutes. Drain broccoli... in a small saucepan over low heat. Add... minutes over low heat, stirring constantly... constantly to prevent lumps. When well... thickened. Season with salt and pepper... Slightly beat egg yolks. Add a third of... Then add yolks slowly to remainder of... Beat egg whites until stiff and batter to... the sauce, then fold in the remainder. P... Place in a pan of hot water and bake at... lightly browned on top.

❦ From Carol Ann's Kitchen ❦
Pauline's Potato Salad

This is my mother's recipe for potato salad. She got it from her mother. My grandmother, mother and aunt all made potato salad just like this. I have always thought that it was the best ever; but, of course, I was always prejudiced to my mother's cooking. My mother and grandmother always said that the secret ingredient in potato salad is celery seed. *Please look for Pauline's Potato Salad in Carol Ann's Deli this week.*

6 medium potatoes, peeled, cooked
  and cubed
8 hard-boiled eggs, cubed
6 green onions, chopped
1 1/2 tsp. salt

3/4 tsp. large-grind black pepper
1 cup mayonnaise
1 Tbsp. Dijon mustard
3/4 cup pickle relish
1 1/2 tsp. celery seed

Combine mayonnaise, mustard, pickle relish, salt, pepper and celery seed. Add cubed potatoes, eggs and green onions, and mix carefully and thoroughly. Chill for at least four hours. Makes 8 servings.

History

While clergy nourish the souls of their community, my father provided the sustenance that nourished their bodies. He spent his days as a purveyor of food stuffs, stocking grocery shelves with canned goods and tending the produce he sold with gentle devotion.

Born December 13, 1910, on a farm south of Ashland, Kansas, Merrill Seth Steele moved to Greeley, Colorado, in 1926 with his father, Seth Robert Steele, mother, Olive Amelia McNary Steele, three brothers, George Edward, Robert Eugene, and Albert Lee, and two sisters, Evis Vesta and Elma Effie. Although a farmer at heart, Merrill began his grocery career as a sacker and meat cutter in a small corner market in Greeley, a teenage school boy looking for work.

Merrill Steele   *Albert Steele*

During the early years of the Depression, circa 1931, O. P. Skaggs hired my father as a store manager in Denver, Colorado. The Skaggs family owned and operated markets in ten western states. Their business genius founded the forerunners of today's retail giants Safeway and Rite Aid. Working for Skaggs was not an easy task for up-and-coming-young store managers who were thrown into the aisles with only two instructions: "Polish the apples and don't lose any money."

My father worked about a year for O. P. Skaggs then moved to the small farming town of Eaton, Colorado, where he worked for Longley's Market. Surviving meagerly on a diet of bread and cheese, Merrill saved his pennies for eight years to accumulate enough cash to purchase a business that sold merchandise salvaged from train wreckage. He opened Steele's Cash Food Markets in 1940, at age 29, with his brother, Albert, age 21.

Since credit cards didn't exist in the 1930s and 1940s, many grocers permitted their customers to run a tab. This practice allowed many familes to survive during this difficult time. Markets that included the phrase "Cash and Carry" in their name "carried" their customers via a charge account until they could provide the "cash" to pay. Our market was "cash" only. The brothers' explanation for only accepting cash: "If we're not

Steele's Cash Food Market, 113 East Oak Street, Fort Collins, Colorado, circa 1945

involved in the lending business and not charging interest on what's owed, we can give our customers lower prices."

AL STEELE

Steele's Cash Market opened with forty corner markets vying for grocery dollars in a town with a population of 12,251—stiff competition. To compete, corner markets provided exceptional and very personal customer service. Today, sackers ask if we'd like help out to our cars. In the 1940s, carry-out service meant your groceries were carried home, your canned goods were put in the pantry, and your perishables in the icebox.

Each little market had a personality all its own, as the independent grocery owner wore his heart on his sleeve. When you walked through the turnstiles of a grocery store, the owner's individual style bounced off every nook and cranny, so shoppers patronized a market where they felt right at home.

My father and uncle shunned glamour, so the first Steele's was a simple, no frills establishment where efficiency ruled, and the slogan "Lowest Average Price Everyday" governed all decisions of consequence. As young children, my father explained this important pricing philosophy to us: "There are items some grocery stores price below their wholesale cost to fool their customers into thinking they have low prices— like mayonnaise, ketchup, and bananas. But items like pickles are priced for profit—a big profit. We believe all products should have the same percentage mark up. That's why it says 'Lowest Average Price Everyday' on our building. We calculate our operating costs and price all items with the same percentage mark up so we cover our operating costs and make only a 'fair' profit."

Merrill Steele tending the produce he sold.

Markets in the 1940s averaged about 5,000 square feet in size. We owned a smaller one. The aisles were so narrow shoppers could only travel in one direction. This market had a white metal ceiling that looked as if it had survived a severe case of hail damage. White metal molding capped plain white walls. Cans stocked meticulously in pyramid fashion crept up the walls from the shelf tops and said: "This market is operated by perfectionists. See how precisely we're balanced." The wooden floor, worn bare in many spots, had been trampled down from years of use. No fancy light fixtures illuminated the store, just simple light bulbs spaced evenly in a grid-like pattern. Air conditioning was unheard of, but Steele's Cash Food Market did have ceiling fans to keep stale air circulating.

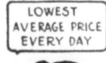

MERRILL STEELE

The most notable feature was the bargain bin—home to the weekly advertised specials. Positioned at the rear of the store, constructed out of cheap plywood, and painted brown, this homely, wooden, six-foot long contraption became our customers' favorite spot. No aimless wandering to find the weekly specials. Our sale items were located in one convenient place. My father used to say, "Keeping that 'bargain bin' stocked is like feeding a hungry horse with an eyedropper—it has a beginning but the end is no where in sight."

The Steele's Bargain Bin— always a customer favorite

My fondest memory of the original Steele's on Oak Street is the donut machine. Stationed next to the entrance, the alluring smell of frying fritters seduced any one passing by. The donut ladies, Martha Bennett and Agnus Daffin, mixed the ingredients for the dough. Their magic hands poured the dough into a funnel on top of the machine. Then, this inventive contraption measured out the exact amount of dough required for a single donut by compressing the batter through a donut-shaped mold. The dough dropped into individual holding cells that rotated in a circular pattern in hot grease. This apparatus held and fried a dozen donuts at a time. When the donuts had traveled full circle in the sizzling grease, a hidden spatula would pop up and flip them over so their other side could be fried. Once the cooking process was complete, a donut lady would remove the donuts, dip them in frosting, and top them with chopped nuts, shredded coconut, or candy sprinkles.

Many a youngster stood spellbound observing this process. More importantly, if you were present when the donuts came out of the fryer but before they'd been iced, the donut lady would let you select your favorite frosting and topping. In my childhood, a good day meant eating a donut from the donut machine.

On my childhood visits to the market, my father could either be found checking or working in his office. Two check stands, which consisted of bulky, splinter-infested counters and separate register stands, reeked of efficiency. In those days, cashiers punched keys to ring up an order. To charge a customer 29 cents meant simultaneously pushing the 20 cent key and the 9 cent key. These registers only rang as high as $5, but this accommodated 1940s prices. Cigarettes cost a dime a pack; lemons, 19 cents a dozen; lard, 10 cents a pound; sugar, a nickel a pound; a bar of Ivory soap, a dime; and all soft drinks were a nickel a bottle. The registers calculated only three types of transactions—cash, for customer orders, no sale, to open the register, and paid out, for compensating vendors for delivered merchandise. These registers did not have the capability to tally sales tax, sales by department, or track inventory.

But despite the simplicity of the times, the check stands were still congested. An adding machine positioned at the end of one counter served as back up to ring up orders when customer lines got too long. Storage bins held cardboard boxes for packing up groceries since the brown grocery bag was used sparingly in the 1940s and 1950s.

If we didn't find my father in the check stands, he'd be in his office. A trip to this cubbyhole was an interesting adventure. Makeshift stairs, crammed inside pint-size quarters that required adults to hunch over, twisted up to a rickety catwalk that stretched precariously over the back room. While this bridge leading to the office had hand railings on either side to steady any pedestrian, it shook when you walked across it. I'm sure the sheer sight of such a structure would cause today's Occupational Safety and Health inspectors to start ticketing. Employees summoned to the office literally walked the gangplank.

The office loomed over the market from its second-story perch. A lattice-work window provided a bird's eye view of the goings on below, allowing my dad and Uncle Albert to work in their office while still keeping a close eye on business. A stalwart black safe with a crank handle stood sentry in the corner protecting our cash. Hanging a bit off center the only wall decoration was a calendar picturing Marilyn Monroe, half clad and voluptuous, ruby lips puckered into a seductive greeting. As a young girl, I avoided looking at this embarrassing photo, dumbfounded that such a picture hung in our market.

The back room, a grocerman's Stonehenge, was a maze of cardboard boxes stacked up like pillars as high as a grown man could reach. A conveyor belt stretched along the back wall, transporting boxes unloaded from the truck to their place among the columns or to the basement, the store's main warehouse. Positioned on the north wall, a long narrow sink functioned as produce prep area and a wooden counter as work space for packaging bulk foods like flour and sugar.

The dark, dank, and mysterious basement smelled tomb-like and foreboding. Wall-to-wall rows of boxes, organized with the same precision as a troop of marching soldiers, stretched the full length of this cellar. Yet despite its orderly appearance, shadows lurked in every corner.

The important task of egg candling took place in the basement. Farmers delivered eggs from the chicken coop directly to the market often in exchange for merchandise. Determining if these eggs were salable became the market's sole responsibility. I remember the egg candler as a simple wooden box about one-foot square. A peep hole provided a glimpse into the candler where a cup-shaped egg holder sat inside about three inches from the hole. Positioned a few inches behind the cup was a light bulb. The task of candling required that each individual egg be placed by hand into the cup. By switching on the light bulb and peering through the peep hole, a grocer could see shapes inside the egg's shell. If a solid mass was present, it meant an embryo had developed, and the egg was discarded.

Stealing has historically been a significant problem for grocers. In fact, today the average supermarket loses over a quarter of a million dollars annually from pilferage. Since most supermarkets work on a one to two percent profit margin, a significant theft problem can cause a corner market to close its doors. To combat this today, supermarket owners install high-tech security systems to monitor vulnerable theft areas. But back then, grocers used the store's attic for surveillance.

When my father thought we were mature enough to keep secrets, he showed us the market's security system. "You can't tell anyone about this place. When cash is missing, this is where we watch to find out who is stealing."

Merrill Steele, circa 1964

Typical of unfinished attics, the floor consisted of two-by-fours spaced every foot or so and separated by insulation. Planks of wood stretched across the two-by-fours to an area just above the registers where a piece of plywood had been strategically situated. A hole had been poked through the ceiling, providing anyone laying on the plywood full view of the registers below.

On the occasion when enough cash was missing to worry my father, he would appear to leave the store in the evening like he was going home for supper. But instead, he would slip into the alley, climb a telephone pole that carried him to the store's roof, and enter the attic through a heating unit that sat on top of the market. He'd tip toe across the planks to the spot just above the cash registers and lay down, quietly watching through the peep hole, to see who helped themselves to the store's cash. His explanation for doing this: protecting his livelihood. "I want to catch the real culprit and not mistakenly accuse anyone of stealing."

When Steele's opened, it didn't have a frozen foods section. A small freezer case was added in the late 1940s. We did have a small dairy case where milk was sold in bottles and butter in wooden cartons. We had a meat department and a walk-in cooler where sides of beef hung from hooks. In those days, butchers cut every piece of meat sold in our market. If you needed a special cut, the butcher would custom cut your order right off the carcass. Meat was cut on wooden butcher blocks, unheard of in today's markets, and the floor was covered with saw dust to absorb any bloody drippings.

My Uncle George, a World War II Marine, was called to serve in the Korean War. When he returned in 1952, he and my dad bought Longley's Market in Eaton, Colorado. Under George's leadership, Steele's Food Store provided the sustenance that nourished the bodies of the Eaton community for over two decades.

In June, 1956, my father purchased the Franklin School building erected in 1886–87. His public comments regarding the purchase: "I bought the site for investment purposes and plans for the property remained indefinite." Construction of the Mountain Avenue store did not begin until 1962, and this location opened for business in November of 1963.

The new Mountain Avenue store seemed monstrous at the time—a full 11,000 square feet in size. The building, also, housed a 2,000 square-foot bakery, owned and operated by Russell Hamilton, and a 720 square-foot beauty shop, owned and operated by Nell Muhrer. The parking lot accommodated 85 cars. Customers appreciated this addition as the Oak Street store did not have a parking lot. This modern new store had wider aisles (at least customers could travel in two directions), five check stands, and a large frozen foods section. Now that's not surprising considering the increasing number of frozen items bombarding the American consumer.

The opening ad promoted this new location as providing every known convenience to make shopping at Steele's the comfortable, convenient, and practical way to buy groceries in Fort Collins. Aisles were easily identified to speed the housewife in a hurry. Five check stands and beautiful decor added comfort for the lady who had time to browse and shop for the numerous bargains on name-brand items priced to fit her budget.

My father began planning another location in the early 1970s. This facility, opened in May, 1974. This 38,000 square-foot supermarket contained

George Steele and the Eaton store

ten check stands, an expanded frozen foods section, and a modern service and self-service meat department managed by Kenneth Walsh.

State-of-the art for its time, this market had seven-foot wide aisles and the parking lot accommodated 250 cars. For the first time in 1974, Steele's began selling chef-prepared foods, offering their customers a new convenience. The Steele's kitchen prepared homemade potato salad, Jell-O®, and coleslaw daily. Valuing the importance of fresh fruits and vegetables, produce buyers purchased the pick of the crop as soon as it became available. Store hours were 8.00 a.m. to 8:30 p.m. week days, and we were closed on Sundays.

My dad passed away in October, 1979, leaving his son, Robert, and wife, Pauline, to continue the traditions he had established. Robert managed the Foothills location, and Pauline oversaw operations at Mountain.

My mother died September 8, 1974. After her death, my husband, Russ, and I joined the firm. The second generation took the reins in a competitive and brutal environment.

Steele's Cash Market on Mountain Avenue, 1963

Foothills store, May, 1974

Inundated by the continual arrival of new products to the grocery shelves, the Foothills location was remodeled in 1984 to increase shelf space for all the latest food fads and to add a seafood department and a full-fledged, sit-down deli.

Feeling the effects of intensifying competition from chain stores, the family decided that increasing its market share was paramount in remaining competitive in the market place. In 1985, the Mountain location was remodeled, expanding the store to 17,000 square feet and adding a delicatessen. Steele's puchased the on-site bakeries, owned and operated by Ed and Thelma Fleener in 1987.

Russ and Carol Kates with Robert Steele, Foothills office

An additional location in Windsor was acquired in 1989. In order to provide the people of Windsor with more services, this building was remodeled on two separate occasions.

In 1991, the family partnered with Ed Horejs, a local pharmacist to incorporate in-store pharmacies in its facilities.

By the end of the 1980s, chain stores had increased their focus on general merchandise and non-food items, like pet food and cosmestics, prepared take-home entrees and salads, and ethnic and natural foods. To stay abreast of the changing industry, the family built another state-of-the-art facility. This 43,000-square foot supermarket, designed to give customers a one-stop shopping experience, included a pharmacy, dry clearners, post office, and video department. The expanded sit-down deli even included Chinese take-out.

Still feeling the pinch of mounting pressure from chain stores, the family believed that annual sales needed to exceed 100 million dollars to compete with warehouse club stores and mass merchandisers. To accomplish this end, two additional locations were acquired in 1998—one in Fort Morgan and the other in Niwot, Colorado.

Following extensive research of all the latest services available in supermarkets, a state-of-the-art facility opened in December, 1998. With over 63,000 square feet and 8-foot wide aisles, this market had room to stock any product imaginable and had a modern, fully equipped home-meal replacement department that provided time-starved customers with a healthy alternative to fast food. While the focus was still on comfort, convenience, and exceptional customer service, the family added a new dimension to the shopping experience—fun. The dairy section came complete with cows that mooed and chickens that clucked. The customer of the 21st century wanted to be entertained. The professionally designed interior had a farm motif and a down-home country feel.

Over the course of the 20th century, Steele's, like all corner markets, evolved and changed to meet the needs of its customers. The past teaches us that the format of the market will change, companies will come and go, but food will always be produced, distributed, and consumed by a society whose needs are always changing.

For over six decades, the Steele family provided the sustenance that nourished the bodies of its community, constantly adapting to the ever-changing market place and shifts in the eating habits of the American people, yet steadfast in its desire to remain true to the basic principles of its founder.

Ed Fleener, master baker

Steele's Bakery cake decorators

Carol Ann's Deli—Foothills location

Left: Steele's Windsor Market was acquired in 1989. Above: Windsor produce department.

Left: Steele's Harmony Market, 1991; Above: Betty Swann helps a customer, Mountain Pharmacy

Steele's Niwot Market, 1998

Courtesy Fort Collins Public Library

Drake Steele's store, 1998; Above: Carol Ann's Kitchen

Dairy Products and Cheese.   3

Baked Brie.   5

Cream Cheese Holiday Wreath.   5

Warm Artichoke Dip with Asiago Cheese Bread.   6

Carol Ann's "Super Bowl" Dip.   7

"Super Bowl" Super Nachos   8

Carol Ann's Layered Mexican Dip   9

Shrimp and Scallop Salsa.   10

Russ' Fool-Proof Hot Wings   11

Carol Ann's Blue Cheese Dressing.   11

Smoked Salmon Quesadillas   12

Crab Cakes with a Pineapple Salsa   13

Four Cheese Fondue   14

Three Cheese Toasts with Sun-Dried Tomatoes.   15

Carol Ann's Spinach Dip   15

Focaccia Bread with Tomatoes and Mozzarella   16

These appetizers are perfect for entertaining.

Tips for Buying and Storing Dairy Products

Shopping

Like all perishables, dairy products should be one of the last items you purchase. Dairy products should be cold to the touch when you put them in your cart. Also, when selecting dairy products, pick containers that have not been damaged in any way or that leak.

It is important to check dates to be sure products have not expired. If your market continually has close-dated product, it is a sign that items are not selling quickly enough to ensure freshness.

The "Sell-By" date is the last day the manufacturer recommends a product be sold. While milk may still be good a few days after this date, buy dairy products that have at least 7 days before they reach their "Sell-By" date. The "Best if Used By" date means that the manufacturer does not feel the product will be safe to consume after that date. Never buy dairy products that are at or passed this date.

Checking Out

It is usually when you reach the check stand that you discover whether any dairy products you've selected have leaks. If you have product that leaks, insist that the cashier get you a replacement. Ask the sacker to bag all your dairy products in the same bag. This helps product stay cooler on the ride home and makes the job of putting your groceries away easier.

Using and Storing Dairy Products at Home

Refrigerate your dairy products as soon as you get home. Shelf-stable milk can be stored in your pantry but should be refrigerated as soon as it is opened.

Containers of dairy products should be tightly closed after use and put immediately back into the refrigerator. Never leave dairy products out on your kitchen counter any longer than necessary and never more than 2 hours. Once opened, butter should be covered while stored in the refrigerator. If you've put milk or cream in a pitcher for serving, don't return unused product back to its original container.

Freezing Butter

If your supermarket has a special on butter and you buy a large quantity, it can be frozen for later use. To freeze butter, wrap it tightly in aluminum foil or place it in ziplock freezer bags.

Safe Refrigeration Times

Butter, opened	1 to 2 weeks	Butter, frozen	6 to 9 months
Margarine, opened	4 to 6 months	Half-and-Half, opened	10 days
Milk, opened	5 days	Sour Cream, opened	2 to 4 weeks
Cream: light, heavy, table, whipping	10 days	Yogurt, opened	7 to 10 days
		Frozen Yogurt, unopened	6 weeks

Tips for Buying and Storing Cheese

Shopping

Buy only pasteurized solid cheese. If unpasteurized milk is used in making hard cheese, the package should be marked "aged 60 days" or longer. Don't buy moldy cheeses, with the exception of some blue cheeses or expensive Brie that ripen with harmless molds.

Using and Storing Cheese at Home

Cheese should be refrigerated immediately upon arriving home. Store it in the original package until opened. After opening, rewrap cheese in moisture-proof wrap like aluminum foil, an airtight container, or a zip-lock bag. Keep your cheese in your meat and cheese drawer where it will not be exposed to light.

When mold appears on solid cheese, cut off the mold, along with a half-inch piece surrounding it. What remains should be safe to consume.

Cheese should be served at its recommended serving temperature, which will vary according to type of cheese. Moist, soft cheese, like cottage cheese or mozzarella, should not be left out of the refrigerator for longer than 2 hours.

Freezing Cheese

Hard, natural cheeses can be frozen. Cut into 1-inch thick, 1-pound sections and wrap tightly in plastic. Frozen cheese will keep for 6 to 8 weeks and should be thawed in the refrigerator. Allow 1 to 2 days for cheese to thaw. It loses some of its texture during freezing and, therefore, should be used for cooking.

Safe Refrigeration Times

Cottage cheese, opened	10 to 30 days
Cream or Neufchatel cheese, opened	2 weeks
Hard or wax-coated cheeses like	
Cheddar, Edam, Gouda, or Swiss: unopened	3 to 6 months
opened	3 to 4 weeks
sliced	1 to 2 weeks
Ricotta cheese, opened	5 days
Processed cheese food products	3 to 4 weeks

Baked Brie

SERVES 6

Simple to prepare and delicious. A perfect hors d'oeuvres for the holidays.

1 whole mini Brie or Camembert (15-ounces)
1 tablespoon butter, cut into thin slices
2 tablespoons slivered almonds
2 tablespoons brown sugar

Preheat the oven to 350 degrees. Place cheese on an ovenproof serving dish, cover with a moist paper towel, and bake for 10 minutes. Remove the paper towel. Top with butter and almonds and sprinkle with brown sugar. Broil 6 inches from the heat until bubbly, watching closely to prevent burning. Brown sugar will caramelize very quickly. Serve immediately with thin slices of sourdough baguettes or water crackers.

*L*egend has it that the French Emperor, Charlemagne, first tasted Brie at a monastery in Reuil-en-Brie during the eighth century. Charlemagne fell instantly in love with this soft, creamy cheese. The favorites of kings soon become the favorites of us common folk.

Cream Cheese Holiday Wreath

MAKES ABOUT 4 CUPS

Coating the cream cheese with parsley instead of nuts gives the wreath a festive flair. Make a holiday bow from red pepper strips as a special garnish.

Brie has its best flavor when perfectly ripe. Select one that is plump and resilient to the touch. Its rind may show some pale brown edges. Ripened Brie has a short life and should be eaten within a few days.

2 packages (8-ounces) cream cheese, softened
1 package (3-ounces) cream cheese, softened
½ cup jarred roasted sweet red peppers, drained
1 teaspoon minced garlic
½ teaspoon salt
½ pound bacon, crisply fried and crumbled
½ cup smoked almonds, chopped
½ cup green onions, thinly sliced
Fresh parsley, snipped

In a food processor, blend cream cheese, roasted red peppers, garlic, and salt until smooth. Add bacon, almonds, and green onions and process until combined. Cover and refrigerate 1 hour. On a serving platter, spoon cream cheese mixture into a circle. With hands, mold into a smooth wreath shape (mixture will be soft). Coat the wreath with parsley. Cover with plastic wrap and refrigerate until firm. Serve with crackers.

Warm Artichoke Dip
with Asiago Cheese Bread

MAKES 1 LOAF AND 4 CUPS OF DIP

The Rock Bottom Brewery in Denver serves this on their appetizer menu. I tried it one evening and found it delicious. I recreated it at home. This one is addictive!

FOR THE ASIAGO CHEESE BREAD

2 cups all-purpose flour
2 teaspoons baking powder
1 tablespoon sugar
½ teaspoon salt
8 tablespoons butter
1 cup grated Asiago cheese
½ cup green onions, thinly sliced
1 teaspoon dried dill weed
¾ cup milk + 2 tablespoons milk
2 eggs, lightly beaten
1 teaspoon minced garlic

Preheat the oven to 350 degrees. Grease a 9-inch loaf pan. In a large bowl, combine flour, baking powder, sugar, and salt. Using a fork, cut in butter until the mixture resembles coarse crumbs. Blend in cheese, green onions, and dill. In a small bowl, combine milk, egg, and garlic and pour into the flour mixture. Stir just until the flour mixture is moistened. Pour into the loaf pan. Bake for 50 to 60 minutes, or until the top is golden brown and the loaf shrinks slightly away from the sides of the pan. Let bread cool 10 minutes before removing. Serve warm with Warm Artichoke Dip.

FOR THE DIP

1 can (14-ounces) water-packed artichoke hearts, drained and chopped
1 cup sour cream
1 cup mayonnaise
1 cup grated Asiago cheese
½ cup green onions, thinly sliced
Cayenne pepper to taste

Preheat the oven to 350 degrees. Combine artichoke hearts, sour cream, mayonnaise, Asiago cheese, and green onions in a small baking dish. Season to taste with cayenne pepper. Mix thoroughly. Place in an oven-proof baking dish and bake about 20 minutes, or until heated through.

The invention of mayonnaise is credited to the French chef of Duke Richelieu in 1756. While the Duke was off fighting the British at Port Mahonnaise, his chef was at home preparing a victory feast. Realizing he had no cream in the kitchen with which to make a sauce, the chef used olive oil instead. He named the new culinary masterpiece "Mahonnaise" in honor of the Duke's victory over the British.

Don't forget to pick up Asiago cheese. It's the secret ingredient. Asiago is a semi-firm Italian cheese. It comes in small wheels with glossy rinds. It's yellow interior has many small holes. Young Asiago is a table cheese. When aged over a year, it becomes hard enough for grating. You can find shredded Asiago cheese in the deli cheese section at your supermarket. I prefer DiGiorno®.

6

Carol Ann's "Super Bowl" Dip

MAKES ABOUT 3 CUPS DIP

*I*n the grocery business the Super Bowl is like an important holiday. When the Broncos played in the Super Bowl, Steele's got hammered. That's grocery lingo for "sales were beyond expectations." You need real food to cheer for your favorite team. Go, Broncos!

1 round, firm loaf unsliced sourdough bread, about 8 to 10 inches in diameter
1 round, firm loaf sliced sourdough bread, about 8 to 10 inches in diameter
4 tablespoons olive oil
2 tablespoons butter, melted

FOR THE BREAD BOWL AND BREAD CUBES

Preheat the oven to 350 degrees. Slice off the top of unsliced loaf of bread and set aside. Hollow out the insides with a small paring knife, leaving a ½-inch thick shell. Cut the removed bread into 1-inch cubes, or larger. Cut sliced loaf into 1-inch cubes, or larger. In a small bowl combine olive oil and butter. Brush bread cubes with the oil mixture until evenly coated. Place cubes on a cookie sheet and bake for 10 to 15 minutes, turning once, until golden brown. Remove from the oven and set aside.

FOR THE DIP

½ cup sour cream
1 cup shredded Cheddar cheese
1 package (8-ounces) cream cheese, softened
½ cup chopped green onions
1 can (4-ounces) mild green chile peppers, chopped and drained
1 teaspoon Worcestershire® sauce

In a large bowl, combine sour cream, Cheddar cheese, cream cheese, green onions, green chile peppers, and Worcestershire® sauce. Mix well. Spoon the dip into hollowed bread. Replace the top of loaf. Wrap filled loaf with several layers of aluminum foil. Set loaf on a cookie sheet and bake at 350 degrees for 1 hour and 10 minutes, or until the cheese filling is melted and heated through. To serve, remove the foil wrapping and put loaf on a serving dish with bread cubes arranged around it for dipping.

"Super Bowl" Super Nachos

SERVES 6 TO 12

½ pound chorizo sausage
½ pound lean ground beef
¾ cup white onion, chopped
1 can (16-ounces) refried beans
Your favorite tortilla chips
2 cups shredded Monterey Jack cheese, or to taste
2 cups shredded Cheddar cheese, or to taste

Remove casing from chorizo sausage. In a large heavy skillet, place chorizo sausage, ground beef, and onion and sauté over medium heat until meat is lightly browned. Drain off grease.

Preheat the oven to broil. Spread refried beans evenly on a large oven-proof platter, about 10 X 15 inches, and top with tortilla chips, forming a peak in the center of the platter. Spread the meat mixture evenly over tortilla chips and then smother with shredded cheeses, evenly covering as many tortilla chips as possible. Place the platter about 5 inches beneath the broiler and cook until cheese is melted and bubbly.

GARNISHES

1 cup of your favorite salsa
¼ cup green onions, thinly sliced
Pickled jalapeño slices, to taste
1 can (2¼-ounces) sliced black olives
Carol Ann's guacamole, see recipe on Page 266.
Sour cream

Drizzle salsa over nachos and garnish with green onions, pickled jalapeño slices, and sliced black olives. Mound guacamole and sour cream on top of nachos. Serve immediately.

To compete with the chains, independent grocers have promotional events to not only attract customers but to make the grocery shopping experience more fun. For example, in the late 1980s, Steele's invited Tony Dorsett, Sammy Winder, and Steve Watson for an autograph signing party. Customers lined up a block long.

To keep tortilla chips fresh, store them in an air-tight container in a cool, dark place.

Chorizo sausage comes in a casing, which should be removed before using. To remove the casing: use a sharp knife to make a full-length slit down the sausage and peel off the casing.

Carol Ann's Layered Mexican Dip

SERVES 12

I've been making layered dip for years. My guests never tire of this one.

Dave Pace began bottling salsa in 1947. He perfected his formula and began selling it commercially in grocery stores in 1948. Salsa sales skyrocketed in the 1970s and exploded during the 1980s. By 1991, U. S. sales of salsa outsold ketchup by $40 million.

1 package (8-ounces) cream cheese, softened
2 cups sour cream
1 package (¼-ounce) Old El Paso® Taco Seasoning Mix
3 avocados
2 tablespoons lemon juice
Lettuce leaves, washed and dried
2 plus cups shredded Cheddar or Colby cheese
1 tomato, diced
6 green onions, chopped
1 can (2¼-ounces) sliced black olives
Your favorite tortilla chips
Your favorite salsa

In a large bowl, blend cream cheese, sour cream, and taco seasoning mix until evenly mixed and set aside. If you have trouble getting a nice consistency, you can use your mixer, but do not blend for too long. Mash avocados until slightly lumpy, add lemon juice, and blend thoroughly.

Cover a serving platter with lettuce leaves. Spread avocado mixture evenly over lettuce leaves. Layer with cream cheese mixture, spreading evenly over avocado. Top with cheese by mounding it into a heap so that it forms a peak. Garnish with tomato, green onions, and black olives. Serve with tortilla chips and salsa.

In 1942, avocados cost 5¢ each.

CAROL ANN'S DAD

Most potato and tortilla chips have a freshness date stamped on the package. Always check dates when buying this product. I examine the package carefully to ensure the contents have not been damaged and the chips are not broken into small, unusable pieces.

If your supermarket has only rock-hard avocados, place them in a paper bag with an apple to speed the ripening process.

shrimp and Scallop Salsa

SERVES 6

Serve with blue corn tortilla chips.

¼ pound small shrimp
¼ pound bay scallops, rinsed
½ cup water
1 cup water
1 cup frozen corn, cooked
3 green onions, thinly sliced
¼ cup red onion, finely diced
1 jalapeño pepper, cored, seeded, and finely diced
3 tomatoes, cored and diced
1 avocado, peeled, seeded, and diced
¼ cup fresh cilantro, finely chopped
½ teaspoon minced garlic
1 teaspoon dried oregano
¼ teaspoon ground cumin
1 tablespoon fresh lime juice
Salt to taste

TO PREPARE SHRIMP

Purchase precooked, frozen shrimp. Thaw according to package directions. Remove tails, chop, cover, and refrigerate at least 1 hour.

TO PREPARE SCALLOPS

In a large skillet, poach bay scallops in ½ cup water over medium-high heat for about 3 minutes, stirring frequently, or until scallops are cooked through. Remove scallops from the skillet. Cool and chop. Cover and chill at least 1 hour.

FOR CORN

In a small saucepan, bring 1 cup water to boil over medium-high heat. Add frozen corn and cook according to package directions. Drain and chill at least 1 hour.

In a large bowl, combine shrimp, scallops, corn, green onions, red onion, jalapeño pepper, tomatoes, avocado, cilantro, garlic, oregano, cumin, lime juice, and salt to taste. Mix gently. Cover and chill at least 1 hour.

Packages of scallops often leak on the way home from the market. Ask the sacker to bag them separately in plastic.

To ensure your cilantro stays fresher a bit longer, try placing it in a glass of water. Cover it with a plastic bag, securing the bag to the glass with a rubber band, and then refrigerate. The water should be changed every 2 to 3 days.

Russ' Fool-Proof Hot Wings

SERVES 4 TO 6

Serve with icy-cold celery sticks and blue cheese dressing.

2 ½ pounds chicken drumettes
1 cup milk
1 ½ cups flour
1 ½ cups corn meal
Vegetable oil for frying chicken drumettes
1 bottle SchWings® Buffalo Hot Wing Sauce

Place milk in a small bowl. In a medium bowl, combine flour and corn meal until well blended. Place flour mixture on a plate. Dip each drumette in milk and then coat with flour. Heat vegetable oil in a large electric skillet or deep fryer to 370 degrees. Vegetable oil should be 1 to 1 ½-inches deep for skillet frying. If using a deep fryer, fill with vegetable oil according to directions. Deep fry drumettes, a few at a time, until nicely browned and crisp, about 12 to 17 minutes. Remove and drain on a paper towel. Transfer fried drumettes to a large covered container. Drizzle SchWings® to taste over drumettes. Snap the cover tightly on the container and shake vigorously until drumettes are evenly coated. Add more SchWings® to taste and shake again, evenly coating drumettes with sauce.

 *Be sure to pick up SchWings®. It's the secret ingredient.*

Carol Ann's Blue Cheese Dressing

MAKES ABOUT 3 CUPS

1 cup mayonnaise
1 cup sour cream
1 cup blue cheese, crumbled
¼ cup + 2 tablespoons white vinegar
2 teaspoons minced garlic
1 teaspoon salt
½ teaspoon large grind black pepper

In a medium bowl, combine mayonnaise, sour cream, blue cheese, vinegar, garlic, salt, and pepper and whisk until blended. Cover with plastic wrap and refrigerate until time to serve.

Buffalo wings originated in Buffalo, New York, in 1964 in the kitchen of the Anchor Bar, located near the foot of Main Street and the Buffalo River, consequently the name "anchor." Frank and Theresa Bellissimo owned and operated this establishment, and the Buffalo wing was not only devised but also served by Mrs. Bellissimo herself. This gastronomical treat became so famous that in 1977 the City of Buffalo designated July 29 as "Chicken Wing Day."

Karen Deitesfeld, a Colorado resident, hosted a party attended by a New York advertising executive. A typical New Yorker, this gentleman knew his wings and insisted her hot wing sauce was better than the Anchor Bar's. He encouraged Ms. Deitesfeld to bottle and sell her hot wing sauce, and she's been doing it ever since under the SchWings® label. SchWings®— better than the original.

smoked Salmon Quesadillas

SERVES 12 TO 16 AS AN APPERTIZER
OR 6 TO 8 AS A LIGHT SUPPER

Serve with your favorite salsa.

> 8 ounces goat cheese, softened
> 6 ounces cream cheese, softened
> ½ cup sour cream
> 2 tablespoons red onion, finely chopped
> ½ teaspoon fresh dill, minced
> 8 (8-inch) flour tortillas
> 8 ounces peppered smoked salmon, flaked
> Olive oil

In a small bowl, blend goat cheese, cream cheese, sour cream, onion, and dill until well mixed. Spread the cheese mixture evenly over 4 tortillas. Lay one-fourth salmon evenly over the cheese mixture on each tortilla. Place remaining tortillas on top of salmon, pressing down gently. Using a pastry brush, coat a large non-stick skillet very lightly with olive oil. Heat the skillet over medium-high heat. When hot, add 1 quesadilla to the skillet and cook until brown spots appear on the bottom of tortilla, about 1 minute. Using a spatula, turn quesadilla and cook the other side in the same way. Transfer to a cutting board, allowing to cool 1 minute. Cook remaining quesadillas. Cut into wedges and serve immediately.

Dill will not look crisp even when fresh. Look for bunches with deep green leaves with no sign of rot or yellowing.

Rinse dill and pat dry with paper towels. Chop off the thick stem. Using cooking shears, mince dill to desired size.

During high school, I did the payroll. Back then, we calculated payroll on an adding machine by multiplying hourly wage by number of hours worked. My father paid in cash, which we placed in white envelopes.

I did this in the afternoons, so my mornings were free. One day, my friend, Sharon Smith, and I decided to go up to Horsetooth Reservoir for a swim. My brother and his girlfriend, Christie Coffman, joined us. My brother and Christie swam out to one of the islands. When it came time for me to get to work, they hadn't returned, so Sharon and I rented a boat to retrieve them. On the way back, the boat ran out of gas and we had to push it back to the marina. We overextended our rental time. Since we had no more money, the owner made us clean boats to pay our way—a disgusting affair.

I was late to work. My fate—"How could you be so irresponsible? Our employees depend on their money. You're fired!" I learned early on—in business, there are no excuses. And, if you rent a boat that runs out of gas, it's probably not your fault!

Crab Cakes with a Pineapple Salsa

SERVES 6

You can use canned crab meat for this recipe, but the crab cakes taste better when you use Alaskan King crab legs. To cook crab legs, see recipe on Page 212.

I found this early recipe for crab cakes delightful. It's from The New Art of Cookery Made Plain and Easy, *authored By a Lady (Hannah Glasse) in 1792. "Having taken out the Meat, and cleaned it from the Skin, put it into a Stew-pan, with half a Pint of White Wine, a little Nutmeg, Pepper, and Salt over a slow Fire; throw in a few Crumbs of Bread, beat up one Yolk of an Egg with one Spoonful of Vinegar, throw it in, and shake the Sauce-pan round a Minute, then serve it up on a Plate."*

TO ASSEMBLE THE CRAB CAKES

    1 cup bread crumbs
    2 large eggs, beaten
    3 tablespoons mayonnaise
    2 tablespoons green bell pepper, cored, seeded, and finely diced
    2 tablespoons red bell pepper, cored, seeded, and finely diced
    2 tablespoons red onion, finely diced
    2 tablespoons celery, finely diced
    1 tablespoon fresh parsley, snipped
    1 teaspoon minced garlic
    ½ teaspoon salt
    ¼ teaspoon dry mustard
    ¼ teaspoon cayenne pepper
    3 cups fresh crab meat – about 6 King crab legs

In a medium bowl, mix together 1 cup bread crumbs, eggs, mayonnaise, green and red bell peppers, red onion, celery, parsley, garlic, salt, dry mustard, and cayenne pepper. Stir in crab meat, mixing thoroughly. Cover and chill mixture at least 2 hours or overnight.

The secret to making great pineapple salsa is a sweet pineapple. Leaves on the crown should be fresh, with a deep green color. Pull gently on the leaves. If the leaves can be easily removed with gentle pressure, the pineapple is ripe. The stem end of a fresh pineapple will have a sweet aroma. Highly colored pineapples will have a sweeter taste because they were picked ripe.

FOR THE PINEAPPLE SALSA

    2 cups fresh pineapple, cored, peeled, and chopped
    ¼ cup red bell pepper, cored, seeded, and diced
    ¼ cup green bell pepper, cored, seeded, and diced
    ¼ cup red onion, diced
    ½ jalapeño pepper, minced
    2 tablespoons green onions, thinly sliced
    2 tablespoons fresh cilantro leaves, snipped
    1 tablespoon lime juice

In a medium bowl, combine pineapple, red and green bell peppers, red onion, jalapeño pepper, green onions, cilantro, and lime juice and toss gently. Cover and refrigerate for 2 to 4 hours. Makes about 3 cups.

continued next page

TO COOK AND SERVE THE CRAB CAKES

> 2 cups bread crumbs
>
> 3 tablespoons olive oil

Shape crab mixture into 12 small cakes. Evenly coat each cake with the remaining bread crumbs. You may not need to use all the bread crumbs. Heat olive oil in a large skillet over medium heat. For an electric skillet, heat at 350 degrees F. Cook crab cakes until brown and crisp, about 5 minutes per side. To serve, top each crab cake with pineapple salsa, allowing some salsa to fall onto the plate.

Four Cheese Fondue

MAKES ABOUT 6 CUPS

Simple to prepare and perfect on cold winter nights. Originated by Swiss peasants to use up hardened cheeses, fondue is the perfect way to use your leftover cheese.

> 1 cup shredded fontina cheese
>
> 1 cup shredded Swiss cheese
>
> 1 cup grated Asiago cheese
>
> 3 tablespoons all-purpose flour
>
> 2 cups chardonnay wine
>
> 1 teaspoon minced garlic
>
> 1 cup grated Parmesan cheese
>
> White pepper to taste

In a large bowl, toss the fontina, Swiss, and Asiago cheeses lightly with flour. Pour chardonnay wine into the fondue pot and heat over medium-low heat until hot. Add garlic. Add the cheese mixture, a handful at a time, stirring constantly, and waiting until each addition melts before adding the next. Add Parmesan cheese, stirring until melted. Season to taste with white pepper.

SERVE WITH

> Assorted breads cut into bite-size pieces
>
> Cherry tomatoes
>
> Sweet Italian sausage, cut into 1-inch slices and fried until browned and cooked through

K raft debuted Cheez Whiz® on July 1, 1953. A survey of American housewives revealed over 1,304 possible ways to use this new product. And that doesn't count the creative approaches their children discovered.

Heating fondue slowly ensures it will not become rubbery. If your fondue becomes too thick, increase the heat, add a little wine, and stir vigorously.

A ceramic pot works best when making cheese fondue.

Three Cheese Toasts
with Sun-Dried Tomatoes

MAKES ABOUT 36 PIECES

This can be prepared in about 15 minutes. Tapenade makes a nice substitution if you don't like sun-dried tomatoes.

> 1 loaf French or sourdough baguette, cut into ¼-inch slices
> 3 tablespoons olive oil
> 1 cup feta cheese, crumbled
> 1 cup ricotta cheese
> 1 cup shredded mozzarella cheese
> 1 teaspoon minced garlic
> White pepper to taste
> 10 sun-dried tomatoes, drained and quartered

Preheat the oven to 300 degrees. Arrange bread slices on a baking sheet. With a pastry brush, lightly brush the tops with olive oil. Bake until bread is golden brown, about 3 to 4 minutes. Remove from the oven and set aside. Increase the oven temperature to 350 degrees. In a medium bowl, blend cheeses and garlic. Season with white pepper. Mound 1 teaspoon of the cheese mixture onto each bread slice. Top with sun-dried tomato quarter. Cover with an additional teaspoon of the cheese mixture. Bake until cheese begins to melt. Serve immediately.

Carol Ann's Spinach Dip

MAKES ABOUT 7 CUPS

> 1 package (10-ounces) frozen spinach, thawed and squeezed dry
> 1 cup mayonnaise
> 1 cup sour cream
> 2 cups grated Parmesan cheese
> 2 cups shredded Monterey Jack cheese
> 6 teaspoons minced garlic
> ½ teaspoon large grind black pepper

Transfer spinach from the freezer to the refrigerator the night before to thaw. Preheat the oven to 350 degrees. In a medium bowl, combine mayonnaise, sour cream, Parmesan and Monterey Jack cheeses and mix until well blended. Be sure thawed spinach is squeezed as dry as possible before proceeding. Add spinach, garlic, and pepper. Mix well. Place the cheese mixture in a 1-quart ovenproof casserole dish. Bake the dip uncovered for 15 minutes, or until the mixture is bubbly.

On March 6, 1930, a chilling date in our nation's history, Birds Eye® conducted "the Springfield Experiment" in 18 grocery stores in Springfield, Massachusetts, introducing 26 frozen items to the American consumer. The initial Birds Eye® line featured 26 items, including 18 cuts of frozen meat, spinach and peas, a variety of fruits and berries, oysters, and fish fillets. The birth of retail frozen foods got a slow start due to the lack of freezer facilities in grocery stores. But in 1934, Birds Eye® contracted with the American Radiator Corporation to manufacture inexpensive, low-temperature, retail coolers. In 1944, they leased the first insulated railroad cars designed for frozen food distribution, allowing frozen foods to be shipped all across the country.

Focaccia Bread
with Tomatoes and Mozzarella

SERVES 6

This makes a wonderful appetizer for an Italian meal or a nice accompaniment with a Caesar salad.

> 2 medium tomatoes, peeled, seeded, and diced into small pieces
> 1 focaccia bread or 12 slices of fresh Italian bread, cut ½-inch thick
> 5 teaspoons garlic paste
> ¼ cup olive oil
> 3 tablespoons fresh oregano, minced
> Freshly ground black pepper
> 1 cup shredded mozzarella cheese

USING FOCACCIA BREAD

Preheat the oven to 400 degrees. Remove bread from the package. Using a metal spatula, spread focaccia with garlic paste and brush with olive oil. Top with oregano and tomatoes and season with pepper. Sprinkle with mozzarella cheese and bake 8 to 10 minutes, or until cheese is bubbly. Serve immediately.

USING ITALIAN BREAD

Toast bread on both sides. Using a metal spatula, spread toasted bread with garlic paste and brush with olive oil. Top with oregano and tomatoes and season with pepper. Sprinkle with mozzarella cheese and place under the broiler of an oven for a few seconds to melt cheese.

Although a trendy new arrival on the supermarket artisan bread scene, focaccia bread is as old as recorded history. Before ovens were invented, this flat bread was baked on hot stones over a mound of ashes.

When buying fresh oregano, select bright green bunches with no sign of wilting or yellowing. Oregano will keep up to 3 days when refrigerated in plastic containers. Oregano compliments tomato-based dishes.

Core and make an X in the top of tomatoes for easy peeling. Drop into boiling water for 10 seconds and remove. Peel tomatoes and immerse in icy cold water to retard cooking. Set aside.

Maui Onion and Tomato Salad 19

Carol Ann's Caesar Salad 20

Romaine Salad with a Twist 21

Toss It Greek Style 22

Special Occasion Spinach Salad 23

Spinach Salad with a Sweet-and-Sour Dressing 24

Spinach Salad with a Mustard Dressing 25

My Kids' Favorite Pasta Salad 26

Spaghetti in a Salad? 27

Grilled Chicken and Penne Pasta Salad 28

Three Cheese Tortellini and Veggie Salad 29

Dilled Shrimp and Angel Hair Pasta Salad 30

Warmed Shrimp in a Tarragon Cream Sauce 31

Back to the Seventies Taco Salad 33

Cobb Salad a la Carol Ann 34

Blackened Salmon Salad 35

Rice Salad with a Medley of Veggies 37

Jazzed-Up Green Bean Salad 38

Chicken and Cantaloupe Salad 39

Luau Chicken Salad 40

Chinese Chicken Salad 41

Pauline's 24-Hour Salad 42

Great food begins with shopping, especially when preparing salads. For tips on getting the freshest produce, see Page 299.

salads

Maui Onion and Tomato Salad

SERVES 4

On our last night of a romantic week-long vacation in Maui, my husband and I dined on the beach, watching whales splash playfully in the ocean while the sun blushed a flamingo fan across the horizon. Following is my version of the salad we had that evening.

In Hawaii, they use the Maui onion. If your supermarket doesn't carry this variety, a good substitute is a sweet Texas, Vidalia, or Walla Walla onion.

FOR THE DRESSING

> 3 tablespoons balsamic vinegar
> ½ teaspoon salt
> 1 teaspoon large grind black pepper
> 1 teaspoon minced garlic
> 1 teaspoon Dijon mustard
> 3 tablespoons olive oil

In a small bowl, combine balsamic vinegar, salt, pepper, garlic, and Dijon mustard. Whisk to blend. While continuing to whisk, slowly add olive oil. Set aside.

FOR THE SALAD

> 1 head leaf lettuce, washed, dried, and torn into bite-size pieces
> 6 ripe tomatoes, sliced
> 1 to 2 medium Maui onions, peeled and thinly sliced
> 4 ounces blue cheese, crumbled

For tips on picking the freshest, ripest tomatoes see Page 335.

Cover 4 salad plates with leaf lettuce. In a circular pattern, place a layer of onion rings on top of lettuce. Repeat the same pattern with a layer of 5 to 6 slices of tomato. Sprinkle each salad with blue cheese. Drizzle dressing over salad. Do not toss. Serve immediately.

CAROL ANN'S DAD

The most succulent, flavorful tomatoes are "vine-ripened". Sometimes it is easier to slice tomatoes using a bread knife. The serrated teeth won't tear the skin.

Carol Ann's Caesar Salad

SERVES 4 TO 6

This is one of our favorite green salads. For special occasions, try sprucing it up with thinly sliced mushrooms and bacon bits.

FOR THE DRESSING

> 2 coddled egg yolks
> ½ tube anchovy paste
> 1 heaping teaspoon minced garlic
> 1 heaping teaspoon Dijon mustard
> 2 tablespoons fresh lemon juice
> 1 teaspoon Worcestershire® sauce
> ½ teaspoon salt
> ½ teaspoon freshly ground (or large grind) black pepper
> ¼ cup red wine vinegar
> ½ cup olive oil

Coddle eggs by immersing them in boiling water for 10 seconds. Separate eggs, reserving yolks, and discarding whites. In a small bowl, combine egg yolks, anchovy paste, garlic, mustard, lemon juice, Worcestershire® sauce, salt, pepper, and vinegar. Whisk ingredients until smooth. While continuing to whisk, slowly add olive oil. Cover and refrigerate until ready to serve.

FOR THE SALAD

> 2 heads romaine lettuce, washed, dried, and torn into bite-size pieces
> Grated Parmesan cheese to taste (I use ½ to 1½ cups depending upon my mood.)
> Croutons

To prepare romaine lettuce, rinse thoroughly, pat dry with towels. (A salad spinner reduces time spent in prepping lettuce. If you don't have one, it's a great investment.) Place romaine lettuce in a large salad bowl. Add Parmesan cheese and croutons and toss gently. Whisk dressing again and pour over romaine lettuce, adding just enough to moisten. Toss again. Serve immediately. This salad wilts quickly once mixed with dressing.

Milk was not always pasteurized. Currently, egg producers are beginning to pasteurize eggs. The American Egg Board advises that eggs that have been pasteurized in their shells are safe to use without cooking in recipes. Pasteurization kills salmonella bacteria that may be present inside the shell. Look for the letter "P" on egg cartons. This designates the eggs have been pasteurized and are safe to use raw.

I've heard many a tale about the origination of the Caesar Salad. But research credits restaurateur, Caesar Cardini, of Tijuana, Mexico, with creating the first salad prepared tableside in 1924, adding a flamboyant ambiance to his restaurant's dining experience. The International Society of Epicures in Paris voted his dish "the greatest recipe to originate from the Americas."

The Caesar salad became a staple in supermarket delis when grocers began prepackaging all the fixings for this all-time American favorite in the 1990s.

When making Caesar salad, I prefer to pick up anchovy paste rather than canned anchovy fillets. The paste is easier to combine with the other dressing ingredients, and it has a milder flavor.

Romaine Salad with a Twist

SERVES 6

This recipe adds a new twist to the traditional tossed salad.

FOR THE DRESSING

> 1 jar (6-ounces) marinated artichoke hearts
> ¼ cup balsamic vinegar
> 2 tablespoons fresh chives, chopped
> 1 tablespoon lemon juice
> 1 tablespoon Dijon mustard
> 2 teaspoons honey
> 5 tablespoons mayonnaise
> ½ cup olive oil

Don't refrigerate cherry tomatoes until they are bright red in color. Refrigerating tomatoes before they reach maturity retards the ripening process.

Chop marinated artichoke hearts and place in a food processor or blender along with marinade. Add balsamic vinegar, chives, lemon juice, Dijon mustard, and honey. Blend until the ingredients are smooth and well mixed. Add mayonnaise and blend again. Add olive oil and blend to a smooth consistency. Cover and chill dressing for 1 hour.

When purchasing chives, look for ones with a uniform green color with no signs of wilting or yellowing. When stored in plastic and refrigerated, fresh chives will keep up to a week.

FOR THE SALAD

> 2 heads romaine lettuce, washed, dried, and
>   torn into bite-size pieces
> 1 small red onion, thinly sliced
> 1 basket cherry tomatoes, washed and sliced in half
> 1 can (15-ounces) water-packed artichoke hearts,
>   chopped and drained
> ½ to 1 cup grated Parmesan cheese

In a large bowl, combine romaine lettuce, red onion, cherry tomato halves, chopped artichoke hearts, and grated Parmesan cheese. Toss with dressing. Serve immediately.

Toss it Greek Style

SERVES 6

I first ate this salad at a Denver restaurant. I thought it was fantastic. I love re-creating my favorite restaurant fare at home.

FOR THE DRESSING

> ¼ cup red wine vinegar
> ¼ teaspoon dried oregano
> ¼ teaspoon salt
> ¼ teaspoon large grind black pepper
> ¼ cup plus 1 tablespoon olive oil

Capers should be rinsed before using to remove any excess salt.

In a small bowl, combine red wine vinegar, oregano, salt, and pepper and whisk to blend. While continuing to whisk, slowly add olive oil. Cover and refrigerate until ready to serve.

FOR THE SALAD

> 24 cherry tomatoes, halved
> ½ cup chopped red onion
> 1 can (14-ounces) water-packed artichoke hearts, quartered
> 2 tablespoons capers
> 24 kalamata olives, pitted
> 6 to 12 peperoncini, whole or cut into bite-size pieces, depending on size
> 2 heads romaine lettuce, washed, dried, and torn into bite-size pieces

Romaine with rust, oversized butts, or large, milky ribs is not good quality. Select romaine that is cut close to the leaf stems and is free of browning. Good romaine will have deep green leaves all the way down to its center.

CAROL ANN'S DAD

In a large salad bowl, layer cherry tomatoes, red onion, artichoke hearts, capers, kalamata olives, and peperoncini. Place romaine lettuce on top of the other ingredients and cover with a damp paper towel. Refrigerate until ready to serve.

> 4 ounces crumbled feta cheese

Just before serving, add feta cheese to the salad. Pour dressing over the salad and toss.

Lettuce should always be torn. Cutting it with a knife turns the edges brown faster.

Special Occasion Spinach Salad
with a Raspberry Vinaigrette Dressing

SERVES 6

While the combination of ingredients is unusual, this makes a tasty addition to any special occasion meal.

*F*lavored vinegars became popular in the 1980s and began popping up on American grocery shelves in the 1990s. Any fruit juice that contains a lot of sugar can be used to make vinegar, including bananas, oranges, pineapples, blueberries, and raspberries.

FOR THE DRESSING

½ cup raspberry white wine vinegar
1 tablespoon Dijon mustard
1 teaspoon minced garlic
¼ teaspoon salt
Large grind black pepper to taste
¾ cup canola oil

In a small bowl, combine raspberry vinegar, Dijon mustard, garlic, salt, and pepper. Slowly pour in oil, whisking until blended. Cover and refrigerate until ready to serve

FOR THE SALAD

4 cups spinach leaves, washed, dried, and torn into bite-size pieces
1 head romaine lettuce, washed, dried, and torn into bite-size pieces
1 pint fresh strawberries, hulled and sliced
4 ounces blue cheese, crumbled
3 tablespoons sliced almonds, toasted

In a large salad bowl, combine spinach, romaine lettuce, strawberry slices, blue cheese, and toasted almonds. Drizzle with dressing. Toss and serve immediately.

Wash strawberries first and then hull them. If they are hulled before they are washed, they absorb too much water and become mushy.

To toast nuts, place on a baking sheet in a 350-degree preheated oven for 5 to 10 minutes, or until golden brown. Watch closely as nuts turn from golden brown to black very quickly. I personally prefer to toast nuts by sautéing them in a small skillet that has been lightly coated with butter. For this method, stir frequently over medium heat for 5 to 7 minutes.

Spinach Salad with a Sweet-and-Sour Dressing

SERVES 6

My entire family loves this salad. The first time I tasted this treasure was at a Denver restaurant called Toby's Jug. Although no longer in business, I remember Toby's Jug as one of the first restaurants in Denver to serve a spinach salad.

FOR THE DRESSING

> 1 cup corn oil
> 1 cup cider vinegar
> ⅓ cup ketchup
> 1 medium onion, chopped
> ⅓ cup honey
> ½ teaspoon salt
> 2 tablespoons tamari sauce

In a blender, combine corn oil, cider vinegar, ketchup, onion, honey, salt, and tamari sauce and process until thoroughly mixed. May be refrigerated 3 days. Cover and refrigerate until ready to toss.

FOR THE SALAD

> 1 bag (10-ounces) fresh spinach, rinsed, drained,
>   and refrigerated until crisp
> 1 can (8-ounces) water chestnuts, drained and sliced
> 4 hard-boiled eggs, sliced
> 1 bag (16-ounces) fresh bean sprouts
> 1 pound bacon, fried crisp, drained, and crumbled
> 1 cup shredded Cheddar cheese

In a large salad bowl, layer spinach, water chestnuts, hard-boiled eggs, bean sprouts, crumbled bacon, and shredded Cheddar cheese. Cover with damp paper towel and refrigerate at least 1 hour. This salad will keep nicely 4 hours in the refrigerator. When ready to serve, toss salad lightly. Toss again, adding dressing to moisten all ingredients according to individual preference.

The beginnings of La Choy Food Products date back to 1920 when two University of Michigan friends formed a partnership. Wally Smith, a Detroit grocer, and Ilhan New, a Korean, began growing bean sprouts in a bathtub and selling the sprouts in jars. By 1922, they were sold in cans.

When buying bean sprouts, examine the package carefully. Look for crisp sprouts whose buds are attached. Avoid slimy, dark, or musty-smelling sprouts. Sprouts have a short life. It's best to buy them a day ahead of use.

Tamari sauce is a dark sauce made from soybeans. It is thicker than soy sauce and has a distinctively mellow flavor. If you don't have tamari sauce on hand, you can substitute soy sauce, but it will slightly alter the flavor.

Spinach Salad with a Mustard Dressing

SERVES 6

FOR THE DRESSING

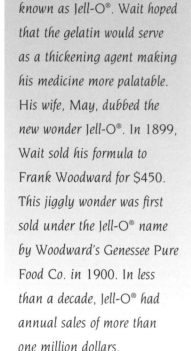

A cough syrup manufacturer, Pearle B. Wait, who in a 1897 attempt to invent cough and laxative formulas, stumbled upon the fruit-flavored gelatin later known as Jell-O®. Wait hoped that the gelatin would serve as a thickening agent making his medicine more palatable. His wife, May, dubbed the new wonder Jell-O®. In 1899, Wait sold his formula to Frank Woodward for $450. This jiggly wonder was first sold under the Jell-O® name by Woodward's Genessee Pure Food Co. in 1900. In less than a decade, Jell-O® had annual sales of more than one million dollars.

2 hard-boiled eggs, chopped
¼ cup red wine vinegar
5 tablespoons heavy cream
1 tablespoon Dijon mustard
1 teaspoon minced garlic
½ teaspoon salt
1 tablespoon large grind black pepper
¼ cup olive oil

In a medium bowl, combine eggs, red wine vinegar, heavy cream, Dijon mustard, garlic, salt, and pepper and whisk until smooth. While continuing to whisk, slowly add olive oil. Cover and refrigerate until ready to toss salad.

FOR THE SALAD

1 bag (10-ounces) spinach, rinsed, drained,
   and refrigerated until crisp
½ pound bacon, fried crisp, drained, and crumbled
¼ pound mushrooms, thinly sliced
1 cup shredded Swiss cheese
1 can (8-ounces) sliced water chestnuts
½ cup black olives, sliced
½ cup green onions, sliced

In a large bowl, combine spinach, crumbled bacon, mushrooms, Swiss cheese, water chestnuts, black olives, and green onions. Toss, add mustard dressing, and toss again until ingredients are evenly coated.

If you want to use fresh water chestnuts, select ones with no sign of shriveling. Simply peel the water chestnut like a potato, then slice to desired size.

I use button mushrooms for this recipe. Look for ones that are firm and evenly colored with tightly closed caps. If the gills are showing, the mushrooms are passed their prime. Avoid specimens that have soft spots or a dark-tinged surface.

My Kids' Favorite Pasta Salad

SERVES 6

When you want to please the kids in the family, this is a winner.

FOR THE DRESSING

    5 hard-boiled eggs, chopped
    1 cup celery, finely chopped
    6 gherkin pickles, finely chopped
    ½ cup white onion, chopped
    1 ½ cups mayonnaise
    ¼ cup juice from pickles
    Salt to taste
    Pepper to taste

In a small bowl, combine eggs, celery, gherkin pickles, onion, mayonnaise, pickle juice, salt, and pepper. Mix well.

FOR THE SALAD

    12 ounces rotini, cooked al dente and drained

Cook rotini al dente according to package directions or see Tips for Cooking Pasta on Page 241. Drain, rinse with cool water, and drain again.

    ½ pound Monterey Jack cheese, cut in ½-inch cubes
    ½ pound cooked ham, cut in ½-inch cubes

In a large bowl, place rotini, add dressing, and toss. Cover and chill overnight. Just before serving add cheese and ham and mix lightly. .

    Fresh parsley, chopped
    Paprika

Garnish with chopped parsley and paprika.

During my childhood, my brother and I would trek off to our neighborhood market to purchase Kool-Aid® for our summer Kool-Aid® stands. This miracle drink was developed by Edwin Perkins from a fruit syrup. Perkins began marketing his syrup under the name Fruit Smack in 1920. Inspired by the success of Jell-O®, he concentrated his syrup into a powder in 1927, packaged it in envelopes, and dubbed it Kool-Ade. Little did he know, way back then, how many children would start their entrepreneurial careers selling his powdered wonder drink.

One pound of raw shrimp that has been cooked, shelled, de-veined, and coarsely chopped may be substituted for the ham and cheese.

When using celery in a salad, I always remove the strings by snapping the rib at the point where the stalk changes color from green to white. This exposes the strings. Using a small paring knife, gently pull the strings from the stalk.

spaghetti in a salad?

SERVES 6

When I first served this salad to my family, my children were mortified. "Mother, spaghetti in a salad? Where's the sauce?"

1 pound spaghetti, cooked al dente and drained

Break spaghetti in half and cook al dente according to package directions or see Tips for Cooking pasta on Page 241. Drain, rinse with cool water, and drain again. Transfer spaghetti to a large bowl and let sit for 10 minutes.

½ cup bottled Italian dressing
½ cup bottled red wine vinaigrette dressing
1 teaspoon minced garlic
1 teaspoon large grind black pepper
½ teaspoon salt
½ teaspoon dried oregano
½ teaspoon dried basil

Add Italian and red wine vinaigrette dressings, garlic, pepper, salt, oregano, and basil and mix gently. Cover and marinate in the refrigerator overnight.

1 package (6-ounces) frozen snow pea pods, thawed
1 package (10-ounces) frozen green peas, thawed
1 can (14-ounces) water-packed artichoke hearts, drained and quartered
16 cherry tomatoes, washed and cut into halves
⅓ cup grated Parmesan cheese

The next day, add snow pea pods, green peas, artichoke hearts, cherry tomatoes, and Parmesan cheese. Cover and chill at least 2 hours before serving.

*A*ctor, Paul Newman, along with his friend, A. E. Hotchner, had a custom of giving old wine bottles filled with secret-recipe salad dressings to their friends every Christmas. In 1982, the two partners launched Newman's Own® all-natural food products.

Dried herbs are best when used within six months. Mark the opened date on the jar with a black marker.

Grilled Chicken & Penne Pasta Salad
in a Tomato Vinaigrette Dressing

SERVES 4 TO 6

Makes a lovely entrée for a special occasion luncheon.

FOR THE DRESSING

> 1 tablespoon vegetable oil
> 3 medium tomatoes, peeled, halved, and seeded
> 2 teaspoons minced garlic
> ⅓ cup red wine vinegar
> 2 tablespoons lemon juice
> 1 teaspoon salt
> 1 teaspoon large grind black pepper
> ½ cup vegetable oil

In a large skillet, heat 1 tablespoon vegetable oil over medium heat and sauté tomatoes until soft. Remove and place in a food processor or blender. Add garlic, red wine vinegar, lemon juice, salt, and pepper and process until smooth. While blending on a low speed, slowly add the remaining ½ cup vegetable oil to the blender and continue to process until well blended. Cover and refrigerate until ready to toss salad.

> 16 ounces penne pasta, cooked al dente, drained

Cook pasta, al dente according to package directions. For Tips on Cooking Pasta, see Page 241. Drain, rinse with cold water, and drain again.

FOR THE SALAD

> 1 ½ cups green onions, thinly sliced
> 1 medium red bell pepper, cored, seeded, and chopped
> ¾ cup black olives, halved
> 1 can (14-ounces) water-packed artichoke hearts, drained and chopped
> ½ cup chopped red onion
> 3 chicken breasts, grilled and sliced with skin and bones removed

In a large bowl, combine pasta, green onions, red bell pepper, black olives, artichoke hearts, red onion, and chicken. Add 2 cups of the dressing to salad and toss to coat. Serve the remaining dressing on the side.

The salad has evolved over the years. Beginning in the 1980s, Americans started using pasta as an ingredient. This recipe is a perfect example. Not only is pasta eaten cold, but tomatoes are the main ingredient in the dressing.

Steele's began selling chef-prepared pasta salads in the deli in the late 1980s.

Three Cheese Tortellini and Veggie Salad

MAKES ABOUT 12 CUPS

Even tortellini gets into the noodle game in this light, yet scrumptious, salad.

*T*he Bolognese claim to have created tortellini, tiny pasta shaped like a navel. In fact, the citizens of Bologna are so fond of this pasta that a group of citizens formed the Learned Order of the Tortellini dedicated to preserving this noodle. When they meet, these tortellini connoisseurs wear red and gold hats shaped like tortellini, and a golden tortellini charm dangles from ribbons around their neck. When they gather to feast on their favorite food, they never speak a word until every tortellini has been consumed and then only to utter a gentle murmur of appreciation.

> 2 packages (9-ounces) fresh DiGorno® three cheese tortellini, cooked al dente and drained

Cook tortellini al dente according to package directions or see Tips for Cooking Pasta found on Page 241. Drain, rinse with cold water, and drain again.

> 1 teaspoon minced garlic
> ¾ cup bottled olive oil vinaigrette with balsamic vinegar
> ½ cup chopped fresh parsley
> 1 cup sliced green onions
> 1 cup red bell pepper, cored, seeded, and chopped
> 1 jar (6-ounces) marinated artichoke hearts, undrained and cut up
> 4 tablespoons snipped fresh basil

In a large bowl, place cooked tortellini. Add garlic and vinaigrette and toss. Add parsley, green onions, red bell pepper, artichoke hearts with marinade, and basil. Toss again, cover, and refrigerate for several hours or overnight.

> 2 cups broccoli florets

Fill a large saucepan half full of water and place over high heat. Bring to a boil and blanch broccoli until bright green (about 1 minute) and drain. Rinse with cold water and drain again. Cover and refrigerate broccoli, separately from salad, for several hours or overnight.

When buying fresh broccoli, look for tightly closed buds that have an even, deep green color. The stem should be lighter green than the buds and leaves should be crisp.

> ⅔ cup large grated Parmesan cheese
> 16 cherry tomatoes, halved

When ready to serve, add broccoli florets, Parmesan cheese, and cherry tomatoes to salad and toss. Spoon into serving bowls.

Choose basil with evenly colored leaves with no sign of wilting or yellowing.

Dilled Shrimp and Angel Hair Pasta Salad

SERVES 6

Already peeled and de-veined shrimp costs a bit more but, for me, is worth every penny.

FOR THE DRESSING

¼ cup vermouth

2 teaspoons dried parsley

2 teaspoons dried dill

2 tablespoons green onions, thinly sliced

1 tablespoon Dijon mustard

1 teaspoon minced garlic

Large grind black pepper to taste

½ cup olive oil

In a small bowl, combine vermouth, parsley, dill, green onions, Dijon mustard, garlic, and pepper. Whisk constantly until thoroughly combined. While continuing to whisk, slowly add olive oil. Cover and refrigerate until ready to toss salad.

Red and yellow bell peppers can be a bit pricey. To ensure you are selecting the best, look for fresh, firm peppers that are brightly colored and have a thick flesh and a firm, green calyx and stem. Do not buy bell peppers with wrinkled skin or any soft or brown spots.

FOR THE SALAD

16-ounces angel hair pasta, cooked al dente and drained

Cook angel hair pasta according to package directions or see Tips for Cooking Pasta on Page 241. Drain, rinse with cold water, and drain again.

For this recipe, I prefer medium size, 40 to 50 shrimp per pound.

1 ½ pounds shrimp

1 cup red bell pepper, cored, seeded, and diced

1 cup yellow bell pepper, cored, seeded, and diced

1 cup celery, diced

3 cups green onions, thinly sliced

1 jar (6 ½-ounces) marinated artichoke hearts

16 cherry tomatoes, halved

1 cup large grated Parmesan cheese

Salt to taste

For tips on de-veining shrimp, see Page 186.

Peel and de-vein shrimp. Cook shrimp in boiling water, 1 to 2 minutes, until opaque throughout, being careful not to overcook. Immediately rinse cooked shrimp under cold water and drain. In a large bowl, combine angel hair pasta, shrimp, red and yellow bell peppers, celery, green onions, artichoke hearts, tomatoes, and Parmesan cheese. Add salt to taste. Pour dressing over salad, and toss to coat all ingredients evenly. Serve at room temperature.

Warmed Shrimp in a Tarragon Cream Sauce *Over a Bed of Greens*

SERVES 6

I served this at a bridal shower. When you're hosting an elegant luncheon, this will "wow" your guests.

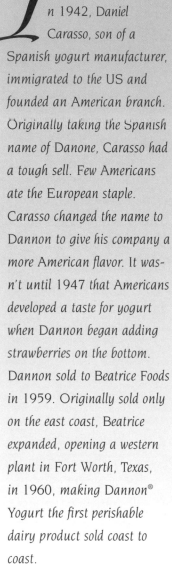

In 1942, Daniel Carasso, son of a Spanish yogurt manufacturer, immigrated to the US and founded an American branch. Originally taking the Spanish name of Danone, Carasso had a tough sell. Few Americans ate the European staple. Carasso changed the name to Dannon to give his company a more American flavor. It wasn't until 1947 that Americans developed a taste for yogurt when Dannon began adding strawberries on the bottom. Dannon sold to Beatrice Foods in 1959. Originally sold only on the east coast, Beatrice expanded, opening a western plant in Fort Worth, Texas, in 1960, making Dannon® Yogurt the first perishable dairy product sold coast to coast.

The secret ingredient in this recipe is fresh tarragon. It is an aromatic herb with a distinctive anise-like flavor. Be sure to stop in the produce department and pick up fresh tarragon.

FOR THE DRESSING

> ½ cup olive oil
> 3 tablespoons red wine vinegar
> 6 tablespoons plain yogurt
> 1 teaspoon Dijon mustard
> 1 teaspoon minced garlic
> ½ teaspoon salt
> ¼ teaspoon large grind black pepper
> Pinch tarragon

In a blender, combine olive oil, red wine vinegar, yogurt, Dijon mustard, garlic, salt, pepper, and tarragon and process until smooth. Cover and refrigerate until ready to toss salad.

FOR THE SAUCE

> 3 pounds shrimp
> 2 tablespoons olive oil
> Reserved shrimp shells
> 1 tomato, chopped
> ⅔ cup dry white wine
> ½ cup water
> ¼ teaspoon salt
> 1 teaspoon minced garlic
> ½ cup heavy cream
> 2 teaspoons dried tarragon
> 2 tablespoons olive oil
> Salt and large grind black pepper to taste

Peel and de-vein shrimp, reserving shells. In a large skillet, heat 2 tablespoons olive oil over high heat. Add shrimp shells and cook, stirring constantly, until they turn pink, about 1 minute. Add tomato, white wine, water, salt, and garlic and bring to a boil. Reduce heat to medium and cook 10 minutes. Add heavy cream and tarragon and simmer 10 minutes longer. Strain sauce into a small saucepan, pressing hard on shells to retrieve as much sauce as possible. Discard shells. Bring the sauce to a boil over high heat. Reduce heat and simmer until sauce is reduced to ⅓ cup and is slightly syrupy, about 10 minutes.

continued next page

FOR THE SHRIMP

In a large skillet, heat the remaining 2 tablespoons olive oil, peeled and de-veined shrimp, and salt over high heat. Add shrimp in 3 to 4 batches and cook until pink and opaque throughout. Do not over cook. When sautéing shrimp, you may need extra olive oil. If so, use an additional 2 tablespoons. In a large bowl, place shrimp, drizzle with tarragon sauce, and season with salt and pepper. Cover with aluminum foil to keep warm and set aside.

FOR THE GREENS

    1 head red leaf lettuce, washed, dried,
       and torn into bite-size pieces
    1 head green leaf lettuce, washed, dried,
       and torn into bite-size pieces

Add dressing to greens and toss. Arrange mixed greens on 6 plates and mound shrimp in center.

In 1989, Fresh Express® in Salinas, California, introduced 'salad in a bag', giving supermarket shoppers a new level of convenience—the instant salad. Fresh Express® designed their 'bag' to control the ingress and egress of oxygen, allowing lettuce to stay fresh for up to two weeks. The first bagged salad contained iceberg lettuce; but by 2000 the variety of lettuces in packaged salads included radicchio, mesclun, and frisee, and their sales topped $1 billion.

When shopping for leaf lettuce, look for whole, unbroken leaves with no wilting or spoilage at either the tip or base of the leaves.

To de-vein shrimp, hold them under a slow stream of cold water and run the tip of an ice pick or sharp knife down their back, scraping out the intestine. Rinse gently to remove any black.

Buy large shrimp with a count of 31–35 per pound.

Back to the Seventies Taco Salad

SERVES 6

The taco salad first became popular in the 1970s. Invite your girlfriends over to reminisce about the good old days and serve this classic.

1 pound ground beef
1 teaspoon minced garlic
1 can (4-ounces) chopped green chiles
1 can (16-ounces) tomatoes
1 teaspoon salt
¼ teaspoon large grind black pepper
1 head iceberg lettuce, washed, dried,
   and torn into bite-size pieces
1 cup grated Cheddar cheese
6 ounces tortilla chips
6 green onions, sliced

GARNISH WITH

Chopped tomatoes, sliced black olives, sour cream, salsa,
   guacamole

In a large skillet, sauté ground beef and garlic over medium heat until meat is browned. Drain. Add green chiles, tomatoes, salt, and pepper and stir. Reduce heat and simmer over low heat uncovered for 30 minutes. Just before serving, arrange lettuce, Cheddar cheese, tortilla chips, and green onions on salad plates. Add ground beef mixture and desired garnishes. Toss and serve immediately.

The first taco recipe written in the English language appeared in California cookbooks in 1914.

Fritos® originated in 1932 in San Antonio, Texas, when candy maker, C. Elmer Doolin, was served a dish of corn chips in a cafe. Doolin paid the cafe owner $100 for a converted potato ricer and a recipe for "Tortillas Fritas" and began producing ten pounds of Fritos® a day. Eventually he moved his operation to Dallas. Fritos® Corn Chips were sold nationally in 1949.

I prefer to buy "extra lean" ground beef when making this recipe. "Extra lean" means for every 100 grams of beef there are less than 2 grams of saturated fat and less than 95 milligrams of cholesterol.

Cobb Salad a la Carol Ann

SERVES 4

FOR THE DRESSING

½ cup vegetable oil
2 tablespoons olive oil
2 tablespoons red wine vinegar
2 tablespoons water
2 teaspoons lemon juice
½ teaspoon Worcestershire® sauce
½ teaspoon Dijon mustard
1 teaspoon minced garlic
¼ teaspoon salt
½ teaspoon large grind black pepper

In a blender, place vegetable and olive oils, red wine vinegar, water, lemon juice, Worcestershire® sauce, Dijon mustard, garlic, salt, and pepper and process until well blended. Cover and chill until ready to toss salad. Makes less than 1 cup.

FOR THE SALAD

1 head red leaf lettuce, washed, dried, and torn into bite-size pieces
1 head green leaf lettuce, washed, dried, and torn into bite-size pieces
2 tomatoes, chopped
3 boneless, skinless chicken breasts, cooked and sliced thin
1 pound bacon, fried crisp and crumbled
1 avocado, sliced
2 hard-boiled eggs, sliced
4 ounces blue cheese, crumbled

Place red and green leaf lettuce on 4 dinner plates and arrange tomatoes, chicken, bacon, avocado, eggs, and blue cheese in rows over lettuce leaves so that they fan the plate. Drizzle approximately ¼ cup of dressing onto each salad. Dressing can be served on the side.

In the wee hours of the morning in 1926, Bob Cobb, owner of the Brown Derby in Los Angeles, was desperate for a midnight snack. Raiding the restaurant's refrigerator, he whipped up a doozy of a salad using leftovers. He shared this late-night treat with Sid Grauman of Grauman's Chinese Theater. Grauman was so taken with the 'leftover' salad that he stopped for lunch at the Brown Derby the next day to order what he named a Cobb Salad. And from that moment on, the Cobb Salad became a popular menu item at the Brown Derby.

Blackened Salmon Salad

SERVES 6

I ate this salad in an Atlanta, Georgia, restaurant while attending the 1996 Olympic games. I thought it deserved a gold medal. When I returned home, I had to duplicate it. I use the same dressing as I do for my Cobb Salad.

FOR THE BLACKENING

4 teaspoons salt
6 teaspoons paprika
2 teaspoons cayenne pepper
1 ½ teaspoons white pepper
1 teaspoon large grind black pepper
¾ teaspoon ground thyme
¾ teaspoon ground oregano
6 salmon steaks
8 tablespoons melted butter

In a small bowl, combine salt, paprika, cayenne pepper, white pepper, black pepper, thyme, and oregano. Dip both sides of fish in spice mixture and rub over salmon steaks to thoroughly cover. Heat a heavy skillet on high heat until extremely hot. Dip spice-covered fish in melted butter and place in the hot skillet. Cook for 4 to 5 minutes and then turn. Cook an additional 4 to 5 minutes on the second side. Remove fish from the skillet, remove the bones and skin, and set aside to cool to room temperature.

FOR THE DRESSING

1 cup vegetable oil
4 tablespoons olive oil
4 tablespoons red wine vinegar
4 tablespoons water
4 teaspoons lemon juice
1 teaspoon Worcestershire® sauce
1 teaspoon Dijon mustard
2 teaspoons minced garlic
½ teaspoon salt
1 teaspoon large grind black pepper

In a blender. combine vegetable and olive oils, red wine vinegar, water, lemon juice, Worcestershire® sauce, Dijon mustard, garlic, salt, and pepper and purée until smooth. Cover and refrigerate until ready to serve salad.

continued next page

Our markets didn't open for business on Sundays until 1988. We struggled long and hard with this monumental decision, cognizant of the fact doing business on Sundays was out of character for our family. Every one of our competitors had been open on Sunday for years, some even operating 24 hours a day. The world was a different place in the fifties and sixties; businesses closed on Sundays. But by the eighties, most supermarkets had succumbed to the pressure of expanding hours. Because of shrinking family incomes, more women had joined the workforce, and Sundays had become an errand day. Family consensus agreed our survival hinged upon opening on Sundays.

One old timer called when the decision to expand our hours was announced. His comment? "Your father is rolling in his grave! I'll never shop at Steele's again!" I wanted to inquire where he would be shopping since every other supermarket in town had been open on Sundays for years. But instead I teased my brother, "I'm glad we installed that rotisserie in Dad's coffin.

(continued on page 36)

FOR THE SALAD

3 heads green leaf lettuce, washed, dried, and torn into bite-size pieces

1 jar baby corn, drained

1 can (16-ounces) water-packed artichoke hearts, drained and quartered

24 peperonconi

2 avocados, peeled and sliced

2 tomatoes, chopped

8 ounces feta cheese, crumbled

To assemble salad, cover 6 dinner plates with green leaf lettuce. Evenly divide baby corn, artichoke hearts, peperoncini, and avocado slices on each dinner plate. Mound one blackened salmon steak and one-sixth of tomatoes in the center of each plate. Sprinkle with feta cheese. Serve with the dressing on the side so it can be added according to individual preference.

Do not wash lettuce until ready to use. Store whole heads in plastic bags. This helps them retain their natural moisture and stay crisp. Do not store lettuce with apples or pears, as these fruits emit ethylene gas that turns lettuce brown.

*If your **avocado** is too hard, place it in a paper bag with an apple to speed the ripening process.*

***Tomatoes** as well ripen more quickly when placed in a paper bag.*

(continued from page 35)
At least when he's rolling in his grave, his bones won't break."

Looking back, this was probably the worst decision we made. Before opening on Sundays, Saturday was a blockbuster day at Steele's. With the extra day, our Saturday business merely split between the two weekend days. I think the old timer was probably right. My father would have resisted the temptation. But then again, who knows?

I believe the trend to stay open seven days a week has contributed to the erosion of family life in our country. Families deserve one day each week when the only activity scheduled on the agenda is spending time together. In addition, the constant worry of standing tall seven days a week is stressful for the business owner. They need a day off, just to rest.

Stores in Europe close on Sundays, and life goes on. My husband traveled to Belgium with our Bakery Production Director to learn more about European-style baking techniques. He arrived on a Saturday night, and on Sunday morning realized he had forgotten to pack a toothbrush. Not a single store in Brussels was open. Surprisingly enough, he survived without a toothbrush until Monday morning when the stores were back in business.

Rice Salad with a Medley of Veggies

SERVES 12

Rice and green bean salads made their debut in the 1960s. Feta cheese was not available in American supermarkets until the 1980s.

ordon Harwell, a Texas produce broker, developed the first converted rice in 1943. The owner of the Mars® candy empire, Forrest Mars, purchased his mill and created the Uncle Ben's® label, now the leading brand of rice in the United States.

FOR THE DRESSING

1 ½ cups feta cheese, crumbled
½ cup red wine vinegar
1 tablespoon dried oregano
1 teaspoon ground cumin
¾ cup corn oil

In a large bowl, combine feta cheese, red wine vinegar, oregano, and cumin and whisk to blend. Feta cheese should be crumbled to the size of a grain of rice. While continuing to whisk, slowly add corn oil. Cover and refrigerate until ready to toss salad.

FOR THE SALAD

4 ½ cups water
2 ½ cups uncooked long-grain white rice
1 teaspoon salt
1 package (10-ounces) frozen corn, thawed and drained
1 cup green bell pepper, cored, seeded, and chopped
1 cup red bell pepper, cored, seeded, and chopped
1 cup red onion, chopped
1 cup green onions, thinly sliced
2 tablespoons fresh chives, chopped

Onions can be a bit tricky to purchase. Do not buy red onions that have dark patches, soft spots, or black mold. Examine the sprout end of red onions carefully. This is the first place spoilage will occur. Do not buy if it has a soft, sunken, yellow top.

In a large saucepan, bring water to a boil over high heat. Stir in rice and salt. Reduce to low heat, cover, and cook 20 minutes, or until rice is tender. Remove from heat and let stand 5 minutes. Transfer to a large bowl, add dressing, and toss. Add corn, red and green bell peppers, red onion, green onions, and chives. Toss and serve immediately.

Jazzed-Up Green Bean Salad

SERVES 6

FOR THE DRESSING

    3 tablespoons balsamic vinegar
    ½ teaspoon lemon juice
    1 teaspoon salt
    ½ teaspoon large grind black pepper
    1 teaspoon minced garlic
    1 teaspoon dry mustard
    ¼ teaspoon paprika
    3 tablespoons olive oil

In a small bowl, combine balsamic vinegar, lemon juice, salt, pepper, garlic, dry mustard, and paprika and whisk to blend. While continuing to whisk, slowly add olive oil. Cover and refrigerate until ready to toss salad.

When shopping for beans, don't just grab a handful. Pick through them and select tender, crisp, well-formed beans. If freshly picked, green beans will have a smooth velvety skin. If the beans inside the pods are visible, the beans were overgrown.

FOR THE SALAD

    4 cups fresh green beans, washed and cut into 1½-inch pieces
    1 cup white onion, chopped
    1 ½ cups canned garbanzo beans, drained
    3 small summer squash, sliced

In a large saucepan, place green beans just enough water to cover. Bring water to a boil over medium-high heat. Reduce heat to medium-low and simmer 20 minutes. Drain and transfer green beans to a large bowl. Add onion and garbanzo beans, toss, and set aside. Steam squash for 3 minutes. Drain and combine squash with the other vegetables. Mix dressing with vegetables and marinate overnight in refrigerator.

    1 cup sour cream

When ready to serve, add sour cream and blend gently.

The fewer green beans in the saucepan, the quicker they cook and the better they taste. If cooking more than one pound, use more than one pan.

Chicken and Cantaloupe Salad
in a Mango Chutney Dressing

SERVES 4

*I*n the first half of the twentieth century, apples, raisins, and nuts were the first fruits found in salad. By the 1990s, even cantaloupe had found its way into salads.

FOR THE DRESSING

¾ cup vegetable oil
½ cup Major Grey® Mango chutney
¼ cup white wine vinegar
3 teaspoons minced garlic
1 tablespoon Dijon mustard
1 tablespoon soy sauce
1 tablespoon sesame oil
½ teaspoon Tabasco® sauce

Place vegetable oil, chutney, vinegar, garlic, mustard, soy sauce, sesame oil, and Tabasco® sauce in a in blender. Puree until smooth. Cover and refrigerate until ready to use.

FOR THE SALAD

3 cups cooked chicken breast, cut into bite-size pieces
    (about 3 boneless, skinless chicken breasts)
3 cups cantaloupe, cut into ½-inch pieces
1 cup celery, thinly sliced
½ cup green onions, thinly sliced
¼ cup roasted, salted cashews
Lettuce leaves, washed and dried

In a large bowl, combine chicken, cantaloupe, celery, and green onions. Just before serving, add cashews to salad. Toss with enough dressing to evenly coat ingredients. Arrange lettuce leaves on four plates. Mound salad on top of lettuce.

When buying your cantaloupe, shop with your nose. A ripe cantaloupe will emit a slight fragrance. It should also yield to gentle pressure on the blossom end, the end opposite the stem.

CAROL ANN'S DAD

Luau Chicken Salad

SERVES 6

This is my version of a salad I enjoyed while on vacation in Hawaii. Treat yourself to a resort lunch right at home. I like to serve this nestled on a bed of lettuce with fresh pineapple spears, mandarin oranges, and red or green grapes.

FOR THE SALAD

6 chicken breasts, cooked, cooled, boned, skinned,
and chopped into bite-size pieces

1 can (5-ounces) water chestnuts, sliced and drained

½ cup chopped macadamia nuts

1 cup celery, sliced

1 can (15½-ounces) pineapple chunks, drained
or 2 cups fresh pineapple, cut into bite-size pieces

In a large bowl, combine chicken pieces, water chestnuts, macadamia nuts, celery, and pineapple chunks.

FOR THE DRESSING

1 cup mayonnaise (more if needed)

1 teaspoon soy sauce

Onion salt to taste

Coarse grind black pepper to taste

In a separate bowl, combine mayonnaise and soy sauce. Add dressing to salad and toss. Season with onion salt and pepper to taste. Cover and chill several hours before serving.

*B*est Foods® introduced a light and cholesterol free mayonnaise in the 1980s. Low-fat mayonnaise was introduced in 1985.

Cut off the top and bottom of a pineapple with a large, sharp knife. Slice off the skin from the top downward. I prefer to remove any remaining eyes with a small paring knife. Cut in a circular motion around the eye and pry it out. Cut the fruit into four wedges and remove the core.

Chinese Chicken Salad

SERVES 4

FOR THE MARINADE

> ½ cup corn oil
> 6 tablespoons white vinegar
> 2 tablespoons dried red pepper flakes
> 3 tablespoons sugar
> 2 tablespoons soy sauce
>
> 4 chicken breasts, cooked, skinned, boned, and shredded
> 2 cups water chestnuts, drained and sliced

In a medium bowl, combine corn oil, white vinegar, red pepper flakes, sugar, and soy sauce. Mix well. Stir in chicken and water chestnuts. Marinate, refrigerated and covered, overnight.

FOR THE SALAD

> 1 head iceberg lettuce, washed, dried, and shredded
> 5 green onions, thinly sliced
> 2 ounces Maifun® Chinese rice noodles, deep-fried according to package directions
> 2 tablespoons toasted sesame seeds

In a large salad bowl, combine lettuce and green onions and refrigerate. Just before serving, deep-fry noodles according to the package directions and place on a paper towel to cool. Drain marinated chicken mixture. Add chicken mixture, noodles and sesame seeds to lettuce. Toss gently and serve immediately.

In 1911, the Corn Products Refining Company introduced the first cooking and salad oil made from corn. Mazola® Oil, the first corn oil made from 100 percent golden corn, came in square, yellow tins decorated with a corn maiden. Salesman introduced Mazola to grocers and homemakers by cooking French fried potatoes on portable stoves in stores to demonstrate its superior frying qualities and flavor.

The secret to cooking Chinese rice noodles is to be sure the oil is hot enough. Test the oil by adding a few noodles. If they puff instantly, the oil is hot enough to continue. Also, it's best to cook the noodles in small batches.

Pauline's 24-Hour Salad

SERVES 10 TO 12

My mother made this salad for Thanksgiving in place of the traditional Waldorf. It can be prepared a day ahead, unlike the Waldorf that should be prepared and served immediately. This salad is perfect for novice cooks who are uncomfortable with the many last minute preparations a Thanksgiving dinner require.

1 egg, slightly beaten
2 tablespoons lemon juice
2 tablespoons sugar
Pinch salt
½ cup whipping cream, whipped, or Cool Whip®
Powdered sugar for sweetening the whipped cream
12 marshmallows, quartered, or 48 mini marshmallows
1 cup pineapple tidbits, drained
1 cup mandarin oranges, drained
1 cup seedless grapes
1 cup bananas, sliced
8 Maraschino cherries, quartered

Place a double boiler over medium heat. Add egg and beat slightly. Add lemon juice, sugar, and salt and mix gently with a fork. Heat over hot but not boiling water. Cook, stirring constantly, about 5 minutes or until mixture thickens. Cool to room temperature and fold in whipped cream or Cool Whip®, marshmallows, pineapple, mandarin oranges, grapes, bananas, and cherries.

I'm Chiquita banana and I'm here to say...." I made my debut in the American supermarket in 1944. In the late 1980s, Oscar Grillo turned me into a woman. By the end of the 20th century, I'm hot stuff and bananas are the No. 1 selling fruit in America.

Bananas should never be refrigerated. Store bananas at room temperature.

This salad will keep 2 to 3 days if properly refrigerated.

Tips for whipping cream: Chill mixing bowl and beaters in freezer about 1 hour. Keep whipping cream chilled until ready to whip. Pour whipping cream into mixing bowl and process at a high speed. Continue whipping until firm peaks form. Add powdered sugar to taste only after peaks have formed.

Jalapeño Chicken Chowder 45

Chicken 'n Cheese Chowder 46

Company's Coming Scallop Chowder 47

Corn Chowder in Warmed Tortilla Bowls 48

Easy Artichoke and Scallop Chowder 49

Hearty Clam Chowder 50

Portuguese Style Vegetable Soup 51

Auntie Beryl's Vegetable Beef Soup 52

Jewish Penicillin—Chicken and Noodles 53

French Onion Soup 54

Cream of Potato Leek Soup 55

Cream of Broccoli Soup 56

Fresh Tomato Bisque with Basil 57

Mushroom Bisque 58

Salmon Bisque 59

Artichoke Langostino Bisque 60

Lobster Bisque 61

Carol Ann's Chili 62

Western Style Chili 63

Chuck Wagon Chili 64

White Bean Chili with Chicken 65

Vegetable Chili 66

Green Chile Stew 67

Thursday's Tutu Beef Stew 68

I love serving soup for supper.

Jalapeño Chicken Chowder

SERVES 8

The year 1930 marked the introduction of the first frozen food by Birds Eye®, the origin of the cream-filled Hostess® Twinkie®, and the creation of the first baking mix for biscuits. Mabel White Holmes created Jiffy® Baking Mix, a baking mix for biscuits in which the only ingredient to be added was liquid. She and her husband, who owned the Chelsea Milling Co., in Chelsea, Michigan, later introduced 18 different mixes for pie crusts, cakes, and muffins.

On a busy day, buy a roasted chicken from the grocery store and cut off the meat. Substitute 2 cups of canned chicken broth for the chicken stock, then add water as necessary to achieve desired thickness.

1 whole chicken	2 bay leaves
2 quarts water	1 teaspoon peppercorns
1 teaspoon salt	Ends of 6 stalks of celery

In a large heavy kettle, place chicken, water, and salt and bring to a boil over medium-high heat. Reduce heat to a simmer. Skim any foam off the top. Add bay leaves, peppercorns, and ends of celery. Simmer 1 hour, or until chicken is done. Remove chicken from the kettle and cool. Skin and bone chicken. Cut into small chunks and set aside. Strain chicken stock through a sieve and pour it back into a holding pot, discarding the celery ends and spices.

8 tablespoons butter
½ cup flour
Reserved chicken stock
1 can (16-ounces) peeled tomatoes
6 stalks celery, diced
1 bunch green onions, thinly sliced
2 jalapeño peppers, seeded and chopped
1 medium onion, chopped
1 green bell pepper, seeded, cored, and diced
1 red bell pepper, seeded, cored, and diced
1 yellow bell pepper, seeded, cored, and diced

In the large kettle, melt butter over medium heat. Add flour and stir until lightly browned. Slowly pour reserved chicken stock into flour paste, stirring constantly to prevent soup from becoming lumpy as it thickens. Add tomatoes, celery, green onions, jalapeño peppers, onion, and green, red, and yellow bell peppers to the broth. Cook for 30 minutes, or until vegetables are barely done.

Cooked chicken, cut into chunks
1 small zucchini, diced
1 small yellow squash, diced
1 can (12-ounces) corn, drained
1 can (15-ounces) black beans, drained and rinsed

Add chicken, zucchini, squash, corn, and black beans. Cook for 5 minutes. Serve with Jiffy® Corn Bread.

Be sure to pick up Jiffy Corn Bread mix. It's easy to prepare and the perfect accompaniment for this chowder.

Chicken 'n Cheese Chowder

SERVES 4 TO 6

I love soup for supper, especially in the winter. I like to serve this with a tossed green salad and a sourdough baguette.

4 tablespoons butter
1 cup carrots, shredded
½ cup onion, chopped
4 tablespoons flour
2 cups milk
2 cups canned chicken broth
3 cups diced, cooked chicken
(about 3 boneless, skinless chicken breasts)
2 tablespoons dry white wine
½ teaspoon Worcestershire® sauce
½ teaspoon celery seed
¼ teaspoon salt
¼ teaspoon large grind black pepper
3 cups shredded Cheddar cheese

In a large saucepan, melt butter over medium heat. Add carrots and onion and sauté until soft but not brown. Blend in flour and cook 1 minute, stirring constantly. Slowly pour in milk and chicken broth and stir until thickened. Let simmer for 5 minutes. Add cooked chicken, wine, Worcestershire® sauce, celery seed, salt, and pepper to stock and blend thoroughly. Add the cheese and stir until just melted. Do not let the soup boil.

If you're in a hurry, purchase pre-shredded carrots found in the produce department of your supermarket.

When selecting chicken, look for the USDA shield. Only buy chicken that is marked Grade A.

*D*r. John Thomas Dorrance, an MIT trained chemist, traveled to Germany to earn his doctorate. While living abroad, he became fond of eating soup. As the nephew of the owner of the Joseph Campbell Preserve Co., Dorrance understood that soup had been a difficult product to manufacture. Because of its weight and bulk, canned soup was expensive to transport. For that reason, only two companies manufactured soup at the end of the 19th century. Dorrance began to wonder if cans of soup were smaller, if they'd be less expensive to ship. He removed the heaviest ingredient in soup, water, and created a version of stronger soup that housewives could mix with water. His brainchild made a fortune for the Campbells® Soup Co. The original flavors of Campbells® soup included tomato, vegetable, chicken, consomme, and oxtail. By 1905, Campbell's® sold 21 flavors of soup.

Company's Coming Scallop Chowder

SERVES 6 TO 8

This chowder is similar to clam chowder, but it uses scallops instead. It's quite rich and very filling. Try it when bay scallops are on sale. A sourdough baguette is a must for dipping in this chowder. The broth is so good you'll savor every drop.

*D*uring the 1700s, fish chowder was a popular dish among the Northeastern Native Americans. Some historical records indicate that mounds of clamshells could be found at their favorite gathering places. The Pilgrims didn't care much for fish, with the exception of eel, and were slow to catch on to eating fish stew.

1 leek, thinly sliced
1 large white onion, chopped
2 stalks celery, thinly sliced
8 ounces mushrooms, cleaned and sliced

In a large bowl, place leek, onion, celery, and mushrooms and set aside.

½ pound bacon, fried crisp and crumbled
2 tablespoons butter
Reserved leek, onion, celery, and mushrooms
1 can (14½-ounces) chicken broth
1 teaspoon large grind black pepper
3 tablespoons fresh parsley, snipped
1 tablespoon fresh thyme, snipped
3 potatoes, peeled and diced

In a large heavy kettle, brown bacon over medium heat until crisp. Remove bacon with a slotted spoon and transfer to a paper towel to drain. Cool, crumble, and set aside. Add butter to the kettle, along with reserved vegetables. Sauté and stir over low heat for 5 minutes. Add chicken broth, pepper, parsley, thyme, and potatoes. Bring soup to a boil, then simmer over low heat for about 20 minutes, or until potatoes are tender.

3 tomatoes, peeled and chopped

Bring a small saucepan of water to a boil. Cut an X in the top of tomatoes and drop in boiling water for 10 to 30 seconds. Remove with a slotted spoon. Peel, remove stems, and chop.

Before slicing leeks, remove the green portion of the leek and separate the layers. Rinse carefully to remove any grit. For tips on cleaning leeks, see Page 325.

2 pounds bay scallops, rinsed and drained
1 cup white wine
1½ cups heavy cream
1 teaspoon salt
¼ teaspoon cayenne pepper

Add tomatoes, crumbled bacon, bay scallops, and white wine and simmer an additional 10 minutes. Do not overcook scallops as they will become tough. Add heavy cream, salt, and cayenne pepper and heat through. Serve immediately.

Corn Chowder in Warmed Tortilla Bowls

SERVES 6

I like to serve this chowder with guacamole and tortilla chips. For a fun and different presentation, line your soup bowls with warmed flour tortillas. If you cook chicken breasts ahead of time, this whole meal can be prepared in about 35 minutes.

2 tablespoons butter
1 cup onion, chopped
1 teaspoon minced garlic
3 cans (17-ounces) creamed corn
1 cup canned chicken broth
2 cups milk
1 can (4-ounces) diced green chile peppers
1 teaspoon ground cumin
½ teaspoon ground white pepper
¼ teaspoon Tabasco® sauce
4 boneless, skinless chicken breasts, cooked and cubed
1 ½ cups shredded Monterey Jack cheese
Flour tortillas

When Hernando Cortez and his conquistadores arrived in the New World on April 22, 1519, they found the Aztecs made flat corn bread. The native name for these breads was tlaxcalli. The Spanish named them tortilla.

In a large heavy kettle, melt butter and sauté onion over medium heat until translucent, about 6 minutes. Add garlic and cook 2 minutes longer. Do not allow onion and garlic to brown. In a blender or food processor, purée creamed corn. The creamed corn should not be completely smooth, but should retain some texture. Add puréed corn and chicken broth to the kettle and simmer gently over medium-low heat for 10 minutes. Stir in milk, green chiles peppers, cumin, white pepper, and Tabasco® sauce. Add chicken and cheese and stir until cheese melts. Place warmed flour tortillas in soup bowls. Ladle soup into tortillas. Serve immediately.

GARNISH WITH

Sour cream, salsa, guacamole, or crumbled corn tortilla chips

To warm flour tortillas, preheat oven to 250 degrees. Wrap 3 to 4 tortillas in aluminum foil and place in the oven for 10 minutes.

Easy Artichoke and Scallop Chowder

SERVES 4 TO 6

An unusual, yet delicious, combination of flavors.

2 medium potatoes, peeled, washed, and diced

In a large saucepan, place potatoes with just enough water to cover. Bring to a boil over medium-high heat and cook potatoes until tender, about 10 to 15 minutes. Drain and set aside.

3 tablespoons butter
1 cup red onion, finely chopped
2 tablespoons lemon juice

In a large kettle, melt butter over medium heat. Add red onion and cook until translucent, about 3 minutes. Add lemon juice to onions and simmer until evaporated.

3 cups canned chicken broth
3 cups milk
1 ½ cups canned (water-packed) artichoke hearts, diced and drained
2 ½ pounds bay scallops, rinsed and drained
¼ teaspoon salt
¼ teaspoon white pepper
⅛ teaspoon cayenne pepper
1 tablespoon fresh chives, chopped

Add chicken broth, milk, artichoke hearts, bay scallops, and cooked potatoes to the kettle. Simmer gently about 4 minutes. Do not boil. Season with salt, white pepper, cayenne pepper, and chives. Ladle soup into bowls and serve immediately.

The first cookbook published in America in 1796 was written by Amelia Simmons. Here is her chowder recipe: "Take a bass weighing four pounds, boil half an hour, take six slices raw salt pork, fry them till the lard is nearly extracted, one dozen crackers soaked in cold water five minutes; put the bass into the lard, also the pieces of pork and crackers, cover close, and fry for 10 minutes; serve with potatoes, pickles, apple-sauce or mangoes; garnish with green parsley."

Scallops often leak on the way home. Ask the sacker to bag them separately in plastic.

Hearty Clam Chowder

SERVES 6

Serve this in bread bowls for a real San Francisco treat.

5 slices bacon, coarsely chopped
⅔ cup green onions, thinly sliced
5 medium potatoes, peeled and cut into ½-inch cubes
⅔ cup green bell pepper, cored, seeded, and chopped
⅔ cup celery, chopped
2 cups water
1 teaspoon minced garlic
1 teaspoon salt
½ teaspoon white pepper
1 teaspoon Worcestershire® sauce
4 drops Tabasco® sauce

In a large kettle, sauté bacon until crisp over medium heat. Add green onions, potatoes, green bell pepper, celery, water, garlic, salt, white pepper, Worcestershire® sauce, and Tabasco® sauce. Cover the kettle and simmer for 15 minutes, or until potatoes are tender.

2 cups fresh clams with juice
2 cups half-and-half

In a separate pan, heat the clams in their juice for 3 minutes, or until tender. Add clams with juice and half-and-half to the kettle and heat, stirring, until piping hot. Do not boil.

TO PREPARE BREAD BOWLS

6 sourdough bread bowls

Cut a circle in the top of a loaf of sourdough bread and scoop out the center to form a bowl. Cut scooped-out bread into bite-size chunks for dipping in the chowder. Serve chowder in a bread bowl, with bread cubes on the side.

 Clams should be added the last 15 minutes of cooking, otherwise they become mushy.

*B*y the middle of the 1800s, fish chowder was a mainstay throughout the northeastern United States. Clams became a popular ingredient in chowders because one simply went to the beach and dug them up.

*B*ringing home the bacon got easier in 1924 when Oscar Meyer® offered the American consumer the first presliced, packaged bacon. As creative packaging became more important to entice the shopper, Oscar Meyer® began wrapping its hotdogs with yellow bands in 1929.

Portuguese Style Vegetable Soup

SERVES 8

This is a spicy vegetable soup that is quite filling and makes a great entrée.

In 1948, V-8® Vegetable Juice Cocktail was introduced by the Campbell® Soup Company.

1 pound hot Italian sausage
1 cup onion, chopped
1 to 2 pounds precooked ham, cut into bite-size pieces
3 medium potatoes, peeled and diced
3 celery stalks, chopped
2 medium carrots, peeled and diced
1 can (4-ounces) chopped mild green chile peppers
1 can (11-ounces) niblet corn, drained
2 cans (15-ounces) kidney beans, drained and rinsed
1 can (15-ounces) Italian-style tomato sauce
1 cup V-8® juice
1 bay leaf
½ teaspoon Tabasco® sauce
¼ teaspoon salt
1 teaspoon large grind black pepper
6 cups water

In a large kettle, sauté Italian sausage and onion over medium heat until sausage is cooked through and onions are tender. Add ham, potatoes, celery, carrots, green chile peppers, niblet corn, kidney beans, tomato sauce, V-8® juice, bay leaf, Tabasco® sauce, salt, pepper, and water. Bring to a boil over high heat, skim foam from the surface, reduce heat, and simmer 2 hours. Remove bay leaf from the soup and serve in soup bowls.

Never buy canned goods with dents.

CAROL ANN'S DAD

For the best flavor, soup should be simmered gently for several hours rather than boiled. Boiling soup can make its ingredients tough and its broth cloudy.

As you finish dicing potatoes, soak them in cold water until ready to use. This keeps them from turning brown. Drain before adding to soup.

Auntie Beryl's Vegetable Beef Soup

SERVES 8

My Auntie Beryl, whose husband was a butcher at the first Steele's, shared her secret for making dynamite vegetable beef soup with me. She used leftover prime rib. I traditionally serve prime rib for Christmas dinner, so December 26th is vegetable beef soup day at my house. When I'm selecting my Christmas prime rib, I get a couple of extra pounds so I'll have plenty of leftovers. Auntie Beryl claimed prime rib bones are the secret ingredient that make this old standby truly spectacular. If I don't have leftover prime rib or if I'm pinching pennies, I use stew meat or sirloin steak.

> *y Aunt Beryl hovered over her stove poking and prodding the food she cooked with gentle devotion, coaxing it to blossom into something spectacular. She taught me that cooking is not just throwing cans into a pot. It is nurturing with tender loving care that which nurtures you.*

    2 pounds leftover prime rib with bones
        Substitutions: 2 pounds stew meat, cut in 1-inch cubes,
        or 2 pounds sirloin steak
    6 cups V-8® juice
    6 cups water
    1 can (16-ounces) peeled tomatoes
    ½ cup chopped onion
    4 teaspoons salt
    2 teaspoons Worcestershire® sauce
    ¼ teaspoon chili powder
    2 bay leaves
    2 packages (10-ounces) frozen mixed vegetables

In a large kettle, place leftover prime rib and bones, V-8® juice, water, peeled tomatoes, onion, salt, Worcestershire® sauce, chili powder, and bay leaves over medium-high heat. Bring to a boil over high heat, reduce heat, and simmer 2 hours. Remove meat and bones and cut meat into bite-size pieces. Strain the broth and skim off any excess fat. Return broth to the kettle. Add meat and vegetables to the broth, cover, and simmer 1 hour.

> *If you decide to use soup bones for this recipe, start them in cold water. Placing them into boiling water seals the bone, preventing flavor and nutrients from being released.*

If using stew meat, spray the kettle bottom with cooking spray and brown the stew meat, sautéing the pieces of meat until evenly browned on all sides. Stew meat will not need to be cut into pieces. If using steak, spray the kettle bottom with cooking spray and brown steak on both sides. Remove and cut steak into bite-size pieces. Then add at the same time you would if using prime rib.

Jewish Penicillin—Chicken and Noodles

SERVES 6 TO 8

I make Jewish penicillin every time someone in my family feels under the weather. It is comforting, easy on the stomach, and is the perfect nourishment for any down-and-out soul.

Another "get well" staple I always keep on hand is Gatorade®. It's is a great pick me up after a good work out and the perfect elixir to replenish fluids during a severe bout of flu. It was invented in 1965 by Dr. Robert Cade at the University of Florida as a drink to rehydrate athletes. Gatorade® made the supermarket scene in 1967.

4 large chicken breasts, with bones and skins on
2 quarts water
¼ cup fresh snipped parsley
4 celery stalks, sliced thin
Tops of celery stalks with leaves
1 carrot, peeled and sliced
1 small onion, chopped
2 teaspoons salt
¼ teaspoon large grind black pepper
1 pound wide egg noodles

In a large kettle, place chicken breasts with just enough water to cover (about 2 quarts). Add parsley, celery, tops of celery stalks with leaves, carrot, onion, salt, and pepper. Cover and bring to a boil over high heat. Reduce to low heat and simmer 2½ hours, or until tender. Remove chicken breasts from the broth, discard skin and bones, and cut chicken meat into bite-size pieces. Discard tops of celery stalks. Return the broth to a rapid boil. Add noodles and cook, uncovered, 7 to 8 minutes. Add chicken meat the last few minutes of cooking.

If you want a clear broth, strain it several times through a sieve.

Ask the sacker to bag your chicken separately in a plastic bag to prevent any juices from seeping on to other products.

French Onion Soup

SERVES 6

Your family will love coming home to this on a cold winter evening. Serve with Spinach Salad with a Sweet and Sour Dressing and French bread.

FOR THE BROTH

6 tablespoons butter
6 large onions, thinly sliced
6 tablespoons Worcestershire® sauce
1 teaspoon salt
1 teaspoon large grind black pepper
¾ cup dry white wine
½ teaspoon dried thyme
½ teaspoon dried basil
3 cans (14½-ounces) beef broth
3 cans water

FOR THE TOPPING

Large grated Parmesan cheese
Sliced mozzarella cheese
Sliced French bread, toasted

In a large kettle, melt butter over medium heat. Add onions and sauté until tender. Add Worcestershire® sauce, salt, pepper, wine, thyme, basil, beef broth, and water. Stir to combine. Simmer at least 60 minutes. The longer this cooks, the better the flavor. Pour the soup into individual ovenproof bowls and sprinkle with Parmesan cheese. Place a slice of toasted French bread in each bowl, then cover the bread with slices of mozzarella cheese. Place under a broiler for a few minutes until lightly browned and bubbly.

To shed fewer tears when slicing onions, cut the root off last, refrigerate before slicing, and peel the onion under cold water.

Don't forget to pick up wine at the liquor store. French onion soup is best when made with wine.

The origin of onion soup dates back to a very hungry King Louis XV who returned late one night to his hunting lodge. All he had on hand was onions, butter, and champagne. He mixed the ingredients together, and French Onion soup was born.

When first introduced, Campbell's® dubbed its chicken noodle soup "Chicken with Noodles." Sales were slow initially until the slip of the tongue on the "Amos 'n Andy" show renamed it Chicken Noodle Soup. Within days, orders for "Chicken Noodle Soup" skyrocketed. Today, Campbell's® uses a million miles of noodles annually in making this particular variety, enough noodles to circle the equator more than 40 times.

Cream of Potato Leek Soup

SERVES 4

The traditional evening meal in France includes soup. This French re-creation is inexpensive, easy to prepare, and down-right delicious.

Vichyssoise, a cold potato soup, was created when King Louis XV of France became worried someone was trying to poison him. He asked a number of servants to taste his food before he ate it. As they passed the soup around, it became cold before it finally reached King Louis. Upon tasting the cool potato soup, King Louis decided he preferred it that way.

4 tablespoons butter
1 ½ cups onion, finely chopped
1 ½ cups leeks, finely chopped
3 green onions, thinly sliced
2 pounds potatoes, peeled and cubed
3 ½ cups canned chicken broth
1 tablespoon dried chives
2 cups half-and-half
1 teaspoon salt
1 teaspoon large grind black pepper

In a large kettle, melt butter over medium heat. Add onion, leeks, and green onions and sauté, stirring frequently, until onion is tender and transparent, about 4 minutes. Add potatoes, chicken broth, and chives. Cover and simmer for 20 to 30 minutes, or until potatoes are tender. Remove potatoes, along with 1 cup broth, and place in a blender or food processor. Purée, then whisk puréed potatoes back into the remaining soup to thicken. Add half-and-half, salt, and pepper and reheat soup until warmed through.

In 1990, Campbell's® introduced Cream of Broccoli soup. Campbell's® launched this variety with a "Get President George Bush to Eat Broccoli" recipe contest. Cream of Broccoli became the company's most successful new soup in 55 years.

Leeks can be sandy. Place cut pieces of leek into a large bowl filled with warm water. Using your fingers, whirl the pieces vigorously to remove any grit. The sand should sink to the bottom. Scoop out the leeks and transfer them to a colander. Rinse and drain thoroughly.

Prolonged exposure to light will turn potatoes green. Do not buy green potatoes. They have a bitter flavor, and eaten in excess, can be toxic.

Cream of Broccoli Soup

SERVES 4

4 tablespoons butter
1 medium onion, chopped
¼ cup flour
2 cans (14½-ounces) chicken broth
1½ pounds fresh broccoli, cut into florets, stems chopped
1 teaspoon salt
1 teaspoon large grind black pepper
2 cups milk
8 ounces shredded Swiss cheese

In a large saucepan, melt butter over medium heat. Add onion and sauté for 10 minutes, or until golden. Add flour, stirring constantly, for an additional minute until thickened. Gradually add chicken broth and broccoli. Bring to a boil, stirring frequently. Cover and simmer 15 minutes, or until broccoli is tender. Purée soup in a blender or food processor. Return soup to the saucepan. Add salt, pepper, and milk. Add enough milk to make soup the consistency you desire, not to exceed 2 cups. I usually add only 1 cup. Reheat, stirring occasionally. Add Swiss cheese and stir until cheese melts.

Look for broccoli with tightly closed buds and crisp leaves. The buds should be an even, deep-green color, and the stems should be a lighter green than the buds.

My father lifted weights and ran two miles a day long before it became popular. One summer while visiting the Grand Canyon he decided to prove his prowess by hiking to the bottom of the canyon—an eight-mile distance one way. Most people hike down, camp overnight at the bottom, and hike out the next day. For us, it was a one-day affair.

The next morning, armed with ham sandwiches on toast and one canteen of water, we set off down the trail. My mother refused to go.

My father took off running dressed in his grocer's uniform—a white shirt, tie, dress slacks, and oxford shoes. He had left his apron at home. My brother and I followed at a normal pace. After a few hours, I got worried about him, so I asked some hikers coming up if they had seen him going down. "Did he have on a necktie?" "Yes, that's him."

We finally met up with him, at the bottom. It had taken him two hours to get down. It took my brother and me four.

After eating ham sandwiches in 120 degrees, I got sick at my stomach and couldn't walk. My dad's solution: "We'll take our belts off, harness her up, and drag her out." The two of them hauled me three miles to the first watering hole.

By this time I felt better. My father, however, taking full advantage of the watering hole, began gulping water like there was no tomorrow until he got sick. He laid in the trail groaning. "Carol Ann, call the mules." My brother continued up the trail, while I stayed nursing my father. It took dad eight hours to crawl out.

I took photos of him lying on the trail to remind him of the error of his ways, but these pictures mysteriously disappeared.

Fresh Tomato Bisque with Basil

SERVES 4 TO 6

Serve this chunky soup with a Caesar salad and a sourdough baguette.

In traditional French cooking, bisque is a thick, smooth shell-fish soup in which the shellfish has been puréed. Chowder is a chunky stew normally made with seafood. Over time, the term bisque has evolved to include any thick, creamy fish, tomato, or vegetable based soup. Even Campbell's® makes a tomato bisque.

2 cups white onion, chopped
3 tablespoons butter
2 pounds ripe tomatoes, peeled, seeded, and chopped
1 bay leaf
2 teaspoons minced garlic
1 teaspoon salt
½ teaspoon large grind black pepper

In a large kettle, sauté onion in butter over medium heat until tender. Add tomatoes, bay leaf, garlic, basil, salt, and pepper and stir to combine. Simmer for 30 minutes or until tender

2 cups half-and-half
1 cup milk
1¾ cups canned chicken broth
¼ cup brandy
2 tablespoons fresh basil, slivered

Discard bay leaf. Add half-and-half, milk, chicken broth, brandy, and basil to the tomato mixture. Cook until just heated through. Ladle into soup bowls.

GARNISH WITH

Buttered croutons
Chopped fresh basil

Dried herbs emit their best flavor when heated while fresh herbs lose their flavor if cooked too long. Add dried herbs at the beginning of cooking and fresh herbs near the end.

To peel tomatoes, *cut an X on the top. Drop them into boiling water for about 10 to 30 seconds. Remove with a slotted spoon. Immediately plunge into cold water to retard cooking. Peel.*
To sliver basil, *roll 3 to 4 leaves into a tight cylinder. Cut into thin strips with cooking scissors.*

Smell the stem end of the tomato. If it's ripe, it will smell like a tomato.

Mushroom Bisque

SERVES 6

Perfect for a light Sunday supper.

4 tablespoons butter
1 pound mushrooms, finely chopped
4 tablespoons onion, finely chopped
4 tablespoons flour

In a large saucepan, melt butter over medium heat. Add mushrooms and onions and sauté for 6 minutes, or until tender. Sprinkle in flour and sauté for 2 to 3 minutes, stirring frequently to avoid lumps.

4 cups canned chicken broth
¾ cup vermouth
1 bay leaf
3 tablespoons cornstarch dissolved in 3 tablespoons water
1 cup heavy cream, warmed
½ teaspoon salt
White pepper to taste

Add chicken broth, vermouth, and bay leaf. Bring mixture to a boil, reduce heat to low, and simmer for 15 minutes. Remove bay leaf. Add cornstarch-water mixture and blend thoroughly. Simmer for an additional 10 minutes, stirring frequently to prevent sticking. Warm heavy cream in a separate saucepan over low heat, being careful not to bring it to a boil. Add warmed heavy cream, salt, and white pepper and blend well.

*C*ampbell's® Cream of Mushroom hit the grocery shelves in 1934, becoming the first canned soup to be used as a sauce. In 1955, Campbell's® home economists developed the recipe for green bean casserole using cream of mushroom soup. This recipe remains today one of the most popular and requested recipes developed using Campbell's® products.

The secret ingredient in this dish is white pepper. Be sure to pick some up. White pepper is used in dishes where dark specks of black pepper would stand out.

When you purchase mushrooms for this recipe, forget what you've learned about snow-white tight caps. Select mushrooms that are dark and old with caps that have opened, exposing their underneath side. These mushrooms have a stronger taste and will enhance the flavor of the soup. You can experiment with different varieties of both mushrooms and herbs.

Salmon Bisque

SERVES 6

The perfect comfort food on cold winter nights.

½ pound fresh salmon
1 cup water reserved from poaching salmon

In a small saucepan, poach salmon over medium heat in just enough water to cover until salmon flakes easily when pierced with a fork, about 5 to 7 minutes. Cool, flake, and set aside, reserving approximately 1 cup of water used for poaching. Add salmon and reserved water to the blender and purée.

4 tablespoons butter
⅓ cup green onions, thinly sliced
1 teaspoon minced garlic
⅓ cup all-purpose flour
2 cups milk
2 cups half-and-half
Salmon purée
½ cup canned tomato purée
3 tablespoons brandy
1 teaspoon salt
1 teaspoon dried dill
¼ teaspoon ground white pepper

When shopping for salmon, always shop with your nose first. Fresh fish never smells fishy. As fish fillets or steaks begin to age, they look dry around their edges, and the edges will change color.

In a large kettle, melt butter over medium heat. Add green onions and garlic and sauté until onions are tender. Blend in flour. Cook, stirring constantly, for 3 minutes. Slowly whisk in milk and half-and-half, stirring constantly until thickened. Add salmon purée, tomato purée, brandy, salt, dill, and white pepper. Simmer for 15 minutes, stirring frequently to keep soup smooth.

Don't forget to pick up wine at the liquor store.

Artichoke Langostino Bisque

SERVES 6

My husband loves lobster bisque. At today's prices, however, it's often not afford-able. I created this recipe using langostinos for the sake of economy. The artichokes add body and flavor. Langostino is the Spanish word for "prawn." Langostinos are very large shrimp.

angostinos are a crus-tacean, sometimes sold as rock shrimp in supermarkets. They are usually found as ingredi-ents in soups and salads.

    1 tablespoon butter
    ½ cup white onion, chopped
    1 can (14½-ounces) water-packed artichoke hearts, drained
    2 teaspoons lemon juice
    1¾ cups canned chicken broth
    1 egg yolk
    2 tablespoons all-purpose flour

In a medium skillet, sauté onion in butter over medium-heat until tender and translucent. Purée artichoke hearts in a blender until finely chopped. Add sautéed onion, lemon juice, chicken broth, egg yolk, and flour to blender. Purée until well combined. Transfer artichoke-purée mixture to a large kettle.

    1 cup heavy cream
    1 cup white wine
    2 tomatoes, chopped
    ¾ cup tomato paste
    1 teaspoon dried chives
    ¾ pound flaked, cooked langostino meat
    ¾ teaspoon cayenne pepper
    ½ teaspoon salt
    White pepper to taste

Add heavy cream, wine, tomatoes, tomato paste, and chives to the kettle. Stir until well combined. Cook over medium heat until heated through, stirring occasionally to blend the ingredients. Add langostino meat, cayenne pepper, salt, and white pepper to taste. Continue to cook over medium heat until heated to serving temperature, about 5 minutes.

Langostinos can be cooked by steaming, boiling, or baking. This shellfish need not be completely cooked through. It is only important that the flesh has begun to firm slightly. Remove the meat from the shell before adding to the bisque.

Lobster Bisque

MAKES 6 PORTIONS

This is an extravagant, delicious recipe. It must be prepared with tender loving care. Its rich flavor is perfect for special occasions like Valentine's Day or Christmas Eve.

Campbell's® introduced their "Labels for Education" program in 1973. This program allowed schools and community groups to redeem Campbell's® labels for audiovisual equipment and other educational materials. Supermarkets served as the collection point for school and groups in their communities. Steele's happily participated in this program, helping Campbell's® make a difference in our schools.

FOR THE LOBSTER TAILS

> 1 gallon water
> 2 lobster tails, about 8 ounces each

Heat water in a large stock pot over high heat to boiling. Drop in lobster tails, cover, and cook for 10 minutes. Remove tails from the pot, reserving 4 cups of water. Let lobster tails cool. Remove shells from lobsters and finely dice meat. Set lobster meat aside, saving shells.

FOR LOBSTER STOCK

> 3 tablespoons unsalted butter
> Reserved lobster shells
> ⅓ cup Cognac
> ½ cup shallots, chopped
> 2 teaspoons minced garlic
> 3 tablespoons tomato paste
> 2 tomatoes, peeled and seeded
> 2 ½ cups white wine
> 4 cups reserved water from cooking lobster tails
> 1 teaspoon dried tarragon
> ½ teaspoon dried thyme
> Pinch red pepper flakes
> 2 bay leaves

In a large skillet, melt 3 tablespoons butter over medium heat. Add lobster shells and pour in Cognac. Heat until Cognac is warm, then light it with a match. When the flames subside, stir in ½ cup shallots, garlic, tomato paste, tomatoes, wine, reserved cooking water, tarragon, thyme, red pepper flakes, and bay leaves. Simmer uncovered at least 30 minutes. Remove bay leaves. Blend broth in a food processor until shallots and tomatoes are liquefied.

See Page 16 for tips on peeling tomatoes.

continued next page

Chopped fresh chives make a nice garnish for this soup.

FOR THE BISQUE

> 3 tablespoons unsalted butter
> 3 tablespoons shallots, chopped
> 3 tablespoons all-purpose flour
> Lobster stock
> 2 cups milk
> 1 ½ cups half-and-half
> Salt to taste
> White pepper to taste
> Reserved lobster meat

In a stock pot, melt 3 tablespoons butter over medium-high heat. Add 3 tablespoons shallots and sauté for 3 minutes. Add flour and stir constantly for 1 minute. Gradually blend in the lobster stock. Stir in milk and half-and-half and heat over medium heat until heated through. Season with salt and white pepper to taste. Stir in reserved lobster meat and continue to warm for several minutes. Serve immediately.

Carol Ann's Chili

SERVES 4

I traditionally make this chili every Halloween. It's a hectic day for mothers, and this dish is easy to prepare. I keep it simmering and ready to feed little trick or treaters whenever they want something that will stick to their ribs. Jiffy® Corn Muffin Mix makes the perfect accompaniment.

> 1 pound lean ground beef
> 1 cup onion, chopped
> 1 can (4-ounces) diced green chile peppers
> 1 can (16-ounces) tomatoes, chopped
> 1 can (16-ounces) kidney or chili beans
> 1 can (8-ounces) tomato sauce
> 1 teaspoon chili powder
> 1 bay leaf
> 1 teaspoon salt
> Large grind black pepper to taste

Garnishes: shredded Cheddar cheese and chopped white onion

In a heavy skillet, sauté ground beef and onion over medium heat until meat is lightly browned and onion is tender. Crumble meat with a fork while it cooks. Drain off fat. Stir in green chile peppers, tomatoes, kidney or chili beans, tomato sauce, chili powder, bay leaf, and salt. Season to taste with pepper. Cover and simmer for 1 hour. Remove bay leaf. Serve in soup bowls and sprinkle with shredded Cheddar cheese and chopped onion.

Western Style Chili

SERVES 8

Serve this chili with warmed tortillas and garnish it with shredded Cheddar cheese. This chili is quite filling!

½ pound dried kidney beans, washed

In a medium saucepan, place beans with just enough water to cover. Bring to a boil over high heat, Reduce heat to low, cover, and simmer for 1 ½ hours or until beans are tender, adding more water if needed.

¼ cup corn oil
2 large onions, chopped
2 large green bell peppers, cored, seeded, and chopped
2 teaspoons minced garlic

In a heavy kettle, heat corn oil over medium heat. Add onions, green bell peppers, and garlic and sauté until onions are transparent.

¼ cup fresh parsley, chopped
1 can (28-ounces) peeled tomatoes
2 ½ pounds beef chuck roast, cut into ½-inch pieces
1 ½ pounds lean pork butt, cut in ½-inch pieces
2 tablespoons chili powder
1 can (4-ounces) chopped green chiles
1 tablespoon salt
1 ½ teaspoons large grind black pepper
2 teaspoons ground cumin

Serve with: warmed tortillas

Garnish with: shredded Cheddar cheese

Add remaining ingredients to the kettle, including any broth from beans. Simmer covered, for 1 hour. Uncover and cook for 30 minutes longer or until thick.

*I*n 1977, chili manufacturers from the state of Texas successfully lobbied the legislature to have chili proclaimed the official 'state food' of Texas. In 1993, the Illinois State Senate passed a resolution proclaiming Illinois as the 'Chilli Capital of the Civilized World', outraging Texans.

Soup will keep for 2 to 3 days if refrigerated and no more than 6 months if frozen.

If you don't plan to eat your soup the same day you make it, do not overcook or over season it. When you reheat it, the ingredients will continue cooking.

Chuck Wagon Chili

SERVES 6

1 tablespoon vegetable oil

2 ½ pounds ground beef, coarsely ground

6 slices bacon, chopped and fried crisp

1 medium onion, chopped

1 green bell pepper, cored, seeded and chopped

1 can (14 ½-ounces) diced tomatoes, including liquid

1 can (4-ounces) diced green chile peppers

1 can (6-ounces) tomato paste

1 cup coffee

⅛ cup chili powder

1 ½ teaspoons ground cumin

½ teaspoon crushed red pepper

1 tablespoon cocoa powder

1 bay leaf

1 orange, halved

> "*Next to music there is nothing that lifts the spirits and strengthens the soul more than a good bowl of chili.*"
> —*author unknown*

Preheat the oven to 350 degrees. In a large skillet, heat vegetable oil on medium-high heat. Add ground beef and sauté for 8 to 10 minutes until browned. Drain off grease. In a large kettle, sauté bacon over medium heat until crisp. With a slotted spoon, remove bacon pieces and transfer to a paper towel to drain. Add onion and green bell pepper to the same kettle and sauté for 3 to 4 minutes, or until tender. Add browned ground beef, bacon, tomatoes, green chile peppers, tomato paste, coffee, chili powder, cumin, crushed red pepper, cocoa powder, and bay leaf. Mix the ingredients together and cook over medium heat for 10 minutes. Pour chili into a large ovenproof casserole. Place orange halves on top of chili, face down, and bake for 1 ¼ hours. Remove orange halves and bay leaf before serving.

Garnish with: shredded Cheddar cheese, chopped white onion, and chopped pickled jalapeño chile peppers.

 In some butcher shops, coarsely ground beef is called chili meat. If your butcher shop doesn't carry coarsely ground beef, ask to have it custom ground for you. Lean ground beef makes a good substitute.

White Bean Chili with Chicken

SERVES 8

A creative serving suggestion is to line soup bowls with flour tortillas.

1 pound Great Northern white beans, rinsed and picked over

In a large heavy kettle, place beans with enough cold water to cover them by at least 3 inches. Cover the kettle and soak beans overnight. The next day, drain beans into a large colander.

2 pounds boneless, skinless chicken breasts

Place chicken in a large heavy saucepan. Add cold water to cover and bring to a boil over high heat. Reduce heat to low and simmer until chicken is tender, about 15 minutes. Drain, cool, and reserve 4 cups of stock. Cut chicken into cubes and set aside.

2 tablespoons olive oil
2 cups onion, chopped
4 teaspoons minced garlic
2 cans (4-ounces) chopped mild green chiles
2 teaspoons ground cumin
1 ½ teaspoons dried oregano
¼ teaspoon cayenne pepper
4 cups chicken stock (reserved from cooking chicken)
4 cups canned chicken broth
1 can (12-ounces) Coors® Light Beer
2 cups shredded Monterey Jack cheese

In the same kettle used for soaking beans, heat olive oil over medium-high heat. Add onions and garlic and sauté until translucent. Stir in green chiles, cumin, oregano, and cayenne. Sauté an additional 2 minutes. Add beans, chicken stock, and canned chicken broth. Bring to a boil. Reduce the heat and simmer until beans are very tender, stirring occasionally, 2 to 4 hours. Add chicken meat, beer, and cheese. Stir until cheese melts. Line soup bowls with flour tortillas. Ladle chili into bowls.

Garnish with: shredded Monterey Jack cheese, sour cream, salsa, and cilantro leaves.

Serve by: lining soup bowls with flour tortillas.

*I*n the late 1800s, chili queens sold a fiery stew made of chiles and beef at open-air chili stands in San Antonio, Texas. Latino women made the chili at home and transported it to the Military Plaza Mercado in colorful wagons. Although the chili was originally made to feed the soldiers, every class of citizen from Mexican boot-blacks to silk-hatted tourists sat side-by-side eating the delicious stew. The sweet smell of mesquite fires kept the chili warm, while for the mere price of 10 cents, chili queens dished up a big plate of chili and beans, with a tortilla served on the side. In 1937, the chili queens were put out of business by the city health department because of their inability to conform to sanitary standards. In 1980, the City of San Antonio instituted an annual "Return of the Chili Queens Festival" in Market Square to honor the state dish.

Vegetable Chili

SERVES 6

While driving in my car, listening to talk radio, I heard a nutritionist discuss the need for more fruits and vegetables in the American diet. I created this recipe to include more vegetables in my family's diet. Here's a chili recipe that tastes so good you'll think it has meat in it.

1 medium-size eggplant, unpeeled and cut into ½-inch cubes
Salt
½ cup olive oil
2 medium yellow onions, diced
4 teaspoons minced garlic
2 large green bell peppers, cored, seeded, and diced
¼ cup olive oil
1 can (28-ounces) crushed tomatoes
1½ pounds Roma tomatoes, chopped
1 tablespoon chili powder
1 teaspoon ground cumin
1 tablespoon dried oregano
1 tablespoon dried basil
2 teaspoons large grind black pepper
1 teaspoon salt
1 teaspoon fennel seed
1¾ cups canned beef broth
1 can (16-ounces) red kidney beans, drained
1 can (16-ounces) garbanzo beans, drained
2 tablespoons fresh dill, chopped
2 tablespoons fresh lemon juice

Place eggplant in a colander and sprinkle with salt. Let stand for 30 minutes. While eggplant is resting, heat ½ cup olive oil in a large kettle over medium heat. Add onions, garlic, and green bell peppers and sauté until softened. Add the remaining ¼ cup olive oil and eggplant and sauté until eggplant is almost tender. Reduce heat to low. Add crushed tomatoes, Roma tomatoes, chili powder, cumin, oregano, basil, pepper, salt, fennel seed, and beef broth. Cook uncovered, stirring frequently, for 30 minutes. Stir in kidney beans, garbanzo beans, dill, and lemon juice and cook another 15 minutes.

If you over salt or spice your soup, add a few slices of potatoes to it. Simmer for 30 to 45 minutes and then remove and discard the potato slices.

Chili joints appeared in Texas at the turn of the century. By the 1920s, they had spread throughout the West; and by the lean Depression years, most western towns had a chili joint. These joints meant the difference between starvation and staying alive for many Americans because chili was cheap and crackers were free. In fact, during the Depression, chili joints have been credited with keeping more people from starvation than the Red Cross.

Eggplants should be firm and hard and feel heavy for their size. Choose ones with a solid deep purple color that extends all the way to the stem without signs of green. Avoid spotted eggplants or ones that are soft or wrinkled.

Green Chile Stew

SERVES 12

4 tablespoons olive oil
2 pounds chuck steak, cut into 1-inch cubes
2 yellow onions, chopped
1 cup red wine
8 cups water
2 carrots, peeled and thinly sliced
2 potatoes, peeled and cut into ½-inch cubes
1 can (7-ounces) chopped green chiles
1 cup canned beef broth
1 ½ teaspoons ground cumin
2 cups Mild Pace® Picante Sauce
½ teaspoon salt
½ teaspoon large grind black pepper

TOPPINGS

1 French baguette, sliced and toasted, 2 slices per serving
4 ounces shredded Cheddar cheese
4 ounces shredded Monterey Jack cheese
Sour cream

*L*egend has it that Will Rogers judged towns by the quality of their chili. He is said to have sampled chili in hundreds of towns spanning the states of Texas and Oklahoma and concluded that the best chili came from a small cafe in Coleman, Texas.

To reduce the fat content in soup, make it a day ahead of time and chill overnight. Remove the hardened fat that forms on the surface before reheating and serving.

In a large heavy kettle, heat olive oil over medium heat. Add steak and onions and sauté 2 to 3 minutes, or until steak is browned. Add wine and water. Bring to a boil, then reduce heat, and simmer for 15 minutes. Add carrots and potatoes, bring stew to a boil, and reduce heat again to simmer. Add green chiles, beef broth, cumin, and picante sauce and simmer for 1 hour. Before serving, season with salt and pepper. Place the stew in individual serving bowls and top each bowl with 2 toasted baguettes slices. Sprinkle with both cheeses and place under the broiler until cheese melts. Top with a dollop of sour cream.

Thursday's Tutu Beef Stew

SERVES 6

If you have a busy afternoon hauling kids around, put the meat on a gentle simmer for 1½ hours. Add the veggies 30 to 45 minutes before dinner.

2 tablespoons vegetable oil

2 pounds beef stew meat, cut in 1½-inch cubes

2 cups hot water

1 teaspoon Worcestershire® sauce

1 teaspoon minced garlic

1 medium onion, sliced

2 bay leaves

1 tablespoon salt

1 teaspoon sugar

½ teaspoon paprika

¼ teaspoon large grind black pepper

6 carrots, peeled and cut into 1-inch pieces

6 new potatoes, scrubbed and halved

1 pound pearl onions, outer skins removed

1 small head of cabbage, washed and cut into eighths

In a Dutch oven, heat vegetable oil over medium heat. Add stew meat and sauté, turning often so the sides are evenly browned. Add hot water, Worcestershire® sauce, garlic, onion, bay leaves, salt, sugar, paprika, and pepper. Cover and simmer for 1½ hours, stirring occasionally to keep from sticking. Remove bay leaves. Add carrots, new potatoes, and pearl onions. Cover and cook for 30 minutes. Add cabbage sections and continue to cook another 15 minutes, or until cabbage is steamed to desired tenderness.

 You can make beef stew with different cuts of meat if you don't mind cutting the meat into pieces. When your supermarket has chuck, rump, or short ribs on special give them a try in stew. They can be quite flavorful when cooked slowly.

 You can conceal the fact you are serving leftovers by placing leftover stews in individual baking dishes, covering them with a pie crust or biscuits, and reheating.

M y mother put on a pot of beef stew every Thursday afternoon before she took me to dancing lessons. Slow cookers had not yet been invented, so during the 1950s my mother made stew on busy afternoons. My father expected a hot meal when he came home from work, and he was never disappointed.

 When I cube meat for stew, I prefer cutting it thicker. Larger pieces hold their shape better and give the stew a better taste.

A fresh cabbage will show no sign of browning. Never buy this vegetable if it has a strong odor.

CAROL ANN'S DAD

Carol Ann's Homemade Sloppy Joes 71

Brats 'n Beer. 72

Ball Park Sausages. 72

Fourth of July Hamburgers 73

Sirloin Steak Sandwich with a Horseradish Sauce 74

Cheese Steak Sandwich. 75

Shredded Beef and Simmered Onion Hoagies. 76

Flank Steaks Gyros in Pita Bread 77

Gourmet Grilled Cheese 78

Tri-Tip Steak Sandwich with a Barbecue Sauce 79

Barbecued Chicken on Onion Rolls. 80

Chicken Salad Sandwiches 81

Piccadilly Circles with Crab Salad and Tomatoes. 82

Crab Salad Sandwiches with Gruyere Cheese. 82

Russ' Reuben Sandwich 83

Brie Lover's Picnic Sandwich 84

French Bistro Ham and Swiss. 85

Four Cheese Pizza with Roma Tomatoes. 86

Veggie Pita Pizzas. 87

Shrimp and Artichoke Pizza 88

These recipes are sure to please when you're in the mood for sandwiches.

DELI

Sandwiches and Pizza

Carol Ann's Homemade Sloppy Joes

SERVES 6

A great autumn supper. Serve with carrot sticks or your favorite raw veggies, fresh fruit, and cheese slices.

When time allows, I like to make everything from scratch. This recipe can be prepared in about 30 minutes and is superior to the canned version of Sloppy Joes.

The origin of the sloppy Joe is as messy as the sandwich. Some say it originated at Sloppy Joe's Bar in Havana while others claim it first appeared in 1936, on the menu of the Town Hall Deli in South Orange, New Jersey. It remains on the menu of the Town Hall Deli today, as the "Original Sloppy Joe." It is a triple-decker sandwich made of layers of ham, tongue, and Swiss cheese, served with Russian dressing on long, thin slices of buttered rye. Yet others credit Sloppy Joe's in Key West, Florida, a favorite hangout of Earnest Hemingway, as inventing this comfort food. Some merely attribute it to the Depression-era habit of making almost anything out of hamburger. The first time I ate this delicacy was in the school cafeteria of my elementary school. I really didn't care who invented it.

2 pounds lean ground beef
2 medium onions, chopped
1 green bell pepper, cored, seeded, and chopped
2 teaspoons minced garlic
3 teaspoons chili powder
2 cans (28-ounces) Italian plum tomatoes, chopped
2 cans (6-ounces) tomato paste
½ cup bottled chili sauce
½ cup canned beef broth
1 ½ teaspoons Worcestershire® sauce
Salt to taste
Pepper to taste

Kaiser rolls

In a heavy large skillet, brown ground beef over medium heat. Cook until meat just begins to lose its pink color, crumbling it with a fork, for about 5 minutes. Add onion, green bell pepper, and garlic. Cook until vegetables begin to soften, stirring occasionally, about 5 minutes. Mix in chili powder and stir 1 minute. Add tomatoes, tomato paste, chili sauce, beef broth, and Worcestershire® sauce. Cook until mixture is thick, stirring occasionally, about 15 minutes. Season to taste with salt and pepper. Serve on Kaiser rolls.

If you are making a sandwich that has a saucy filling, like sloppy Joes, toast the bread before assembling the sandwich.

Brats 'n Beer

SERVES 8

I got this recipe from my sister-in-law, Valerie Kates, while visiting her in Wisconsin. Boiling the sausages in beer cooks them through so they only need browning on the grill.

8 bratwurst sausages
4 cans (12-ounces) Coors® Light Beer

Pour beer into a heavy kettle and bring to a boil. Add brats and boil over medium heat for 30 minutes. Remove brats from beer and brown on all sides on a grill, barbecue, or under a broiler.

SERVE WITH

Hot dog buns	Dill pickles
Sauerkraut	Pickle relish
Mustard	Chopped tomatoes
Ketchup	Chopped onions

The fourth of July is the biggest hot-dog eating day of the year.

Ball Park Sausages

SERVES 6

A fun, creative way to serve your favorite sausage. It's best to use precooked sausages because they take less time to cook.

2 tablespoons olive oil
2 large yellow onions, sliced into ½-inch thick slices
2 green bell peppers, cored, seeded,
    and sliced into ½-inch thick slices
Salt to taste
Large grind black pepper to taste

6 smoked sausages (bratwurst, Polish, or German)
6 poppy seed hot dog buns
Spicy brown or coarse-grain mustard

In a large skillet, place olive oil over medium-high heat. Add onions and green bell peppers and sauté until onions are transparent. Season with salt and pepper to taste. Grill sausages directly over medium heat on your barbecue until browned and no longer pink in the middle, about 8 to 10 minutes. Place each sausage in a toasted poppy seed bun. Add grilled onions and peppers and serve with spicy brown or coarse-grain mustard.

Sausages became standard fare at baseball parks in 1893 when Chris von de Ahe, owner of a St. Louis bar and the St. Louis Browns, began selling sausages with his already sought-after beer. It is estimated that Americans will eat over 27.5 million hot dogs at major league baseball parks in 2005.

Fourth of July Hamburgers

MAKES 4 PATTIES

The Fourth of July just doesn't seem right without traditional American fare. Here's a spruced-up version of an old American favorite that will turn your barbecue into a gourmet feast.

2 pounds ground sirloin steak (or any lean ground beef)
3 tablespoons fresh snipped chives
3 fresh basil leaves, chopped
½ teaspoon red pepper flakes
¼ teaspoon salt
½ teaspoon large grind black pepper
4 tablespoons crumbled blue cheese

In a large bowl, gently mix ground sirloin steak, chives, basil, red pepper flakes, salt, and pepper. Shape beef mixture into 4 thick patties. Make a pocket in the center of each patty, fill with blue cheese, and cover the cheese with the meat so that the burger is stuffed with cheese. Grill patties over a high heat, about 5 minutes per side for medium rare.

SERVE WITH

Sesame seed hamburger buns
Sliced tomatoes
Thinly sliced white onions
Mayonnaise
Ketchup
Dijon mustard

To make the pockets: Form the ground beef into thick patties. Use a steak knife and begin ¼ inch from one edge. Slice down into patty about ¼ inch, then continue to cut across patty to the other side, stopping about ¼ inch from edge. The top should resemble a flap.

Use a meat thermometer to test for doneness. Hamburgers should be cooked to an internal temperature of 160 degrees F.

My father was a task master and taught many a greenhorn how to put in a full day's work. When I attended one of my high school reunions, I ran into a couple of class mates who had worked for Merrill. One said to me with gratitude, "Your father taught me how to work."

My dad didn't teach his children to work; he pounded his never-say-die work ethic into us. This process was not always pleasant. The first day I worked as a cashier was on July 3rd, one of the busiest days of the year. In those days, grocery stores closed on the 4th of July, as did most businesses. I began checking at 9:00 a.m. A continuous string of customers congregated in an endless line at my register all day long. Grocermen are a rare breed—they like long lines.

At 9:00 p.m., after the last of the customers had been helped and I'd put in a 12-hour day with no break, my father locked the market doors and began retrieving money from the registers. Nearing collapse, I took off running, "I'm going to the bathroom. I haven't been since I started checking early this morning." He hollered at me as necessity propelled me towards the restrooms. "Why didn't you call for a relief checker?" Stunned this opportunity was available and angry I hadn't been informed of this possibility, I screamed back, "You didn't tell me I could." I was 17 years old at the time.

Sirloin Steak Sandwich
with a Horseradish Sauce and Grilled Onions

SERVES 6

TO MARINATE THE SIRLOIN

⅔ cup Coors® Light Beer

⅓ cup vegetable oil

1 teaspoon minced garlic

1 teaspoon salt

½ teaspoon large grind black pepper

2 pounds sirloin steak

In a large bowl, combine beer, vegetable oil, garlic, salt, and pepper. Add steak to the beer mixture, cover, and marinate overnight. Drain marinade from steak. Grill steaks in a large skillet over medium-high heat until done to your liking, about 4 to 6 minutes per side. Slice meat into ¼-inch slices.

FOR THE HORSERADISH SAUCE

¾ cup mayonnaise

¾ cup sour cream

2 to 4 tablespoons prepared horseradish

1 ½ teaspoons lemon juice

¼ teaspoon Tabasco® sauce

In a medium bowl, combine mayonnaise, sour cream, horseradish, lemon juice, and Tabasco® sauce and mix thoroughly. Cover and refrigerate until ready to use.

FOR THE ONIONS AND BREAD

2 large onions, thinly sliced

4 tablespoons butter

½ teaspoon paprika

1 loaf French bread, unsliced

In a large skillet, sauté onion rings in butter and paprika until tender, but not brown. Keep onions warm. Cut French bread horizontally, then into thirds. Set aside until ready to assemble sandwiches. Spread the bread with about half of the horseradish sauce. Top bread with steak and onions. Serve open face, with the remaining sauce on the side.

Procter & Gamble introduced Crisco® Vegetable Shortening in 1911. Most women were accustomed to cooking with butter or lard, so the new product was a hard sell. To encourage women to use Crisco®, Procter & Gamble suggested spreading sandwiches with a mixture of Crisco®, egg yolk, Worcestershire® sauce, lemon juice, and vinegar. Sound appetizing? Although Orthodox Jews loved the shortening because it was neither meat nor dairy, sales of Crisco® didn't take off until lard and butter became scarce during World War I.

Cheese Steak Sandwich

SERVES 6

FOR THE MAYONNAISE

> 1 cup mayonnaise
> 1 tablespoon of your favorite barbecue spice
> 2 teaspoons lemon juice
> 1 teaspoon minced garlic
> ¼ teaspoon salt

In a small bowl, combine mayonnaise, barbecue spice, lemon juice, garlic, and salt and whisk until well blended. Set aside. Sauce may be prepared ahead and refrigerated.

FOR THE STEAK

> 3 pounds sirloin steak, cut 1-inch thick
> 2 tablespoons olive oil
> Salt to taste

Preheat the broiler or grill. Pat steaks dry and brush with 2 tablespoons olive oil. Broil or grill steaks over a high heat until seared and well crusted on one side, about 4 minutes. Turn, season with salt, and cook the second side for about 4 minutes for medium rare. Transfer to a cutting board and slice steaks crosswise into ¼-inch thick slices.

FOR THE VEGETABLES

> 2 tablespoons olive oil
> 1 large onion, thinly sliced
> 1 small red bell pepper, cored, seeded,
>   and sliced into julienne strips
> 1 small green bell pepper, cored, seeded,
>   and sliced into julienne strips

In a large sauté pan, heat the remaining 2 tablespoons olive oil over medium heat. Add onion and red and green bell peppers and sauté until soft and starting to brown, about 8 minutes. Remove the pan from the heat and season vegetables with salt. Set aside.

TO ASSEMBLE SANDWICHES

> 8 ounces shredded Cheddar cheese
> 8 ounces shredded Monterey Jack cheese
> 6 steak buns or hoagies

Split the steak buns but do not cut into 2 halves. Spread mayonnaise on both insides of each roll. Add steak slices, top with vegetables, and sprinkle with the cheeses. Place under the broiler, 2 at a time, until cheese melts. Serve immediately.

The Gardenburger® Original Veggie Patty was created in 1981 by Paul Wenner at his vegetarian restaurant, the Gardenhouse, in Gresham, Oregon. He began selling his veggie patty to other establishments, eventually closing his restaurant in 1985 to found Gardenburger, Inc. By 1998, his company had annual sales of more than $100 million dollars.

For more tender meat that's easier to chew, purchase Choice-graded sirloin.

Shredded Beef and Simmered Onion Hoagies

MAKES 6 SANDWICHES

FOR THE BEEF

2 tablespoons butter
2 tablespoons olive oil
1 (3-pound) bottom round roast
Salt to taste
Large grind black pepper to taste
½ cup Cognac
1¾ cups canned beef broth
2½ cups full-bodied red wine

In a Dutch oven, heat butter and olive oil over medium high heat. Sprinkle roast with salt and pepper. Place roast in the Dutch oven and brown evenly on all sides. Pour Cognac into the pan, warm, and flame with a match. Immediately pour beef broth over roast to douse the flame. Add ½ cup wine to the pan, cover, and simmer on low for about 3 hours, adding an additional ½ cup wine every 30 minutes. Remove beef from the pan and let cool to room temperature. Shred beef into small pieces, following the grain of the meat. Return beef to liquid. Heat until warmed.

FOR THE ONIONS

½ cup butter
5 large onions, sliced ¼-inch thick
1 cup full-bodied red wine
½ cup red wine vinegar
½ cup sugar
½ teaspoon salt
1½ teaspoons large grind black pepper

In a heavy large saucepan, melt butter over low heat. Add onions, red wine vinegar, sugar, salt, and pepper and stir well. Cover and cook slowly over low heat, stirring frequently, about 1 hour. Remove the cover and cook 2 hours longer, stirring occasionally.

TO ASSEMBLE SANDWICHES

6 hoagie buns, cut in half lengthwise
12 slices Muenster cheese

Preheat the broiler. Slice French bread in half, lengthwise, but do not cut into 2 pieces. Fill with one-sixth of shredded beef and simmered onions and top with Muenster cheese. Place under the broiler until cheese melts.

The American Vinegar Institute confirmed through research that vinegar has a shelf life of several years. After opening some naturally processed vinegars, a gelatin mass, 'mother of the vinegar,' may form inside the bottle. This mass is harmless and should simply be removed.

To shred meat use two forks and insert the prongs, back sides facing each other, into the center of a portion of meat. Pull the forks gently away from each other causing the meat to break into thin strips. Continue the process until the entire piece has been pulled apart.

76

Flank Steak Gyros in Pita Bread
with Grilled Onions and a Cucumber Sauce

SERVES 4

FOR THE CUCUMBER SAUCE

½ cucumber, peeled, seeded, and cubed
½ cup plain yogurt
½ cup sour cream
2 tablespoons fresh basil, finely chopped
½ teaspoon garlic salt
¼ teaspoon cayenne pepper

The cucumber sauce is best when made with fresh basil. Don't forget to pick it up.

Place the cubed cucumbers in a blender and liquefy. In a small bowl, mix cucumber, yogurt, sour cream, basil, garlic salt, and cayenne pepper. Cover and refrigerate until ready to use.

TO MARINATE THE FLANK STEAK

2 tablespoons olive oil
1 teaspoon onion salt
1 teaspoon garlic salt
1 teaspoon dried basil
1 teaspoon dried oregano
1 teaspoon large grind black pepper
1 beef flank steak, about 2 pounds

Look for cucumbers that are firm and well-shaped with a deep green color. Do not buy this vegetable if it has soft spots or soft ends.

In a small bowl, combine olive oil, onion salt, garlic salt, basil, oregano, and pepper. Spread marinade evenly over both sides of flank steak. Allow flank steak to sit at room temperature about 30 minutes before grilling. Grill flank steak directly over medium heat, turning once, until cooked to the desired temperature, about 10 minutes for rare and 15 minutes for medium. Grilling flank steak longer will dry it out. Remove flank steak from the grill and allow it to rest 2 to 3 minutes. Thinly slice the flank steak on the diagonal across the grain.

FOR THE SANDWICHES

2 large red onions, peeled and cut crosswise in half
2 tablespoons olive oil
4 pita pockets
4 Roma tomatoes, cut crosswise into ¼-inch thick slices
4 lettuce leaves

Lightly brush both sides of onion halves with olive oil. Grill onion halves directly over medium heat, turning once, until tender, about 12 to 14 minutes total. Fill each pita pocket with steak, onion, tomatoes, and lettuce. Drizzle cucumber sauce inside.

Gourmet Grilled Cheese

MAKES 4 SANDWICHES

Easy — and it's the cheesiest! The classic American comfort food.

8 tablespoons butter, softened

8 slices sourdough bread

4 slices Provolone, about 4 ounces

4 thin slices mozzarella cheese, about 4 ounces

4 slices fontina cheese, about 4 ounces

2 ounces crumbled Gorgonzola cheese

8 slices ripe tomatoes

Preheat a large electric skillet to medium heat. Pair up slices of bread for sandwiches. Spread 1 tablespoon of butter on the outsides of each slice of bread. Layer the 4 cheeses on the unbuttered side of the bottom of each sandwich. Place 2 tomato slices on top of cheese. Place the top slice of bread on each sandwich with the buttered side out. Grill the sandwich in a skillet over medium heat until golden brown. Immediately place a lid on top of skillet. After 2 minutes, turn and grill until the second side is golden brown and cheeses are melted. Serve immediately.

The invention of the sandwich is credited to John Montague, the Fourth Earl of Sandwich and patron to Captain James Cook, who explored New Zealand, Australia, Hawaii, and Polynesia in the late 1700s. Legend has it that Montague, a hardened gambler, played cards for hours at a time, refusing to leave the tables for meals. One evening he ordered his valet to bring him salt beef tucked between two slices of toasted bread. This new dish grew in popularity and was named after its inventor, the Earl of Sandwich.

You can use any variety of cheese when making this sandwich, but when selecting cheese consider how it melts. I love fontina cheese in grilled cheese. It has a mild, nutty flavor and melts easily and smoothly.
You want bread with a firm texture when making this sandwich. Sturdier bread will yield a grilled sandwich with a better presentation.

The secret to a good grilled cheese sandwich is buttering the bread evenly. Softened butter works best.

Tri-Tip Steak Sandwich
with a Barbecue Sauce

SERVES 6

FOR THE TRI-TIP RUB

        1 tablespoon large grind black pepper
        2 teaspoons garlic salt
        1 teaspoon dry mustard
        1 teaspoon paprika
        ½ teaspoon cayenne pepper
        2 to 2½ pounds tri-tip beef, cut about 1½-inches thick

In a small bowl, combine black pepper, garlic salt, mustard, paprika, and cayenne pepper. Press the mixture into the surface of the tri-tip, cover with plastic wrap, and refrigerate 3 to 24 hours.

Ketchup was first commerically produced in 1876 by F. & J. Heinz Co.

FOR THE SAUCE

        1 tablespoon olive oil
        ½ cup red onion, finely diced
        1 teaspoon minced garlic
        ½ cup canned chicken broth
        ½ cup ketchup
        ½ cup A-1® Smoky Mesquite Steak Sauce
        2 tablespoons fresh parsley, finely chopped
        1 tablespoon Worcestershire® sauce
        1 teaspoon finely ground coffee
        ½ teaspoon large grind black pepper

In a medium saucepan, warm olive oil over medium heat. Add red onion and garlic and sauté, stirring occasionally until soft, about 5 minutes. Add chicken broth, ketchup, steak sauce, parsley, Worcestershire® sauce, ground coffee, and black pepper. Bring the mixture to a boil, then reduce the heat to a simmer, and cook, stirring occasionally, about 10 minutes. Allow to cool. This sauce is best served at room temperature.

The tri-tip is a less familiar cut of meat but unbelievably tender and delicious. It should never be grilled more than medium rare and should always be cut against the grain into thin slices.

        12 slices sourdough bread, toasted

Preheat the oven to 400 degrees. Grill tri-tips directly over medium heat, turning once, until both sides are seared, about 5 minutes per side. Place seared tri-tips in the oven about 10 minutes to continue cooking to a medium rare. Slice on the diagonal against the grain into thin slices. Place slices of meat on toasted sourdough bread, cover with sauce to your taste, and top with the second slice of toasted sourdough bread. Serve warm.

Barbecued Chicken on Onion Rolls

SERVES 8

On a busy day save time by purchasing a cooked whole-roasted chicken from the deli.
Strip meat from the bones and cut into bite-size pieces.

1 whole cut-up fryer
Water for cooking chicken
1 ¼ cups ketchup
1 ¼ cups water
½ onion, finely chopped
1 teaspoon salt
1 teaspoon celery seed
½ teaspoon chili powder
¼ cup brown sugar, lightly packed
2 drops Tabasco® sauce
¼ cup Worcestershire® sauce
¼ cup red wine vinegar

8 onion rolls

The first recorded sandwich was made in the first century B.C. by a rabbi, Hillel Elder, who originated the Passover custom of sandwiching a mixture of chopped nuts, apples, spices, and wine between two matzohs. This filling, known as harosets, *represents the suffering of the Jews.*

In a large kettle, place whole chicken that has been cut into pieces, cover with water, and heat to boiling over medium-high heat. Simmer chicken about 1 hour, or until cooked. Remove chicken from the kettle and cool. Remove meat from the bones and cut into bite-size pieces. In a large saucepan, combine ketchup, water, onion, salt, celery seed, chili powder, brown sugar, Tabasco® sauce, Worcestershire® sauce, and vinegar, stirring to blend well. Add chicken to sauce and simmer for 1 ½ hours. Serve warm on onion rolls.

Since the chicken is quite saucy, it's a good idea to toast the bread before assembling the sandwich.

Chicken Salad Sandwiches

SERVES 4 TO 8

FOR THE CHICKEN SALAD

> 4 boneless, skinless chicken breasts, cooked
> and cut into bite-size pieces
> Salt to taste
> Pepper to taste
> ¼ cup water

Preheat the oven to 325 degrees. Place chicken breasts in a shallow baking dish, season with salt and pepper, and add water. Bake until chicken breasts are just cooked through, about 45 minutes. Remove from the oven, cool, and cut into bite-size pieces.

> 1 cup green onions, thinly sliced
> 1 cup celery, thinly sliced
> 1 can (8-ounces) water chestnuts, sliced
> 1 cup shredded Monterey Jack cheese

In a large bowl, combine chicken, green onion, celery, water chestnuts, and Monterey Jack cheese.

FOR THE MAYONNAISE

> ¾ cup mayonnaise
> 4 teaspoons Dijon mustard
> 1 teaspoon Worcestershire® sauce
> 1 teaspoon salt
> 4 drops Tabasco® sauce
> 1 cup tomatoes, chopped

In a small bowl, combine mayonnaise, Dijon mustard, Worcestershire® sauce, salt, and Tabasco® sauce. Mix well. Add mayonnaise mixture to vegetable and chicken mixture and mix thoroughly. Add chopped tomatoes to chicken mixture.

FOR THE SANDWICHES

> 1 loaf French bread
> 1 cup shredded Monterey Jack cheese

Slice a loaf of French bread in half lengthwise. Trim any uneven crust from the bottom so that the loaf rests evenly. Place bread, cut side up, on a baking sheet. Spread chicken mixture evenly over the bread, then sprinkle the remaining 1 cup shredded Monterey Jack cheese over top. Bake until cheese is bubbly and lightly browned, about 10 minutes. Cut each loaf half into 4 individual pieces and serve.

Thomas Jefferson, ambassador to France, first introduced the French fry to guests at Monticello after returning from a visit abroad. The popularity of this fare spread like wild fire. Those were the days! Back then, they didn't worry about fat or cholesterol. During the summer of 1853 at Moon Lake Lodge in Saratoga Spring, New York, the standard, thick-cut French fry mutated into a thin, crispy treat—all because of an unhappy customer. Native American George Crum, a chef at this elegant resort encountered a guest who found his French fries too thick for his liking. Since the customer is always right, Crum cut and refried a thinner batch, but the guest again turned his nose up at the portly fries. Irritated, Crum retaliated with a French fry so thin and crisp it couldn't be skewered with a fork. This picky guest, however, became so smitten with the paper-thin, browned potatoes, other diners began requesting the thinner fry. And that's how the Saratoga Chip became a house specialty at Moon Lake Lodge.

Piccadilly Circles
with Crab Salad and Tomatoes

MAKES 12 HALF SANDWICHES

8 ounces light cream cheese, softened
16 ounces imitation crabmeat, shredded
1 tablespoon lemon juice
½ cup mayonnaise
1 tablespoon fresh parsley, minced
¾ cup large grated Parmesan cheese
Cayenne pepper to taste
3 large tomatoes, thickly sliced
6 English muffins, split

Preheat the broiler. In a large bowl, combine cream cheese, crabmeat, lemon juice, mayonnaise, parsley, Parmesan cheese, and cayenne pepper and mix well. Place 1 slice of tomato on each muffin half and spread with crab mixture. Place muffins on a baking sheet and broil 5 inches from the heat source in an oven until sandwiches are heated through and tops are browned.

During the 1960s, Steele's purchased Picadilly Circles® by the truckloads and sold them for a mere 19 cents for a package of twelve. These frozen treats consisted of English muffins, brushed ever so lightly with tomato sauce and then topped with a slice or two of pepperoni and a sprinkling of mozzarella cheese. Many a penny-pinching college student, myself included, survived modestly on these inexpensive mock pizzas.

Crab Salad Sandwiches
with Gruyere Cheese

SERVES 4 TO 6

1 to 1½ loaves sourdough baguette
4 tablespoons melted butter
4 cups imitation crabmeat
1 cup shredded Gruyere cheese
2 green onions, thinly sliced
½ cup mayonnaise
¼ cup sour cream
1 tablespoon lemon juice
Salt to taste
Large grind black pepper to taste

Once opened, mayonnaise will keep about 2 months in the refrigerator.

Preheat the oven to 400 degrees. Split baguettes in half lengthwise. Brush with melted butter. Toast lightly on a cookie sheet. In a large bowl, combine crabmeat, shredded Gruyere cheese, green onions, mayonnaise, and sour cream. Mix well. Season with lemon juice, salt, and pepper to taste and mix again. Spoon crab mixture onto the bottom half of the baguettes. Place on a baking sheet. Bake for 5 to 10 minutes or until hot. Top with the other half of the baguette and serve.

Russ' Reuben Sandwich

MAKES 6 SANDWICHES

Russ prefers to make his Reubens with pastrami, but most Reubens are made with corned beef. This recipe calls for ¼ pound of meat per sandwich. For a really meaty Reuben, use ⅓ pound per sandwich.

1 tablespoon butter
1 ½ pounds pastrami, shaved very thin
12 slices Jewish pumpernickel bread
½ cup prepared Thousand Island Dressing
Your favorite sauerkraut, drained
12 slices Swiss cheese
4 tablespoons butter, divided

In a large skillet, melt 1 tablespoon of butter and sauté pastrami over medium heat until warmed through. Keep pastrami warm.

Pair up slices of bread for 6 sandwiches. Take the top off each sandwich and spread the insides with Thousand Island Dressing. Layer top half of each sandwich with 2 slices of cheese, ¼ pound of pastrami, and a heaping spoonful of sauerkraut. Add the bottom slice to each sandwich. In a large electric skillet, melt 2 tablespoons butter over low heat. Place the sandwiches on the hot skillet and grill, about 2 minutes, cheese side up. With a spatula, remove sandwiches to a plate. Melt remaining 2 tablespoons of butter in the skillet and replace sandwiches, turning them over to grill the other side. Grill until the cheese melts. Remove sandwiches to a platter and cut into halves. Serve piping hot.

*A*lthough the origin of the Reuben sandwich is highly debated, many believe it was created in 1914 at Reuben's Restaurant in New York City. Nebraska Cornhuskers disagree, claiming the sandwich was actually invented in 1922 by grocer, Reuben Kolakofsky, during a poker game at the Blackstone Hotel in Omaha.

The secret to a good Reuben *is to shave the corned beef or pastrami very thin; otherwise, it tends to be tough. Don't buy the meat that is already pre-sliced. Ask the deli clerk to slice it for you—very thin.*

Purchase bread *with a firm texture when making this sandwich. It works best because it is sturdy enough to hold the filling.*

Brie Lover's Picnic Sandwich

MAKES 12 SANDWICHES

This recipe can be made up to 6 hours ahead. Wrap the sandwiches tightly in foil and refrigerate. To take on a picnic, transport the sandwiches in a cooler.

8 tablespoons mayonnaise

4 tablespoons Dijon mustard

2 (24-inch long) sourdough baguettes

14 ounces Brie, sliced, room temperature

1 pound mesquite-smoked turkey, thinly sliced

3 large tomatoes, thinly sliced

2 avocados, thinly sliced

1 head leaf lettuce, washed, dried, and torn into small pieces

12 peperoncinis, halved lengthwise

Salt to taste

Pepper to taste

In a small bowl, mix mayonnaise and Dijon mustard. Cut each baguette in half lengthwise. Spread the mayonnaise mixture on the cut sides of baguettes. Gently spread Brie on the bottom half of each sandwich. Cover Brie with slices of turkey, tomatoes, avocados, lettuce leaves, and peperoncini. Sprinkle with salt and pepper. Cover with tops of baguettes. Cut each baguette diagonally into 6 sandwiches.

*I*n 1988, Oscar Mayer® introduced the Lunchable®, my son's favorite school lunch when he entered second grade.

Brie has its best flavor when perfectly ripe. Look for one that is plump and resilient to the touch. Its rind may show some pale brown edges. Ripened Brie has a short life and should be eaten within a few days.

To ripen tomatoes so they are perfect, place in a paper bag. When the stem ends smells like a tomato, it's ripe.

If you are making sandwiches to be eaten later, pack the tomatoes, lettuce, and peperoncinis separately and add just before eating. Take the avocado along whole, slice just before eating, and add.

Best Foods® is the "best" mayonnaise on a grocer's shelves.

CAROL ANN'S DAD

French Bistro Ham and Swiss

MAKES 6 SANDWICHES

My husband and I ate this sandwich at a little sidewalk café in Paris. I thought it was wonderful. When I returned home, I had to re-create it. I serve it with a green salad, a light vinaigrette dressing, and slices of fresh pears.

1 loaf sliced sourdough bread
Mayonnaise to taste
1 ½ pounds honey-cured ham, thinly sliced
2 to 3 tomatoes, sliced
8 ounces shredded Swiss cheese

The ham sandwich was introduced to the United States around 1840 by Elizabeth Leslie in her cookbook entitled Directions for Cookery. The recipe was simple—ham, bread with butter, and a scant bit of mustard.

Preheat the broiler. Pair up sourdough bread slices into sandwich units. Open each unit so that the insides are facing up. Lightly coat the sandwiches with mayonnaise. Pile shaved ham on inside half of each sandwich and cover with tomato slices. Place the top slice of bread onto each sandwich. Cover with shredded Swiss cheese. Place sandwiches on a cookie sheet and place under the broiler of an oven. Broil the sandwiches until cheese melts and is golden brown. Sandwich top should look similar to the top of French onion soup.

For best results, store your deli meats in zip-lock bags. Deli ham will keep 3 to 5 days in the refrigerator.

To ensure your deli meat is fresh, ask the clerk to shave it thin at the time you purchase it. I always prefer my meats shaved thin.

Four Cheese Pizza with Roma Tomatoes

MAKES 4 SERVINGS

1 package (16-ounces) Boboli® (12-inch Italian bread shell)
1 large green bell pepper, cored, seeded, and chopped
1 cup shredded mozzarella cheese
¾ cup shredded fontina cheese
½ cup grated Parmesan cheese
½ cup crumbled feta cheese
1 tablespoon fresh basil, chopped
3 medium Roma tomatoes, sliced thin
1 tablespoon olive oil
2 teaspoons minced garlic

Preheat the oven to 425 degrees. Place bread shell on a lightly greased cooking sheet. Sprinkle green bell pepper over crust. Top with mozzarella cheese, fontina cheese, Parmesan cheese, and feta cheese; spread cheeses out so they will blend together as they melt. Sprinkle basil over cheeses. Arrange tomato slices on top of cheese. In a small bowl, combine olive oil and garlic. Brush tomato slices with oil mixture. Bake for 10 to 12 minutes or until cheeses are melted and pizza is heated through. Let stand 5 minutes before serving.

Eugene' deChristopher created the Boboli® Italian bread shell in California in 1988, giving cooks the essence of freshly made pizza crusts with the convenience of a prepackaged product.

Leftover pizza will keep 3 to 4 days in the refrigerator.

It is often difficult to purchase ripe Roma tomatoes. Plan ahead when buying this variety. They often need further ripening at home.

Veggie Pita Pizzas

MAKES 8 PIZZAS

FOR THE VEGGIE MIXTURE

4 tablespoons olive oil
1 small red onion, thinly sliced
4 teaspoons minced garlic
1 small yellow bell pepper, cored, seeded, and sliced thin
1 small red bell pepper, cored, seeded, and sliced thin
1 small green bell pepper, cored, seeded, and sliced thin
2 small zucchinis, sliced thin
8 mushrooms, washed, stemmed, and sliced thin
2 teaspoons dried oregano
Salt to taste
Pepper to taste

Preheat the oven to 350 degrees. In a large skillet, heat olive oil over moderately-low heat. Add onion and garlic and sauté until onion is tender. Add yellow, red, and green bell peppers and continue cooking until tender, about 4 minutes. Add zucchini, mushrooms, oregano, and salt and pepper to taste. Continue cooking, stirring frequently, about 2 minutes, or until zucchini is tender. Set aside.

FOR THE PITA PIZZAS

4 (6-inch) whole-wheat pita loaves
Olive oil for brushing pita rounds
Salt to taste
1 ½ cups shredded mozzarella cheese

Halve the pita loves horizontally to form 8 rounds. Arrange the rounds, cut side up, on a baking sheet, and brush the tops lightly with olive oil. Sprinkle the rounds with salt to taste and toast in the middle of the oven for 5 minutes or until rounds are golden and crisp. Sprinkle 1 ½ cups mozzarella cheese on the rounds and bake for 1 minute or until the cheese is melted.

FOR THE TOPPING

2 fresh tomatoes, chopped
4 tablespoons fresh basil, chopped
1 ½ cups shredded mozzarella cheese
8 tablespoons large grated Parmesan cheese

Divide the veggie mixture among the rounds, mounding slightly. Sprinkle with basil and the remaining 1 ½ cups mozzarella and Parmesan cheese. Broil the rounds about 4 inches from the broiler until the cheese melts and is bubbly.

Pizza migrated to America in the last half of the 19th century. It was first introduced in Chicago by peddlers who chanted 'Two cents a chew" as they walked up and down Taylor Street with metal washtubs of pizzas on their heads. In Naples, these "pizza delivery guys" strolled the city carrying cylindrical copper drums on their heads. The drums had a false bottom, which concealed hot charcoal that kept the pizzas warm.

Shrimp and Artichoke Pizza

MAKES 2 PIZZAS. SERVES 6

1 pound fresh or frozen shrimp, peeled, de-veined,
  and tails removed

4 tablespoons olive oil

2 teaspoons minced garlic

1 can (14 ½-ounces) artichoke hearts, drained and cut into sixths

2 packages (16-ounces) Boboli® (12-inch Italian bread shell)

2 cans (14 ½-ounces) pizza-style chunky tomatoes

½ cup green onions, sliced

2 teaspoons dried rosemary

2 cups shredded mozzarella cheese

Preheat the oven to 425 degrees. Thaw shrimp, if frozen. Halve shrimp lengthwise, remove tails, and set aside. In a large skillet, heat olive oil over medium heat. Add shrimp and garlic and sauté for 1 to 2 minutes or until shrimp turns pink, stirring frequently. Cut artichoke hearts in half and then into thirds. Add artichoke hearts to shrimp mixture and cook for 2 minutes. Remove from the heat and set aside. Put Boboli® crusts on a cookie sheets. Spoon 1 can of tomatoes on to each Boboli®. If tomatoes have excess juice, drain before spreading. Drain off the majority of olive oil from shrimp and spoon shrimp mixture over tomatoes. Sprinkle ¼ cup green onions and 1 teaspoon dried rosemary over each Boboli®. Finish each shell by sprinkling 1 cup mozzarella cheese on top. Bake for 10 to 12 minutes, or until mozzarella cheese melts and pizza is heated through.

American soldiers stationed in Italy during World War II brought home a taste for pizza. Roman® Pizza Mix, the first commercial pizza-pie mix, was produced in 1948 by Franc A. Fiorello. Frozen pizzas, marketed by the Celentano Brothers, were first found in grocery stores in 1957.

To de-vein shrimp, hold them under a slow stream of cold water and run the tip of an ice pick or sharp knife down their back, scraping out the intestine. Rinse gently to remove any black.

Tips for Buying and Storing Chicken 91

Divine Chicken Divan. 94

Grilled Lemon Garlic Chicken. 95

Grilled Herbed Chicken. 96

Orange Tarragon Chicken Breasts 97

Chicken with Red Chili Sauce. 98

South-of-the-Border Chipotle Chicken 99

Chili-Rubbed Chicken 100

Whole Roasted Lemon Chicken. 101

Roasted Parsley Chicken. 102

A French Country Dinner. 103

Parisian Chicken Casserole. 104

Chicken Cacciatore 105

German Style Baked Chicken 106

Sesame Chicken. 107

Thai Chicken in a Peanut Sauce. 108

Finger Lickin' BBQ Chicken. 109

Perfect Picnic Fried Chicken 110

Grilled Chicken with a Peach Salsa 111

Chicken and Vegetable Skillet Supper. 112

Sautéed Chicken and Shrimp 113

Chicken Kabobs. 114

Stuffed Cornish Game Hens with Roasted Potatoes . . . 115

From French to Thai, I've created lots of ways to perk up "plain old chicken".

Tips for Buying and Storing Chicken

Shopping

Chicken should feel cold to the touch when it's in the supermarket cooler. Grocery stores do from time to time have trouble with refrigeration, so never purchase a chicken that feels warm. Fresh chicken often sits in a pink liquid. This is mostly water absorbed by the chicken during the chilling process. It is not blood. Most blood is removed during slaughter, and only a small amount of blood remains inside the muscle. While this pink liquid is unattractive, it is not harmful. Always check dates on packages. If the chicken has reached its "Sell-By" date, cook or freeze it that same day. Never purchase product that has passed its "Sell-By" date.

Only purchase chicken that is inspected by the USDA and that bears a shield identifying it as U. S. Grade A. Grades B and C are blemished and are normally used for frozen dinners and canned products.

If purchasing frozen chicken, it should be rock-hard and show no signs of ice crystals or freezer burn inside the package. Choose packages that are below the freezer line in the grocer's case.

Chicken meat can be white or yellow in color. Its pigment does not affect its quality or nutritional value. If chickens are fed substances containing yellow pigment, then the color of their flesh will be more yellow than white. When selecting chicken, shop with your eyes and your nose. Look for meat that is not transparent, blotchy, or dried around the edges. Fresh chicken has a clean smell.

When buying a whole bird, look for a well-shaped chicken. It should have more breast than leg meat. Both the breast and the chicken parts should be moist and plump. NEVER purchase a whole, raw stuffed chicken to cook at home. Poultry should be cooked immediately after stuffing.

When shopping, purchase your dry goods first and refrigerated items last. The less time items like chicken spend outside refrigeration the better.

Checking Out

When checking out, it's best to ask the clerk to bag your chicken separately. If you request to have your order sacked in paper bags, ask to have the chicken double-bagged in plastic as well. Packaged chicken often leaks. Placing it in plastic avoids the possibility of cross-contaminating other foods and keeps any leaking mess contained. Once home, I keep my chicken in plastic bags in the refrigerator as well. This keeps any leakage from spilling out and cross-contaminating foods in the refrigerator.

Storing and Using Chicken at Home

After purchasing, go directly home and put chicken immediately into the refrigerator. If you've purchased fresh chicken, it is best to use it within 1 to 2 days. If you've purchased frozen chicken, it will keep indefinitely; but, personally, I like to use my chicken within 1 to 2 months. Freezing poultry for an indefinite period results in significant moisture loss and affects its tenderness and flavor.

If you are freezing chicken in its original packaging, try over-wrapping it with heavy-duty aluminum foil or putting it into freezer bags. This prevents freezer burn. If you are repackaging chicken into smaller amounts, use airtight freezer containers or freezer bags.

Proper wrapping prevents "freezer burn", which is caused by air getting to the surface of the food. Food that has been burned by freezing has grayish-brown, leathery spots. If your chicken becomes freezer burned, it's best to remove this part either before or during cooking as it will be dry and tasteless.

Using Deli Rotisserie Chicken

If you are buying rotisserie chicken from the deli, be sure it is hot at time of the purchase. Deli-roasted chicken should be eaten within 2 hours after bringing it home. If you'd like to refrigerate it for use the next day, cut it into several pieces and refrigerate it in shallow, covered containers. Rotisserie chicken must be eaten within 3 to 4 days and can be served either cold or hot. When reheating, it's best to bring the chicken to a temperature of 165 degrees F. Chicken should be hot and steaming. It is safe to freeze rotisserie chicken by placing it in freezer bags or airtight containers. It will keep for 4 months, but I prefer not to keep it longer than 30 days.

Defrosting Frozen Chicken

There are three safe ways to thaw chicken: in the refrigerator, in cold water, or in the microwave. Never set chicken out on the kitchen counter to thaw.

The best method is refrigerated thawing. Boneless chicken breasts will thaw overnight if placed in the refrigerator. Whole chickens or chicken pieces with bones take 1 to 2 days or longer. Once thawed, chicken may be kept in the refrigerator 1 to 2 days before cooking. If you've had a crazy week and for some reason have not been able to cook thawed chicken, you must cook it before you can refreeze it.

Chicken can be thawed in cold water. Leave the bird in its airtight package and submerge it in cold water. Change the water every 30 minutes or so to ensure the water is cold. Allow 2 to 3 hours for a 3 to 4-pound package of chicken pieces to thaw and about 1 hour for a 1-pound package of boneless chicken breasts.

If you thaw chicken in the microwave, it must be cooked immediately. Bacteria begins to form when the meat is warm. Not continuing to cook the meat until it is thoroughly cooked is dangerous.

Never cook frozen chicken in a microwave or slow cooker. You can cook it from its frozen state in the oven or on top of the stove. Allow 50 percent more time when cooking frozen chicken in this manner.

Marinating

Chicken should not be marinated for more than 2 days in the refrigerator. If using marinade to baste chicken, bring marinade to a boil in a small saucepan over medium heat before reusing.

Safe Cooking

Whole chickens should be cooked to 180 degrees F. Test by placing a meat thermometer in the chicken's thigh.

Safe Refrigeration Times

Fresh chicken	1 to 2 days
Cooked leftover chicken	3 to 4 days
Cooked chicken casseroles, dishes, or soup	3 to 4 days
Fried chicken	3 to 4 days
Deli-sliced chicken meat	3 to 5 days
Deli rotisserie or fried chicken	3 to 4 days
Unopened chicken sausages	2 weeks provided not exceeding "Sell-By" date
Chicken sausages	7 days after opening
Chicken salad	3 days

Divine Chicken Divan

SERVES 6

This is the dish I traditionally make for friends who have suffered a family tragedy. To me, it's the perfect comfort food for both the body and the soul.

> 3 whole chicken breasts, (6 halves) skin and bones on
> Dried rosemary to taste
> Salt to taste
> Pepper to taste

Preheat the oven to 350 degrees. Sprinkle chicken with rosemary, salt, and pepper. Place chicken in a baking dish and bake uncovered for 1 hour. Cool. Skin, bone, and slice chicken into ½-inch strips and set aside.

> 1 pound fresh broccoli, cut into florets with stems chopped
> 1 slice white onion
> Dash salt

In a large saucepan, place broccoli with just enough water to cover. Add onion and salt and cook over medium-high heat until broccoli is tender, about 10 minutes. Drain and set aside.

> 2 cups water
> ¾ cup raw white rice
> ¼ teaspoon salt
> 2 teaspoons butter

In a large saucepan, bring water to a boil over high heat. Stir in rice, salt, and butter. Reduce heat, cover, and simmer 20 minutes, or until rice is tender. Remove from heat. Let stand covered 5 minutes, or until rice has absorbed water.

FOR THE CHEESE SAUCE

> ¼ cup butter
> ¼ cup flour
> 1¾ cups milk
> ½ teaspoon salt
> ⅛ teaspoon large grind black pepper
> 2 cups shredded Cheddar cheese
> ⅔ cup grated Parmesan cheese

In a large saucepan, melt butter over medium heat, add flour, and stir until smooth. Cook 2 minutes, stirring constantly. Gradually add milk, stirring constantly until thickened. Add salt, pepper, and cheeses. Stir until cheeses melt.

TO ASSEMBLE CASSEROLE

In a 9 X 12-inch ovenproof baking dish, layer chicken, then broccoli, then rice. Pour the cheese sauce over the entire dish. Bake uncovered at 350 degrees for 30 minutes, or until bubbly.

C*hicken Divan originated in the 1950s at a New York restaurant, the Divan Parisienne. In French, divan means a meeting place or great hall. In English, it means sofa. It was originally made with either a mornay or hollandaise sauce. Sofa, to me, implies comfort. Chicken Divan is the perfect comfort food.*

For tips on buying fresh broccoli, see Page 318.

CAROL ANN'S DAD

Grilled Lemon Garlic Chicken

SERVES 4

The first time I ate lemon garlic chicken was in Palm Desert, California, at the Marriott Resort and Spa. I was in a terrible automobile accident in 1987 and should have died, but my husband says I'm too mean too die. My right knee was shattered, and the doctors didn't know if I'd ever walk again. When I was first permitted to exercise after abandoning my wheel chair, walker, crutches, and cane, my husband sent me to a spa for my fortieth birthday. This is my version of my favorite spa recipe.

FOR THE MARINADE

2 tablespoons vegetable oil
3 tablespoons fresh lemon juice
1/8 teaspoon dried thyme
1/8 teaspoon large grind black pepper
1/4 teaspoon Veg-It Vegetable® Seasoning
1 teaspoon minced garlic

4 boneless, skinless chicken breasts

In a large bowl, combine vegetable oil, lemon juice, thyme, pepper, Veg-It® seasoning, and garlic. Whisk to blend. Add chicken, cover, and refrigerate 2 hours. Remove chicken from the marinade. Grill over hot coals 4 to 5 minutes per side, or until chicken is cooked through but not dry.

Worried about your caloric intake? In 1907, a slim figure was considered the sign of ill health. Actress, Lillian Russell, the era's epitome of beauty, weighed in at almost 200 pounds. A longtime friend of Diamond Jim Brady, a voracious eater, Russell could match him forkful for forkful. Brady was known to consume three dozen oysters, a dozen crabs, six or seven lobsters, a steak, a tray of pastries, and two pounds of candy at one sitting. Not only was Russell known for her hearty appetite, rumor has it that she also smoked 500 cigars a month.

An easy way to extract juice from a lemon is to roll the fruit firmly over a hard surface with the palm of your hand. Then cut the lemon in half. Hold it cut side up and squeeze it over a bowl. This keeps the seeds inside the fruit.

If you want to serve this as a sandwich, have the following items on hand: lettuce, tomato, sliced onions, mayonnaise, onion buns. They don't allow mayonnaise or onion buns at the spa.

Grilled Herbed Chicken

SERVES 4 TO 8

This is best when made with fresh herbs. I combine dried and fresh herbs by adding one or two kinds of fresh herbs I happen to have on hand.

FOR THE MARINADE

½ cup olive oil

½ cup fresh lemon juice

1 teaspoon Dijon mustard

4 teaspoons minced garlic

¼ cup chopped fresh parsley

1 teaspoon dried or 1 tablespoon fresh sage

1 teaspoon dried or 1 tablespoon fresh rosemary

1 teaspoon dried or 1 tablespoon fresh tarragon

1 teaspoon dried or 1 tablespoon fresh oregano

1 teaspoon dried or 1 tablespoon fresh chives

½ teaspoon salt

Large grind black pepper to taste

4 to 8 boneless, skinless chicken breasts

In a small bowl, combine olive oil, lemon juice, Dijon mustard, garlic, parsley, sage, rosemary, tarragon, oregano, chives, salt, and pepper. Whisk to blend. Place chicken breasts in a shallow dish and pour the marinade over them. Cover with plastic wrap, refrigerate, and marinate at least 2 hours. Remove chicken breasts from the marinade and place the marinade in a small saucepan. Bring the marinade to a boil over medium heat and set aside. Grill chicken over hot coals for 4 to 5 minutes per side, depending on the thickness of chicken breasts. Brush frequently with the marinade.

Early cooking instructions often would say, "Add a knob of butter the size of a hen's egg. Fanny Merrit Farmer, author of Boston Cooking School Cook Book, *is credited with standardizing measurements; i.e., the cup, tablespoon, and teaspoon.*

When substituting dried for fresh herbs, follow these guidelines: ¼ teaspoon powdered herb = 1 teaspoon dried herb = 1 tablespoon chopped fresh herb.

Food safety regulations currently require that any marinade coming into contact with a meat product be brought to a boil before it is used for basting.

Orange Tarragon Chicken Breasts

SERVES 4

In 1947, entrepreneur, Anthony Rossi, founded the company that would eventually become Tropicana®. He began by selling Florida citrus fruits in gift boxes. Since only large fruit was used in the gift boxes, Rossi saw the smaller fruit going to waste, so he bottled the inferior orange and grapefruit sections in aseptic glass containers. He shipped the jars to hotels and restaurants in refrigerated trucks. Despite his success, Rossi believed he had new markets to explore. In the early 1950s, if Americans wanted orange juice, they could use frozen concentrate or squeeze their own oranges. Although most industry professionals believed distributing fresh juice in large quantities was impossible, Rossi thought otherwise. His answer to the dilemma: flash pasteurization – raising the temperature of the juice over a very short time. A container also had to be developed, so American Can Company was commissioned to create a waxed paper carton in half pint, pint, and quart sizes. By 1953, 2,000 dairies delivered cartons of Tropicana® orange juice to the doorsteps of their customers. Today, Tropicana® is the number 1 selling orange juice in supermarkets.

I love making Lemon Garlic Chicken for my family. It's easy to prepare and gentle on the waistline. But my family likes variety. This recipe delights the palate with a fresh combination of flavors and is just as easy.

> 2 cups Tropicana® orange juice
> 1 cup low-sodium canned chicken broth
> 2 tablespoons fresh tarragon, chopped
> 4 boneless, skinless chicken breasts
> Salt to taste
> Large grind black pepper to taste
> 2 tablespoons butter

In a large skillet, bring orange juice, chicken broth, and tarragon to a boil over medium heat. Season chicken breasts with salt and pepper and place in the skillet. Cook chicken breasts, uncovered, for 15 minutes per side over medium-high heat. Remove chicken breasts from the skillet and set aside. Reduce orange juice and chicken broth mixture over high heat to approximately 4 tablespoons of liquid. Remove the skillet from heat. Stir in butter and blend with the orange sauce. Sauce will turn brown. Arrange chicken on a serving platter. Spoon sauce over chicken and serve immediately.

Fresh herbs should be washed before using. After washing, pat dry with a paper towel.

This recipe is best when made with fresh tarragon. If you don't have any on hand, be sure to pick some up.

To reduce is a culinary term that means to boil liquid at a rapid speed until the volume is reduced by evaporation. This makes the liquid thicker and intensifies the flavor. The resulting mixture is referred to as a "reduction".

Chicken with Red Chili Sauce

SERVES 8

FOR THE MARINADE

    ¾ cup lemon juice

    ½ cup dry white wine

    4 tablespoons olive oil

    2 tablespoons chili powder

    4 teaspoons minced garlic

    3 shallots, chopped

    2 tablespoons soy sauce

    2 tablespoons honey

    1 ½ tablespoons fresh oregano leaves, chopped

    8 boneless, skinless chicken breasts

    Salt to taste

    Large grind black pepper to taste

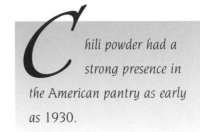

Chili powder had a strong presence in the American pantry as early as 1930.

In a blender, place lemon juice, white wine, olive oil, chili powder, garlic, shallots, soy sauce, honey, and oregano and purèe until smooth. Place chicken breasts in a glass baking dish, smother with the marinade, and turn to coat. Cover and refrigerate chicken breasts overnight. Preheat the barbecue or broiler to medium high. Drain the marinade into a small saucepan, bring to a boil over medium-high heat, remove from heat, and set aside. Season chicken with salt and pepper. Grill or broil chicken breasts until cooked through, about 5 minutes per side. Brush the marinade over chicken breast and transfer to a serving platter. Serve the remaining marinade on the side.

To skin and bone a whole chicken breast: Using your fingers peel off the skin. Located at the wide end of the breast is the wishbone. Using a paring knife, scrape it free and pull it out. Place the breast skin side up on a cutting board. Using the heel of your hand press down firmly in the center so that you break the membrane covering the breastbone and cartilage. Turn breast over. Using a paring knife, cut around the shoulder bones located at the wide end of the breast and remove. Using your fingers loosen the breastbone and cartilage from the flesh and pull out. Slide a paring knife beneath the rib bones and work them loose. Cut the breast in half and trim any uneven edges. To remove the tendon inside the tenderloin: pull the thick end of the tenderloin away from the breast. With a knife scrape against the tendon until it becomes detached.

South-of-the-Border Chipotle Chicken

SERVES 6

While most jalapeños are green, occasionally you will find a red-skinned variety. When red jalapeños are smoke-dried, they're called chipotles.

FOR THE MARINADE

⅔ cup white wine
⅔ cup olive oil
⅔ cup orange juice
⅔ cup fresh lime juice
½ cup ground Chile Caribe
2 tablespoons minced chipotle chiles in adobo sauce
1 tablespoon Chipotle hot sauce
6 teaspoons minced garlic
1 medium white onion, chopped
4 to 5 pounds chicken pieces
Reserved marinade, divided
1 to 2 tablespoons flour

Chile Caribe, chipotle chiles in adobo sauce, and Chipotle hot sauce can be found in the ethnic foods section of supermarkets or specialty food stores.

In a medium-sized bowl, combine white wine, olive oil, orange and lime juices, Chile Caribe, chipolte chiles, Chipolte hot sauce, garlic, and onion and pour into a 15 X 10 X 2-inch baking dish. Add chicken pieces and turn to coat evenly. Cover with plastic wrap and refrigerate at least 2 hours, turning occasionally. Preheat the oven to 325 degrees. Bake chicken in the marinade for approximately 60 minutes, or until almost done. Remove chicken pieces from the marinade and divide the marinade in half. Place half of the marinade in a small saucepan over medium heat. Gradually add enough flour to the saucepan to thicken the marinade to a sauce. Place second half of the marinade in a small saucepan, bring to a boil over high heat, and set aside for basting. Grill chicken until cooked through, turning occasionally, about 10 minutes. Brush with the remaining half of the marinade. Serve chicken on a platter with the thickened sauce on the side.

I prefer to bake my chicken until its almost done and then grill it for flavor only. This keeps the chicken from getting too black.

Chili-Rubbed Chicken

SERVES 4

This dish can be eaten as an entrée, used in chicken fajitas, or served over a salad. I use a Mexican seasoning, Sazon Goya®, found in the ethnic foods section of supermarkets and specialty food stores, in preparing this recipe. Sazon Goya® adds an authentic Mexican flavor to any dish.

FOR THE MARINADE

¼ cup white wine vinegar
¼ cup olive oil
¼ cup orange juice
¼ cup pineapple juice
4 tablespoons yellow onion, diced
1 ½ teaspoons minced garlic
2 teaspoons salt
¼ teaspoon white pepper
1 bay leaf
2 packets Sazon Goya®
4 boneless, skinless chicken breasts

In a large bowl, combine white wine vinegar, olive oil, orange and pineapple juices, onion, garlic, salt, white pepper, bay leaf, and Sazon Goya® and whisk to blend. Add chicken breasts, cover, and marinate for 1 hour in refrigerator. Remove chicken breasts from the marinade. Discard the marinade.

FOR THE RUB

2 tablespoons paprika
2 teaspoons cayenne pepper
2 tablespoons salt
2 teaspoons ground white pepper
2 tablespoons large grind black pepper
2 tablespoons chili powder
2 tablespoons dried oregano
1 tablespoon garlic powder

In a small bowl, combine paprika, cayenne pepper, salt, white pepper, black pepper, chili powder, oregano, and garlic powder. The rub can be stored in an airtight container for up to 6 months. Coat chicken breasts evenly with the rub. Grill over a medium heat for 4 to 5 minutes per side, or until cooked through.

James Dole, cousin of Hawaii governor, Sanford Dole, began growing pineapples on 60 acres north of Oahu in 1901. A relatively unknown fruit at that time, Dole had to educate mainland consumers about this new wonder fruit. Dole's® first pineapples were shipped in tin cans sealed with solder.

If you can't find Sazon Goya®, Emeril® makes a Southwest Essence® that is a good substitute. Emeril® products are available in most supermarkets.

Whole Roasted Lemon Chicken

6 SERVES

My father accepted responsibility for his mistakes no matter what the consequences. An example of just how far he'd go to eat his mistakes occurred one summer on a family vacation. The place and year escape me, but the events will forever stick in my throat.

My mother insisted we always eat breakfast, and on vacations that meant the closest diner. One morning we sat chatting about plans for the day when our breakfast orders arrived. My father had ordered pancakes and hot tea, so the waitress set two small chrome-like pitchers in front of him, both identical in size, shape, and appearance. One held hot water for tea—the other syrup. Without thinking, my father picked up the vessel containing hot water and dumped it onto his pancakes. With our chins on the table, we watched in disbelief as he ate the griddle cakes soaked with hot water. "Dad, get another order!" He responded emphatically, "No! My mistake! They taste fine just like they are."

He did at least ask the waitress for another round of hot water and didn't try to concoct tea with the maple syrup.

12 tablespoons butter, softened
3 teaspoons grated lemon zest
2 tablespoons lemon juice
Salt to taste
White pepper to taste
1 (6-pound) whole chicken
2 tablespoons lemon juice
1 lemon, thinly sliced

Preheat the oven to 325 degrees. Cream butter and lemon zest together. Beat in 2 tablespoons lemon juice. Add salt and white pepper to taste. Loosen the skin of a cleaned chicken by carefully slipping fingers between the skin and the meat. Start at the neck and work down to the drumsticks, being careful not to pierce the skin. Spread half of butter mixture under the skin and pat to smooth butter into a uniform layer. Truss chicken and rub with the remaining butter. Arrange, breast side down, on a rack in a baking pan. Bake for 20 minutes. Turn breast side up and sprinkle with the remaining 2 tablespoons lemon juice. Roast chicken, basting with the pan juices, for 1 to 1 ½ hour, or until its juices run clear when chicken is pricked. Remove from the oven and let stand for 10 minutes before serving. Carve and serve on a large platter. Garnish with lemon slices.

To truss a bird: Use an 18-inch piece of kitchen twine and tie the center around the bird's ankles in such a manner as to fasten the legs together. You will have two equal lengths of twine to loop once around each wing at the elbow joint—the joint between the two meatiest parts of the wing. Bring the ends of the twine over the lower third of the breast and tie as tightly as possible.

To clean a whole chicken: Remove the neck and chicken parts from its cavity. Wash the bird thoroughly, both its outside skin and inside its cavities. Remove any feathers or loose skin on the outside of bird that were not removed during processing.

Roasted Parsley Chicken

SERVES 4 TO 6

1 (5 to 6-pound) roasting chicken
2 tablespoons butter, softened
Salt to taste
Large grind black pepper to taste
2 teaspoons minced garlic
1 bunch parsley, washed and stems trimmed
2 tablespoons butter, softened
Salt to taste
Large grind black pepper to taste
½ cup canned chicken broth
¼ cup lemon juice

Preheat the oven to 325 degrees. Rub the cavity of a cleaned chicken with 2 tablespoons softened butter. Sprinkle the cavity with salt and pepper, rub with garlic, and stuff with parsley. Rub the skin of the chicken with the remaining 2 tablespoons butter and sprinkle with salt and pepper. Place chicken, breast side up, in a roasting pan. Combine chicken broth and lemon juice in a small bowl and pour over the bird. Bake for 20 minutes per pound, about 1 ½ to 2 hours, basting frequently. Chicken is done when juices run clear after piercing the thigh with a sharp skewer. Remove from the oven and let stand 10 minutes before serving. Carve and arrange on a large platter.

To carve a chicken: If the bird has been trussed, remove the twine. Remove any stuffing from cavity. Place bird on cutting board. Using a large fork, hold bird in place. With a carving knife, cut through the skin where the leg is attached to the breast and push leg off until thighbone pops out of its socket. Detach legs from body and transfer to cutting board. Separate the drumstick and thigh by cutting through the ball joint. You can carve the meat off of drumsticks and thighs or eat them like you would when you fry a chicken. Pry the wing from the body with your hand until the joint is exposed, then cut through the joint. To carve the breast, slice the meat parallel to the breastbone. Thinner slices of breast meat will dry out sooner.

Bisquick® is stocked by grocery stores in 1931 with the claim that this mix "Makes Anybody a Perfect Biscuit Maker." General Mills executive, Carl Smith, borrowed a brilliant idea from a dining car chef after taking a train trip from Portland to San Francisco. Just one more example of the food industry philosophy that any good idea is worth recreating. Dining well past normal dinner hours, Smith ordered biscuits with his meal and was surprised when he was served fresh, hot biscuits. He learned that ingredients for the biscuits had been combined much earlier. Smith presented this concept to a General Mills chemist who eventually found a solution to keeping the shortening fresh and the leavening agent powerful in the dry Bisquick® mix.

A French Country Dinner

SERVES 8

Serve with Allouette cheese and sourdough baguette for soaking up every drop of this flavorful broth.

*M*errill developed an unusual way of teaching teenage employees valuable life lessons. Sid Groves relays his experience following a night of guzzling with his friends. Sid's mother, rankled about his hangover, called my father and instructed him to work Sid like a mule as a consequence for a night of partying. So, that's just what my father did, and Sid claims that cured his wild streak.

FOR THE RUB

½ teaspoon salt
½ teaspoon dry mustard
½ teaspoon dry ground mace
½ teaspoon ground cumin
½ teaspoon ground sage
½ teaspoon large grind black pepper

FOR THE DINNER

8 chicken breast halves, with bones and skins on
Vegetable cooking spray
2 medium green bell peppers, cored, seeded, and cut into eighths
1 large onion, peeled and cut into eighths
16 large button mushrooms

FOR THE TOMATO-WINE SAUCE

1 cup Pinot Noir
1½ teaspoons minced garlic
1 can (14½-ounces) stewed tomatoes

Preheat the oven to 350 degrees. In a small bowl, combine salt, mustard, mace, cumin, sage, and pepper. Coat chicken breasts with the rub and place in a 13 X 9-inch baking dish that has been coated with cooking spray. Arrange green bell peppers, onion, and mushrooms around chicken breasts. In a medium bowl, combine Pinot Noir, garlic, and stewed tomatoes and pour over chicken and vegetables. Bake uncovered for 1 hour, or until chicken is done.

I prefer using chicken breasts with bones and skins on for this recipe. It's more difficult to eat, but the bones and skin add more flavor.

Parisian Chicken Casserole

SERVES 4

My favorite type of cuisine is French. This is my own creation of a simple supper my husband and I shared at a romantic little sidewalk café in Paris. The only accompaniments you need with this dish are French bread, a bottle of wine, and, of course, amoré.

> 4 slices bacon, cut into small pieces
> 2 tablespoons butter
> 8 small pearl onions

Preheat the oven to 350 degrees. In a large skillet, fry bacon over medium heat until crisp. Remove and transfer to a paper towel to dry. Crumble into bite-size pieces and set aside. Add butter to the same skillet and sauté onions in butter and bacon drippings until lightly browned. Remove onions from the skillet with a slotted spoon and set aside.

> 1 frying chicken, cut up (2 breasts, 2 legs, 2 thighs, 2 wings)
> Salt to taste
> Large grind black pepper to taste

Season chicken pieces with salt and pepper to taste, then brown in the same skillet. Transfer bacon, onion, and chicken pieces to an ovenproof casserole.

> ½ pound fresh mushrooms, quartered
> ½ small eggplant, peeled and cut into ½-inch strips
> 2 medium tomatoes, peeled and quartered
> 1 small green bell pepper, cored, seeded, and cut into ½-inch strips
> 1 teaspoon minced garlic
> ¼ teaspoon dried thyme
> 1 bay leaf
> ¼ teaspoon dried basil
> ½ cup white wine

Be sure your heaviest produce, like eggplant, is placed on the bottom of your sack. Always put soft produce, like tomatoes, on the top.

Add mushrooms, eggplant, tomatoes, green bell pepper, garlic, thyme, bay leaf, and basil to the same skillet. Sauté over medium heat for three minutes while slowly adding white wine. Arrange vegetables around and over chicken pieces in the casserole dish. Cover and bake for 60 minutes. Remove bay leaf and serve.

Chicken Cacciatore

SERVES 4

Serve polenta with this dish, Page 225. It's the traditional accompaniment.

Chicken cacciatore originated in the countryside of central Italy. Cacciatore means 'hunter's style.' The dish originated during the Renaissance when the only people who enjoyed poultry were the well-to-do who hunted it for sport.

> 1 cup all-purpose flour
> 1 teaspoon salt
> ½ teaspoon large grind black pepper
> 4 pounds of your favorite chicken pieces
> 5 tablespoons olive oil

In a medium-sized bowl, combine flour, salt, and pepper. Wash chicken pieces and pat dry with paper towels. Dip chicken pieces in seasoned flour, shaking off any excess. In a large skillet, sauté chicken in hot olive oil over medium-high heat until browned, cooking in batches if necessary to avoid crowding. As chicken pieces brown, remove and transfer to a plate.

> 2 cups white onion, finely chopped
> 2 teaspoons minced garlic
> 1 can (16 ounces) peeled tomatoes, chopped
> 2 cups green bell peppers, cored, seeded, and chopped
> 2 bay leaves
> 1 cup Merlot wine
> ½ pound mushrooms, sliced with stems trimmed
> 1 jar (4-ounces) pimientos, drained

In the same oil, sauté onion and garlic until golden. Return chicken pieces to the pan and add tomatoes, green bell pepper, bay leaves, and Merlot wine. Cover the skillet and simmer for 30 minutes, or until chicken pieces are tender. Add mushrooms and pimientos and cook for an additional 10 minutes.

This dish has the best flavor when it's cooked a day ahead. If you cook it ahead, be sure to undercook it slightly and reheat slowly to finish the cooking process.

> 2 tablespoons cornstarch
> 1 to 2 tablespoons cold water

Make a cornstarch paste by dissolving cornstarch in 1 to 2 tablespoons cold water. Stir cornstarch paste into the skillet and cook 1 to 2 minutes, stirring constantly until sauce thickens. Remove bay leaves and serve over your favorite pasta.

German Style Baked Chicken

SERVES 4 TO 6

This recipe is a real hit with kids.

FOR THE CHICKEN

> 4 boneless, skinless chicken breasts
> Vegetable oil for brushing chicken breasts
> Salt to taste
> Large grind black pepper to taste

Preheat the oven to 325 degrees. Place chicken breasts in a baking dish, brush lightly with vegetable oil, and sprinkle with salt and pepper. Bake 1 hour, or until done. Do not overcook. Cut chicken breasts into bite-size pieces and set aside.

FOR THE SAUCE

> 5 tablespoons butter
> 5 tablespoons all-purpose flour
> 1 cup canned chicken broth
> $\frac{2}{3}$ cup milk
> $\frac{1}{2}$ teaspoon lemon juice
> $\frac{1}{4}$ teaspoon salt
> $\frac{1}{4}$ teaspoon large grind black pepper
> Dash nutmeg

In a heavy sauce pan, melt butter over medium-low heat. Gradually add flour, stirring frequently, about 3 minutes. Slowly add 1 cup chicken broth and milk and stir. Increase heat and bring to a boil. Reduce heat and simmer until thickened, about 10 minutes. Blend in lemon juice, salt, pepper, and nutmeg.

FOR THE CASSEROLE

> $\frac{1}{4}$ cup canned chicken broth
> 1 package (16-ounces) egg noodles, cooked al dente and drained
> Reserved sauce
> $\frac{2}{3}$ cup grated Parmesan cheese
> 1 teaspoon paprika

Moisten the bottom of a casserole dish with the remaining $\frac{1}{4}$ cup chicken broth. Layer the casserole dish with noodles, then chicken, and smother with sauce. In a small bowl, combine Parmesan cheese and paprika and sprinkle over the top of the casserole. Increase heat on the oven to 350 degrees. Bake until bubbling and golden brown, about 30 minutes.

My father could be a bit hot headed and would often get his dander up when things went haywire. When this occurred, he'd storm home to unload on my mother. She would let him vent and then say, "Now, Dad. Let's talk this through." My mother was a terrific sounding board. In fact, Liz Case claims: "Your father would have been nothing without your mother." I've come to realize as I've aged that people behind the scenes have more of an impact than they're given credit for.

Cook noodles al dente according to package directions or see Tips for Cooking Pasta on Page 241.

Sesame Chicken

SERVES 6

I love ordering Sesame Chicken at our local Vietnamese restaurant, Young's. It's one of my favorite spots for Oriental fare. This is my version of that tasty dish.

TO MARINATE CHICKEN

 3 teaspoons soy sauce
 3 teaspoons Marsala wine
 6 boneless, skinless chicken breasts, cut into bite-size pieces

In a large bowl, combine soy sauce and Marsala wine. Add chicken breasts and marinate at room temperature about 30 minutes.

SOY SAUCE MIXTURE

 ¾ cup sugar
 ¼ cup soy sauce
 2 ½ tablespoons rice vinegar
 4 teaspoons Marsala wine
 1 cup canned chicken broth

In a medium bowl, combine sugar, soy sauce, rice vinegar, Marsala wine, and chicken broth. Blend and set aside.

 ⅓ cup vegetable oil
 2 egg whites, lightly beaten
 ¼ cup cornstarch
 1 teaspoon minced garlic
 2 teaspoons crushed red pepper
 Reserved soy sauce mixture
 Reserved chicken
 ¼ cup sesame seeds
 Rice noodles, cooked according to package directions
 6 green onions, thinly sliced

In a wok, heat vegetable oil over medium-high heat. Right before cooking chicken, add egg whites and cornstarch to chicken mixture and stir until well blended. Cook chicken mixture in 3 batches until golden on all sides, about 3 minutes per batch. Remove chicken with a slotted spoon and transfer to paper towels to drain. Cover with foil to keep warm.

Discard all but 2 tablespoons vegetable oil from the wok and reduce heat to medium. Add garlic and red pepper and sauté for about 1 minute. Add soy sauce mixture, increase heat to medium-high, and cook until sauce thickens, about 15 minutes. Add reserved chicken and sesame seeds and stir until coated. Serve over rice noodles and garnish with sliced green onions.

*I*rma Rombauer, *a widow, wondering how she would support herself after her husband's death, self-published* The Joy of Cooking *in 1931. To date, this famous cookbook has sold over 10,000,000 copies.*

Don't forget to pick up Marsala. It's the secret ingredient, adding a rich, smoky flavor to this dish.

Thai Chicken in a Peanut Sauce

SERVES 6

4 tablespoons butter
2 pounds boneless, skinless chicken breasts, cut into thin strips
2 cups carrots, peeled and thinly sliced on the diagonal
3 stalks celery, thinly sliced on the diagonal
2 packages (8-ounces) bean sprouts
3 green onions, thinly sliced
1 teaspoon minced garlic
2 tablespoons soy sauce
¾ cup heavy cream
½ cup creamy peanut butter
1 teaspoon salt
½ teaspoon large grind black pepper
6 quarts water
2 packages (6-ounces) rice noodles
½ cup sliced almonds, toasted
2 green onions, thinly sliced

In a large non-stick skillet, melt butter over medium-high heat. Add chicken and sauté for 1 to 2 minutes, or until meat turns white and cooks through. Remove chicken and set aside.

Reduce heat to medium-low. Add carrots, celery, bean sprouts, green onions, and garlic and sauté for 3 to 5 minutes, or until vegetables are tender, stirring frequently. Add soy sauce and cook for 1 minute, stirring occasionally.

Increase heat to medium, add heavy cream, and bring to a boil. Reduce heat and simmer for 2 minutes, stirring occasionally. Add peanut butter, salt, and pepper and stir until peanut butter has melted. Add sautéed chicken. Keep mixture warm on low heat while noodles cook.

In a large kettle, bring 6 quarts water to a boil over high heat. Add rice noodles and cook per package directions until done (about 3 to 5 minutes).

To serve, mound noodles on 6 dinner plates. Ladle chicken with sauce in center of noodle and garnish with toasted almonds and green onions.

According to legend, a St. Louis physician encouraged George A. Bayle, Jr., the owner of a food products company, to process and package peanut paste in 1890. The doctor wanted the protein substitute for his patients with poor teeth who couldn't chew meat. Dr. John Harvey Kellogg, wanting a vegetarian source of protein, also experimented with peanut butter for his patients. His brother, manager of their sanatorium, Western Health Reform Institute, opened the Sanitas Nut Co. to produce peanut butter for grocery stores. In 1895, the Kelloggs' patented the 'Process of Preparing Nut Meal.'

To toast nuts, place on a baking sheet in a 350-degree preheated oven for 5 to 10 minutes, or until golden brown. Watch closely as nuts turn from golden brown to black very quickly. I personally prefer to toast nuts by sautéing them in a small skillet that has been lightly coated with butter. For this method, stir frequently over medium heat for 5 to 7 minutes

Finger Lickin' BBQ Chicken

MAKES 12 PIECES

FOR THE BARBECUE SAUCE

1 bottle (12-ounces) chili sauce
1 bottle (12-ounces) water
1 can (10¾-ounces) tomato puree
¼ cup Worcestershire® sauce
¼ cup cider vinegar
¼ cup tightly-packed brown sugar
1½ cups white onion, chopped
1 teaspoon minced garlic
1½ teaspoons dry mustard
1 teaspoon large grind black pepper

*P**aper napkins first appeared in 1925.*

In a medium saucepan, combine all ingredients over medium-high heat. Fill the chili bottle with water and shake to free any remaining sauce. Pour water into the sauce. Bring the sauce to a boil. Simmer, uncovered, stirring often to prevent scorching, about 1 hour. Let cool before serving. Makes about 3 cups of sauce.

I precook my chicken prior to barbecuing to ensure the meat is done and to avoid a charred finished product. For extra flavor, add a handful of mesquite chips to the coals.

TO MARINATE THE CHICKEN

3 chicken breasts, 3 thighs, 3 legs, 3 wings
½ cup fresh lemon juice (about 3 lemons)
1 teaspoon chili powder
1 teaspoon large grind black pepper
4 teaspoons minced garlic
Oil for coating rack

Preheat the oven to 325 degrees. Rinse chicken under cold water and pat dry with a paper towel. In a small bowl, combine lemon juice, chili powder, pepper, and garlic and whisk to blend. Place chicken pieces in a large bowl and smother with the marinade, tossing to coat. Cover with plastic wrap and refrigerate until 1 hour before grilling.

Recipes like this one make me happy I was born after the paper napkin was invented. Be sure to pick up paper napkins. This one is really messy!

Bake chicken breasts and thighs for 40 minutes, legs for 14 minutes. Only cook wings on the barbecue. Lightly oil a grill rack and arrange chicken on the rack, skin side up, so that most of the chicken is not directly over the coals. Dark-meat pieces should be closer to the coals than the white meat. Grill, covered for 10 minutes. Brush with barbecue sauce and continue grilling, covered, another 5 minutes. Turn chicken skin side up. Brush with barbecue sauce, cover, close the vents, and grill 5 minutes. Serve with extra sauce on the side. Adding sauce too soon can cause burning.

Perfect Picnic Fried Chicken

SERVES 4 TO 6

FOR THE MARINADE

2 cups buttermilk
¼ cup Dijon mustard
2 teaspoons onion salt
2 teaspoons garlic salt
2 teaspoons dry mustard
2 teaspoons cayenne pepper
1 teaspoon large grind black pepper
8 pieces cut-up chicken, skinned

In a large bowl, combine buttermilk, Dijon mustard, onion salt, garlic salt, dry mustard, cayenne pepper, and black pepper and whisk to blend. Place chicken pieces in the bowl and coat with the marinade. Refrigerate and marinate at least 2 hours.

3 cups all-purpose flour
1 tablespoon baking powder
2 teaspoons onion salt
2 teaspoons garlic salt
2 teaspoons dry mustard
2 teaspoons cayenne pepper
1 teaspoon large grind black pepper
2½ cups peanut oil

In a large bowl, whisk flour, baking powder, onion salt, garlic salt, dry mustard, cayenne pepper, and black pepper. Place the flour mixture in a 13 X 9 X 2-inch glass dish. With the marinade still clinging to chicken pieces, add chicken pieces to the flour mixture and turn, thickly coating each piece. Let chicken pieces stand in the flour mixture 30 to 60 minutes, turning chicken occasionally to recoat. Pour oil into a large electric skillet to a depth of about 1 inch. Heat peanut oil over medium-high heat to 350 degrees. Gently shake off any excess flour coating. Add chicken pieces, skin side down, to peanut oil. Fry until golden brown, turn chicken over with tongs, and fry the second side until golden brown. Reduce heat to medium-low, approximately 300 degrees, and continue to fry until chicken is cooked through. Serve chicken warm or at room temperature.

*I*n the early days when our budget was tighter than my mother's girdle, we didn't enjoy Sunday afternoon picnics. Instead, my father proposed a different kind of family outing—stocking shelves. Dad hauled cases of canned goods from the back room, Mom sliced them open with a knife, and my brother and I did the stocking. We were too little to read, so we stacked the cans on the shelves according to their labels. We amazed our mother with our expert picture identification skills, even distinguishing the subtle differences between cut and French green beans.

If you drain the chicken pieces on a rack rather then on paper towels, the crust will stay crisper longer.

After flouring chicken, chill for 1 hour. The coating will adhere better during frying.

Grilled Chicken with a Peach Salsa

SERVES 6

This is a great dish to make when Colorado peaches are in season.

If you place peaches in a paper bag, they will ripen in about a day.

FOR THE SALSA

2 cups fresh or frozen peaches, chopped
½ red bell pepper, cored, seeded, and chopped
1 ripe avocado, seeded, peeled, and chopped
3 green onions, thinly sliced
1 teaspoon finely shredded lime zest
Juice of one fresh lime
1 to 2 tablespoons fresh cilantro, snipped

In a bowl, combine peaches, red bell pepper, avocado, green onions, lime zest, lime juice, and cilantro. Cover and refrigerate until chicken is ready to serve.

A good peach will have a well-defined crease, a sweet fragrance, and feel soft to the touch. See Page 310 for more information.

FOR THE MARINADE

1 cup chardonnay wine
2 teaspoons finely shredded orange zest
⅓ cup orange juice
2 tablespoons olive oil
2 tablespoons fresh rosemary, snipped
1 bay leaf

6 boneless, skinless chicken breasts

In a medium bowl, combine wine, orange zest, orange juice, olive oil, rosemary, and bay leaf. Place chicken in a shallow dish, pour marinade over chicken, cover with plastic wrap, and refrigerate at least 1 hour. Drain chicken, reserving marinade. Place the marinade in a small saucepan over medium-high heat and bring to a boil. Set aside. Grill chicken, about 5 minutes per side, or until chicken is tender and no longer pink. Brush occasionally with marinade while grilling. Serve chicken with salsa.

CAROL ANN'S DAD

To peel thick-skinned fruits, cut a small amount of the peel from the top and bottom of the fruit. Place the fruit on a cutting board and cut off the peel in strips from top and bottom.

Chicken and Vegetable Skillet Supper

SERVES 6

I started making this dish in the 1970s. This is the first recipe I created which used wine as an ingredient. This entrée is easy to prepare and I love the color contrasts—carrot orange, zucchini green, and tomato red.

1 can (10¾-ounces) chicken broth
1 cup dry white wine
3 tablespoons minced onion
1 bay leaf
¼ teaspoon dried rosemary, crushed
6 boneless, skinless chicken breast halves
3 small carrots, peeled and halved lengthwise into strips
6 small zucchinis, quartered lengthwise into strips
1 can (16-ounces) peeled tomatoes, chopped, with juices

In a large skillet, combine chicken broth, wine, onion, bay leaf, and rosemary. Bring to a boil over medium-high heat. Place chicken breasts in the boiling liquid. Reduce heat to medium-low, cover, and simmer for 10 minutes. Add carrots and cook 10 minutes longer. Add zucchinis, tomatoes, and juice from tomatoes and cook another 10 minutes.

My mother, Pauline, was a bit of a perfectionist. She taught me one very valuable life lesson--practice makes perfect. This rings true in every area of our lives from playing the violin to mastering the game of tennis. Cooking is no exception. You can't be a good cook if you don't work at it. Although my mother had a limited repertoire of recipes, she had perfected every one. I've been making this dish since the 1970s. Following in my mother's footsteps, this one is down pat.

When I first started making this recipe, supermarkets didn't sell boneless, skinless chicken breasts. I used whole. Now, the boneless, skinless breast has become the most popular poultry product in American supermarkets because it is low in fat and cooks quickly.

Sautéed Chicken and Shrimp

SERVES 6

FOR THE CHICKEN AND SHRIMP

¼ cup olive oil

18 ounces boneless, skinless chicken breasts, cut into ½-inch strips

¼ cup olive oil

12 ounces shrimp, peeled and de-veined

2 teaspoons minced garlic

1 teaspoon crushed hot red pepper

2 tablespoons tomato paste

1 cup dry white wine

¾ cup canned chicken broth

Salt to taste

I like using large shrimp, 31–35 count per pound, for this recipe.

In a large skillet, heat ¼ cup olive oil over medium-high heat and sauté chicken strips for several minutes. Remove from the pan, transfer to a plate, and cover with aluminum foil to keep warm. To the same skillet, add an additional ¼ cup olive oil and sauté shrimp for several minutes, or until they turn pink. Remove, transfer to the plate with chicken, and cover to keep warm. To the same skillet, add garlic and red pepper and sauté, but do not brown. Mix in tomato paste and stir until smooth. Add wine, stir to combine, and cook until mixture is reduced to ¼ cup. Stir in chicken broth and salt to taste. Add chicken and shrimp to the sauce, stirring to coat evenly. Do not simmer, but keep warm.

FOR THE VEGETABLES

6 tablespoons olive oil

1 large white onion, sliced

1 large green bell pepper, cored, seeded, and cut into strips

1 large red bell pepper, cored, seeded, and cut into strips

2 large tomatoes, cored, peeled, seeded, and cut into wedges

Salt to taste

¼ cup fresh parsley, chopped

2 tablespoons fresh basil, chopped

2 tablespoons fresh oregano, chopped

This recipe is served over pasta or rice. Don't forget to pick up your favorite pasta or rice if you don't have some in your pantry.

In another large skillet, heat the remaining 6 tablespoons olive oil over medium-high heat and sauté onion until translucent. Add green and red bell peppers, tomatoes, salt, parsley, basil, and oregano. Cook until heated through and combine with chicken and shrimp mixture. Serve over pasta or rice.

Chicken Kabobs

SERVES 4

This makes a great summer supper. Making your own kabobs is a piece of cake.

VINAIGRETTE MARINADE

    4 tablespoons safflower oil
    4 tablespoons rice vinegar
    4 tablespoons sparkling mineral water
    3 tablespoons lime juice
    2 tablespoons Dijon mustard
    4 tablespoons green onions, thinly sliced
    2 tablespoons fresh chives, chopped
    16 grinds white pepper
    Veg-It® seasoning to taste

In a large bowl, combine safflower oil, vinegar, sparkling water, lime juice, Dijon mustard, green onions, chives, white pepper, and Veg-It® and whisk to blend.

KABOBS INGREDIENTS

    1 red bell pepper, cored, seeded,
      and cut into 1-inch square pieces
    1 medium zucchini, cut on the diagonal in 1-inch pieces
    1 yellow squash, cut on the diagonal in 1-inch pieces
    8 mushroom caps, washed and stems trimmed
    4 boneless, skinless chicken breast halves
    Vinaigrette Marinade

Fill a kettle half full of water and bring to a boil over high heat. Place red bell pepper pieces in a strainer, lower the strainer into boiling water, and blanch until no longer raw but still crisp. Remove red bell peppers, drain, and cool in a large bowl of ice water. Cut each chicken breast into 2 pieces and then into 5 pieces. Place all vegetables and chicken pieces in a large bowl and cover with vinaigrette marinade. Cover bowl with plastic wrap, refrigerate, and marinate for 2 hours, turning 2 to 3 times. Preheat charcoal grill or broiler. Remove chicken and vegetables from the marinade and thread onto skewers. Place the marinade in a small saucepan, bring to a boil over high heat, and set aside. Grill over hot coals or broil kabobs for 10 minutes, or until done, turning frequently and basting with the heated marinade. Serve over rice.

Perrier made its debut in the American supermarket in 1976. Before that time, who could imagine we'd be buying bottled water to drink. By 1979, Americans had tripled their consumption of bottled water.

To blanch is a culinary term that means to plunge food briefly into boiling water and then into cold water to stop the cooking process. This process firms the flesh and sets the color and flavor. It can also be used to loosen skin.

I like to thread my vegetables and chicken on separate skewers. This ensures that both are cooked just enough. Thread the skewers loosely. Cramping the chicken and vegetables makes it difficult for them to cook evenly.

Stuffed Cornish Game Hens
with Roasted Potatoes

SERVES 6

Cornish game hens turn any gathering into an elegant affair. When you want to impress your guests, this is a sure winner.

TO PREPARE STUFFING

Always stuff just before roasting — never ahead of time. Stuffing that sits in an uncooked bird is a breeding ground for bacteria.

> 12 tablespoons butter
> ¾ cup green onions, thinly sliced
> 3 packages (10-ounces) frozen spinach, thawed and drained
> 1 pound mushrooms, stems removed and sliced
> 1 cup ricotta cheese
> ¾ cup grated Parmesan cheese
> 1 teaspoon dried thyme
> 1 teaspoon minced garlic
> ¾ teaspoon salt
> ½ teaspoon large grind black pepper

Preheat the oven to 425 degrees. In a large skillet, melt butter over medium heat. Add green onions and sauté for 2 minutes. Squeeze spinach as dry as possible and add to green onions along with mushrooms. Increase heat to high and cook mushrooms, stirring frequently, until browned and the pan is dry. Cool slightly and stir in ricotta cheese, Parmesan cheese, thyme, garlic, salt, and pepper.

To tie legs and wings: See tip on Page 101.

TO PREPARE HENS

> 6 Cornish game hens
> Salt to taste
> 12 red new potatoes
> 3 tablespoons melted butter
> Salt to taste
> Pepper to taste

You need kitchen twine for this recipe. Don't forget to pick some up.

Wash hens thoroughly and pat dry with paper towels. Season inside of the cavities with salt. With skin side up and drumsticks facing you, gently separate the skin from the breast meat by loosening it with your hands. Gently slip fingers between the skin and the meat. Divide the stuffing mixture evenly under the skin of each hen. Tie legs and wings closely to the body with string. Place hens in a shallow roasting pan with potatoes. Brush with melted butter and sprinkle with salt and pepper. Roast, basting frequently with the pan drippings, until hens are nicely browned and potatoes are tender, about 60 minutes. Serve immediately.

NEW as a NEWS FLASH

COAST-TO-COAST HOOK-UP

Florida . . . Texas . . . California—every state in America's "sun belt"—sends something to our Produce Department . . . something that will add to the health and happiness of your family. Fresh fruits and vegetables—full-flavored and vitamin-rich—are here in vast variety awaiting the pleasure of your family. Put two or three on tonight's dinner program.

BUTTER
Guaranteed
Lb. 37¢

LOWEST FOOD PRICES

NEW CABBAGE, lb. . . . . . 2½¢
RADISHES, Bu. 3¢

P & G SOAP
Giant bars
4 for **19¢**

DASH Granulated
Giant size **53¢**
Large size **27¢**

Folger's Coffee
Mountain grown
1 lb. **31¢**   2 lb. can . . . . **61¢**

HI-VALUE COFFEE, lb. . . . . . . 19¢
GROUND FRESH   GUARANTEED

MATTEE
BRAZILIAN TEA, 1-4 lb. . . . . 19¢
Try this new delicious tea from Brazil

WHEATIES
2 for **21¢**

SOFTASILK CAKE FLOUR
26¢

NO. 1 MEXICAN
TOMATOES
lb. **11¢**

GREEN ONIONS,
2 bunches . . . . 9¢

Spinach California Curly Leaf . . . . lb. **5¢**
Rhubarb, lb. . **10¢**   **Endive,** bunch . **5¢**
Asparagus Calif. . . . . lb. **17¢**

AVOCADOS, each . . . . 5¢
New Potatoes, lb. . . . . 5¢
Mustard Greens, bunch . . . . 5¢
Cauliflower, lb. . . . . 10¢

WASHINGTON DELICIOUS
lb. **5½¢**

The New Improved
OLD DUTCH CLEANSER
3 cans for **20¢**

HORSE 'N BUGGY
PANCAKE FLOUR
5 lb. bag . . **23¢**

AMAIZO
GOLDEN SYRUP
5 lb. pail . . . . **32¢**

CRISCO
3 lb. can
75¢

JUICE ORANGES, 2 doz. . . . . 25¢

CHEESE Armour's American . . . . . . 2 lb. box 59¢

BLUE BONNET
SALAD DRESSING Qts. . . . . **35¢** Pts. . . . . **24¢**
HEINZ KETCHUP 14 oz. bottle . . . . . . **22¢**

Del Monte
Peaches
No. 2½
22¢

Del Haven Sliced or Halves
PEACHES, No. 2½ cans . . . . . 19¢
Libby
DELUXE PLUMS, No. 1 cans . . . . 10¢
Libby's Sliced
PINEAPPLE, 15 oz. cans . . . . 15¢
Del Haven
KADOTA FIGS, No. 1 cans . . . . 11¢

Royal Rio
GRAPEFRUIT, No. 2 cans . . . . . 11¢
Marshall's
BLACKBERRIES, heavy syrup . . . 15¢
All Good
PEARS, No. ½ cans . . . . . 22¢

FRUIT COCKTAIL
No. 1 tall
2 for **25¢**

Del Monte Vacuum Packed
CORN
12 oz.
12¢

CHAMPION PEAS, medium cans . . 10¢
GARDEN SPINACH, No. 2½ cans . . 14¢
Phillipps
PORK & BEANS, No. 2½ cans, 2 for 27¢
Del Monte
TOMATO JUICE, medium cans, 3 for 20¢
Kuner's
CUT BEETS, No. 2½ cans, 2 for . . 21¢

Continental
NOODLE SOUP
3 pkgs. for **25¢**

Franco Am.
Spaghetti 9¢

Fancy Pink
SALMON
No. 1 tall **21¢**

Wilson's Certified
CORNED BEEF
12 oz. can . . . . **25¢**

DASH DOG FOOD
3 cans for **25¢**

GOLDEN WEST FLOUR

Vitamin Enriched   Fully Guaranteed
98 lbs. . . . . . **3¹⁵**   48 lbs. . . . . **1⁶³**   24 lbs. . . . . **85¢**

HI-VALUE FLOUR
Made by Omar   Guaranteed
98 lbs. **2⁸⁷**   48 lbs. **1⁴⁹**   24 lbs. **79¢**

BEEF ROAST Tender, corn fed . . . . . lb. 27¢
Lamb Shoulder Roasts . . lb. 23¢

Ground Beef Lean Fresh ground . . . . lb. **20¢**
Bacon Sliced Armour's Star . . . . lb. **35¢**
Bacon in the piece Morrell's Best . . . . lb. **27¢**

CHEESE Colo. full cream . . . . lb. 29¢
Aged, 2 years . . . . lb. **47¢**

Fresh Southern Catfish . . . . lb. **35¢**
Ocean Perch Boneless . . . . lb. **29¢**
Prido Shortening All purpose shortening . . . . . lb. **18¢**
Oysters New Jersey Selected . . . . pint **41¢**

Get More for Food Stamps at Steele's

Clapp's Baby Food Strained All kinds . . . . 3 for **20¢**
American Salt 26 oz. round box . . . . 2 for **11¢**
Excell **Crackers** . . . . 2 lbs. **18¢**   Excell **Grahams** . . . 2 lbs. **21¢**
Zee Tissue 4 roll pack . . . . **19¢**

March 19, 1942

Tips on Buying and Storing Turkey 119

Carol Ann's Thanksgiving Turkey 121

Pauline's Old-Fashioned Oyster Stuffing 122

My Favorite Thanksgiving Stuffing 123

Corn Bread Stuffing with Sausage and Jalapeños 125

I love preparing Thanksgiving dinner. It's my favorite holiday. I like serving the following accompaniments with my turkey:

Caesar Salad – Page 20

Pauline's 24-Hour Salad – Page 42

Cranberry Salad – Page 371

Garlic Mashed Potatoes with Jalapeños and Cheddar Cheese – Page 232

Fresh Green Beans with Herbs – Page 220

Old-Fashioned Candied Yams – Page 236

Auntie Beryl's Pumpkin Pie – Page 295

Talking Turkey
Tips on Buying and Storing Turkey

The debate over whether to purchase a fresh or frozen turkey can best be answered by the amount of space you have in your refrigerator for storage and the time required for safe thawing. If you shop ahead of time, it is safer to purchase a frozen turkey. If you purchase your turkey 1 to 2 days before cooking, you can feel safe purchasing a fresh bird.

 I personally prefer to purchase a name brand fresh turkey the day before I plan to use it. I have had good luck with Butterball®, Honey Suckle®, and Red Bird® brands. Many supermarkets advertise rock-bottom specials on turkeys at Thanksgiving. Be extra careful when purchasing really cheap birds because often times they are defective. I prefer to stick with well-known brand names to ensure a quality turkey.

Some bone-in poultry carries the term "basted" or "self-basted" on its label. I prefer to avoid these products because they are injected or marinated with a solution that contains butter or some other edible fat, broth, stock, or water plus spices and other flavor enhancers.

When calculating how much to buy, plan between 1 to 1 ½ pounds per person, depending on the amount of leftovers you'd like to have. If you're feeding 12 people, plan to purchase a 12 to 16-pound turkey.

Storing

Frozen turkeys are available year-round. If I've bought a frozen turkey on sale, I never keep it in my freezer more than two months. Mark your purchase date on it with a black marker.

Fresh turkeys are readily available around the holidays but should be cooked within a few days of purchase. Store a fresh turkey in its original wrapping in the refrigerator until ready to use.

Thawing Frozen Birds

Turkeys must be thawed before cooking. The preferred method for thawing a turkey is in the refrigerator at a temperature of 40 degrees F or lower. Allow 24 hours of thawing time for every 5 pounds of turkey. A 16-pound bird will take a little more than three days to defrost.

Turkeys can be thawed in cold water. Place the bird in your kitchen sink and fill it with cold water. The water must be changed every 30 minutes to ensure it remains cold. Allow 30 minutes per pound if thawing in cold water. A 16-pound bird will take 8 hours to defrost.

Storing Leftover Turkey

Refrigerate leftover turkey within 2 hours. Cut turkey into smaller pieces, slicing meat off the breast. Wings and legs may be left whole. Place in shallow containers and store in the refrigerator. Discard the carcass.

Freezing Leftover Turkey

To freeze leftover turkey meat, place it in airtight freezer containers or freezer bags. I prefer not to store a frozen turkey for more than 2 months.

Safe Refrigeration Times

Fresh turkey	1 to 2 days
Cooked leftover turkey	3 to 4 days
Cooked turkey casseroles, dishes, or soup	3 to 4 days

Carol Ann's Thanksgiving Turkey

The night before cooking your turkey, remove giblets from the cavity. Rinse thawed turkey thoroughly, both inside the bird's two cavities and the outside skin. During rinsing, remove any pinfeathers or loose skin that might have been missed in processing. Scrape any remaining innards from the cavity. Pat bird dry and place it in a roaster, cover with damp paper towels, and refrigerate until ready to stuff. Remove giblets from the wrapper, wash, place in a covered container, and refrigerate.

When ready to stuff, lightly salt the large cavity. Gently spoon in stuffing, lightly filling both cavities to capacity. If the large cavity has a band of skin across the tail, push drumsticks under the tail. It is not necessary to fasten the opening. If there is no skin, close the opening by placing skewers across it and lacing it shut with a cord. Tie the drumsticks to the tail. Dental floss works well for lacing.

Preheat the oven to 325 degrees. Place turkey, breast side up, on a roasting rack in a roasting pan. Rub the skin thoroughly with vegetable oil or butter. Using a food thermometer is the only way to ensure your turkey has reached its proper temperature. Insert the thermometer in a thigh muscle—do not touch the bone. Cap the turkey loosely with aluminum foil, pressing the foil lightly at the drumstick and breast ends. Do not allow the foil to touch the top or sides of the turkey. You can test your turkey to see if it is cooked to the appropriate temperature in several different places. Turkey should be cooked to 180 degrees F between the breast and innermost part of the thigh or 170 degrees F in the thickest part the of breast. Cook thighs and wings until they reach 180 degrees F in thickest part of meat. The stuffing inside your turkey should reach 165 degrees F.

Roasting time by weights:

6 to 8 pounds	3 ½ to 4 hours
8 to 12 pounds	4 to 4 ½ hours
12 to 16 pounds	4 ½ to 5 ½ hours
16 to 20 pounds	5 ½ to 6 ½ hours
20 to 24 pounds	6 ½ to 7 ½ hours

During the last 2 hours of cooking, baste the turkey occasionally with pan juices. Before meat thermometers, cooks knew a turkey was done when its drumsticks moved up and down and twisted easily in the socket. Let your bird stand 15 minutes out of the oven before you carve it.

You can place a piece of cheesecloth inside the cavity before stuffing your turkey. When you remove the cloth, all the stuffing will come out at once.

Pauline's Old-Fashioned Oyster Stuffing

SERVES 8 TO 10

This is the recipe my mother made every Thanksgiving. If you're fond of oysters, you'll love this one.

¼ cup butter
½ cup white onion, chopped
½ cup celery, chopped
1 bay leaf
6 cups dry bread cubes, Pepperidge Farm®
   Herbed Seasoned Crushed Stuffing
1 tablespoon dried parsley
2 beaten eggs
1 pint raw oysters, chopped, liquid reserved
1 teaspoon poultry seasoning
1 teaspoon salt
¼ teaspoon large grind black pepper
Reserved oyster liquid
Milk
Butter (optional)

In a large skillet, melt butter over medium heat. Add onion, celery, and bay leaf and sauté until vegetables are tender. Discard bay leaf. In a large bowl, combine bread cubes and parsley in a large bowl. Pour butter mixture over bread cubes and mix thoroughly. In a medium bowl, combine eggs, oysters, poultry seasoning, salt, and pepper. Place oyster liquid in a measuring cup and add enough milk to make ⅓ cup. Add oyster liquid to the oyster mixture and mix gently. Pour over the bread mixture and mix thoroughly. If stuffing is too dry, add additional milk or melted butter until desired moistness is achieved. Makes enough stuffing for a 10-pound turkey.

My mother taught me to prep the vegetables for stuffing the night before. This makes Thanksgiving morning go much smoother. Place chopped celery and onion in covered containers and refrigerate until it's time to assemble the stuffing.

For this dish, I buy freshly shucked oysters in pint containers from the fish section of the supermarket. Fresh oysters should be refrigerated in their liquor and kept no more than 1 or 2 days.

*G*ot leftovers? In 1954, the holiday season had melted into the new year like a snowman welcoming spring, yet the C. A. Swanson Co. had railroad cars full of unsold frozen turkeys that were overstaying their welcome.

A Swanson employee named Gerry Thomas had a brilliant idea for the thawing birds, although his fellow employees snickered at its sheer absurdity: package the turkey in a partitioned metal tray, along with all the trimmings—dressing, gravy, cornbread, peas, and sweet potatoes—then sell the dinner frozen. Thomas dubbed his brainchild the TV dinner. Initially, Swanson made fewer than 6,000 of these frozen feasts, but within a year they had shipped more than ten million.

My Favorite Thanksgiving Stuffing

SERVES 8 TO 10

Apricots originated in China over 4,000 years ago.

12 ounces dried apricots, diced
1 cup Grand Marnier®

In a small saucepan, place apricots and 1 cup Grand Marnier® over medium heat and bring to a boil. Remove from heat and set aside.

Turkey liver and heart

In a small saucepan, place turkey liver and heart in just enough water to cover and simmer over low heat for 30 minutes. Set aside.

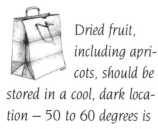

Dried fruit, including apricots, should be stored in a cool, dark location — 50 to 60 degrees is best. A good container for storing is a mason jar. Minimizing their exposure to light preserves color and vitamins.

½ cup butter
2 cups white onion, chopped
2 cups celery, chopped
½ pound bulk pork sausage
24 ounces Pepperidge Farm® Herb Seasoned Crushed Stuffing
1 cup slivered almonds
¼ cup butter
3 cups canned chicken broth
½ cup Grand Marnier®
½ teaspoon dried thyme
½ teaspoon salt
Large grind black pepper to taste

In a large skillet, melt ½ cup butter over medium heat. Add onion and celery and sauté for 10 minutes, or until vegetables are tender. Transfer to a large mixing bowl and set aside.

Cook pork sausage in the same skillet, crumbling with a fork, until sausage is no longer pink. Remove from heat, drain any excess grease, and add to the onion mixture. Finely dice turkey liver and heart and add to the onion mixture. Add stuffing mix, apricots with liquid, and slivered almonds to the onion mixture. Mix thoroughly. Heat the remaining ¼ cup butter and chicken broth in a small saucepan over medium heat just until butter melts. Pour over stuffing mixture and add the remaining ½ cup Grand Marnier®, thyme, and salt. Mix well to evenly moisten stuffing. Season to taste with pepper. Makes enough stuffing for a 20-pound turkey.

Don't forget to stop by the liquor store and pick up a bottle of Grand Marnier®.

continued next page

FOR THE TURKEY

1 turkey (about 20 pounds) ready to cook, see Page 121.
2 oranges, cut in half
¼ cup butter, softened to room temperature
1 teaspoon dried thyme
Salt to taste
Large grind black pepper, to taste

Preheat the oven to 325 degrees. Follow directions for washing turkey found on Page 121. Squeeze juice from oranges evenly over outside of turkey and in neck and body cavities. Spoon stuffing loosely into the cavities. Set aside extra stuffing. Close cavities with small trussing skewers. Place turkey on a roasting rack in a roasting pan, breast side up. Spread butter over the skin of turkey and sprinkle with thyme, salt, and pepper to taste. Cover with aluminum foil, pressing the foil lightly at drumstick and breast ends. Avoid letting the foil touch the top or sides. Roast for 3 hours. Remove the foil and roast, basting occasionally until juices run clear when meaty part of the thigh is pierced with a sharp skewer, about 3 more hours. Bake leftover stuffing in a covered baking dish at 325 degrees for 30 minutes

The average American ate approximately 20 pounds of turkey a year in 1990 compared with 2 pounds per year in 1930.

For a smoother Thanksgiving morning, chop the onions and celery the night before. Place them in covered containers and refrigerate until it's time to stuff your bird. This stuffing is so good you will want to extract every drop of it from your turkey. Try inserting a piece of cheesecloth into the bird's cavity before stuffing. When you remove the cloth, all the stuffing comes magically out at once.

Leftover stuffing will keep 3 to 4 days in the refrigerator. Place in an airtight container and refrigerate no more than 2 hours after dinner.

Corn Bread Stuffing with Sausage and Jalapeños

SERVES 10 TO 12

This stuffing stays quite moist when baked in the oven as a casserole. Sausage and jalapeños give it a Southwestern flair.

1 pound kielbasa sausage, diced
2 tablespoons unsalted butter
1 cup white onion, chopped
1 cup celery, chopped
1 bunch (about 9) green onions, thinly sliced
1 cup fresh parsley, chopped
6 cups Pepperidge Farm® Corn Bread Stuffing
1 jalapeño pepper, seeded and minced
1 ½ teaspoons dried sage, crumbled
1 teaspoon poultry seasoning
1 ½ teaspoons dried thyme, crumbled
1 ½ teaspoons dried oregano, crumbled
1 teaspoon dried rosemary, crumbled
1 bay leaf, crumbled
2 teaspoons salt
1 ½ teaspoons large grind black pepper
Butter for greasing casserole dish
2 large eggs, beaten
2½ cups turkey stock or canned chicken broth

Preheat the oven to 325 degrees. In a heavy medium skillet, sauté sausage over medium-high heat until it just begins to brown. Add butter and stir until melted. Add onion, celery, and green onions and sauté until tender. Mix in chopped fresh parsley. Set aside. In a large bowl, place corn bread stuffing. Add sausage mixture, jalapeño pepper, sage, poultry seasoning, thyme, oregano, rosemary, bay leaf, salt, and pepper and mix thoroughly. Butter a casserole dish. In a small bowl, combine eggs and broth. Add egg mixture to corn-bread mixture. Mix thoroughly. Transfer to a prepared baking dish. Cover tightly with foil. Bake dressing 30 minutes. Uncover and bake until top is dry to the touch, 30 to 45 minutes more.

*P*epperidge Farm® products were the brainchild of Connecticut housewife, Margaret Rudkin. Learning her sons had an allergy to commercial breads that contained preservatives and artificial ingredients, she experimented with baking preservative-free bread. Ultimately, she perfected a whole-wheat loaf that contained only natural ingredients. She started a small business out of her kitchen selling her "Pepperidge Farm" bread to local grocers. After World War II and its shortages and rationing ended, Mrs. Rudkin opened the company's first modern bakery in Norwalk, Connecticut, and began producing dinner rolls, stuffing, and oatmeal breads. Mrs. Rudkin always took the first bite—holding tenaciously to her principles of quality.
I never use anything but Pepperidge Farm® stuffing.

Although usually made from pork, you can find really tasty kielbasa sausages made from turkey. My son prefers the turkey.

Get Your Hands on These SUPER SAVINGS

Copr. Advertisers Exchange Inc. 1955

You save two ways when you shop at STEELE'S! First, you get item-by-item economy because we make every price a low price! Second, you get the BONUS BARGAINS made possible by our constant search for the best food buys of the week . . . every week! Quite naturally, this all adds up to SUPER SAVINGS on the total cost of your food order. Yes indeed—everytime you shop here, you get big savings right in the palm of your hand. Come see. Come get your hands on this week's SUPER SAVINGS!

NONE SUCH MINCE MEAT 9 oz. Package **25¢**

DROMEDARY PITTED DATES 1 Lb. Pkg. **33¢**

PETER PAN CREAMY PEANUT BUTTER 18 oz. Jar **49¢**

PINEAPPLE
ROYALTY CRUSHED 7 oz. CAN **7¢**

APRICOTS
DELMONTE HALVES NO. 2½ CAN **29¢**

ROYAL GELATIN
6 FLAVORS 3 FOR **10¢**

ARMOUR'S CHOPPED HAM 12 oz. TIN **45¢** **ARMOUR'S CHOPPED BEEF** 12 oz. TIN **29¢**

Every Day Low Prices

Blubill SALAD DRESSING Qt.	39c	Hersheys CHOCOLATE BITS 6 oz	21c
Kraft FRENCH DRESSING 8 oz	21c	Hersheys COCOA lb	63c
Sqnaire RUSSIAN DRESSING 8 oz	29c	Maxwell INSTANT COFFEE 4 oz	$1.61
French's MUSTARD 8 oz	9c	Spam CHEESE lb	$1.00
Starfree VINEGAL Qt	25c	Log Cabin SYRUP 12 oz	29c
Del Monte CATSUP 14 oz	18c	Nucoa MARGARINE M oz	51c
Gerber's Strained BABY FOOD 3 for	15c	Pard Dog Food 3 for	27c
Gerbers Chopped BABY FOOD Each	10c	Vic Dog Food 3 for	25c
Gerbers Strained MEATS Each	21c	Friskies Dog Food 3 for	27c
GERBERS CEREALS 1 pkg	15c	FRISKIES Cubes 4 pkg	77c

Derby Tamales 15¢
CHILI 16 oz **23¢**

KRAFTS VELVEETA CHEESE SPREAD 2 lb. Box **75¢**

FRYERS
Cut Up Grade "A" lb. **47¢**
20 DOZEN BOUGHT FOR THIS SALE—GET YOURS EARLY

LAMB ROAST
Swift's Premium lb. **39¢**

Rival Bacon
3 lbs. **99¢**

BEEF LIVER
Select Baby Beef lb. **33¢**

SAUSAGE
German or Big Links lb. **59¢**

SAUSAGE IS OUR SPECIALTY

Ground Beef 3 lbs	89c	Lamb Steaks	49c
Italian Sausage home made lb	69c	Swiss Steak	59c
Pan Sausage fresh 3 lbs	99c	Cudahy Hams	49c

Cauliflower HOME GROWN Lb. **10¢**

JONATHAN APPLES Colorado Lb. **10¢**

SUNKIST **LEMONADE** Not Frozen 6 oz. can **10¢**

HERSHEY KISSES **25¢**

BAKING CHOCOLATE Hersheys, 8 oz. **47¢**

SPIC & SPAN Large **25¢**

STEELE'S
CASH FOOD MARKET
LOWEST AVERAGE PRICE EVERY DAY

WESSON OIL Pint **33¢** Quart **63¢**

September, 29, 1953

Picky About Pork 129

Pork Chops with a Peach and Crab Apple Chutney 131

Hand-Me-Down Pork Chops and Spanish Rice 132

Grilled Tequila Pork Chops with an Avocado Salsa 133

Baked Pork Chops in a Tomato Chutney Sauce 134

Pork Loin Chops Drizzled with a Mango Sauce 135

Artichokes and Pork Chops in a Wine Cream Sauce . . . 136

Pork Chops Florentine. 137

Pork Chops with a Lemon Dill Sauce 138

Rosemary Pork Loin Chops. 139

German-Style Smoked Pork Chops 140

Pork Tenderloin with Wild Mushrooms. 141

Grilled Honey Sesame Pork Tenderloin. 142

French Style Roast Pork 143

My Husband Loves His Baby Back Ribs 144

Spicy Country Style Ribs. 145

Peachy Polynesian Country Style Ribs 146

Barbecued Spareribs with a Chutney Sauce 147

Jamaican Jerk Barbecued Ribs 148

Smoked Holiday Ham with a Bourbon-Mustard Glaze. . 149

When you're pondering pork, here's what I've got in store.

Pork

Picky About Pork

Is Pork Graded?

Pork is inspected and graded either "Acceptable" or "Utility". All fresh pork sold in supermarkets is "Acceptable." It does not have the quality grading differences that are available with beef products.

Shopping

When buying pork, look for cuts with a small amount of fat on the outside and meat that is firm with a grayish pink color. Pork will have better flavor and tenderness if it has a small amount of marbling. Choose packages that are cold and tightly wrapped without tears or punctures. Pork should not be blotchy. Spots indicate that it has begun to spoil. Make your pork selection, along with other perishables, last.

Check for dates on packages. Many stores mark packages with a "Sell-By" date. Never buy product that has expired. Use or freeze products with a "Sell-By" date within 3 to 5 days of purchase. Strictly observe "Use-By" days specified by packers.

Checking Out

Ask the sacker to bag your pork separately in plastic bags to contain any leakage that might cross-contaminate other foods.

Storing and Using Pork at Home

Pork products should be refrigerated at 40 degrees F immediately upon arriving home. Use or freeze fresh pork within 3 to 5 days.

It is safe to freeze pork in its original packaging or repackage it in zip-lock freezer bags. If freezing in the original package, it is best to over-wrap the package with aluminum foil to avoid freezer burn. When air reaches the surface of food, it causes grayish-brown, leathery spots known as freezer burn. Portions damaged by freezer burn should be cut away either during or after cooking. Frozen pork should be used within 3 to 4 months. It is not necessary to wash raw pork before cooking.

Thawing Frozen Pork

Pork can be safely thawed in the refrigerator, in cold water, or in the microwave. The preferred method is the refrigerator. Pork chops will thaw in 1 day. Whole roasts will take 2 days or longer. Once thawed, pork can be kept safely in the refrigerator for 3 to 5 days. To defrost in cold water, do not remove the packaging which must be airtight.

If wrapped in butcher paper, place the pork in a leak-proof bag, then put it in a large bowl in your kitchen sink and fill it with cold water. The water should be changed every 30 minutes to ensure it stays cold. Small packages will defrost in about 1 hour using this method. A 3 to 4-pound roast may take 2 to 3 hours. If you use the microwave for thawing, the pork must be cooked immediately.

It is safe to cook frozen pork in the oven, on the stove, or grill without thawing it first. Cooking times may take 50 percent longer. Frozen pork should not be cooked in a slow cooker.

Marinating Pork

Pork can be marinated in the refrigerator in a covered container up to 5 days. Boil any marinade that has been in contact with raw meat before using it to baste cooked pork. Discard any leftover marinade.

Safe Cooking Temperature and Practices

The most important factor in using pork safely is thorough cooking. Pork must be cooked to an internal temperature of 160 degrees F to eliminate disease-causing bacteria. For best results, use a meat thermometer.

It is not safe to partially pre-cook pork and then refrigerate it to finish cooking later. However, it is safe to partially pre-cook pork and then immediately transfer it to a hot grill to finish.

Safe Refrigeration Times

Fresh pork roasts, steaks, chops, or ribs	3 to 5 days
Fresh pork liver or variety meats	1 to 2 days
Home-cooked pork, soups, stews, or casseroles	3 to 4 days
Ham, fully-cooked, whole	7 days
Ham, fully-cooked, half	3 to 5 days
Ham, fully-cooked, sliced	3 to 4 days
Bacon	7 days
Sausage	1 to 2 days
Smoked breakfast links, patties	7 days
Summer sausage labeled "Keep Refrigerated"	3 months, unopened
Summer sausage labeled "Keep Refrigerated"	3 weeks, opened
Lunch meats, opened	3 to 5 days
Lunch meats, unopened	2 weeks

Pork Chops with a Peach and Crab Apple Chutney

SERVES 6

FOR THE CHUTNEY

1 onion, diced
1 tablespoon vegetable oil
1 teaspoon balsamic vinegar
¼ teaspoon curry powder
1 can (32-ounces) peaches, drained and diced, syrup reserved
12 whole spiced crab apples, drained, cored, and diced
2 tablespoons Grand Marnier®

According to German tradition, partaking in a roast pork dinner on Christmas Eve will prevent evil and bring prosperity in the New Year.

In a small skillet, cook onion in 1 tablespoon vegetable oil over low heat, stirring, until softened. Add 1 teaspoon balsamic vinegar and ¼ teaspoon curry powder to onions. Transfer mixture to a small bowl and blend in peaches, crab apples, and Grand Marnier®. Set aside.

FOR THE PORK CHOPS

¾ teaspoon curry powder
1 ½ teaspoons salt
1 ½ teaspoons large grind black pepper
6 pork chops
2 tablespoons vegetable oil
¾ cup reserved peach syrup
3 teaspoons balsamic vinegar

Since fruits are acidic, you should cook them in a nonreactive pan— stainless steel, nonstick coated, or enameled cast.

In a small dish, mix ¾ teaspoon curry powder, salt, and pepper. Rub mixture on both sides of pork chops. In a large skillet, heat 2 tablespoons vegetable oil over medium-high heat and brown pork chops on both sides, about 3 minutes per side. Pour off excess fat and reduce heat to low. Add reserved peach syrup and 3 teaspoons balsamic vinegar. Cover and simmer until pork chops are cooked through, about 10 minutes. Transfer pork chops to a serving platter. Boil pan juices until thickened, about 1 minute, and then spoon over pork chops. Serve with peach and crab apple chutney mixture.

Hand-Me-Down Pork Chops and Spanish Rice

SERVES 6

This is a recipe my Grandmother Gladys handed down to my mother, and she, in turn, shared with me. My grandmother's recipe called for green bell pepper instead of chopped green chile peppers and regular tomatoes instead of plum. This takes no time at all to prepare.

6 pork chops
2 tablespoons vegetable oil
1 teaspoon salt
½ teaspoon chili powder
¼ teaspoon large grind black pepper
¾ cup uncooked long-grain rice
½ cup onion, chopped
1 can (4-ounces) chopped green chile peppers
1 can (28-ounces) plum tomatoes, chopped

Trim excess fat from pork chops. In a large electric skillet, slowly brown chops in vegetable oil, about 15 to 20 minutes. Drain off excess fat. In a small bowl, combine salt, chili powder, and pepper and sprinkle over chops. Add rice, onion, green chile peppers, and tomatoes and stir to combine. Cover and cook over low heat, about 40 minutes, stirring occasionally.

My Grandmother Gladys had the knack for turning the dullest day into one packed with laughter. She loved secrets, cheating at cards, and telling stories. She claims the secret ingredient in this recipe is chili powder.

If any cans or packages you bring home from the market show any signs of leakage, mold, cloudy liquid, or rust or if the liquid spurts out when opened, don't take any chances. Throw it out.

Grandma Gladys says, "Be sure to pick up chili powder. It's the secret ingredient!"

Grilled Tequila Pork Chops
with an Avocado Salsa

SERVES 6

When I created recipes for our ads, it seemed like pork chops were always on sale. It got difficult to find new and different ways to fix that old standby. This recipe is one of my favorites—it turns plain old pork chops into a gourmet's delight.

TO MARINATE PORK CHOPS

¼ cup tequila
½ cup lime juice
½ cup red onion, chopped
2 tablespoons sesame oil
1 teaspoon ground cumin
6 boneless pork loin chops, cut 1 ½-inches thick, fat trimmed

In a small bowl, combine tequila, lime juice, red onion, sesame oil, and cumin. Blend well and reserve 2 tablespoons. Place pork chops in a shallow dish, covering with marinade. Cover pork chops with plastic wrap and refrigerate 2 to 4 hours, turning occasionally.

FOR THE SALSA

4 Roma or plum tomatoes, chopped
1 avocado, chopped
4 green onions, thinly sliced
¼ cup red onion, chopped
1 serrano pepper, seeded and finely chopped
1 jalapeño pepper, seeded and finely chopped
1 tablespoon fresh cilantro, snipped
1 teaspoon minced garlic
½ teaspoon salt
2 tablespoons reserved marinade

In a small bowl, combine tomatoes, avocado, green onions, red onion, serrano and jalapeño peppers, cilantro, garlic, salt, and reserved marinade. Cover and refrigerate until time to serve.

TO GRILL PORK CHOPS

½ cup jalapeño jelly

Drain pork chops and grill on a grill rack over high heat for 8 to 11 minutes or until juices run clear, turning once and brushing with jalapeño jelly during the last 5 minutes. Serve with salsa.

*I*n the 18th century, citrus juice was found to prevent scurvy, a disease which devastated the British Navy. Britain began importing limes from Jamaica to counter the disease. Limes became the citrus of choice for British sailors, and that's how they came to be called "limeys."

To store a cut avocado: Keep the seed in the vegetable, brush lightly with lemon juice, wrap tightly with plastic wrap, and refrigerate.

Baked Pork Chops in a Tomato Chutney Sauce

SERVES 6

This is a perfect dish to savor on a cold, autumn night when the wind howls and the rain washes the earth. I like to serve it with Baked Acorn Squash, recipe on Page 234.

6 pork chops

FOR THE SAUCE

¾ cup ketchup
¼ cup lemon juice
2 heaping teaspoons brown sugar
2 teaspoons Worcestershire® sauce
½ cup water
¾ cup Major Grey® Mango Chutney

Preheat the oven to 350 degrees. In a small saucepan, combine ketchup, lemon juice, brown sugar, Worcestershire® sauce, water, and mango chutney and bring to a boil over medium heat. Lower the heat and simmer for 20 minutes. Place pork chops in a single layer in a baking dish and cover with the sauce. Bake, uncovered, for 1 ½ hours.

Chutney originated in India where it is served with almost every meal either as a relish with curry dishes or a sauce for hot dishes. The British brought chutney back to England during the Colonial era. Major Grey's Chutney® became the British standard for excellence.

Different supermarkets have different terminology for pork chops. Select chops that are labeled pork loin center-cut chops, rib chops, or loin chops. "Center-Cut" means it comes from the center of the loin, the best part of the pig.

Pork Loin Chops Drizzled with a Mango Sauce

SERVES 4

FOR THE MANGO SAUCE

1 medium mango, peeled and cored
1 tablespoon vegetable oil
1 tablespoon minced garlic
1 jalapeño pepper, seeded and minced (about 1 tablespoon)
⅓ cup fresh basil leaves, thinly slivered
1 cup canned chicken broth
1 ½ tablespoons brown sugar
1 tablespoon soy sauce
¾ cup reserved mango puree
Salt to taste
Large grind black pepper to taste

Purée mango in blender and set aside. Heat vegetable oil in a medium skillet over medium heat. Add garlic, jalapeño pepper, and basil. Sauté until basil wilts, about 1 minute. Add chicken broth, brown sugar, and soy sauce. Bring to a boil, stirring occasionally. Reduce heat to low and simmer 2 minutes. Gradually whisk in mango purée. Simmer until sauce thickens and coats spoon, about 5 minutes. Season to taste with salt and pepper.

FOR MEAT

4 pork loin chops, cut about 1-inch thick

Prepare barbecue or preheat broiler. Grill over hot coals or broil pork loin chops until just cooked through, about 5 to 7 minutes per side. Transfer to plates and drizzle warmed mango sauce over pork chops.

Plan ahead when making this recipe. Most supermarkets sell hard mangoes and you need to ripen them at home. Leave the fruit at room temperature until the skin yields to pressure but does not feel mushy. For tips on picking mangoes, see Page 308.

CAROL ANN'S DAD

When slivering basil, I like to roll 3 to 4 leaves into a tight cylinder and then cut thin strips with my cooking scissors.

Artichokes and Pork Chops in a Wine Cream Sauce

SERVES 6

FOR ARTICHOKES

> 3 large artichokes
> Water for boiling artichokes

Cut off stem and top one-third of artichoke hearts and pull off lower, outer petals. Wash thoroughly. Cut in half. Fill a large kettle full of water and bring to a boil over high heat. Add artichokes, cook for 20 minutes, and drain well.

FOR PORK CHOPS

> 6 loin pork chops, cut 1-inch thick
> Salt
> Pepper
> ½ cup flour
> 2 tablespoons vegetable oil
> 1 ½ cups white onions, sliced
> 4 teaspoons minced garlic
> 1 beef bouillon cube dissolved in ¾-cup water
> 1 ½ tablespoons fresh thyme, snipped

Preheat the oven to 350 degrees. Season pork chops with salt and pepper and coat with flour. In a large skillet, pan brown pork chops in vegetable oil. Remove pork chops from the skillet and drain excess fat. Sauté onions and garlic over medium heat until golden. Add bouillon cube dissolved in hot water and 1 ½ tablespoons thyme and bring to a boil. Place pork chops in a large ovenproof casserole dish. Cover pork chops with artichokes and onion mixture. Bake for 1 hour, or until pork chops are tender and cooked through. Add cream sauce the last 10 minutes of baking.

FOR THE CREAM SAUCE

> 2 tablespoons Dijon mustard
> 1 cup white wine
> 2 cups half-and-half
> ½ teaspoon fresh thyme, snipped

In the same skillet used for browning pork chops, add Dijon mustard, white wine, half-and-half, and the remaining ½ teaspoon thyme, and simmer for 10 minutes. Set aside.

Morton Salt® began looking for an advertising slogan in 1911. An ad agency designed a container depicting a little girl holding an umbrella in one hand and a salt container in the other to let customers know that Morton Salt® wouldn't get clumpy even in damp weather. Morton settled on the slogan, "When it rains, it pours." The umbrella girl was introduced by Morton in 1914 and given a new look in 1921, 1933, 1941, 1956, and 1968.

When selecting an artichoke, look for one with tightly packed, crisp leaves. As they age, the leaves of an artichoke spread apart. Check the cut end. A black end means the artichoke has been stored too long.

Pork Chops Florentine

SERVES 6

3 packages (10-ounces) frozen spinach
6 pork loin chops
6 tablespoons butter
3 tablespoons grated onion
6 tablespoons flour
1 ¼ cups canned chicken broth
1 ¼ cups milk
¼ teaspoon salt
6 grinds white pepper
2 egg yolks, lightly beaten
Thawed spinach, with liquid squeezed out
1 cup grated Swiss cheese
4 tablespoons grated Parmesan cheese

A la Florentine means in the style of Florence. This term refers to dishes that contain spinach combined with Mornay sauce. Some historians believe that Catherine de Medici, the Italian wife of Henry II of France, made the Florentine-style of cooking popular when she introduced it to the Court of France.

The night before, set spinach in refrigerator to thaw. Once spinach thaws, squeeze out any liquid, place in a large bowl, and set aside.

In a large lightly-greased skillet, brown pork chops over medium heat. Reduce heat, cover, and cook until tender, about 30 minutes. Keep warm.

In a medium saucepan, melt butter over medium heat. Add grated onion and sauté until tender. Add flour and cook over low heat for 3 minutes, stirring frequently. Slowly add chicken broth and milk and continue to stir until sauce thickens. Season with salt and pepper.

Place egg yolks in a separate bowl. Stir ¼ cup sauce into egg yolks and then add the yolk mixture to sauce, stirring until smooth and thick.

In the large bowl containing spinach, add 1 cup sauce and mix thoroughly. Spread the spinach mixture over the bottom of a large greased shallow casserole. Arrange pork chops on top of spinach. Add Swiss cheese to the sauce and simmer over low heat until cheese melts. Pour the remaining sauce over pork chops, sprinkle with Parmesan cheese, and bake, uncovered, at 400 degrees for 15 minutes, or until the Florentine is bubbly and lightly browned.

When I grate onions, I prefer to use a metal grater with perforated sharp-edged holes and a handle rather than a food processor. Peel the onion and slice ¼ inch off the top. Grate the onion with a gentle up and down motion just like you would cheese. When finished, slice off the rough edge, place remaining onion in zip-lock bag, and refrigerate.

Pork Chops with a Lemon Dill Sauce

SERVES 6

FOR THE SAUCE

½ cup mayonnaise
½ cup sour cream
½ cup Dijon mustard
½ cup fresh lemon juice
8 teaspoons fresh dill, minced
1 teaspoon large grind black pepper

In a small bowl, combine mayonnaise, sour cream, Dijon mustard, lemon juice, dill, and pepper. Place pork chops in a dish so that they fit tightly and pour half the sauce over pork chops. Cover with plastic wrap and refrigerate for 6 hours. Refrigerate remaining half of the sauce in a covered container.

6 pork chops
Reserved sauce

Remove pork chops from the sauce and discard used marinade. Grill pork chops for 10 minutes per side over medium hot coals, or to desired doneness. Just before removing pork chops from the grill, brush lightly with part of the remaining dill sauce. Serve additional sauce on the side.

*H*ellmann's® originally produced two different mayonnaise recipes. One became so popular that Hellmann® put a blue ribbon around it to set it apart. The "ribbon" version was in such demand that Hellmann® designed the "Blue Ribbon" label for its larger glass jars.

Rosemary Pork Loin Chops

SERVES 4

Serve with garlic mashed potatoes and a Caesar salad.

FOR THE MARINADE

> ½ cup olive oil
> 1 tablespoon minced garlic
> 2 tablespoons fresh rosemary, chopped
> 1 tablespoon fresh thyme, snipped
> 4 bay leaves, crumbled
> 2 teaspoons large grind black pepper
> 4 (5-ounce) boneless pork loin chops, cut 1-inch thick

In a shallow glass baking dish, combine olive oil, garlic, rosemary, thyme, bay leaves, and pepper. Add pork chops and turn to coat. Cover and chill at least 3 hours.

Pork, like beef, will have better flavor and tenderness if it has a small amount of marbling.

FOR REDUCED BROTH MIXTURE

> 1 can (14½-ounces) chicken broth
> 2 teaspoons tomato paste

In a medium saucepan, combine chicken broth and tomato paste and bring to a boil over medium-high heat. Cook until reduced to ¾ cup, about 20 minutes. Set aside.

FOR PORK CHOPS

Scrape off excess marinade from pork loin chops into a heavy, large skillet and heat over medium high. Add pork chops and sauté until cooked through, about 5 to 7 minutes per side. Transfer pork loin chops to a platter and keep warm.

Shallots should be plump, firm, and well shaped. Avoid this product if it shows any signs of black mold or if it is wilted or sprouting.

FOR THE SAUCE

> 2 tablespoons olive oil
> 2 tablespoons shallots, minced
> 1 teaspoon minced garlic
> ¼ cup cooking sherry
> Reduced broth mixture
> ¼ cup half-and-half

Add olive oil, shallots, and garlic to the same skillet used for pork loin chops and sauté for 1 minute. Add cooking sherry and boil until reduced to a glaze, stirring constantly, about 1 minute. Add reduced broth mixture to sauce, bring to a boil, and reduce heat to medium. Stir in half-and-half gradually and simmer until the sauce thickens. Spoon the sauce onto plates and top with pork loin chops.

German-Style Smoked Pork Chops
with Sauerkraut, New Potatoes, and Polish Sausages

SERVES 6

A delicious combination of flavors when you're in the mood for German cuisine.

FOR THE SAUERKRAUT

    2 quarts sauerkraut
    2 tart apples, peeled, cored, and thinly sliced
    1 cup dry white wine
    1 cup apple cider
    1 tablespoon peppercorns, lightly crushed
    Salt to taste

Smoked sausages will dry out quickly. Be careful not to overcook them.

Place sauerkraut in a colander and rinse well. Drain thoroughly and transfer to a large kettle. Add apples, white wine, apple cider, peppercorns, and salt. Cover and simmer over a low heat for 2½ hours, adding more wine or cider if liquid cooks down.

    1 pound polish sausage, sliced diagonally into ½-inch pieces
    6 smoked pork chops

In a large non-stick skillet, brown sausage slices over a medium heat until cooked through. Remove sausage slices with a slotted spoon, transfer to paper towels, and set aside. Reserve drippings in skillet.

After sauerkraut has cooked 1 hour, place smoked pork chops on top of sauerkraut. Cover and continue cooking for remaining 1½ hours.

Once I bring sausages home from the market, I don't like to keep them any longer than 1 to 2 days.

    6 small new potatoes
    3 tablespoons butter, melted
    4 tablespoons fresh parsley, chopped

About 30 minutes before sauerkraut is done, place new potatoes in a medium saucepan with just enough water to cover. Bring to a boil over high heat, reduce the heat to medium, and boil gently for 10 to 15 minutes, or until potatoes are tender. Remove from the saucepan and cool. In a small saucepan, melt butter over low heat. Add parsley and stir gently. Remove from heat and roll potatoes in parsley-butter mixture and set aside.

With a potato peeler, remove a thin strip around the center of each potato.

Reheat sausage drippings in the same skillet over high heat. Add enough sauerkraut to the skillet to cover to a ½-inch depth. Brown sauerkraut until crisp. Mound the remaining sauerkraut on a large serving platter. Arrange pork chops, sausage slices, and new potatoes around the mound. Place the fried sauerkraut on top.

Pork Tenderloin with Wild Mushrooms

SERVES 6 TO 8

I make this with portabello and oyster mushrooms, however, cremini, shitake, or enoki mushrooms would be good substitutes. This makes a lovely special occasion entrée.

*U*ntil the 1980s, pork tenderloin was sold as part of a bone-in loin roast. Now it's available as a separate cut. It has become a popular cut because it cooks quickly, is very low in fat, and the results are always quite tender.

3 teaspoons large grind black pepper
2 teaspoons coarsely ground sea salt
1 tablespoon coriander seeds
1 teaspoon ground cumin
2 pounds pork tenderloin, trimmed of fat and any silver skin
Cooking spray
1 tablespoon olive oil
2 tablespoons balsamic vinegar

In a small bowl, combine pepper, sea salt, coriander seeds, and cumin. Rub pork tenderloin with spices on all sides and wrap in plastic wrap. Refrigerate for 4 hours or overnight. Preheat the oven to 350 degrees. Lightly spray a baking dish with cooking spray. Remove the pork tenderloin from the plastic wrap and place it in the baking dish. Rub with 1 tablespoon olive oil, place in the oven, and roast for 15 minutes. Pour 2 tablespoons balsamic vinegar over the pork tenderloin and roast for 30 minutes, turning meat occasionally to baste in pan juices. Cook the pork tenderloin until it reaches an internal temperature of 155 degrees, or just until barely pink at the center. Do not overcook. Remove pork tenderloin from the oven, baste, and let stand for 10 minutes before slicing into ½-inch thick pieces.

For tips on cleaning and storing mushrooms, see Page 327.

FOR THE MUSHROOMS

3 tablespoons olive oil
3 tablespoons butter
3 shallots, finely chopped
1 pound portabello mushrooms, stemmed, trimmed, and thinly sliced
1 pound fresh oyster mushrooms, stemmed, trimmed, and thinly sliced (may substitute 4 ounces dried oyster mushrooms)
12 fresh sage leaves, thinly sliced
1 cup white wine
Freshly ground black pepper

When buying sage, look for a fresh color and aroma. Sage has gray-green leaves and a musty mint smell. When refrigerated in plastic, it will keep about 4 days.

In a large sauté pan, heat 3 tablespoons olive oil and butter over medium heat. Add shallots, mushrooms, and sage, and sauté for 5 minutes, or until mushrooms are tender. Add wine to deglaze the pan, scraping up any brown bits. Sauté until the liquid is reduced by half. Season sauce with freshly ground black pepper. Place sliced pork tenderloin on a platter and spoon mushrooms around the slices.

Grilled Honey Sesame Pork Tenderloin

SERVES 6

This entrée can be prepared in under 30 minutes. If you have a busy day, marinate the meat in the morning or the night before.

FOR THE MARINADE

- ½ cup Coors® Light Beer
- 3 tablespoons sesame seeds
- 3 tablespoons honey
- 2 tablespoons Dijon mustard
- ½ teaspoon large grind black pepper
- 2 teaspoons minced garlic

2 pounds pork tenderloin

In a small bowl, combine beer, sesame seeds, honey, Dijon mustard, pepper, and garlic and blend thoroughly. In a large bowl, place tenderloin and pour marinade over meat. Cover with plastic wrap, and marinate in the refrigerator for at least 2 hours, turning meat occasionally.

Remove tenderloin from marinade, reserving marinade. Transfer marinade to a small saucepan and bring to a boil over medium-high heat. Remove and set aside.

Vegetable cooking spray

Coat a grill rack with cooking spray. Place tenderloin on the grill over medium-high coals (about 350 to 400 degrees). Grill tenderloin, with grill lid closed, about 25 to 30 minutes, or until a meat thermometer inserted into thickest part of the tenderloin registers 160 degrees. Turn and baste tenderloin occasionally with reserved marinade. Slice diagonally across the grain into thick slices.

According to legend, in 1382 the Duke of Burgundy, Philip the Bold, gave the town of Dijon a coat of arms with the motto "MOULT ME TARDE" based on Multum Ardeo — I ardently desire. As the story goes, the town's many mustard makers adopted the motto, eventually shortening it to Moul-tarde—to burn much. Another legend recounts that King Charles VI gave the citizens of Dijon a coat of arms bearing the motto "MOULT ME TARDE", meaning off to battle. The opponents of the Dijon army encountered the motto but missed the "ME" in the middle and believed they were going to battle with an army of mustard makers.

Store tightly sealed liquid honey in a cool dry place for 6 months. Write the opened date on your honey with a black marker.

When refrigerated, honey crystallizes, forming a gooey, grainy mass. Placing the opened jar in a microwave oven at 100 percent power for about 30 seconds can reliquefy honey. The time will vary depending upon the amount of honey left in the container. You can also place it in a pan of hot water over low heat for 10 to 15 minutes.

French Style Roast Pork

SERVES 8

This recipe is heavenly. I like to serve it with a green salad, a light vinaigrette dressing, a French baguette, and a small selection of French cheeses, like Boursin, Brie, or Camembert.

1 (4 to 4½-pound) pork butt or loin roast
1 teaspoon minced garlic
4 tablespoons unsalted butter, softened
2 tablespoons Dijon mustard
1 teaspoon dried thyme
½ teaspoon large grind black pepper
1 cup canned chicken broth
1 cup dry white wine
2 tablespoons apricot jam

Preheat the oven to 350 degrees. Cut five deep slits in roast with a sharp knife and insert minced garlic into the slits. Place roast in a shallow roasting pan. In a small bowl, combine butter, Dijon mustard, thyme, and pepper. Spread this mixture evenly over roast. In a small saucepan, heat chicken broth, white wine, and apricot jam together over low heat until apricot jam dissolves. Pour this mixture over roast and cook, uncovered, on the center rack of the oven until cooked through, about 1½ hours for a pork loin roast or 2½ hours for a pork butt roast (20 minutes per pound). Temperature on a meat thermometer should read 150 to 160 degrees when roast is done.

B*efore receiving my learner's permit, Sunday was my favorite day of the week. Back then, businesses closed on Sundays. Members of the Catholic Church directly across the street from the Mountain Avenue store were permitted to park in our lot while they worshipped, but services concluded about lunch time, leaving our parking lot empty—an oasis for the learning-to-drive children of a grocer. Come Sunday afternoon following a flawlessly prepared dinner of roast beef, mashed potatoes, and gravy, my brother and I headed to the market with our father who always spent Sunday afternoons holed up in his office buried in book work. Dad would hand over the keys to his beat-up 1954 blue and white Dodge, and we'd figure eight around the parking lot to our heart's content, the grinding gears rasping out in protest. My father never took the time to wash his car, and he used the back seat as a brief case. Consequently, the old Dodge grew quite dusty and cluttered. No matter how filthy she became, driving her around in circles kept us occupied for hours.*

If you want to serve Camembert with this roast, choose one that is plump and soft to the touch. Avoid ones with hardened edges. This is a sign the cheese may be overripe. When passed its prime, Camembert becomes runny and bitter.

A bone-in pork loin roast will have more flavor then a boneless roast but needs to cook slightly longer.

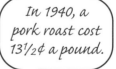
In 1940, a pork roast cost 13½¢ a pound.

CAROL ANN'S DAD

My Husband Loves His Baby Back Ribs

SERVES 4

My husband loves baby back ribs. I struggled with preparing them properly until one of our chefs shared his recipe with me. Anyone can make dynamite baby back ribs following this method. Cooking time for this dish is 90 minutes.

> 4 pounds baby back ribs
>   (approximately one-half slab per serving)
> Salt
> Pepper

Preheat the oven to 450 degrees. Season ribs with salt and pepper. Place, meaty side down, in a shallow roasting pan and roast at 450 degrees for 30 minutes. Remove ribs from the oven, drain excess fat from the pan, and turn meaty side up. Lower the oven temperature to 350 degrees and continue roasting for 30 minutes. Reduce heat to 300 degrees and roast an additional 30 minutes. During the last 30 minutes of roasting, spread barbecue sauce over both sides of ribs, turning and basting until ribs are tender and glazed.

FOR THE SAUCE

> 1 can (6-ounces) tomato paste
> ¼ cup ketchup
> 1 cup water
> 2 tablespoons white vinegar
> ¼ cup lemon juice
> ⅓ cup brown sugar
> ¼ cup Worcestershire® sauce
> ½ teaspoon ground allspice
> 2 teaspoons minced garlic
> ⅔ cup fresh onion, minced
> 1 ½ teaspoons salt

While ribs are roasting, in a medium saucepan, combine tomato paste, ketchup, water, white vinegar, lemon juice, brown sugar, Worcestershire® sauce, allspice, garlic, onion, and salt and simmer over a low heat for approximately 30 minutes.

Denmark is one of the world's three largest pork exporters. Believe it or not, Denmark developed the baby back rib in the early 1980s to crack into the lucrative Japanese market. This style of rib is smaller and more delicate than the traditional American sparerib.

Back ribs come from the back or loin of the pig and are often called loin back ribs. They have more meat than spareribs and are not as fatty. Baby back ribs are a narrower slab of back ribs and are sometimes called riblets.

Plan to purchase 1 pound of baby back ribs per person.

Spicy Country Style Ribs

SERVES 6

FOR CAROL ANN'S SPICY BARBECUE SAUCE

I usually purchase two country-style ribs or 8 to 12 ounces per person.

¾ cup chili sauce

1 tablespoon red wine vinegar

⅓ cup Lea & Perrins® Steak Sauce

1 tablespoon garlic juice

2 teaspoons dry mustard

1 tablespoon minced jalapeño pepper

2 tablespoons horseradish

1 tablespoon Louisiana-style hot sauce

2 tablespoons molasses

2 cups ketchup

In a medium bowl, combine chili sauce, red wine vinegar, steak sauce, garlic juice, mustard, jalapeño pepper, horseradish, hot sauce, molasses, and ketchup and whisk to blend. Sauce can be refrigerated up to one week but is best when made 24 hours before using. Bring sauce to room temperature before serving or using in cooking.

FOR THE RIBS

2 gallons water

⅛ cup Tabasco® sauce

2 teaspoons salt

2 teaspoons black pepper

⅛ cup cayenne pepper

3 onions, sliced

6 pounds country-style ribs

In 1979, spareribs cost $1.39 per pound.

CAROL ANN'S DAD

In a large heavy kettle, place water, Tabasco® sauce, salt, black pepper, cayenne pepper, and onions. Bring ingredients to a boil and reduce to a simmer. Add ribs and simmer for 15 minutes. Turn off heat and let ribs stand in water for 1 hour. Preheat the oven to 350 degrees. Coat ribs with the spicy barbecue sauce and place them in a baking pan. Bake ribs for 20 minutes, turn them over, coat the other side with the spicy barbecue sauce, and continue baking for another 20 minutes.

Peachy Polynesian Country Style Ribs

SERVES 6

TO MARINATE

> 1 cup dry sherry
> ½ cup soy sauce
> 1 teaspoon minced garlic
> 2 tablespoons dry mustard
> 1 teaspoon ground ginger
> 4 to 6 pounds country-style ribs

In a small bowl, combine dry sherry, soy sauce, garlic, mustard, and ginger and whisk to blend. Pour over ribs and marinate at least 4 hours in the refrigerator. Best if marinated overnight. While marinating, occasionally turn and baste ribs.

TO COOK RIBS

Remove ribs from marinade and transfer marinade to a small saucepan. Bring marinade to a boil over medium-high heat and set aside. Place ribs in a shallow roasting pan and brush with marinade. Bake for 1 ½ hours at 350 degrees, basting with the marinade and turning occasionally.

FOR PEACH SAUCE

> 1 cup peach jelly or preserves
> ¼ cup lemon juice
> 2 tablespoons soy sauce
> 2 tablespoons horseradish

In a saucepan, place peach jelly or preserves, lemon juice, soy sauce, and horseradish and bring to a boil over medium heat. Reduce the heat and simmer for 5 minutes. Spoon the sauce over ribs and return to the oven for 5 minutes to glaze. Serve additional sauce on the side.

Country style ribs are cut from the shoulder blade and are the meatiest of all ribs, with less bone than either the sparerib or the baby back.

At the age of 12, Merrill became responsible for running his family's farm while his father, Seth Steele, traveled the country buying oil and gas leases. It's amazing to me as an adult to watch the immature antics of 12 year olds and know that at that same age my father had the obligations of a grown man. He worked hard his entire life from before sunrise to long after the sun went to bed. Looking back, I don't believe he ever had the luxury of learning how to play. Consequently, he had one wish. He wanted to die working. I used to tease him that we'd put the following caption on his tombstone: Here lies Merrill Steele. Died with his apron on.

Be careful what you wish. On a Friday afternoon, October 12, 1979, while working at our market on Mountain Avenue, my father realized he was in the throes of a heart attack. He ran down the stairs from his second-story office and out to the parking lot to his car. He never walked anywhere. He drove himself home to my mother, Pauline, who summoned the ambulance to take him to the hospital. He died the next evening on October 13.

The last time I visited him was only days before. Since his birthday fell on December 13, I questioned him whether or not he'd been born on a Friday. He had only one response to my question. "I'm not sure. All I know is the 13th has always been a bad day for me."

Barbecued Spareribs with a Chutney Sauce

SERVES 4

*E*dmund McIlhenny, a New Orleans banker, received some dried tabasco peppers as a gift from a soldier returning from Mexico shortly after the Mexican War. McIlhenny liked the flavor the peppers gave his food, so he saved some seeds and planted them in his wife's garden.

The tabasco pepper is a small, very hot red chile that originated in the Mexican state of Tabasco.

Determined to turn the peppers into income, he devised a spicy sauce, packaged it in 350 used cologne bottles, and began sending samples to wholesalers. By 1870, McIlhenny secured a patent for Pepper Sauce, eventually naming his sauce, Tabasco®.

FOR THE SAUCE

1 ½ cups Major Grey® Mango Chutney
½ cup bottled chili sauce
4 tablespoons vinegar
2 teaspoons dry mustard
3 tablespoons Worcestershire® sauce
1 teaspoon onion powder
Several dashes Tabasco® sauce

In a medium saucepan, combine chutney, chili sauce, vinegar, mustard, Worcestershire® sauce, onion powder, and Tabasco® sauce. Cook and stir over medium heat until heated through.

3 to 4 pounds lean pork spareribs
Salt

Cut ribs into serving-size pieces. In a large kettle, place ribs with just enough water to cover, and bring to a boil. Reduce heat, cover, and simmer about 1 hour, or until meat is tender. Drain ribs. Sprinkle with salt. Place ribs meaty side down, on the rack of an uncovered grill, directly over medium coals. Grill 5 minutes. Brush with the chutney sauce. Grill an additional 5 minutes. Turn ribs meaty side up, brush with the chutney sauce, and grill 5 more minutes.

Plan to purchase 1 pound of spareribs per person.

Jamaican Jerk Barbecued Ribs

SERVES 4

During a trip to Jamaica, my husband and I had Jamaican-style jerk ribs. They were mouthwatering. Upon returning home, I created this recipe to bring a touch of Jamaica to Colorado.

FOR THE MARINADE

1 onion, finely chopped
2 jalapeño peppers, finely ground
2 teaspoons dried thyme
1 teaspoon salt
1 ½ tablespoons sugar
1 teaspoon ground allspice
½ teaspoon ground nutmeg
½ teaspoon ground cinnamon
1 teaspoon large grind black pepper
3 tablespoons soy sauce
1 tablespoon white vinegar
2 tablespoons red wine vinegar

In a small bowl, combine onion, jalapeño peppers, thyme, salt, sugar, allspice, nutmeg, cinnamon, pepper, soy sauce, white and red wine vinegars and whisk to blend.

4 pounds pork spareribs
1 ½ cups barbecue sauce

Coat ribs evenly on both sides with marinade. Refrigerate for at least 4 hours. Preheat the oven to 350 degrees, place ribs in a roasting pan and bake for 1 hour and 15 minutes. During the last 15 minutes of cooking, brush ribs with your favorite barbecue sauce.

*W*hite distilled vinegar is the most commonly used vinegar. This distilled alcohol is derived from sugar cane, corn grains, molasses, etc. Rice vinegar is made through the alcoholic fermentation of sugars derived from rice or rice concentrate.

If you are in a hurry, a food processor is good for chopping and/or mincing onions and peppers.

Smoked Holiday Ham with a Bourbon-Mustard Glaze

SERVES 10 TO 14

For holidays, I prefer to purchase a spiral-cut, smoked ham. The spiral cut holds the slices together for an impressive presentation and is easy to serve. A smoked ham is fully cooked. To be fully cooked, the U. S.D.A. requires the ham's internal temperature reach 148 degrees F for 30 minutes to minimize any danger of disease. Smoking is the preferred method for accomplishing this and it yields a very flavorful, tender ham.

1 5 to 7-pound smoked, spiral cut ham, bone in

Preheat the oven to 325 degrees. Place ham, fat side up, on a rack in a shallow pan. Do not cover or add water. Roast for 1 ¾ hours.

FOR THE GLAZE

¼ cup honey
½ cup Dijon mustard
2 cups brown sugar
½ cup bourbon
½ teaspoon large grind black pepper

In a small saucepan, combine honey, Dijon mustard, brown sugar, bourbon, and pepper and cook over medium heat until sugar melts. During the last 30 minutes of roasting, remove fat from the bottom of the pan and spoon the glaze over ham. Continue baking, basting occasionally with the glaze. Baste ham with all the glaze before finally removing from the oven for serving.

Ham is labeled "Partially Cooked" or "Fully Cooked." Whichever kind you buy, it is always wise to strictly follow the packer's heating instructions.

When purchasing a bone-in ham, allow one-half (½) pound per person.

For an 8 to 10-pound smoked ham, cook 2 to 2 ¼ hours. For a 10 to 14-pound smoked ham, cook 3 ½ to 4 hours.

All eyes turn to

OUR SUPER BUYS!

SHORTENING Mrs. Tucker's *With Coupon on Page 8 of This Coloradoan* **47¢** 3 lb. Tin

Betty Crocker CAKE MIX 3 Varieties Pkg. **23¢**

Chase & Sanborn **COFFEE** Lb. **79¢**	ARMOUR'S **TREET** Pure Pork 12 oz. Can **29¢**	Pillsbury **PANCAKE FLOUR** 3 Lb. Pkg. **39¢**

Downy Flake Do Nuts Frosted Doz. **43c**

Kuner's Cut GREEN BEANS, 16 oz.	18c	Campbell's TOMATO SOUP, 10½ oz.	10c
Kuner's Cut WAX BEANS, 16 oz.	19c	Campbell's, 10½ oz. VEGETABLE SOUP, 2 for	25c
Kuner's Tender Garden PEAS, 16 oz. can	18c	Campbell's Beef Noodle SOUP, 10½ oz.	15c
Kuner's Cream Style CORN, 16 oz. can	16c	Stokes' CHILI with Beans, 15 oz.	27c
Kuner's TOMATO JUICE, 46 oz.	25c	Armour's TAMALES, 16 oz.	22c
Kuner's Red KIDNEY BEANS, 15 oz.	13c	Armour's CHOPPED BEEF, 12 oz.	33c
Kuner's CHILI BEANS, 15 oz.	13c	Armour's CORNED BEEF, 12 oz.	49c
Kuner's TOMATOES, 16 oz.	14c	Armour's CHOPPED HAM, 12 oz.	49c
Kuner's KRAUT, 14 oz. can	12c	DRIED BEEF, 2½ oz.	29c
Sunshine PIMENTOS, 2 oz.	10c	Swanson's Boned CHICKEN, 5 oz. can	37c

HAMS SKINLESS DEFATTED Whole or Shank Half LB. **55¢**
500 lbs. at this low price

BEEF LIVER SELECT BABY BEEF lb. **33¢**

RIVAL BACON 3 lbs. **99¢**

WIENERS 5 lb. box **$1.95**

BACON ENDS 12 lb. box **$1.49**
While 480 lbs. last

SHURFINE **MILK** TALL CANS **10¢**	SHURFINE **FLOUR** 25 LB. BAG **$1.89**	Ground Beef Pure 3 lbs. 89c	Swiss Steak U.S. Choice lb. 59c
		Bulk Lard 4 lbs. 59c	Country Links Pork lb. 59c
		Italian Sausage Home-made lb. 69c	Pan Sausage lbs. 3 lbs. 99c

Swans Down Angel Food Mix Pkg. **49c**

Cherry Pie Mix Wilderness No. 2 can **25c**

Margarine Gold Coin lb. **18c**

Salad Dressing Blubit Quart **39c**

Shurfine Vinegar Cider Gallon **75c**

Cut Green Beans Nancy Jo, 16-oz. 2 for **23c**

Belmont Mixed Fruit No. 2½ can **29c**

Del Monte Tuna Chunk style 6½ oz. can **29c**

Shurfine Red Salmon 1-lb. can **69c**

NO. 1 TEXAS **YAMS** Lb. **8¢**

POTATOES No. 1 Red 10 lbs. **27c**

CRANBERRIES Lb. **25¢**

JONATHAN **APPLES** Lb. **15¢**

SUNKIST ORANGES 2 doz. lb. **13c**

BANANA SQUASH lb. **8c**

DEL MONTE FREESTONE **PEACHES** 16 oz. Can **25¢** Del Monte **Apricots** No. 2½ can **37c**	**OXYDOL** Contains Oxygen Bleach Lrg. Pkg. **23¢** **Oxydol** Giant Size **59c**	Northern **TISSUE** Roll **5¢** NORTHERN **Towels** Roll **16c**

Friskies Dog Food Cubes or Meal 5-lb. Bag **77¢**

STEELE'S CASH FOOD MARKET
LOWEST AVERAGE PRICE EVERY DAY

Vets Dog Food 1-lb. Cans 3 for **25¢**

September 22, 1965

When Meat Matters   153

Old-Fashioned Beef and Rice Casserole   156

Spicy Skillet Cube Steaks   157

Meat Loaf Good Enough for Company   158

Scandinavian Style Meatballs   159

Hearty Spaghetti Sauce   160

Easy Barbecued Brisket   161

London Broil   162

Fiesta Round Steak   163

Chuck Steak Stew with Summer Vegetables   164

Poor Man's Roast Feast   165

Grilled Tri-Tip Roast   166

Beef Chop Suey   167

Grilled Ball-Tip Steaks with a Horseradish Glaze   168

The Kates Family Mother's Day Shish Kabobs   169

Steak and Tomato Kabobs with a Tomatillo Sauce   170

Marinated Sirloin Steak with a Spicy Salsa   171

Russ' Teriyaki Steak   172

My Husband's Favorite Father's Day Steak   173

New York Strips Smothered with Mushrooms   174

New York Steaks with Barbecued Vidalia Onions   175

New York Pepper Steaks   176

Sirloin Steak with Skewered Vegetables   177

Sirloin Tip Roast   178

T-Bone Steaks with a Green Peppercorn Butter   179

Chili-Rubbed Rib Eye Steaks with Carol Ann's Salsa . . .   180

Uncle Eddie's Standing Prime Rib Roast   181

Grilled Lamb Chops   182

When what's for dinner is beef, this chapter is packed full of mouth-watering meals.

When Meat Matters

Grades of Beef

When buying beef, I consider three things—flavor, juiciness, and tenderness. The marbling in beef, white flecks of fat within the meat muscle, determines its flavor—the more the better.

Beef sold in retail outlets is graded Prime, Choice, or Select. Prime beef has more marbling and, therefore, more flavor. It is the most tender and juicy grade of beef, however, it is higher in fat content. Since only 2 to 3 percent of beef grades out as Prime, it is the most expensive. Choice beef is less expensive than Prime but still has good flavor and tenderness. Select beef has the least marbling, is tough, and lacks flavor. Most supermarkets sell either Choice or Select. Their top line of beef is Choice, however, when advertising special prices, they usually discount Select.

I prefer purchasing Choice-graded beef. I never purchase Select. My palate finds it tough and flavorless. On special occasions, I will often spend the extra money for Prime. I never purchase a Prime-graded standing rib roast, as the Choice grade has enough marbling to ensure a tasty roast. I prefer tenderloins and filet mignons in Choice grade as well. Prime in these cuts is too mushy.

Aging

The best beef is aged. There are two processes for aging beef—dry and wet. "Wet-aged" means the beef is locked in plastic with a bit of water and left for 21 to 28 days. "Dry-aged" means the beef hangs in a cooler so that the blood drains out of the beef. Dry-aging takes from 10 days to 6 weeks. This process yields a very lean, tasty, and dense steak. If you're looking for the very best cut of beef, purchase "dry-aged" Prime beef. It is not safe to age beef at home.

Labeling on Ground Beef

Some ground beef products are labeled "lean" and "extra lean". "Lean" means that for every 100 grams of beef there are less than 10 grams of fat, 4.5 grams or less of saturated fat, and less than 95 milligrams of cholesterol. "Extra Lean" means for every 100 grams of beef there are less than 2 grams of saturated fat and less than 95 milligrams of cholesterol. Deciding which one to purchase is a "no-brainer".

Choosing a Meat Market

I like to shop at a reputable butcher shop where I can have my meat cut to order and where I can be assured of good quality beef. Some chain stores will cut meat to order, however, experienced butchers more likely work during the day. If you want meat custom cut, shop during the day if possible. I prefer to purchase Choice meat, therefore, I look for markets that sell Choice.

Today, most chain supermarkets cut their beef in one central location and ship it packaged to surrounding stores. It is possible meat will have already been packaged for a few days before it arrives at its destination. If you buy your meat at a chain store, it is important to choose product that looks fresh.

Beef should be bright cherry red, without brown spots. While some butchers may tell you spots don't effect the beef, spotting indicates the meat has started to spoil. If your market normally has several packages of spotted beef, it's an indication that meat is not selling quickly enough to ensure freshness. Be wary of these markets. Packages of spotted meat will often be on sale and marked "Manager's Special."

Shopping

When shopping, make your meat selection last. Shop with your eyes. Look for bright cherry red meat that does not have brownish blotches. Look for packages that are cold to the touch and tightly wrapped with no tears or punctures. Occasionally packages of meat may have a red liquid. This is not blood. Beef is about three fourths water. This liquid is natural moisture from the beef.

Check for dates on packages. Many stores mark packages with a "Sell-By" date. Never buy product that has expired. Frozen beef is safe to use if it has passed its "Sell-By" date provided it was frozen prior to that date. Strictly observe "Use-By" dates specified by packers.

Checking Out

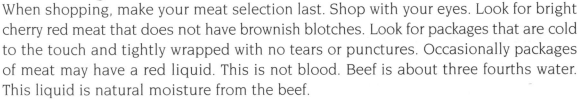

Ask the sacker to bag your meat separately in plastic to contain any leakage that might cross-contaminate other foods.

Storing and Using Beef at Home

Beef should be refrigerated at 40 degrees F immediately upon arriving home and should be used within 3 to 5 days (1 to 2 days for meats like sweetbreads, tongue, or tripe). If you do not plan to use beef within this time frame, freeze it.

It is safe to freeze beef in its original packaging or repackage it in zip-lock freezer bags. If freezing in the original package, it is best to over-wrap the package with aluminum foil to avoid freezer burn. When air reaches the surface of food, it causes grayish-brown, leathery spots known as freezer burn. Portions damaged by freezer burn should be cut away either during or after cooking. Frozen beef should be used within 9 to 12 months.

It is not necessary to wash raw beef before cooking. Any bacteria present on the surface will be destroyed in the cooking process.

While many recipes suggest bringing steaks to room temperature before grilling, steaks should not be removed from the refrigerator more than 30 minutes before grilling.

Thawing Frozen Beef

Beef can be safely defrosted in the refrigerator, in cold water, or in the microwave. The preferred method is the refrigerator. Ground beef, stew meat, and steaks will thaw in 1 day. Bone-in parts and whole roasts will take 2 days or longer. Once thawed, beef is safe to keep in the refrigerator for 3 to 5 days. To defrost in cold water, do not remove the packaging. To use this method, the packaging must be airtight or put into a leak-proof bag. This method is not suitable for product wrapped in butcher paper only. Place the beef in a large bowl in your kitchen sink and fill it with cold water. The water should be changed every 30 minutes to ensure that it stays cold. Small packages of beef will defrost in about 1 hour. A 3 to 4-pound roast may take 2 to 3 hours. If you use the microwave for defrosting, the beef must be cooked immediately.

Marinating Beef

Beef can be marinated up to 5 days in the refrigerator. Boil any used marinade before brushing it on cooked beef. Discard any uncooked marinade.

Safe Cooking Times

Hamburger should be cooked to an internal temperature of 160 degrees F. Use a meat thermometer to ensure meat has reached an adequate temperature. It is safe to cook steaks and roasts medium rare (145 degrees F). If using a meat thermometer, the following temperature readings indicate doneness: 145 degrees F for medium rare, 160 degrees F for medium, and 170 degrees F for well done.

Safe Refrigeration Times

Fresh beef roast, steaks, chops, or ribs	3 to 5 days
Fresh beef liver or variety meats	1 to 2 days
Ground beef	1 to 2 days
Home cooked beef, soups, stews, or casseroles	3 to 4 days
Deli-prepared convenience meals	1 to 2 days
Beef hot dogs, unopened	2 weeks
Beef hot dogs, opened	7 days
Lunch meats, opened	3 to 5 days
Canned beef products, opened	3 to 4 days
Jerky, refrigerated	2 to 3 months

Old-Fashioned Beef and Rice Casserole

SERVES 4 TO 6

1 ½ pounds ground beef

2 tablespoons vegetable oil

1 cup onion, chopped

1 cup celery, chopped

1 cup green bell pepper, cored, seeded, and chopped

1 cup uncooked rice

1 can (28-ounces) peeled tomatoes, chopped

1 cup water

2 teaspoons salt

1 ½ teaspoons chili powder

½ teaspoon Worcestershire® sauce

1 teaspoon large grind black pepper

1 cup black olives, cut in half

Hamburger Helper® hit the grocery shelves in 1970. I'm an old-fashioned girl. I like to make everything from scratch, so I've never used this one.

Preheat the oven to 325 degrees. In a large skillet, brown ground beef over medium heat, crumbling meat with a fork. With a slotted spoon, remove ground beef and set aside. To the same skillet, add vegetable oil and heat. Add onion, celery, green bell pepper, and rice. Cook, stirring occasionally, until lightly browned. Add tomatoes, water, salt, chili powder, Worcestershire® sauce, pepper, and ground beef. Bring to a boil and add olives. Pour rice and the ground beef mixture into a 2-quart casserole and cover. Bake 45 minutes to 1 hour.

When exposed to oxygen, ground beef will become a rosy red color. Sometime you may find the center of a package of ground beef has darkened. This is not harmful. This is the result of lack of exposure to oxygen. If you have concerns about ground beef, check the smell. It should be fresh, not sour, and the meat should feel moist not slimy.

Spicy Skillet Cube Steaks

SERVES 4

This is a great dish to make when you're pinching pennies.

*O*rtega® began canning chiles in Ventura, California, at the end of the 19th century.

2 tablespoons cornmeal
¼ teaspoon garlic powder
¼ teaspoon ground cumin
¼ teaspoon dried oregano
⅛ teaspoon salt
⅛ teaspoon onion powder
⅛ teaspoon ground red pepper
4 lean beef cube steaks, about 4 ounces each
Vegetable cooking spray
¼ cup plus 2 tablespoons tomato sauce
1 can (4-ounces) chopped green chile peppers, drained
1 large ripe tomato, cut into 16 wedges

In a large bowl, combine cornmeal, garlic powder, cumin, oregano, salt, onion powder, and red pepper. Dredge steaks in cornmeal mixture. Coat a large non-stick skillet with vegetable cooking spray and place over medium heat. Add steaks and cook approximately 5 minutes per side, or until browned. Remove steaks from the skillet. Drain off drippings and wipe skillet with a paper towel. Combine tomato sauce and green chiles in the skillet and bring to a boil. Return steaks to the skillet, cover, reduce heat to low, and simmer 10 minutes, or until steaks are tender. Add tomato wedges, cover, and simmer until tomatoes are heated through.

When I was a young girl and my family was on a tight budget, we ate cube steaks quite frequently. A cube steak is an inexpensive, flavorful cut of beef that is taken from the top or bottom round. It is tenderized (or cubed) by running it through a butcher's tenderizing machine once or twice. If not tenderized, the cube steak would be too tough to eat. When I'm watching my pocket book, I shop for cube steak.

Meat Loaf Good Enough for Company

SERVES 8 TO 10

Serve with garlic mashed potatoes and a Caesar salad. This ground beef mixture also makes great meatballs. Serve meatballs with your favorite marinara sauce. Yields 2 to 3 dozen meatballs. Leftover meat loaf makes great sandwiches.

4 tablespoons butter
¾ cup onion, finely chopped
½ cup celery, finely chopped
½ cup green bell pepper, cored, seeded, and finely chopped
½ cup red bell pepper, cored, seeded, and finely chopped
2 teaspoons minced garlic
¼ cup fresh chives, finely chopped

In a large heavy skillet, melt butter over medium heat and add onion, celery, green and red bell peppers, and garlic. Cook, stirring often, until vegetables are tender, about 10 minutes. Add chives and continue to cook about 1 minute. Set aside to cool. Then cover and refrigerate, about 1 hour.

1 teaspoon salt
1 teaspoon large grind black pepper
½ teaspoon ground white pepper
¼ teaspoon cayenne pepper
1 teaspoon ground cumin
3 eggs, well beaten
½ cup ketchup
½ cup half-and-half
2 pounds lean ground beef chuck
   (if not available, use lean ground beef)
1 pound country-style sausage
¾ cup fine bread crumbs
Reserved vegetables

Preheat the oven to 375 degrees. In a mixing bowl, combine salt, black pepper, white pepper, cayenne pepper, cumin, and eggs and beat. Add ketchup and half-and-half. Blend thoroughly. Add ground beef, sausage, and bread crumbs to the egg mixture. Then add the reserved vegetables and mix thoroughly with your hands, kneading for several minutes. Form the mixture into an oval, approximately 15 X 5 X 3 inches, resembling a long loaf of bread. Place meat loaf in a baking dish and place this dish inside a larger pan. Fill a small saucepan with water and bring to a boil. Pour boiling water into the larger pan until it reaches halfway up the side of the baking dish. Place both dishes in the oven and bake for approximately 60 minutes. Remove the baking dish from the water bath and let meat loaf set for 15 minutes before slicing and serving.

After the United States entered World War II, grocery items were rationed. Different items were assigned ration points, and each person received 12 points per week. In 1943, porterhouse steak was assigned 12 points, while a pound of ground beef only 7. This probably explains the popularity of meat loaf, meat balls, and stuffed bell pepper among my parents' generation. I was never crazy about meat loaf, but Meat Loaf Good Enough for Company turns this ordinary entrée into a gourmet delight.

To prevent meat loaf from cracking, try rubbing a small amount of water on the top and sides before placing in the oven.

Scandinavian Style Meatballs

SERVES 4

Swedish potato sausage is a specialty meat that is available during the holidays. A good substitute for Swedish potato sausage is country-style pork sausage.

½ pound Swedish potato sausage
½ pound lean ground beef
1 medium onion, minced
⅔ cup milk
½ cup bread crumbs
1 egg
¼ teaspoon thyme
Salt to taste
Large grind black pepper to taste

In a large bowl, combine Swedish potato sausage, ground beef, onion, milk, bread crumbs, egg, thyme, salt, and pepper and mix. Knead lightly with hands. Shape the mixture into small round balls using one rounded teaspoon of the meat mixture.

Olive oil or vegetable cooking spray for greasing skillet
2 cups hot water
4 chicken bouillon cubes

In a large heavy skillet, add olive oil and heat. Add meatballs and brown on all sides. Drain off any excess grease from the skillet and add 2 cups hot water and bouillon cubes. Cover and simmer 1 hour.

2 tablespoons flour
1 cup water
6 rounded tablespoons sour cream
½ teaspoon dried dill weed
1 package (8-ounces) extra-wide egg noodles, cooked al dente and drained

Remove meatballs from the pan and keep warm. To the same pan, add flour and stir until smooth. Add the remaining 1 cup water or enough water to bring sauce to desired consistency. Heat to a boiling point and boil 1 minute. Stir in sour cream and dill and return meatballs to the pan. Heat thoroughly and serve over cooked noodles.

To prevent meatballs from falling apart when you cook them, try refrigerating them for 20 minutes before cooking.

You can freeze uncooked meatballs on a baking sheet, then place them in a zip-lock freezer bag, and store them in the freezer for 3 months.

Be sure to pick up Swedish potato sausage. It's the secret ingredient.

Hearty Spaghetti Sauce

MAKES ENOUGH SAUCE TO SERVE 8

Serve over ziti with a Caesar salad and garlic bread. This sauce can be prepared in about 30 minutes. Minimum simmering time is 30 minutes, but the longer it simmers, the better the flavor.

2 pounds sweet Italian sausage

2 pounds lean ground beef

4 tablespoons butter

1 large yellow onion, chopped

1 medium green bell pepper, cored, seeded, and diced

4 stalks celery, thinly sliced

2 cans (28-ounces) peeled tomatoes, chopped

2 tablespoons dried oregano

2 tablespoons dried basil

2 teaspoons salt

1 teaspoon large grind black pepper

1½ cups dry red wine

2 cans (6-ounces) tomato paste

In a large heavy skillet, brown sausage and ground beef over medium heat. Drain and set aside. In a large kettle, melt the butter over medium heat. Add onion, green bell pepper, and celery and sauté until limp, about 5 minutes. Stir in sausage, beef, tomatoes with liquid, oregano, basil, salt, pepper, wine, and tomato paste. Simmer covered for 30 to 40 minutes.

A Frenchman, who powered his entire operation with just one horse, built the first pasta factory in America in Brooklyn in 1848. He spread strands of spaghetti out on the roof to dry in the sunshine.

To "chop" means to cut food into bite-size pieces. When I refer to "chop", I cut the food the same size as peas. To "dice" means to cut smaller than "chop". When I "dice", I cut food into about ⅛-inch pieces. "Minced" is smaller than "diced".

Ground beef *should be used within 1 to 2 days of purchase.*

Refrigerate **cooked pasta** *in an airtight container for up to five days. Because cooked pasta will continue to absorb flavors from sauces or oils, it should be stored separately from the sauce.*

160

Easy Barbecued Brisket

SERVES 6

I've been making barbecued brisket with this recipe for over 30 years. I've never found a better one. Brisket comes out tender and flavorful every time.

FOR THE SPICE MIXTURE

2 tablespoons liquid smoke
1 teaspoon garlic salt
1 teaspoon onion salt
2 teaspoons celery seed
1 ½ teaspoons salt
2 teaspoons Worcestershire® sauce
2 teaspoons large grind black pepper

1 (3 to 4-pound) brisket, fat trimmed
1 cup or more of your favorite barbecue sauce

In a small bowl, combine liquid smoke, garlic salt, onion salt, celery seed, salt, Worcestershire® sauce, and pepper. Cover both sides of brisket with the spice mixture. Place brisket in a 13 X 9-inch baking pan, cover with foil, and marinate in the refrigerator overnight.

Bake, covered, in a slow oven, 300 degrees, for 5 hours. After 4 hours, add barbecue sauce and continue to bake covered for 1 additional hour. Baste occasionally. Let meat sit for 15 minutes, then slice on the diagonal. Serve as a main course or on onion buns for sandwiches.

During cattle drives in the late 1800s, cattle barons fed their cowpokes brisket, a tough, stringy cut. The cooks on cattle drives soon learned that if they cooked the brisket for 5 to 7 hours at a low temperature (approximately 200 degrees), it would be tender and delicious. Tell me, how does one measure temperatures over a camp fire?

Don't skimp on the cooking time. Brisket must be cooked slowly for a long period of time.

The brisket is a cut of meat that is taken from underneath the first five ribs of the breast. It is normally sold without the bone. It has two cuts. The flat cut has minimal fat and is usually more expensive. The point cut has more fat.

In most supermarkets, liquid smoke is located in the same section as steak sauces.

London Broil

SERVES 4 TO 6

FOR THE MARINADE

 1 ½ teaspoons salt

 1 teaspoon sugar

 1 scant tablespoon minced dried onion

 ½ teaspoon dry mustard

 ½ teaspoon dried rosemary

 ¼ teaspoon ground ginger

 1 teaspoon large grind black pepper

 ¼ cup lemon juice

 ½ cup vegetable oil

 1 teaspoon minced garlic

 ¼ cup soy sauce

 3 tablespoons honey

 2 tablespoons white vinegar

 1 ½ to 2 pounds flank steak

*L*ondon broil is not an English creation, but rather North American. The first written recipe for this dish appeared in print in the United States in 1931.

In a blender, place salt, sugar, onion, mustard, rosemary, ginger, pepper, lemon juice, vegetable oil, garlic, soy sauce, honey, and vinegar and blend until smooth. Place London broil in a shallow baking dish and smother with marinade. Cover with plastic wrap and marinate in the refrigerator 2 to 3 hours, turning several times. Grill over medium coals for 10 to 15 minutes per side, depending upon thickness. To serve, carve in very thin slices diagonally across the grain.

Don't skimp on marinating time when making London broil. Also, it should be cooked quickly and is best when cooked to medium-rare. Slicing across the grain is paramount for tenderness.

Supermarkets will often advertise London broil as a special. This is a misunderstood term. Originally intended as nomenclature for quickly pan-broiling steaks, it currently means a thin, less tender cut from the flank. This cut comes from the underside of beef just below the sirloin and short loin. When making London broil, purchase flank steak.

Fiesta Round Steak

SERVES 4 TO 6

We went to church as a family every Sunday morning, but Sunday afternoons my father returned to the store to catch up on book work. When my brother and I tagged along as kids, he'd treat us to a raw hot dog from the meat market. We'd gobble down this delicacy with enthusiasm.

In reading the paper today, July 3, 2005, one letter to the editor entitled Eat holiday veggies stated: "Recent government warnings suggest this year's top threat is food poisoning from inadequately grilled hamburgers and hot dogs." It's remarkable my brother and I are still alive considering the number of raw wieners we've ingested! I tried to calculate the number of times my father placed our lives in jeopardy: once a week for (let's be conservative) four years. Goodness gracious! I've probably eaten over 208 raw hot dogs. I am grateful I grew up during times when we weren't afraid of everything we put in our mouths.

2 pounds round steak, cut into ½-inch strips
⅓ cup flour
1 teaspoon salt
½ teaspoon large grind black pepper

1 large onion, sliced
1 can (16-ounces) peeled tomatoes, chopped
1 can (4-ounces) diced green chile peppers
¼ pound fresh sliced mushrooms

1 can (14½-ounces) beef broth
1 tablespoon molasses
3 tablespoons soy sauce

In a small bowl, combine flour, salt, and pepper. Dredge steak strips in the flour mixture and place in a Dutch oven.

Layer onion slices, tomatoes with juice, green chile peppers, and mushrooms on top of steak.

In a medium-sized bowl, combine beef broth, molasses, and soy sauce. Pour the broth mixture over vegetables and steak strips. Bake covered at 325 degrees for 2½ to 3 hours.

When round steak is on sale, give this one a try. It turns a plain, inexpensive cut of meat into a delicious meal.

Chuck Steak Stew *with Summer Vegetables*

SERVES 6

This is a nice dish to prepare ahead of time and simmer on the stove.

3 pounds of chuck steaks, about ½-inch thick,
    cut into 6 servings
Salt to taste
Large grind black pepper to taste
6 large ripe tomatoes, chopped
1 large onion, thinly sliced
2 cups fresh corn kernels cut from 4 fresh ears of corn
2 cups fresh green beans, cut into 1-inch pieces
8 ounces whole small mushrooms,
    washed with stems trimmed
2 tablespoons fresh basil, slivered
3 teaspoons minced garlic
2 tablespoons fresh thyme, snipped and divided
¾ bottle dry white wine
1 can (14½-ounces) beef broth

Season steaks with salt and pepper. In a large bowl, combine tomatoes, onion, corn, green beans, mushrooms, basil, and garlic. Mix to combine. Spoon one third of the vegetable mixture into a Dutch oven or large kettle and top with half the steaks. Sprinkle with 1 tablespoon thyme. Spoon half the remaining vegetable mixture over steaks, layer with remaining steaks, and sprinkle with remaining 1 tablespoon thyme. Top with remaining vegetable mixture. Pour in wine and beef broth. Liquid should be enough to just cover the meat. Bring to a simmer over medium heat and cover tightly. Reduce heat to low. Cook, stirring occasionally, until meat is tender, about 3 to 3½ hours.

20 small new red potatoes, scrubbed but not peeled
3 medium red bell peppers, cored, seeded,
    and cut lengthwise into 1-inch wide strips
¼ cup olive oil
Salt to taste
Large grind black pepper to taste

About 1 hour before serving, preheat the oven to 450 degrees. Place potatoes and red bell pepper strips in a roasting pan and toss with olive oil. Season with salt and pepper. Roast, stirring occasionally, until potatoes are tender, about 45 to 60 minutes.

To serve, skim any fat from the surface of the braised meat sauce. On a dinner plate, place a piece of steak, a serving of potatoes and red bell peppers, then spoon the vegetables and broth on top. Serve immediately.

To remove kernels from the cob: First peel off the husks and remove the silk. Slice off the bottom and place the bottom end on a cutting board. Using a sharp knife, cut straight down the cob. To retain the shape of the whole kernel, only cut 2 or 3 rows at a time. One ear of corn should yield about ½ cup of kernels.

This dish can be prepared in your slow cooker. To convert a recipe to a slow cooker, increase the cooking time by 50 percent.

Only buy beef that has a cherry-red color.

CAROL ANN'S DAD

Poor Man's Roast Feast

SERVES 8 TO 10

When you're budget is so tight it squeaks, this marinade turns an inexpensive cut of meat into a delicious entrée.

Vinegar is an excellent ingredient for marinades because it is a natural tenderizer. It should never be used without combining it with vegetable or olive oil, because used alone it will cook meat. It is, also, a natural food preservative.

FOR THE MARINADE

2 tablespoons vegetable oil
1 medium onion, chopped
1 teaspoon minced garlic
⅓ cup soy sauce
1 teaspoon ground ginger
1 teaspoon ground allspice
1 teaspoon dried rosemary
3 tablespoons red wine vinegar
2 tablespoons brown sugar
1¼ cups canned beef broth

4 pounds chuck roast, approximately 1½-inches thick

In a heavy skillet, place vegetable oil over medium heat, add onion, and sauté until translucent. Add garlic, soy sauce, ginger, allspice, rosemary, red wine vinegar, brown sugar, and beef broth and bring to a boil. Remove from heat and cool. Place roast in a deep glass container. Pour marinade over roast, cover with plastic wrap, and refrigerate overnight, turning occasionally. Broil roast over medium coals for 30 to 45 minutes, depending upon thickness.

The best cut to buy for pot roast is the chuck roast. Shopping in a meat market can sometimes be confusing because the names on packages don't correspond with the cuts referred to in your cookbook. Chuck roast might be called chuck top blade roast, top chuck roast, chuck shoulder pot roast, or chuck mock tender roast.

Grilled Tri-Tip Roast

SERVES 4 TO 6

FOR THE MARINADE

> 2 teaspoons minced garlic
> 1 cup vegetable oil
> ½ cup soy sauce
> ¼ cup Worcestershire® sauce
> ¼ cup Dijon mustard
> ¼ cup lemon juice
> 2 teaspoons large grind black pepper
>
> 2 pounds tri-tip roast

In a large glass baking dish, combine garlic, vegetable oil, soy sauce, Worcestershire® sauce, Dijon mustard, lemon juice, and pepper. Pierce tri-tip roast several times to allow the marinade to penetrate into the interior of the roast. Cover with plastic wrap and marinate for 24 hours in the refrigerator, stirring occasionally and turning to coat all sides. Grill over medium coals for 15 minutes per side, turning, and basting frequently with the marinade.

The tri-tip roast originated in the late 1950s in a Safeway store in Santa Maria, California, when a summer replacement butcher, Larry Viegas, was cutting meat for hamburger and stew meat. That particular day, the store had an over-abundance of lower-end meat, so the market manager placed a triangular chunk on a rotisserie and discovered this tender, flavorful marvel. It slowly became a California favorite. It's called the tri-tip because it comes from the point where the sirloin, sirloin tip, and loin cuts intersect.

The tri-tip can also be called a sirloin tri-tip, a triangle steak, or a triangle roast. It has less marbling and is not as tender as a top sirloin steak, but it has good flavor. When purchasing this cut, choose one that is less than ³/₄- inch thick.

Beef Chop Suey

SERVES 4

Although the Chinese cooking style can be a bit puzzling, even a novice can make authentic beef stir-fry following this simple recipe.

FOR THE BEEF MARINADE

> 2 teaspoons sherry
> 3 tablespoons soy sauce
> 2 teaspoons Worcestershire® sauce
> 2 teaspoons minced garlic
> 1 tablespoon minced ginger
> 1 teaspoon salt
> Dash of pepper
> 1 ½ pounds sirloin steak, sliced in ⅛ to ¼-inch strips

In a large bowl, combine sherry, soy sauce, Worcestershire® sauce, garlic, ginger, salt, and pepper. Add beef and marinate at least 1 hour.

FOR THE VEGETABLES

> 1 cup frozen Chinese pea pods, thawed
> 1 cup carrots, peeled and thinly sliced on the diagonal
> 1 cup celery, thinly sliced on the diagonal
> 1 cup cauliflower, sliced
> 1 cup fresh bean sprouts

Fill a large saucepan with 1 cup water and bring to a boil over medium-high heat. Drop Chinese pea pods, carrots, and celery into boiling water and parboil 1 minute. Remove and set aside. Drop cauliflower in the same water and parboil 1 ½ minutes. Remove and set aside. Drop bean sprouts in the same water and remove immediately (1 second). Drain, saving ½ cup of water.

> 3 tablespoons peanut oil
> Reserved vegetables
> 3 tablespoons peanut oil
> Marinated beef strips
> Reserved vegetables
> Boiled marinade
> ½ cup water reserved from vegetables

Heat a wok or large skillet over high heat. Add 3 tablespoons peanut oil and reserved vegetables and sauté 1 minute. Remove and set aside.

Reheat the pan and add the remaining 3 tablespoons peanut oil. Remove beef strips from the marinade, add to the wok, and sauté until cooked through, about 5 minutes. Transfer marinade to a small saucepan and bring it to a boil over high heat. Set aside. Add vegetables to wok and mix well. Add marinade and ½ cup reserved vegetable water and cook 1 minute, or until heated through. Serve over steamed rice.

---

*T*he Chinese fortune cookie was invented in 1916 by George Jung, founder of the Hong Kong Noodle Co. in Los Angeles, California.

At age 23, I gave my first dinner party. Using a Chinese theme, my menu included beef chop suey, fried rice, sweet and sour pork, and egg rolls made from scratch. The egg rolls put my culinary skills to the test. I started preparing these delicacies at 10:30 a.m. and finally finished at 10:30 p.m., leaving my kitchen a disheveled, chaotic mess. My guests raved about the meal, but I've often wondered if their delight was the result of the late dinner hour.

Grilled Ball-Tip Steaks
with a Horseradish Glaze

SERVES 4

FOR THE MARINADE

½ cup red wine vinegar
½ cup firmly-packed brown sugar
¼ cup ketchup
¼ cup soy sauce
2 tablespoons Worcestershire® sauce
1 teaspoon Dijon mustard
1 teaspoon minced garlic

2 pounds ball-tip or top sirloin steaks
1 teaspoon large grind black pepper

In a large bowl, combine red wine vinegar, brown sugar, ketchup, soy sauce, Worcestershire® sauce, Dijon mustard, and garlic and mix well. Sprinkle both sides of steaks with pepper and rub in with the palm of your hand. Place steaks in the marinade, cover with plastic wrap, and refrigerate 24 hours, turning occasionally. Remove steaks from marinade. Transfer marinade to a small saucepan, bring to a boil over high heat, and set aside. Grill ball-tip steaks over medium-hot coals to the desired doneness, about 8 minutes per side, brushing occasionally with the marinade.

FOR THE GLAZE

2 heaping teaspoons prepared horseradish
1 teaspoon green onions, thinly sliced
¾ cup sour cream

In a small bowl, combine horseradish, green onions, and sour cream. The last three minutes of cooking time, spread the glaze on top of steaks. Continue cooking 3 minutes until glazed.

Steele's was the only grocery store in town to sell ball-tip steaks, which are cut from a trimmed round-tip roast. The ball tip is a relatively unknown cut. Most major supermarkets don't carry it. We credit Kenneth Walsh, a partner in Steele's and the manager of our meat department, with developing the ball tip and introducing it to our customers—they loved it. There are only 3 pounds of ball tip in each cow. When we'd put ball tips on sale, we'd sell 10,000 pounds—that's 3,333 cows. In order to ensure we had sufficient quantities for a sale, Monfort required that we order this steak months in advance.

If you have a good butcher shop near you, ask your butcher if he has ball tips. They're flavorful and, oh, so tender.

The Kates Family Mother's Day Shish Kabobs

SERVES 4 TO 6

There aren't many gifts a mother will appreciate more on Mother's Day than having her family prepare a meal for her on her special day. This includes doing the dishes, of course. Here's what the Kates family fixes for me on Mother's Day. It's simple enough that the whole family can get involved in the process.

*S*hish kabob comes from the Turkish word sis meaning small piece and kebabi meaning to roast. Although authorities debate the actual beginnings of shish kabobs, some credit Medieval Turkic soldiers who threaded meat on their swords and roasted it over open fires with creating this dish.

RUSS' RECIPE FOR MARINADE

½ cup soy sauce
½ cup bourbon
1 teaspoon minced garlic
2 tablespoons sugar
½ teaspoon ground ginger

2 pounds ball-tip or sirloin steaks, cut into 1 ½-inch cubes

In a large bowl, combine soy sauce, bourbon, garlic, sugar, and ginger. Cover and marinate steak cubes in the refrigerator for 2 to 3 hours.

12 large mushrooms, washed and stems removed
12 cherry tomatoes
12 small pearl onions, peeled
2 large green bell peppers, cored, seeded, and cut into 8 to 12 squares
1 bottle Marie's® Lite Italian Dressing

Peeling pearl onions is a tedious job. Using the tip of a sharp paring knife, pull the skin off. Then peel off any membrane beneath it.

In a large bowl, place mushrooms, cherry tomatoes, onions, and green bell pepper cubes and cover with Marie's® Lite Italian Dressing. Cover with plastic wrap and marinate for 2 to 3 hours in the refrigerator, basting occasionally. Place steak cubes and vegetables on skewers in an alternating pattern—steak cube, mushroom, cherry tomato, onion, green bell pepper cube—and then repeat the pattern. Barbecue over medium coals for about 15 minutes, or until done to your taste. Serve over rice.

This recipe is served over rice. Be sure to add rice to your shopping cart.

Steak and Tomato Kabobs
with a Tomatillo Sauce

SERVES 4 TO 6

One of my very favorites!

FOR THE SAUCE

> 10 tomatillos
> 2 cups water
> 1 avocado
> ½ cup sour cream
> 4 dashes Tabasco® sauce
> 1 tablespoon lime juice
> 1 teaspoon minced garlic
> ½ teaspoon salt

Remove husks and stems from tomatillos. Boil tomatillos in 2 cups water until soft and water has evaporated. Place tomatillos in a blender and purée until smooth. Pit and peel avocado and place in the blender. Purée until smooth. Add sour cream and purée until smooth. Season with Tabasco® sauce, lime juice, garlic, and salt. Pour the mixture into a small bowl, cover, and refrigerate until ready to use.

FOR THE RUB

> 2 teaspoons dry mustard
> 2 teaspoons onion salt
> 2 teaspoons garlic salt
> 2 teaspoons chili powder
> 1 teaspoon paprika
> 1 teaspoon ground coriander
> 1 teaspoon ground cumin

FOR THE SKEWERS

> 2 pounds ball-tip (sirloin) steaks
> 16 large tomatoes

In a medium bowl, combine mustard, onion salt, garlic salt, chili powder, paprika, coriander, and cumin. Cut steaks into 1½-inch pieces and coat with the rub. Thread metal skewers by alternating tomatoes and steak. Grill kabobs directly over medium heat, turning once, for 8 to 10 minutes. The skin of tomatoes will be lightly charred.

Choose firm dry tomatillos that fit tightly in their husks.

If you refrigerate tomatillos in a paper bag, they will keep up to 1 month.

To serve: Spread sauce on a large platter and lay grilled kabobs over the tomatillo sauce.

Marinated Sirloin Steak *with a Spicy Salsa*

SERVES 4 TO 6

FOR THE MARINADE

2 cups olive oil
½ cup cider vinegar
½ cup red wine
1 teaspoon dried rosemary
½ teaspoon dried thyme
1 teaspoon dried oregano
1 tablespoon crushed red pepper
1 ½ teaspoons minced garlic
¼ cup Dijon mustard
2 pounds sirloin steaks

In a large bowl, combine olive oil, cider vinegar, red wine, rosemary, thyme, oregano, crushed red pepper, garlic, and Dijon mustard. Blend well. Add steaks, cover with plastic wrap, and marinate overnight in the refrigerator.

SPICY SALSA

2 tablespoons butter
1 teaspoon minced garlic
1 medium onion, chopped
2 green onions, chopped
1 jalapeño pepper, minced
1 teaspoon dried basil
6 tomatoes, chopped
½ cup Dijon mustard
2 cups canned chicken broth

It's a good idea to wear gloves when handling peppers.

In a large saucepan, melt butter over medium heat. Add garlic, onions, green onions, jalapeño pepper, basil, and tomatoes. Cover the pan and cook for 5 minutes. Add Dijon mustard, stir, and cook for 3 minutes. Add chicken broth and bring mixture to a boil. Reduce heat to low and simmer for 1 to 1 ½ hours, or until a pourable sauce is achieved.

TO GRILL STEAKS AND PREPARE VEGETABLE SKEWERS

2 zucchini, cut into ½-inch thick pieces
2 yellow squash, cut into ½-inch pieces
1 red bell pepper, cored, seeded, and cut into 1¼-inch cubes

Scratches or bruises on the skin of zucchini and yellow squash will not hurt the quality. Don't buy these vegetables if their skin is pitted or their texture is spongy.

Remove steaks from the marinade and transfer the marinade to a small saucepan. Bring the marinade to a boil over high heat and set aside. Thread vegetables onto skewers and brush with the marinade. Grill steaks for 6 to 8 minutes on each side, or until the desired doneness is achieved. Grill vegetable skewers until tender, turning often, about 5 minutes a side. Arrange steaks and grilled vegetables on a serving platter and ladle the spicy salsa on top.

Russ' Teriyaki Steak

SERVES 4

I first began eating teriyaki steak in the 1970s. It is still an old favorite. This is my husband's recipe for teriyaki marinade that is also excellent with chicken.

FOR THE MARINADE

> ½ cup soy sauce
> ½ cup bourbon
> 2 tablespoons sugar
> 1 teaspoon minced garlic
> ½ teaspoon ground ginger
>
> 2 pounds sirloin steak

In a large bowl, combine soy sauce, bourbon, sugar, garlic, and ginger and stir until sugar is dissolved. Add steaks, cover with plastic wrap, and marinate 4 hours in the refrigerator, turning occasionally. Pierce steak with a fork when turning to encourage the marinade to penetrate meat. Grill steak over medium-hot charcoal for 5 to 6 minutes per side, or until cooked to the desired temperature.

In Japanese, "teri" means "gloss," and "yaki" are broiled foods. In Japan, when food is teriyaki it has been brushed with a sweet glaze. In the United States, we use it more as a marinade.

The sirloin is the cut of beef that lies between the tender short loin and the tougher round. You will see some differences in tenderness with this cut. The meat cut closer to the short loin will be more tender than cuts made closer to the round. Top sirloin is a continuation of the tender top loin muscle of the short loin. The bottom sirloin is part of the sirloin tip muscle found in the round. If you want a more tender sirloin, buy top sirloin.

My Husband's Favorite Father's Day Steak
Smothered with Shitake Mushroom Sauce

SERVES 6

Even though our eating habits have changed dramatically over the years, most men still love a good steak. In fact, Father's Day is the biggest beef-eating day of the year. My husband's favorite cut is a New York, and this is his favorite preparation.

SHITAKE MUSHROOM SAUCE

> 1 pound fresh shitake mushrooms, sliced into ½-inch strips, stems removed and set aside
> 3 tablespoons butter
> 3 tablespoons peanut oil
> 1 teaspoon minced garlic
> 8 rounded teaspoons Grey Poupon® Country Dijon mustard
> 2 cans (10½-ounces) Campbell's® Double Strength Beef Broth, divided
> ½ cup heavy cream
> Salt to taste
> Large grind black pepper to taste

In a large heavy skillet, place butter and peanut oil over medium heat, add sliced mushrooms, stems, and garlic, and sauté until tender. Add mustard and 1 can of beef broth. Mix thoroughly, increase heat to high, and boil until reduced by half. Add second can of beef broth in small portions, boiling until the sauce is reduced by half, about 20 to 30 minutes. Add heavy cream and boil until the sauce thickens. Season with salt and pepper to taste. Remove stems before serving.

> 6 New York strip steaks, cut 1 to 1 ½-inches thick
> Salt to taste
> Large grind black pepper to taste

Preheat the grill to high. Season steaks with salt and pepper. Grill over hot coals 5 to 8 minutes per side, or until cooked to the desired temperature, about 5 minutes per side for medium rare. Serve sauce on the side.

My father's neckties were ugly as sin. It was during the magical Christmas season that these hideous monstrosities maneuvered their way into his closet. His ties, similar to some accessory you'd find on someone making "the worst dressed list," were bestowed upon him as Christmas gifts by a slightly colorblind female customer whose name I can no longer recall. The ties, however, remain unforgettable. Every Christmas Eve, my father came home from the market bearing an assortment of gifts from vendors, employees, and customers. Although the gifts and givers varied year to year, without fail among his mighty bounty dwelled an elongated tie box. We'd all gather around as he opened up the box for a peek at his latest white elephant. He'd laugh and comment what an eyesore she'd unearthed this year. "She's outdone herself. Really. Where does she find these things?" Come December 26th, he'd proudly put on his newest tie and head off to work where he no doubt thanked the Tie Lady for finding such a beauty.

Spring and fall are the seasons when fresh shiitakes are most plentiful.

Smothered New York Strip Steaks

SERVES 4

FOR THE GREEN CHILE SAUCE

>   4 tablespoons olive oil
>   2 cups onion, chopped
>   1 can (7-ounces) chopped mild green chile peppers
>   ½ teaspoon dried oregano
>   1 tablespoon fresh cilantro, chopped
>   ½ teaspoon salt
>   1 teaspoon Tabasco® sauce

In a large skillet, place olive oil over medium-high heat. Add onion and sauté until soft. Add green chile peppers, oregano, cilantro, salt, and Tabasco® sauce and simmer for 5 minutes. Remove from the heat, cover, and keep warm in a very low-temperature oven.

FOR THE MUSHROOMS

>   4 tablespoons butter
>   12 large mushrooms, thinly sliced
>   ½ teaspoon salt
>   ½ teaspoon liquid smoke

In another large skillet, melt butter over medium heat. Add mushrooms and sauté until soft. Add salt and liquid smoke and mix thoroughly. Keep warm until steaks are ready to serve.

FOR STEAKS

>   4 (8-ounce) New York strip steaks
>   Salt to taste
>   Large grind black pepper to taste

Preheat the grill to high. Season steaks with salt and pepper to taste. Grill over hot coals 5 to 8 minutes per side, or until cooked to desired temperature, about 5 minutes per side for medium-rare.

TO SERVE

Transfer steaks to a serving platter. Divide the mushroom mixture over top and smother with the green chile sauce.

I always preferred my steaks thick — 1½ inches is perfect.

CAROL ANN'S DAD

New York Steaks
with Barbecued Vidalia Onions

SERVES 4

FOR THE MARINADE

6 cloves garlic
1 teaspoon salt
½ teaspoon ground cumin
½ teaspoon large grind black pepper
⅓ cup fresh lime juice
2 tablespoons olive oil

4 New York strip steaks, about 8 to 10 ounces each, cut 1-inch thick

Place garlic cloves, salt, cumin, pepper, lime juice, and olive oil in a blender and process until garlic cloves are finely chopped and mixture is smooth. In a large bowl, place steaks and cover with the marinade. Leave steaks at room temperature and marinate for 15 to 30 minutes.

Preheat the grill. When ready to cook, remove steaks from the marinade and arrange on a hot grate. Grill over hot coals about 5 to 8 minutes, or until cooked to the desired temperature, about 5 minutes per side for rare.

2 large Vidalia onions, peeled, ends sliced off, and cut in half crosswise
3 tablespoons olive oil
Salt to taste
Large grind pepper to taste

Brush onion slices with olive oil and place on hot grate. Grill onions until nicely charred, about 4 minutes per side, seasoning with salt and pepper.

Arrange steaks and onion halves on a serving platter.

*M*y favorite steak sauce is Pickapeppa®, also known as Jamaican ketchup, created in 1921 in Shooters Hill, Jamaica. Pickapeppa®, readily available in supermarkets, is a unique blend of tomatoes, onions, sugar cane, vinegar, mangoes, raisins, tamarinds, peppers, and spices. This tasty sauce is aged in oak barrels for one full year before bottling.

If your supermarket doesn't have Vidalia onions, Maui or Texas sweet onions make a good substitute.

The New York steak is also called a New York strip steak and shell steak. Depending on the region you live in, it can also be marketed as a Kansas City strip steak, a sirloin club steak, or a strip steak. This cut comes from the most tender section of beef, the short loin, and is the boneless top loin muscle.

New York Pepper Steaks

SERVES 4 TO 6

1 tablespoon black peppercorns, crushed
1 tablespoon butter, softened
½ teaspoon minced garlic
1 tablespoon vegetable oil
2 pounds New York strip steaks, cut ½ to ¾-inches thick

½ cup red wine
¼ cup brandy
1 cup heavy cream
1 ½ teaspoons Dijon mustard
Salt to taste
2 tablespoons fresh parsley, snipped

In a small bowl, combine peppercorns, butter, and garlic. Spread evenly on both sides of steaks. In a heavy skillet, heat vegetable oil over medium-high heat. Add steaks and brown on both to the desired temperature. Allow about 5 minutes per side for rare and 7 to 8 minutes per side for well-done. Place on a serving platter and cover with aluminum foil to keep warm.

To the same skillet, add red wine and brandy. Cook over high heat, scraping all the juices off the bottom, until the liquid is reduced to ¼ cup. Add heavy cream and mustard and continue cooking until further reduced and thickened. Season to taste with salt. Just before serving, stir in parsley. Drizzle the sauce over steaks and serve.

Whose recipe is this, anyway? Several chefs take credit for the origination of steak "au poivre". E. Lerch claimed he created this dish working as a chef at the Restaurant Albert on the Champs-Elysees. M. Deveau disputed this fact, arguing he created it while working at Maxim's in 1920. M. G. Comte asserted he made this as a house specialty at the Hotel de Paris in Monte Carlo in 1910, and O. Becker claimed he prepared it in 1905 at Palliard's.

The peppercorn is a berry that grows in grapelike clusters on the pepper plant. It is picked when not quite ripe and then dried until it shrivels and its skin turns dark brown to black. It has a strong, sweet flavor with a hint of sweetness. When buying peppercorns, the best are the Tellicherry and the Lampong.

Marinated Sirloin Steak
with Skewered Vegetables

SERVES 4

Serve with Carol Ann's Rice Pilaf, Page 235.

FOR THE MARINADE

½ teaspoon dry mustard
½ teaspoon dried marjoram
½ teaspoon dried oregano
½ teaspoon dried basil
1 cup canned beef broth
2 tablespoons red wine vinegar
2 teaspoons vegetable oil
1 tablespoon Worcestershire® sauce

16 ounces top sirloin steak

In a small bowl, combine mustard, marjoram, oregano, and basil. Slowly add beef broth, stirring to avoid lumps. Add red wine vinegar, vegetable oil, and Worcestershire® sauce, blending well. Place beef in a shallow dish, pour marinade over meat, and cover. Marinate in the refrigerator 2 to 3 hours, turning about every 45 minutes.

3 medium zucchini squash, cut into ¾-inch slices
1 large green bell pepper, cored, seeded,
  and cut into 1¼-inch cubes
1 large red bell pepper, cored, seeded,
  and cut into 1¼-inch cubes
1 large red onion, cut into eighths and then each eighth
  cut into halves

Thread vegetables onto 4 metal skewers, alternating vegetables.

Remove meat from the marinade. Transfer marinade to a small saucepan and bring to a boil over medium-high heat. Remove from heat. Brush vegetable skewers with the marinade. Grill sirloin 4 to 5 inches over medium-hot coals for 6 to 8 minutes per side. Grill vegetable skewers along side meat, turning frequently, being careful not to burn. Vegetables should be browned but still crisp. Brush meat and vegetables once per side with the marinade during grilling process.

*W*orcestershire® sauce was originally an Indian recipe, brought to Britain by Lord Marcus Sandys, a former governor of Bengal. In 1835, Sandys appeared at the emporium of chemists John Lea and William Perrins on Broad Street in Worcester and asked them to make the recipe for him. Lea and Perrins mixed a batch for Sandys in a wooden barrel, but the results were so fiery they banned it to the cellar. Months later, Lea and Perrins came across the forgotten barrel. Before throwing it out, they decided to give it a taste.

The results—the sauce had mellowed into a delightful seasoning. Lea and Perrins bought the recipe from Sandys and began commercially producing it in 1838.

Sirloin Tip Roast
with Balsamic Vinegar and Rosemary

SERVES 6

Cuddle up in front of a fire on a cold winter evening and enjoy. Serve with sourdough or French bread for dipping in the broth and a green salad.

1 (3-pound) sirloin-tip roast

3 teaspoons minced garlic

1 cup balsamic vinegar

2 tablespoons fresh rosemary, chopped

1 large onion, peeled and thinly sliced

Salt to taste

Large grind black pepper to taste

1 can (16-ounces) peeled tomatoes, chopped, all juices reserved

Poke roast in several places with a thin-bladed knife and insert garlic into the holes. In a large ceramic dish, combine balsamic vinegar and rosemary. Add roast and turn to coat completely. Cover and refrigerate overnight. Preheat the oven to 300 degrees. In a small roasting pan, spread onion slices, place roast on top, and pour the remaining marinade over roast. Season roast with salt and pepper to taste. Add tomatoes and juices. Cover the dish tightly with aluminum foil. Cook roast until it is easily pierced with a fork and its juices run clear, about 3½ hours. Remove roast from the oven and let it rest 5 to 10 minutes before carving. Serve sliced meat with onions, tomatoes, and pan juices.

There may be some grease in the pan juices. Remove grease, before serving. A grease mop works well for this task. Available in specialty kitchen stores or the cookware section of department stores, it looks like a miniature rag mop made with absorbent white strips. Brush it over the surface of soup or stock, and its strips absorb floating grease. Grease mops can be washed in the dishwasher.

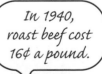

In 1940, roast beef cost 16¢ a pound.

CAROL ANN'S DAD

The secret to this recipe is using fresh rosemary. It's needle-shaped leaves are flavored with hints of pine and mint. More flavor will be released from this herb if you chop it fine. If you only have dried rosemary in your pantry, be sure to pick up fresh.

T-Bone Steaks
with a Green Peppercorn Butter

SERVES 4

For convenience sake, I prefer using the already prepared roasted red bell peppers that you purchase at the supermarket.

1 teaspoon minced garlic
2 strips roasted red bell peppers, drained and minced
3 teaspoons green peppercorns, drained and minced
2 teaspoons fresh rosemary, minced
4 tablespoons unsalted butter, softened
¼ teaspoon salt
2 teaspoons fresh lemon juice

2 T-bone steaks (about 1 pound each and cut 1-inch thick)
1 tablespoon olive oil
Refrigerated butter mixture

In a small bowl, combine garlic, roasted red bell peppers, green peppercorns, and rosemary. Cut butter into 4 chunks and add to the garlic mixture. Add salt and lemon juice. Beat the mixture until well blended and smooth. Transfer the butter mixture to a 4-inch wide sheet of plastic wrap. Roll the plastic wrap around the butter mixture, then shape the package with your fingers into a log-shaped roll, the diameter of a quarter. Refrigerate for at least 1 hour.

Preheat the broiler or prepare coals for grilling. Lightly coat steaks with olive oil on both sides. Broil or grill until seared and well crusted on one side, about 5 minutes. Turn and cook the other side for another 3 minutes for medium-rare or 4 minutes for medium. Transfer the steaks to a cutting board and carve steaks into ½-inch thick slices and divide among 4 warm plates. Remove the butter mixture from the refrigerator and slice into eighths. Place 2 slices of the butter mixture on top of each portion. Serve immediately.

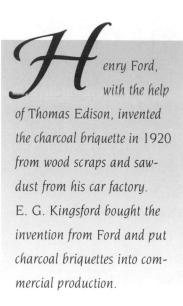

*H*enry Ford, with the help of Thomas Edison, invented the charcoal briquette in 1920 from wood scraps and sawdust from his car factory. E. G. Kingsford bought the invention from Ford and put charcoal briquettes into commercial production.

Be sure to pick up green peppercorns. It's the secret ingredient. Peppercorns are berries that grow in grape-like clusters on the pepper plant. Green peppercorn is a soft, underripe berry that is normally preserved in brine.

Green peppercorns are normally found on the same aisle as pickles. They should be refrigerated once opened. If packed in brine, they will keep 1 month; if packed in water, 1 week.

Chili-Rubbed Rib-Eye Steaks
with Carol Ann's Salsa

SERVES 4

This is my version of chili-rubbed steak. I like to serve it with a homemade salsa. You can use this recipe with any cut of steak, but my preference is the rib eye because of its exceptional flavor and tenderness.

FOR THE RUB

¼ cup dried red chilies, made into a fine powder
¼ cup paprika
2 tablespoons coarse sea salt
1 tablespoon sugar

4 (8-ounce) rib-eye steaks, cut 1-inch thick
Vegetable spray for coating barbeque

To make red chili powder, place 8 dried red chilies in a grinder, blender, or coffee grinder. Grind in small batches, until powdered. If using fresh chiles, preheat the oven to 350 degrees. Using a small paring knife, cut stems off chiles and discard. Cut chiles open along the long side. Remove seeds and place peppers on a baking sheet. Roast about 5 minutes. Cool thoroughly before making into powder.

In a large bowl, combine chili powder, paprika, salt, and sugar. Dip steaks into the powder, rubbing the powder evenly over steaks, and transfer to another dish. Cover with plastic wrap and refrigerate 6 to 8 hours. Spray the barbecue with non-stick spray. Grill steaks over medium heat to the desired doneness, about 5 to 7 minutes per side, turning occasionally to prevent rub from burning.

In 1954, Americans' favorite meal included fruit cup, vegetable soup, steak and potatoes, peas, rolls with butter, and pie a la mode.

Carol Ann's Salsa

1½ pounds plum tomatoes, seeded and chopped
¾ cup red onion, chopped
Juice of 1 lime
2 jalapeño peppers, seeded and minced
1½ teaspoons minced garlic
Chopped fresh cilantro to taste
Salt to taste

The rib-eye is a boneless steak that is sometimes called Spencer or Delmonico. It is known for its rich, juicy flavor. When buying this cut, select steaks with a good amount of marbling.

In a medium bowl, combine tomatoes, red onion, lime juice, jalapeño peppers, and garlic. Season to taste with cilantro and salt. Cover and chill 1 hour before serving.

Uncle Eddie's Standing Prime Rib Roast

SERVES

My Uncle Eddie gave me this recipe years ago. Following this recipe, prime rib comes out medium-rare, juicy, and perfect every time. This recipe is designed for high-altitude cooking.

> 1 standing rib roast, any size
> Salt to taste
> Large grind black pepper to taste

To eat dinner at 7:00 p.m. start at 3:00 p.m. Preheat the oven to 400 degrees. Lightly salt and pepper roast and place in a large roasting pan, rib side up. Put roast in the oven and cook uncovered at 400 degrees for 1 hour. Turn the oven off after 1 hour. DO NOT OPEN THE OVEN DOOR. Leave roast in the oven, and it will continue cooking. About 45 minutes before serving, turn the oven to 325 degrees and cook another 45 minutes.

Uncle Eddie warns that the secret to this preparation is in NOT OPENING THE OVEN DOOR. Current food safety regulations warn the oven temperature should never fall below 140 degrees during the time the oven is turned off. Back in Uncle Eddie's day they didn't have safety regulations.

My Uncle Eddie worked at the first Steele's on Oak Street. He eventually moved to Denver and opened his own butcher shop on the corner of University and Orchard in southeast Denver, called Ed's Cherry Crest Meats. My Uncle Eddie was so picky about his meat he paid an inspector a penny a pound to hand select meat at the slaughterhouse. Uncle Eddie taught me the importance of marbling in beef to ensure a juicy, tender piece of meat.

It's a good idea to order your prime rib at least 1 week ahead. That way you can be sure your butcher will have the size you want.

CAROL ANN'S DAD

Bone-in prime ribs are the most flavorful. I purchase ½ pounds of prime rib for every serving. If serving 8 people, get a 4-pound roast.

To carve a prime rib: Remove any string from the roast. If you have cooked a bone-in roast, place it on a cutting board on its side so that the bones are on your left-hand side. Using one hand, steady the roast with a fork. Cut a serving slice from the roast by slicing horizontally across the meat toward the bones. Then remove the slice from the roast by cutting downward parallel to the bones. Slices are normally ½-inch thick. Transfer slice to serving platter. You can serve the rib bones with the meat if your guests are so inclined. I prefer to save them and any leftover meat to make Vegetable Beef Soup, see Page 52.

Grilled Lamb Chops
with a Warmed Tomato Relish

SERVES 4

I have found it difficult to find a preparation for lamb that pleases everyone in my family. This one is a keeper.

FOR THE MARINADE

    ¼ cup olive oil
    ¼ cup balsamic vinegar
    1 teaspoon salt
    ½ teaspoon large grind black pepper
    8 lamb chops, cut 1 ½-inches thick
    3 teaspoons minced garlic
    1 tablespoon fresh rosemary, chopped

In a small bowl, combine olive oil, balsamic vinegar, salt, and pepper and mix well. Place lamb chops in a dish so that they fit tightly together. Coat lamb chops with garlic, cover with marinade, and sprinkle with rosemary. Cover with plastic wrap and refrigerate for 2 hours. While lamb chops are marinating, prepare ingredients for the relish.

TO BEGIN THE WARMED TOMATO RELISH

    2 tablespoons olive oil
    ¾ cup yellow bell pepper, seeded, cored, and chopped
    ¾ cup red onion, chopped

In a large non-stick skillet, heat olive oil over medium heat. Sauté yellow bell pepper and red onion until limp. Remove from the skillet and set aside.

    Vegetable cooking spray

Lamb chops are best prepared in a grill pan and cooked on top of the stove, but they can be barbecued. Spray a non-stick grill pan with cooking spray and grill the chops over high heat, about 4 minutes per side for medium-rare.

TO FINISH THE WARMED TOMATO RELISH

    2 tablespoons lime juice
    1 cup tomato, chopped
    ¾ cup lightly-packed arugula, chopped
    1 teaspoon fresh rosemary, chopped
    1 teaspoon fresh thyme, chopped

When chops are almost cooked, add lime juice, tomato, arugula, rosemary, and thyme to the pepper-onion mixture, stirring gently. In the same skillet, return the relish to medium heat and cook until heated through. Relish should be warm but be careful not to overcook. Garnish lamb chops with relish and serve immediately.

*C*an you imagine making this recipe in a pan that doesn't have a non-stick bottom? We can thank a DuPont chemist, who in the process of trying to develop a refrigerant, accidentally created Teflon.

Lamb is graded like beef – prime, choice and good. Prime lamb will have thick, well-shaped eye muscles in the loin and rib cuts. Only 10 percent of lamb is graded prime. The majority of lamb sold in a supermarket is choice.

When buying lamb, look for moist, brightly colored meat that is not slimy or sticky. The fat should be waxy white in color and should not be chalky looking.

Tips for Buying and Cooking Fish and Seafood   185

Honey Glazed Salmon with Tomato Salsa   188

Herbed Grilled Salmon.   189

Bourbon Basted Salmon.   189

Vermouth Grilled Salmon   190

Grilled Teriyaki Salmon Steaks.   191

Grilled Salmon with a Basil Cream Sauce   192

Sautéed Dover Sole in a Chardonnay Sauce   193

Grilled Tuna Steaks in a Sake Marinade   194

Kid-Friendly Orange Roughy Parmesan   195

Red Snapper Puerto Vallarta Style.   196

Blackened Rock Cod   197

English Style Fish and Chips   198

Teriyaki Halibut with an Asian Tartar Sauce   199

Mahi-Mahi with a Mushroom Dill Sauce   200

Pan-Grilled Swordfish Steaks.   201

Grilled Swordfish with a Dijon Dill Sauce.   202

Tilapia in a Crème Fraîche Sauce.   203

Tarragon Lobster Tails   204

Shrimp and Crab Bake   205

Szechuan Shrimp.   206

Shrimp Scampi a la Carol Ann.   207

Cajun Shrimp.   208

Caramelized Sea Scallops with a Chile Cream Sauce . .   209

Hibachi-Style Sautéed Bay Scallops   210

Stone Crab Claws   211

Alaskan King Crab Legs with a Light Lemon Mayonnaise   212

Sesame Seed Encrusted Cape Capensis Fillets   213

Bouillabaisse   215

I've created a recipe for almost every kind of fish or seafood your supermarket might have on special.

DELI

Fish &
Seafood

Tips for Buying and Cooking Fish and Seafood

Shopping

Always buy fresh fish or seafood that has been refrigerated or properly iced. The best seafood is the freshest, no more than 2 to 3 days out of the water.

When shopping for fresh fish, shop with your eyes and sense of smell. Fresh fish never smells "fishy" but has a fresh, mild odor. Fish only smells "fishy" or like ammonia when it starts to decompose.

The skin of whole fish should be shiny, almost metallic, with color that has not faded. As fish decompose, the skin coloring becomes less distinct. Scales should be brightly colored and tightly attached to the skin. The gills of fresh fish are red and free from slime. Gills on fish that have passed their prime have faded to a light pink color and may appear gray or somewhat brown or green. If the head is still on the fish, the eyes should be bright, clear, and full and will bulge slightly.

Dressed fish should have firm, elastic flesh and should not have separated from the bones. When pressed, the flesh of fresh fish should spring back.

When buying shellfish, like mussels, clams, or oysters, look for clean, whole shells that have not been chipped, broken, or smashed. Shells need to be tightly closed and never open. A gaping shell means the animal is dead. Also, ask your fishmonger to pack shellfish in ice for the ride home.

If you're buying frozen fish, again shop with your nose. There should be no "fishy" odor. Avoid packages that are torn or perforated. Frozen fish should be solidly frozen and show no signs of discoloration which may indicate freezer burn. Look for wrappings that are tight with no air spaces between the fish and the wrappings.

Shrimp are sold according to the number in a pound known as the count. Jumbo shrimp range 21-25 per pound, extra large—26-30, large—31-35, medium—36-42, small—51-60, extra small—61 and over. When making peel-and-eat shrimp or shrimp cocktail, larger shrimp are preferable. For shrimp salads or other dishes, a smaller shrimp is better. When shrimp is on sale, be sure to check the count your grocer advertises.

When buying canned tuna, I much prefer white or albacore packed in water. Tuna labeled as light, dark, or blended has a stronger flavor.

When shopping, purchase your dry goods first and refrigerated items last. The less time items like fresh fish spend outside refrigeration the better.

Checking Out

When checking out, it's best to ask the clerk to bag your fish separately. If you request to have your order sacked in paper bags, ask to have the fish double-bagged in plastic as well. Some fresh fish, especially scallops, often leak. Placing it in plastic avoids leaks that can cross-contaminate other foods and keeps any leaking mess contained. Once home, I often keep scallops in plastic bags in the refrigerator as well. This keeps any leakage from spilling out and cross-contaminating foods in the refrigerator.

Storing Shellfish at Home

Shellfish must be kept cold and moist up until you cook them, but they also need to breathe. Once you get home, remove shellfish from its package and place in a large bowl. Put a wet paper towel on top of the shellfish and refrigerate.

De-veining shrimp

Unless you are cooking with very small shrimp, they must be de-veined. The intestinal tract on medium to large shrimp runs down their back and is quite unappetizing. To de-vein shrimp, hold them under a slow stream of cold water and run the tip of an ice pick or sharp knife down their back, scraping out the intestine, yet leaving the shrimp intact. Rinse gently to remove any black from the shrimp.

Scallops

Always rinse scallops before using.

Mussels

Frozen mussels are usually cleaned before freezing. If you are buying fresh mussels, they need to be cleaned before cooking. Using a stiff brush, place mussels under a slow stream of cold water and scrub the shells. Then, fill a large bowl with cold water and a few tablespoons of cornmeal. Add the mussels and soak them about 20 minutes. The mussels will take in fresh water and expel any dirt. Mussels have a beard, the stringy group of fibers located between the shells, which must be removed. Gently pull the fibers from the mussel. If the beard is stubborn and difficult to remove, a pair of pliers works well.

Clams

Fill a large bowl with cold water and soak clams for about 20 minutes before cooking.

Storing

The best fish and seafood is the freshest, no more than 2 to 3 days out of the water. Therefore, I always buy fresh fish the same day I use it. Fish will keep 1 to 2 days in the refrigerator. Once cooked, fish will keep for 3 to 4 days in the refrigerator. Smoked fish, like lox, will keep up to 14 days refrigerated. Once opened, canned fish or seafood should be discarded after 3 to 4 days in the refrigerator.

If you are freezing fish in its original supermarket packaging, it's best to over-wrap it with aluminum foil to prevent freezer burn. Fish fillets freeze nicely in sealed zip-lock freezer bags. Before closing the bag, force the air out through a small opening and then quickly finish closing the bag, locking the zip tightly. Whole fish with the skin on are best frozen first dipped in ice water to form a protective glaze over the fish, and then wrapped in freezer paper.

Seafood should be frozen as rapidly as possible, therefore, it is important to thoroughly pre-chill seafood before freezing. Have the temperature of the freezer at 0 degrees F. Place seafood in small packages and spread them out to allow the cold air to circulate evenly.

With the exception of shrimp, frozen fish should be used within 1 to 2 months.

Thawing

To thaw frozen seafood or fish, place fish in its package in a large bowl in the sink. Fill the bowl with cold water and keep a slow stream of cold water running into the bowl. Removing fish or seafood from its package and thawing it directly in cold water may damage its color and flavor.

Cooking

Fish should be cooked until it's opaque, or until it flakes easily when pierced with a fork.

Honey Glazed Salmon
with Tomato Salsa

SERVES 4

FOR THE SALSA

> 2 medium ripe tomatoes, coarsely chopped
> 3 tablespoons red onion, finely diced
> 2 tablespoons fresh parsley, snipped
> 1 teaspoon red pepper flakes
> 2 tablespoons red wine vinegar
> 2 tablespoons olive oil
> ¼ teaspoon salt
> ¼ teaspoon large grind black pepper

In a medium bowl, combine tomatoes, red onion, parsley, red pepper flakes, red wine vinegar, olive oil, salt, and pepper. Cover and refrigerate 1 hour, or until ready to serve.

FOR THE SALMON AND THE GLAZE

> 1 cup cooking sherry
> ¼ cup Dijon mustard
> ½ cup honey
> 1 tablespoon chili powder
> ¼ teaspoon salt
> ½ teaspoon large grind black pepper
> 4 salmon steaks

In a small saucepan, reduce sherry over high heat to ½ cup syrup. In a small mixing bowl, combine Dijon mustard, honey, chili powder, salt, and pepper and add to the sherry syrup. Mix thoroughly, remove from heat, and let rest at room temperature about 1 hour. Brush salmon with the glaze and grill over medium coals about 5 to 7 minutes per side depending upon thickness, or until salmon flakes easily when pierced with a fork.

Salsa should be served on the side in a gravy boat and spread to taste over salmon steaks.

*B*etter Homes and Gardens *published its first article on dieting in 1932.*

Copper River salmon, known for its rich flavor, has become the darling of salmon connoisseurs. It is available towards the end of May and its season lasts about 30 days. It's a bit pricey but worth every penny.

Herbed Grilled Salmon

SERVES 4

I ate this dish at Scot's in San Francisco. It was heavenly, so I asked the chef how he prepared it. This is my version of Scot's Herbed Grilled Salmon.

8 tablespoons fresh parsley, finely chopped
4 tablespoons fresh chives, finely chopped
2 tablespoons fresh basil, finely chopped
1 tablespoon fresh rosemary, finely chopped
4 tablespoons fresh dill, finely chopped
4 tablespoons butter, divided
4 salmon steaks, cut ¾ to 1-inch thick

In a small bowl, combine parsley, chives, basil, rosemary, and dill. In a small saucepan, melt butter over medium-low heat. Brush one side of salmon steaks with half the melted butter and press herb mixture tightly into meat. Place salmon steaks, herb side down, on a hot grill. While steaks cook, brush the other side of salmon steaks with the remaining butter and press the herb mixture tightly into meat. Grill salmon steaks about 5 minutes per side, or until salmon is opaque throughout or meat flakes easily when pierced with a fork.

I love salmon that has been cooked on cedar planking. Pacific Northwestern Native Americans discovered this method of cooking many years ago. They cooked salmon on damp cedar planks and found it enhanced the flavor of their fresh fish.

If you don't have a cedar plank, consider purchasing one. It's works nicely with this recipe.

Bourbon Basted Salmon

SERVES 4 TO 6

2 pounds salmon fillets, de-boned
½ cup brown sugar
6 tablespoons bourbon
6 tablespoons green onions, thinly sliced
6 tablespoons soy sauce
4 tablespoons vegetable oil
Vegetable oil for brushing grill
Reserved bourbon marinade

Place salmon, skin side down, in a shallow baking dish. In a small bowl, combine brown sugar, bourbon, green onions, soy sauce, and vegetable oil. Mix well. Divide marinade into 2 equal portions. Reserve one-half for basting. Pour the second half of the bourbon marinade over salmon, cover, and marinate 1 hour in the refrigerator. Brush the insides of a fish basket with vegetable oil. Remove salmon from the bourbon marinade and discard used marinade. Place salmon in the basket and close securely. Grill salmon in the basket over hot coals, turning once until opaque throughout, about 7 minutes per side, or until the salmon flakes easily when pierced with a fork. Baste with reserved bourbon marinade during cooking.

There are several varieties of North American salmon. Ninety percent come from Alaskan waters. The best Pacific salmon is Chinook or king salmon. High in fat, its flesh is soft in texture and ranges in color from off-white to bright red. Pacific salmon are in season spring through fall.

Vermouth Grilled Salmon

SERVES 4

This marinade is mild yet leaves the salmon very moist, emphasizing its natural flavor.

FOR THE MARINADE

½ cup dry vermouth

½ cup vegetable oil

2 tablespoons lemon juice

¾ teaspoon salt

¼ teaspoon large grind black pepper

½ teaspoon dried thyme

½ teaspoon dried marjoram

¼ teaspoon dried sage

1 tablespoon dried parsley

4 salmon steaks

During the 1980s, America saw an increase in farm-raised seafood, including mussels, crawfish, trout, oysters, catfish, salmon, striped bass, and tilapia.

In a medium bowl, combine vermouth, vegetable oil, lemon juice, salt, pepper, thyme, marjoram, sage, and parsley. Place salmon steaks in a shallow baking dish and pour the marinade over fish. Cover and refrigerate salmon steaks 2 to 3 hours.

Remove salmon steaks from the marinade and grill over medium-hot coals for 7 to 8 minutes per side, or until salmon is opaque throughout and flakes easily when pierced with a fork.

When buying fresh fish, shop with your nose. Fresh fish never smells fishy.

CAROL ANN'S DAD

Washing your hands in cold water before handling fish helps prevent your hands from smelling fishy.

Grilled Teriyaki Salmon Steaks

SERVES 4

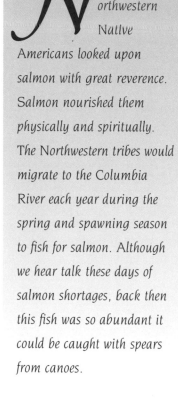

*N*orthwestern Native Americans looked upon salmon with great reverence. Salmon nourished them physically and spiritually. The Northwestern tribes would migrate to the Columbia River each year during the spring and spawning season to fish for salmon. Although we hear talk these days of salmon shortages, back then this fish was so abundant it could be caught with spears from canoes.

FOR THE MARINADE

2 cups soy sauce
¾ cup brown sugar
1 teaspoon dry mustard
1 teaspoon minced garlic
⅛ cup fresh parsley, finely chopped
¼ cup red wine

4 (8-ounce) salmon steaks

FOR THE BUTTER SAUCE

3 tablespoons butter
2 tablespoons lemon juice

FOR THE GARNISH

2 lemons, wedged

In a small saucepan, combine soy sauce, brown sugar, dry mustard, garlic, and parsley. Heat the mixture over low heat until sugar is dissolved. Add wine and stir to combine. Pour sauce into a large bowl. Add salmon steaks and coat them thoroughly. Cover and marinate salmon steaks in the refrigerator for 4 hours.

When time to grill, in a small saucepan, place butter and lemon juice over a low heat until butter is melted. Grill salmon steaks over medium coals for 4 to 6 minutes, depending upon thickness, basting with lemon and butter mixture and turning once. Salmon is done when opaque throughout, or when meat flakes easily when pierced with a fork. Garnish with wedges of lemon.

Atlantic salmon has a high-fat flesh that is pink in color and succulent. Because of industrial pollution in both North American and European tributaries, the Atlantic salmon is diminishing. Canada provides most of the Atlantic salmon, which is in season summer to early winter.

Grilled Salmon
with a Basil Cream Sauce

SERVES 4

4 salmon steaks, cut about 1-inch thick
2 tablespoons olive oil
1 fresh lemon, cut in half
Salt to taste
Large grind black pepper to taste

Preheat the grill to high. Place salmon steaks on a platter and brush both sides with olive oil. Squeeze fresh lemon juice on each side and then season with salt and pepper. Set steaks aside.

FOR THE BASIL CREAM SAUCE

20 fresh basil leaves
⅓ cup white wine
2 teaspoons minced garlic
1 cup heavy cream
1 tablespoon fresh lemon juice
2 tablespoons butter
½ teaspoon salt
¼ teaspoon large grind black pepper

In a blender, combine basil, white wine, and garlic and process at a slow speed to a smooth purée. Transfer the purée to a small heavy saucepan and stir in heavy cream. Bring to a simmer over medium heat and cook until reduced by half, about 10 minutes. Whisk in lemon juice and butter. When butter has melted, remove from heat and season with salt and pepper. Cover and keep warm.

TO GRILL AND SERVE

When ready to grill, arrange salmon steaks on a hot grate and grill 4 to 6 minutes, depending upon thickness. Turn salmon steaks once using a long spatula and grill another 4 to 6 minutes, or until fish flakes easily when pierced with a fork. Transfer steaks to a serving platter and drizzle basil cream sauce over steaks.

The Cuisinart® Food Processor was introduced at the National Housewares Exposition in 1973.

The amount of farm-raised salmon sold in the United States is increasing. Although raised in salt water, the flesh of this fish is not as flavorful as wild salmon and it has a different texture.

Sautéed Dover Sole in a Chardonnay Sauce

SERVES 4 TO 6

Clarence Birdseye pioneered the freezing of fish in 1914 after he observed that fish caught in Labrador froze instantly when exposed to air and, once defrosted weeks later, tasted fresh.

6 Dover sole fillets
½ cup flour
6 tablespoons butter

Coat fish fillets with flour and shake off the excess. In a large skillet, melt 6 tablespoons butter over medium heat. Add fillets and lightly sauté both sides, turning once. Fish is done when it flakes easily when pierced with a fork. Transfer to a plate and keep warm in a very low oven.

1 cup chardonnay wine
2 tablespoons green onions, thinly sliced
1 teaspoon minced garlic
¼ cup heavy cream
⅛ teaspoon salt
Pinch cayenne
2 tablespoons butter

Deglaze the skillet with chardonnay wine. Add green onions and garlic and cook until chardonnay wine is reduced by half. Add heavy cream, salt, and cayenne pepper. Simmer the sauce over low heat, stirring often, until thickened. Whisk in the remaining butter, 1 tablespoon at a time. Spoon the sauce over fish and serve immediately.

It's a good idea to buy fresh fish the same day you plan to eat it.

In the United States most of the fish marketed as Dover sole is actually flounder. Often referred to as fillet of sole, popular members of the flounder family are dab, English sole, and plaice. Flounder is a white fish with a fine texture and delicate flavor. True Dover sole is found only in coastal waters from Denmark to the Mediterranean Sea. It has a delicately flavored flesh and a fine, firm texture. Dover sole is imported to the United States frozen.

To deglaze means: After food has been sautéed and the food and any excess fat has been removed, a small amount of liquid is added to the pan. The browned bits of food on the pan's bottom are loosened by stirring.

Grilled Tuna Steaks in a Sake Marinade

SERVES 4

FOR THE MARINADE

    1 cup soy sauce
    ½ cup sesame oil
    ½ cup lime juice
    ¼ cup sake
    2 teaspoons minced ginger
    2 teaspoons minced garlic
    2 tablespoons red pepper flakes

In a small bowl, combine soy sauce, sesame oil, lime juice, sake, ginger, garlic, and red pepper flakes.

    4 tuna steaks, cut about ¾-inch thick,
      about 6 ounces each
    Cooking spray for oiling grill

Place tuna steaks in a glass dish large enough to hold them in a single layer. Pour marinade over steaks. Cover and refrigerate at least 30 minutes. Lightly oil the grill and light the fire, allowing coals to get very hot or set gas grill on high. Place tuna steaks on a hot grate and cook about 5 minutes until grill marks appear. Turn and grill an additional 5 minutes on the other side. Remove tuna steaks from the grill while they are still rare in the middle or they will become dry. Serve immediately.

Supermarkets go sushi in 1986 when Advanced Fresh Concepts imported trained sushi chefs into kiosk spaces, prepping and selling fresh-made sushi in ready-to-serve packages. When Steele's opened its Harmony market in 1991, fresh-made sushi was available in Carol Ann's Deli.

Two reasonably priced cooking sakes are Sho Chiku Bai or Hakushika. If these aren't available, ask the liquor store clerk for a suggestion.

Tuna is found in temperate waters around the world. There are numerous varieties of tuna: albacore, bluefin, yellowfin, and bonito. Albacore tuna has a mild flavor and the lightest flesh—white with a hint of pink. It is the most expensive canned tuna. Yellowfin has a pale pink flesh and a stronger flavor then albacore. Bluefins have a lighter flesh, but as they age, their flesh turns dark red and their flavor gets stronger. Bonitos have the strongest flavor. Tuna has a rich-flavored, firm-textured, flaky, tender flesh that is moderate to high in fat. Depending upon the variety, fresh tuna is available seasonally beginning in late spring and ending in early fall. Frozen tuna is available year-round and is sold both in a steak and fillet cut.

Kid-Friendly Orange Roughy

SERVES 4

I started making this dish for my children when they were quite young to introduce them to eating fresh fish. The cheesy topping compliments the fish nicely and makes fish really kid-friendly.

Children are kept safe from harm in supermarkets today. Grocery carts even come with seat belts to prevent little shoppers from tumbling to the floor. In my childhood days, however, our market provided a never-ending source of danger for creative young minds.

I learned to be a risk taker using the store's conveyor belt for a roller coaster. This conveyor belt, an old-fashioned porter, stretched along the wall of the back room and carried boxes unloaded from the truck across the back room to the top of the basement stairs, where it plunged down one story into a dark, dank cellar. The steep wooden stairs, a bit lop-sided and splintery, became the perfect hill for a conveyor-created roller coaster.

We used emptied cardboard boxes for cars. Finding the right size box was important—our childish bodies had to fit inside the box with little room to spare for an oversized box might derail and send us flying. I'd place my box on the conveyor belt about six feet before it dropped down to the basement and get into my "car." My brother would set me in motion with a shove. Down I'd go, leaning into the wall for dear life as this magical mover lunged to the cellar. Then, it was my brother's turn, and I'd provide the power to get his car moving. What did I learn from this experience? You can do it if you think you can.

> 2 pounds orange roughy fillets
> Butter for coating baking dish
> Juice of 1 fresh lemon

Place fillets in a buttered baking dish in a single layer. Squeeze juice from lemon into a small bowl. Brush fillets with lemon juice. Let set for 20 minutes.

> ½ cup grated Parmesan cheese
> 4 tablespoons butter, softened
> 3 tablespoons mayonnaise
> 2 green onions, thinly sliced
> ¼ teaspoon salt
> Large grind black pepper to taste
> Dash Tabasco® sauce

Preheat the broiler. In a small bowl, combine Parmesan cheese, butter, mayonnaise, green onions, salt, pepper, and Tabasco® sauce. Place fillets on a broiler pan and broil 3 to 4 inches from the heat source for 5 minutes. Turn and broil an additional 2 minutes. Spread cheese mixture over fish and broil an additional 2 minutes, or until cheese mixture is golden brown. Watch cheese topping carefully so you don't overcook.

Orange roughy is low in fat, has firm white flesh, and a mild flavor. If you want fresh, shop at a specialty fish market or an upscale grocery. Most supermarkets sell it frozen.

If you've had a busy day and forgot to soften your butter, try grating it. This will hasten the softening process and leaves a better consistency than popping it in the microwave.

Red Snapper Puerto Vallarta Style

SERVES 6

I *first ate red snapper while vacationing in Puerto Vallarta with my husband. I loved it! This is my version of red snapper Puerto Vallarta style.*

TO MARINATE THE FISH

> 6 red snapper fillets
> ½ cup fresh lime juice
> 1 teaspoon salt
> 2 teaspoons minced garlic

Place fillets in a shallow glass dish. In a small bowl, combine lime juice, salt, and garlic. Pour the marinade over fillets, cover with plastic wrap, and marinate them in the refrigerator for 2 hours.

FOR TOMATO MIXTURE

> 1 fresh Anaheim pepper, seeded and minced
> 1 fresh jalapeño pepper, seeded and minced
> 3 pounds fresh tomatoes, peeled and chopped
> 2 tablespoons tomato paste
> 2 bay leaves
> ¼ teaspoon dried oregano
> ¼ teaspoon dried thyme
> 2 tablespoons fresh cilantro, chopped

In a small bowl, combine Anaheim and jalapeño peppers, tomatoes, tomato paste, bay leaves, oregano, thyme, and cilantro. Set aside.

> 3 tablespoons olive oil
> 2 medium onions, thinly sliced
> Reserved tomato mixture

In a large electric skillet, heat olive oil over medium heat. Add onions and sauté until transparent. Add tomato mixture to the skillet and stir to blend thoroughly. Reduce heat and simmer for 10 minutes.

Remove tomato mixture from the skillet and transfer to a large saucepan. Keep tomato mixture warm over low heat until time to serve.

> 3 tablespoons butter

Ten minutes before serving, heat butter in the same skillet over medium-high heat. Remove fillets from the marinade and sauté for 2 to 3 minutes per side, turning once. Fish is done when it flakes easily when pierced with a fork. Place fillets on a serving platter and cover with the warm tomato sauce.

If you don't know if your fish is cooked, you can gently place a knife in the thickest part, pry open the flesh, and take a peek. Fish is done when it is opaque throughout and flakes easily. You can also use a food thermometer. A general guideline for fish is 135 degrees F. For fish like tuna that you prefer less cooked, try 120 degrees F.

There are many species of snapper. This saltwater fish is found in United States waters from the Gulf of Mexico up the coast to North Carolina. The better known species are the gray snapper, mutton snapper, schoolmaster snapper, and yellowtail snapper. The most popular is the red snapper, named because it has reddish pink skin and red eyes. The flesh of the red snapper is low in fat with a firm texture. Fresh snapper is available year-round with a peak season in the summer. Some markets will sell rockfish as "Pacific snapper" or "red snapper."

Remember to wear gloves when handling chile peppers.

Blackened Rock Cod

SERVES 8

This blackening recipe can be used with any fish or chicken breasts. I prefer using it with the Hawaiian fish, ono, when it's available. It's also great with boneless, skinless chicken breasts.

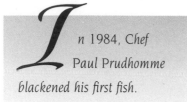

I n 1984, Chef Paul Prudhomme *blackened his first fish.*

FOR THE BLACKENING

 4 teaspoons salt
 6 teaspoons paprika
 2 teaspoons cayenne pepper
 1 ½ teaspoons white pepper
 1 teaspoon large grind black pepper
 ¾ teaspoon dried thyme
 ¾ teaspoon dried oregano

In a small bowl, combine salt, paprika, cayenne pepper, white pepper, black pepper, thyme, and oregano. Mix well.

FOR THE FISH

 8 skinless cod fillets, 8 to 10 ounces each
 8 tablespoons butter, melted

Put spices on a plate large enough to hold fillets and spread into an even layer. Dip both sides of fish in the spice mixture and rub spices over fish, coating evenly. Heat a heavy skillet over high heat until extremely hot. Run your kitchen or stove fan on high speed. Place melted butter in a large shallow bowl. Dip spice-covered fish in melted butter and place directly onto the hot skillet. Cook for 2 minutes and turn. You may drizzle an additional teaspoon of butter on fillets as they cook if you wish. Fish is done when it flakes easily when pierced with a fork.

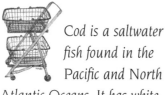

Cod is a saltwater fish found in the Pacific and North Atlantic Oceans. It has white, firm, mild-flavored flesh and is considered lean. It is available year-round and comes whole or in large pieces. Haddock, hake, and pollock are close relatives of cod.

Tips for chicken: If you're making blackened chicken breasts, purchase boneless, skinless breasts. Follow above cooking instructions but increase cooking time to 8 minutes per side for chicken breasts.

This blackening combination is extremely spicy. If you prefer a milder flavor, reduce the cayenne pepper to 1 teaspoon. These spices are enough to make 8 servings. Place any unused blackening in an airtight container and store in your pantry. It will stay fresh for up to 6 weeks.

English Style Fish and Chips
with a Homemade Tartar Sauce

SERVES 6

On a trip to London, my husband and I spent a cold, rainy evening in an English pub. No wonder the English are so fond of their Fish and Chips. It's the perfect comfort food on drizzly evenings. Season with malt vinegar. Chips is the English term for French fries.

FOR THE TARTAR SAUCE

> ¾ cup mayonnaise
>
> 1 teaspoon Dijon mustard
>
> 2 tablespoons sweet pickle relish
>
> 1 hard-boiled egg, chopped
>
> Large grind black pepper to taste

In a small bowl, combine mayonnaise, Dijon mustard, pickle relish, egg, and pepper to taste. Serve on the side with fish. Cover with plastic wrap and refrigerate until ready to serve.

FOR THE FISH

> 1 ½ cups flour
>
> 1 ½ cups flat Coors® Light Beer
>
> 3 tablespoons malt vinegar
>
> 1 ½ teaspoons baking soda
>
> Salt to taste
>
> Large grind black pepper to taste
>
> Vegetable or canola oil for frying
>
> 30 ounces cod fillets, ½-inch thick
>   and cut into serving size portions

In a medium-sized bowl, whisk flour, beer, malt vinegar, and baking soda until well blended. Season batter generously with salt and pepper. Cover and let stand at room temperature. Pour oil into a heavy electric skillet to a depth of ½ inch. Heat oil to 350 degrees. Dip fish into batter, remove, and allow excess batter to drain back into the bowl. Place fish in hot oil and fry until golden brown on both sides and cooked through, about 3 minutes per side. Transfer fish to paper towels and drain. Repeat dipping and frying fish until all the pieces have been fried. Arrange fish on a platter and serve with malt vinegar, tartar sauce, and French fries.

If you make your French fries from scratch, let the cut potatoes stand in cold water one hour before frying. Dry thoroughly before frying and try sprinkling them with flour, which makes them turn a golden brown. The secret to good French fries is to fry them twice. The first time, fry them for only a few minutes and then drain off the grease. The second time, fry them until golden brown.

The secret to frying is to be sure the oil is hot enough. Test the oil by dropping a small piece of fish into the oil. If the oil sizzles when fish is added, it's hot enough to begin. Don't overcrowd fish. It is best to fry fillets in small batches.

Teriyaki Halibut
with an Asian Tartar Sauce

SERVES 6

FOR THE MARINADE

6 tablespoons corn oil
⅓ cup soy sauce
4 green onions, thinly sliced
1 teaspoon minced garlic
2 tablespoons sugar
¼ teaspoon ground white pepper
1 tablespoon sesame seeds

6 halibut steaks, cut 1-inch thick

In a small bowl, combine corn oil, soy sauce, green onions, garlic, sugar, white pepper and sesame seeds. Place halibut steaks in a shallow baking dish and pour marinade over fish. Cover and marinate in the refrigerator 4 to 6 hours.

FOR THE TARTAR SAUCE

1 cup mayonnaise
1 teaspoon soy sauce
1 green onion, thinly sliced
¼ teaspoon sesame seeds

In a small bowl, combine mayonnaise, soy sauce, green onion, and sesame seeds and whisk to blend. Cover with plastic wrap and refrigerate until ready to serve.

Prepare the grill. Remove halibut steaks from the marinade, place on a hot grate, and grill over medium coals 5 to 7 minutes per side, or until fish flakes easily when pierced with a fork.

Hellmann's® Mayonnaise flourished in the east, while Best Foods, Inc., introduced mayonnaise to California consumers. As both companies expanded, inevitably Best Foods, Inc., purchased Hellmann's® in 1932. To this day, Hellmann's® Mayonnaise is sold east of the Rockies, and Best Foods® Mayonnaise is sold to the west.

Halibut, a member of the flatfish family, is found in northern Pacific and Atlantic waters. It is low in fat and has white, firm, mild flavored flesh. Available year-round, it is more abundant from March to September. Halibut is sold either fresh or frozen in fillets and steaks.

Mahi-Mahi
with a Mushroom Dill Sauce

SERVES 4 TO 6

2 pounds mahi-mahi fillets, cut 1-inch thick
Large grind black pepper
2 tablespoons butter, softened

Preheat the oven to 400 degrees. Cut fillets into 6 serving-size pieces and season with pepper. Rub fish with 2 tablespoons softened butter and place in a buttered shallow baking pan.

3 tablespoons butter, softened
1 cup green onions, thinly sliced
3 tablespoons butter, softened
1 pound fresh mushrooms, thinly sliced
¼ cup fresh dill, minced

Mahi-mahi is a dolphinfish and not the dolphin that is a mammal. Also called dorado or dolphinfish, mahi-mahi is found in warm waters throughout the world. It is a moderately fat fish with firm, flavorful flesh. It can be purchased in steaks or fillets.

In a large skillet, melt 3 tablespoons of butter over medium heat. Add green onions and sauté for 1 minute, stirring occasionally. Add the remaining 3 tablespoons of butter and mushrooms to the skillet and continue to sauté until mushrooms have absorbed butter. Add dill and mix thoroughly. Remove the skillet from heat.

Pour the mushroom mixture over fish and bake, basting occasionally with the pan juices, for 8 to 10 minutes for every inch of thickness.

Bake 10 minutes for each inch of thickness. To determine width for cooking, measure fillets at the thickest part.

Pan-Grilled Swordfish Steaks

SERVES 4 TO 6

FOR THE LEMON JUICE MIXTURE

> 3 tablespoons lemon juice
> 4 teaspoons minced garlic
> ¼ teaspoon salt
> Large grind black pepper to taste
> 3 teaspoons fresh oregano, chopped
> ¼ cup olive oil

In a small bowl, blend lemon juice, garlic, salt, pepper, and oregano and beat with a fork until salt dissolves. Slowly add ¼ cup olive oil and continue beating with a fork and set aside.

> Olive oil for coating grill pan
> 2 pounds swordfish steaks, cut 1-inch thick

Heat a grill pan over medium-high heat. Lightly coat the grill pan with olive oil. Pan should be hot enough to sizzle when fish is placed on the grill. Place swordfish steaks on the grill. When a thin, dark crust forms on the heat side of fish, turn with a spatula. Continue cooking the second side until crust marks have formed on both sides.

> Lemon juice mixture
> 1 tablespoon small capers, rinsed

Preheat an electric skillet to high. The skillet should be large enough to accommodate swordfish steaks without crowding. Transfer swordfish steaks from the grill pan to the electric skillet. Immediately pour the lemon juice mixture over swordfish steaks and continue cooking on high heat, turning once, until fish flakes easily when pierced with a fork. Remove steaks and garnish with capers.

Caper berries are the fruit of flower buds from the caper bush, which grows in the southern United States, the Mediterranean, Canada, and Great Britain. Capers are either pickled in vinegar or preserved in brine and used as a condiment. The Romans used them to season fish sauces. They can also be used to flavor rice and meatballs and as a garnish for pizzas. Capers go well with mustard and horseradish.

Capers are found on the pickle aisle of most supermarkets.

The grill pan is used to put grill marks on the swordfish. Finish cooking the fish in the electric skillet.

Grilled Swordfish
with a Dijon Dill Sauce

SERVES 4

FOR THE DIJON DILL SAUCE

½ cup Dijon mustard

⅓ cup sour cream

¼ cup sugar

⅓ cup white wine vinegar

½ cup olive oil

2 tablespoons fresh dill, chopped

¼ teaspoon salt

½ teaspoon large grind black pepper

In a blender or food processor, combine Dijon mustard, sour cream, sugar, and white wine vinegar. Slowly add olive oil and process at a slow speed until ingredients are well blended. Transfer the sauce to a covered container, fold in dill, salt, and pepper, and refrigerate until ready to serve.

FOR THE MARINADE

¾ cup mayonnaise

¼ cup olive oil

1 teaspoon minced garlic

3 teaspoons fresh parsley, snipped

½ cup sour cream

2 pounds swordfish steaks, cut 1-inch thick

In a small bowl, combine mayonnaise, olive oil, garlic, parsley, and sour cream. Place fish in a large shallow baking dish and coat with the marinade. Cover and refrigerate at least 2 hours, turning fish several times to coat. Remove swordfish steaks from the marinade and discard used marinade. Grill swordfish steaks over medium-hot coals turning once, 5 to 7 minutes per side, or until fish flakes easily when pierced with a fork. Place swordfish steaks on a serving platter and smother with Dijon dill sauce.

*I*n 1905, Richard Hellmann, a German immigrant, opened a delicatessen in New York City. His wife's recipe for mayonnaise was featured in salads. It became so popular that Hellmann began selling it in "wooden boats" that were used for weighing butter.

Swordfish is found in temperate waters throughout the world. It has firm, dense, meat-like flesh, a mild flavor, and is moderately fat. It is one of the more popular fish in the United States. Fresh swordfish is available from spring to early fall. It is available frozen year-round. Supermarkets sell it in steaks and chunks.

Tilapia in a Crème Fraîche Sauce

SERVES 6

I normally buy 1 tilapia fillet per person, but this recipe is so good, we like to have seconds so I buy 1½.

FOR THE FISH

8 (6-ounce) tilapia fillets
1 teaspoon fresh thyme, chopped
1 teaspoon large grind black pepper
½ teaspoon salt
Cooking spray

Sprinkle fish with thyme, black pepper, and salt. Heat a large nonstick electric skillet to medium-high heat. Coat lightly with cooking spray. Place fish in the skillet and cook 1 minute on each side.

The flesh of tilapia has a fine texture and is white, sweet, and low in fat. It is sometimes called St. Peter's fish and, in Hawaii, is called the Hawaiian sun fish.

FOR THE SAUCE

1 cup low-sodium chicken broth
5 small portobello mushrooms, thinly sliced
⅓ cup sundried tomatoes, drained and cut into ⅛-inch strips
1½ cups fresh spinach, washed and dried
4 tablespoons crème fraîche
4 tablespoons Dijon mustard

Add chicken broth to the skillet and bring to a boil. Cover, reduce heat, and simmer 5 minutes. Add mushrooms, sundried tomatoes, and spinach and cook, uncovered, 1 minute or until mushrooms are tender. Remove fish from pan and transfer to serving platter. Cover with aluminum foil to keep warm.

Add crème fraîche and mustard to the pan and whisk until well combined. Cook 1 minute, or until heated through. Serve sauce on the side or pour over fish.

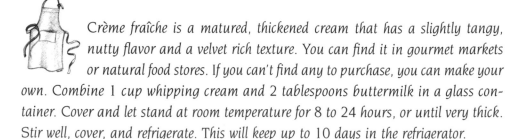

Crème fraîche is a matured, thickened cream that has a slightly tangy, nutty flavor and a velvet rich texture. You can find it in gourmet markets or natural food stores. If you can't find any to purchase, you can make your own. Combine 1 cup whipping cream and 2 tablespoons buttermilk in a glass container. Cover and let stand at room temperature for 8 to 24 hours, or until very thick. Stir well, cover, and refrigerate. This will keep up to 10 days in the refrigerator.

Tarragon Lobster Tails

SERVES 6

6 (6 to 8-ounce) lobster tails

Set lobsters shell side down on a cutting board. Using kitchen shears, make a lengthwise slit in the lobster tails. Remove the gills. Preheat the broiler. Arrange lobsters shell side up on a broiler pan.

4 tablespoons dry sherry
1 tablespoon dried tarragon
1 tablespoon fresh parsley, snipped
4 tablespoons butter, melted
½ teaspoon lemon zest

In a small bowl, combine sherry, tarragon, parsley, 4 tablespoons butter, and lemon zest and mix well. Brush the inside of each lobster tail with the butter mixture. Place lobster tails under the broiler for 6 to 8 minutes, or until meat is tender and the shells are red. A lobster tail will curl when it is done and the shell may char from the broiler.

1 lemon, cut into wedges
12 tablespoons butter, melted

Place lobster tails on a serving platter, garnish with lemon wedges, and serve the remaining melted butter at each place setting in individual cups.

*W*hen the English first landed in Plymouth, lobsters were quite abundant. Historical records indicate this crustacean would wash up on the beaches at Plymouth, Massachusetts, in such numbers that lobsters laid two feet deep on the water's edge. In 1622, when new settlers would arrive, Governor William Bradford apologized. The only food he had to offer them was lobster.

There are two main varieties of lobster sold in the United States. The most popular is the Maine lobster, found off the Atlantic coast of the Northern United States and Canada. Spiny lobsters, also called rock lobsters, are found in waters off the coasts of Florida, Southern California, Mexico, Australia, New Zealand, and South Africa. The Maine lobster has claws; the spiny lobster does not. Outside of California and Florida, most spiny lobster meat sold in supermarkets is in the form of frozen tails, usually labeled "rock lobster tails."

The secret to serving an attractive lobster tail is to remove the tail in one piece from the shell. To accomplish this, place a small knife under the meat, loosen it from the shell, and remove gently.

Shrimp and Crab Bake

MAKES 6 SERVINGS

FOR THE CHEESE SAUCE

¼ cup butter

½ pound fresh mushrooms, washed, stemmed, and sliced

1 teaspoon minced garlic

2 green onions, chopped

¼ cup flour

½ teaspoon large grind black pepper

⅔ cup milk

½ cup shredded Cheddar cheese

⅔ cup white wine

According to the 1995 edition of the Encyclopedia Americana, *there are over 4,500 different species of crabs.*

In a skillet, melt butter over medium heat. Add mushrooms, garlic, and green onions and sauté over medium heat for 5 minutes. Remove from heat and stir in flour, pepper, and milk. Return to medium heat and slowly bring mixture to a boil, stirring frequently. Add ½ cup cheese and stir until melted. Blend in white wine and remove from heat.

1 pound imitation crabmeat

1 pound small shrimp, cooked, peeled, de-veined, and tails removed

1 can (14 ½-ounces) water-packed artichoke hearts, drained and cut into sixths

2 ½ cups shredded Cheddar cheese

Cheese sauce

2 tablespoons bread crumbs

1 tablespoon butter, melted

If you want to use fresh crab in this recipe, 4 pounds of crab in the shell should yield about 1 pound of meat.

In a large mixing bowl, combine crabmeat, shrimp, artichoke hearts, the remaining 2 ½ cups Cheddar cheese, and the cheese sauce. Mix well. Pour into a buttered 2-quart casserole. Melt butter in a small sauté pan over medium-low heat. Add bread crumbs to butter and mix well. Sprinkle bread crumbs on top of the casserole. Bake uncovered at 375 degrees for 30 minutes, or until bubbly and lightly browned.

A general rule of thumb is 1 pound of whole, raw shrimp will yield ½ to ¾ pound of cooked meat.

Szechuan Shrimp

SERVES 4

2 tablespoons peanut oil
1 pound large raw shrimp, shelled and de-veined
¼ cup green onions, minced
¼ teaspoon ground ginger
½ teaspoon minced garlic
2 tablespoons dry sherry
2 tablespoons soy sauce
2 teaspoons sugar
½ teaspoon salt
2 to 3 tablespoons ketchup
2 tablespoons chili sauce
1 teaspoon red pepper flakes

In a wok or large heavy skillet, heat peanut oil over medium-high heat. Add shrimp, green onions, ginger, and garlic and sauté until shrimp are pink. Add sherry, soy sauce, sugar, and salt. Mix well. Blend in ketchup, chili sauce, and red pepper flakes. Mix thoroughly. Serve over piping hot white rice.

For this recipe, purchase shrimp with a count of 31–35 per pound. Do not buy frozen shrimp that have dry spots on their shells. This is a sign of freezer burn. Except for black tiger, black spots on their shells are a sign of spoilage. Signs of yellow or grit on the shells could mean the shrimp have been bleached to remove black spots.

Do not thaw frozen shrimp until the day before you plan to use them.

China has five main cooking styles, each attributed to a region. Cantonese, from the Southeastern region, is famous for its meat roasting and grilling, fried rice, Bird's Nest and Shark's Fin Soup. Fukien, the East Coast, is known for its seafood dishes and its many varieties of soups. Peking-Shantung, the Northeastern region, is acclaimed for its subtle, artful use of seasonings and, of course, Peking Duck. The Honan province, Central China, is known for its sweet-and-sour cooking, while Szechuan-Hunan, Western China, is famous for its hot and spicy dishes. Mandarin and Shanghai are not regional distinctions, but terms used to identify cooking styles. The word mandarin means "Chinese official", and this style of cooking suggests an aristocratic cuisine that combines the best from all the regions. Shanghai cooking is a sophisticated combination of all the styles.

shrimp Scampi a la Carol Ann

SERVES 4

8 ounces spaghetti cooked al dente and drained

Cook spaghetti al dente according to package directions or see Tips for Cooking Pasta on Page 241.

⅓ cup clarified butter
1 tablespoon shallots, finely chopped
1 ½ teaspoons minced garlic
12 large raw shrimp, shelled and de-veined
2 tablespoons brandy
¼ teaspoon dried oregano
¼ teaspoon dried basil
½ teaspoon fresh parsley, minced
¼ cup dry white wine
¾ cup fresh tomatoes, diced
Salt to taste
Large grind black pepper to taste

Supermarkets sell both farm-raised and wild shrimp. Gulf whites have pale shells, are usually wild, and have an excellent taste. Mexican whites are also tasty but are more often farm-raised. Gulf pink or brown shrimp are normally wild and not as large as whites. They have a pinkish or brown shell. Black tiger shrimp is most commonly sold in supermarkets. These shrimp are from Asia and usually farm raised.

In a large skillet, place butter, shallots, and garlic and sauté over medium heat for 2 minutes, or until transparent but not brown. Add shrimp and sauté for 3 to 4 minutes or until shrimp turn pink. Slowly pour brandy into the skillet and cook for 30 seconds. If your skillet is quite hot, the brandy will ignite. Therefore, add it very carefully to avoid being burned. Add oregano, basil, parsley, white wine, and tomatoes and simmer 5 minutes. Season to taste with salt and pepper. Serve over spaghetti.

To clarify butter, melt butter in a sauté pan over medium heat. Remove from heat and let sit for 5 minutes. Skim off foam that has formed on the top and discard.

For tips on de-veining shrimp, see Page 186.

Cajun Shrimp

SERVES 4

2 pounds large shrimp

Wash the shrimp. Remove shells and de-vein, leaving tail intact. Spread shrimp out in a large shallow baking dish.

FOR THE MARINADE

8 tablespoons butter

½ cup olive oil

½ cup chili sauce

1 lemon, sliced

2 teaspoons minced garlic

2 tablespoons lemon juice

1½ tablespoons Worcestershire® sauce

1½ tablespoons liquid smoke

½ tablespoon fresh parsley, finely chopped

1 teaspoon paprika

1 teaspoon dried oregano

1 teaspoon red pepper flakes

½ teaspoon Tabasco® sauce

Salt to taste

Large grind black pepper to taste

In a medium saucepan, combine butter, olive oil, chili sauce, lemon slices, garlic, lemon juice, Worcestershire® sauce, liquid smoke, parsley, paprika, oregano, red pepper flakes, Tabasco® sauce, salt, and pepper to taste. Heat over low heat until warm. Pour over shrimp. Cool, cover, and refrigerate for several hours, basting and turning every 30 minutes. Preheat the oven to 300 degrees. Leave shrimp in the baking dish and bake for 20 minutes. Turn shrimp over after 10 minutes and continue baking the remaining 10 minutes. Serve in soup bowls with French bread to dip in the sauce.

*I*n case you've ever been confused about the differences between the Cajun and Creole style, experts offer the following explanation: Cajun cooking is a combination of French and Southern cuisines. This style uses a dark roux and plenty of animal fat. Creole cooking places an emphasis on butter and cream. Some foodies maintain that Cajun cooking uses more spices, while Creole uses more tomatoes. Both use filé powder and the "holy trinity"—chopped green peppers, onions, and celery.

Before storing, fresh uncooked shrimp should be rinsed under cold running water. Drain well, cover tightly, and refrigerate. Stored in this manner they will keep up to 2 days.

Once cooked, shrimp will keep for 3 days.

Caramelized Sea Scallops
with a Chili Cream Sauce

SERVES 4 TO 6

FOR THE CHILI CREAM SAUCE

> 1 teaspoon chili powder
> Juice of 1 ½ limes
> ¾ cup sour cream
> Salt to taste

In a small bowl, combine chili powder, lime juice, sour cream, and salt. Blend thoroughly, cover with plastic wrap, and refrigerate. Preparing sauce first allows the flavor to mellow.

FOR THE SCALLOPS

> 2 pounds sea scallops, rinsed and drained
> 4 tablespoons fresh parsley, snipped
> Salt to taste
> Large grind black pepper to taste
> ¼ cup olive oil or less

On a flat surface, arrange scallops with the flat side down. Sprinkle with parsley, salt, and pepper. Heat enough olive oil to just cover the bottom of a large non-stick skillet over high heat until olive oil begins to smoke. Reduce heat to medium-high and place scallops in the skillet seasoned side down. Do not disturb them for 2 to 3 minutes. This allows the sugars in the scallops to caramelize. Turn and sear the opposite side for 1 to 3 minutes longer, depending on the size of the scallops.

> Chili cream sauce
> Green onions, thinly sliced

Transfer to a serving platter, drizzle with chili cream sauce, and garnish with green onions. Serve immediately.

Scallops are very perishable. I recommend eating them the day you buy them. Sea scallops are sometimes soaked in water and tripolyphosphate. This does extend their shelf life. If available, buy unsoaked or "dry" scallops. They have a superior flavor and brown nicely. If scallops have a pure white color, they have probably been soaked.

My father had an interesting way of handling young shoplifters. A large Catholic family lived across the street from our Mountain Avenue store, and as fate would have it one sultry summer day, Merrill caught one of the sons stealing. My father explained to the young whipper-snapper that when you were caught shoplifting at Steele's you had a choice of consequences. His options—a call to the police, a call to his parents, or dealing directly with Mr. Steele. It isn't hard to guess which consequence the boy picked.

Dad believed there was a lesson to be learned in each and every life event, so he lectured the juvenile about honesty. My father could be a bit long winded when he had his dander up, so the discourse became quite lengthy. Following the chat, came the math lesson—how much the 10 cent candy bar the boy had pocketed would cost the store. The answer—$2.50. For every item stolen from a market, 25 of the exact same item must be sold to recover the cost of the lost item.

Hibachi-Style Sautéed Bay Scallops
with an Asian Tartar Sauce

SERVES 6

FOR THE TARTAR SAUCE

    1 cup mayonnaise
    1 teaspoon soy sauce
    1 green onion, thinly sliced
    ¼ teaspoon sesame seeds

In a small bowl, combine mayonnaise, soy sauce, green onion, and sesame seeds. Cover with plastic wrap and refrigerate until ready to serve. Serve as an accompaniment on the side.

FOR THE SCALLOPS

    2 tablespoons butter
    2 tablespoons peanut oil
    1 tablespoon soy sauce
    1 tablespoon lemon juice
    1 teaspoon sesame seeds
    ¼ teaspoon salt
    ¼ teaspoon large grind black pepper
    2 pounds bay scallops, rinsed and drained

In a large non-stick skillet, heat butter and peanut oil over medium-high heat. Add soy sauce, lemon juice, sesame seeds, salt, and pepper to the skillet and stir. Add scallops to the skillet in small batches and cook about 1½ minutes per side until cooked through. Remove to a plate and keep warm. When all scallops are cooked, return to the skillet, and heat through before serving.

After visiting the United States, a group of Chinese businessmen took home a bucket of bay scallops from Nantucket. They began cultivating their find. As a result, farm-raised bay scallops are now sold everywhere. Their flavor is not as good as wild scallops, but they are much more affordably priced.

Scallops can be cooked so that their interior remains cool, creamy, and almost raw or cooked through. If you cook them longer, don't cook them to the point they become rubbery. Smaller scallops will usually cook in about 2 minutes. Larger bay and sea scallops will usually cook in 3 to 4 minutes.

Scallops have a sweet smell. Avoid scallops that appear dry or have brown edges. The off-white, cork-shaped Northeastern bay scallop is thought to be the most flavorful. It is found in a small area between Long Island and Cape Cod and has a short season—November through February. This is the best scallop for eating raw.

Stone Crab Claws

SERVES 4

> 6 gallons water
> 4 pounds stone crab claws
> 8 tablespoons butter, melted

Fill a large kettle with 6 gallons of water. Bring water to a full boil and drop crab claws into boiling water. Return water to a full boil and cook crab claws for 3 minutes. Remove crab claws from water and drain. Most supermarkets sell claws that are precooked. They only need to be heated through to serve. Serve melted butter at each place setting in individual cups.

Use a shell cracker, a pair of pliers, or a hammer to crack the claws. Crack the stone crab claws by placing the claw horizontally on a cutting board and striking lightly with a hammer in the center of the claw. Once the claw is cracked, the crabmeat can be removed easily.

Tips on freezing crab: Crabmeat, if cooked fresh and picked from the shell, can be wrapped airtight and frozen at 0 degrees for up to 2 months. Thaw crab only in the refrigerator. Do not thaw at room temperature and do not refreeze.

When cooking with partially cooked crab, the best results are obtained by thawing crab legs and using the meat in cold dishes or by adding the meat to hot dishes only at the last moment, cooking just until heated through, then serving immediately.

Alaskan King Crab Legs
with a Light Lemon Mayonnaise

SERVES 4

Along with warm melted butter, I like to serve crab legs with a light lemon mayonnaise. This sauce and butter go nicely with freshly steamed artichoke hearts — see Page 219 — and fresh French bread.

FOR THE LIGHT LEMON MAYONNAISE

>2 eggs
>5 tablespoons fresh lemon juice
>2 tablespoons Dijon mustard
>1 cup corn oil
>1 cup light olive oil
>1 ½ teaspoons lemon zest
>½ teaspoon large grind black pepper
>1 teaspoon dried dill
>½ teaspoon dried tarragon

In a blender, combine eggs, lemon juice, and Dijon mustard and process at a slow speed for 15 seconds. With the machine running, slowly pour in corn and olive oils and process until the mayonnaise is thick. Transfer to a bowl. Fold in lemon zest, pepper, dill, and tarragon. Cover and refrigerate at least 2 hours before serving.

Crab legs can be boiled, steamed, or broiled for 4 minutes. I prefer boiling.

FOR THE KETTLE

>6 gallons water
>½ cup chardonnay wine
>2 bay leaves
>2 teaspoons minced garlic
>2 lemon wedges
>4 pounds frozen Alaskan King crab legs

Fill a large kettle with water and bring to a boil. Add chardonnay wine, bay leaves, garlic, and lemon wedges to boiling water. Add 2 pounds crab legs to the kettle and boil for 4 minutes. Remove crab legs immediately. Add remaining 2 pounds to the kettle, boil for 4 minutes, and remove. Cool.

In planning to serve crab for dinner, a general rule of thumb when determining serving quantities is 4 pounds of crab in the shell will yield about 1 pound of cooked crabmeat (4 servings). Most Alaskan King crab legs sold in supermarkets are slightly precooked, then frozen. Ask your fishmonger if the crab you are purchasing has been slightly cooked. This is important because it is easy to overcook precooked crab.

If you purchase crab legs frozen, they can be stored in your freezer until thawed. If the crabmeat has begun to thaw, it should be cooked and eaten on the same day as purchased.

Sesame Seed Encrusted Cape Capensis Fillets
with Summer Vegetables

SERVES 6

FOR THE VEGETABLES

12 small new red potatoes, washed and cut in half

2 small zucchini, trimmed and quartered lengthwise, then cut into 1 ½-inch strips

1 small yellow squash, trimmed and quartered lengthwise, then cut into 1 ½-inch strips

3 tablespoons olive oil

1 red bell pepper, cored, seeded, and cut into 1 ½-inch strips

1 tablespoon shallots, finely chopped

Salt to taste

Large grind black pepper to taste

¼ cup reserved cooking liquid

4 tablespoons fresh lemon juice

3 tablespoons fresh parsley, chopped

Cape Capensis is part of the Hake family and is considered a specialty fish in Europe. This fish is caught in nets in deep waters off the coast of South Africa. It's firm flesh, mild flavor, and white color can be compared to Orange Roughy. Capensis are bluish-gray in color, with silvery sides and white bellies. Weighing in between 2 to 4 pounds, Cape Capensis have large mouths, a lower protruding jaw, and sharp teeth.

Fill the bottom of a steamer pan with water and bring to a boil. Place potatoes on the steamer rack over boiling water and steam for 10 minutes. Add zucchini and yellow squash and steam an additional 5 minutes. Remove vegetables from the steamer rack, drain water from the steamer, and reserve ¼ cup liquid. In a large non-stick skillet, heat olive oil over medium-high heat. Add red pepper strips and shallots and sauté until wilted. Add potatoes, zucchini, yellow squash, salt, and pepper and cook stirring constantly 1 minute. Add cooking liquid, lemon juice, and parsley. Toss over medium heat for about 1 minute and serve with fish fillets.

continued next page

When steaming vegetables, be sure the water level does not rise above the basket. This makes the vegetables soggy.

FOR THE CAPENSIS FILLETS

    2 large egg whites

    2 tablespoons water

    Dash Tabasco® sauce

    ½ teaspoon salt

    ½ teaspoon white pepper

    2 jars (2 ¼ ounces) sesame seeds

    4 skinless Cape Capensis fillets, cut in half

    3 tablespoons olive oil

    2 lemons, cut in wedges

In a medium mixing bowl, beat egg whites briefly with a wire whisk, adding water, Tabasco® sauce, salt, and white pepper. Place sesame seeds in a large flat dish big enough to hold a single fillet. Dip fillets one at a time in the egg mixture to coat. Remove any excess egg mixture and pat both sides of fillets with sesame seeds, making certain the seeds stick.

Heat olive oil in a large non-stick skillet over medium-high heat. Add enough fillets so they do not overlap. Cook until golden brown on one side, about 2 minutes. Turn and cook about 2 minutes on the second side. Cooking time varies according to thickness of fish. Fillets are done when they flake easily when pierced with a fork. As fillets are cooked, transfer to a warm platter. Serve with vegetables and garnish with lemon wedges.

Cape Capensis is hard to find. If your supermarket ever has it in stock, be sure to give it a try. This dish is delicious.

The sesame seeds will turn brown during the cooking process.

Bouillabaisse

SERVES 6

Serve with Caesar salad, sourdough baguette, and white wine.

FOR THE STOCK

> 1 gallon water
> ½ cup canned chicken broth
> ⅓ cup clam juice
> 1 pinch saffron
> 1 can (16-ounces) peeled tomatoes, chopped
> 1 can (12-ounces) tomato paste with Italian seasoning
> ½ cup Pernod liqueur
> ½ cup chardonnay wine
> 6 tablespoons butter

In a large heavy kettle, place water, chicken broth, and clam juice over high heat and bring to a boil. Add saffron, tomatoes, tomato paste, Pernod, chardonnay wine, and butter. Reduce heat to low and simmer for 15 minutes.

> ½ cup olive oil
> 1 onion, chopped
> 4 celery stalks, chopped
> 2 carrots, chopped
> 1 teaspoon minced garlic
> ½ teaspoon large grind black pepper
> ½ teaspoon fennel seeds
> 3 bay leaves

In a large sauté pan, heat olive oil on medium-high heat until hot. Add onion, celery, carrots, garlic, pepper, fennel seeds, and bay leaves. Sauté vegetables for 4 to 6 minutes, or until onions are transparent. Add vegetables to the stock, stir, and bring to a boil.

FOR THE FISH

> 1½ pounds Manilla clams, thoroughly scrubbed
> 2 pounds green-lipped mussels, thoroughly scrubbed
> 6 small lobster tails
> 1 pound jumbo shrimp
> 1½ pounds rock cod, cut into 6 pieces

With the stock boiling, add clams, mussels, lobster tails, shrimp, and rock cod. Cook fish for 3 to 4 minutes, or until clams and mussels have opened their shells and the rest of the seafood is done. Lobster tails will curl, rock cod will flake easily.

Bouillabaisse is a classic Provencal fisherman's stew. It dates back to the ancient Greeks (170-230 A.D.), where legend has it that Venus served a fish stew to her husband, Vulcan, to lull him to sleep while she consorted with Mars. I always make bouillabaisse for my husband on his birthday.

You don't have to use the seafood specified in this recipe. If you'd like to substitute other ingredients, get creative.

Shells on clams and mussels should be tightly closed. Gaping shells mean the animal is dead.

For tips on cleaning clams and mussels, see Page 186.

Ask the fishmonger to pack your clams and mussels in ice.

For Mom always the BEST

HER FAVORITE FOODS!

CLOSED SUNDAYS

Surprise her with her favorite menu, served in style on Mother's Day. STEELE'S anticipates her preferences with a selection of famous brands foods' rated "right for Mom." You'll like our wide choices and STOREWIDE LOW PRICES. They all add up to a terrific treat for Mom!

Shurfine Milk 13 Oz. Can **27¢**

HUNGRY JACK FLAKY
BISCUITS 9½ Oz. Package **19¢**

Taco Shells Old El Paso 12 Shells **35¢**

SKILLET MAGIC
Dinners Pkg. **35¢**

OLDEN GRAIN
Macaroni & Cheese 7¼ Oz. **27¢**

BOOTHS
Perch Fillets 1 Lb. **69¢**

PILLSBURY
Flour 25 Lb. Bag **$4.50**

USDA Choice Beef Chuck Steaks Lb. **69¢**	USDA Choice Beef Swiss Steaks Lb. **79¢**
USDA Choice Beef Round Bone Roasts Lb. **79¢**	USDA Choice Beef Chuck Roasts Lb. **69¢**
Lean Fresh Ground Beef 3 Lbs. **$2.65**	USDA A Grade Taste Treat Turkeys Lb. **59¢**
Bar S All Meat Wieners Lb. **79¢**	Bar S Sliced All Meat Bologna Lb. **79¢**
Economy Pak Sliced Halibut Lb. **$1.29**	Booth's Breaded Shrimp Lb. **$1.79**
Home Made Ham Salad Lb. **89¢**	Well Trimmd Beef Tongues Lb. **59¢**
Bar S Sliced Bacon Lb. **99¢**	Boneless Cooked Bar S Hams Lb. **$1.49**

Hunts Pears Halves in Heavy Syrup 15 Oz. Cans **28¢**

Shurfine Cake Mix 4 Flavors Pkg. **33¢**

Krafts Cheese American 1 Lb. Pkg. **69¢**

Mile High Dill Pickles Whole or Hamburger Quart **39¢**

Majesty Pork Shoulder Picnics 1 Lb. Can **$1.39**

Signature Cherry Peppers 22 Oz. **29¢**

Tomatoes Mexican Lb. **50¢**
Hot House Leaf Lettuce Lb. **37¢**
California Avocados Each **35¢**

Cauliflower Calif. Lb. **45¢**
Washington Winesap Apples Lb. **29¢**
Washington Delicious Apples Lb. **30¢**

Cabbage Texas Lb. **12¢**
Arizona Yams Lb. **25¢**

Onions New Texas Yellow Lb. **10¢**

NESTLES
Quik 2 Lb. **95¢**
Lipton Tea Bags 48's **67¢**
Margarine Shurfresh Lb. **39¢**

BEECH-NUT STRAINED
Baby Food **10¢**
Beech-Nut Junior Foods **15¢**

Lux Liquid 13' Off 22 Oz. **45¢**
Electra-Sol 33 Oz. **68¢**
Hilex Bleach Gallon **45¢**

HUNTS
Ketchup 14 Oz. **25¢**
SHURFINE
Mustard 16 Oz. **28¢**
HOME STYLE
Bread 16 Oz. Loaf **29¢**
ROYAL
Gelatin Pkg. **10¢**
Lucky Whip 8 Oz. **93¢**
SCOT
Towels Large Roll **39¢**
Dixie Paper Plates 100's **73¢**
Diamond Foil 25 Ft. **25¢**

Pillsbury Pancake Mix 2 Lb. Pkg. **45¢**

BORDO
Pitted Dates 1 Lb. **49¢**

Fab King Size Package **$1.25**

IRISH SPRING
Soap Bath Size **22¢**

SHURFINE
Coffee 2 Lb. Can **$1.85**

KRAFTS
ITALIAN DRESSING 8 Oz. **35¢**

Hamilton Bakery
FRESH DAILY
BAKERY SPECIALS

DILLY BREAD **52¢**
Butterscotch Brownies **15¢** Ea.
Mother's Day Cakes
Meringue Shells **15¢** Ea.

One of Colorado's Finest Bakeries

STEELE'S CASH MARKET
309 WEST MOUNTAIN

May 9, 1974

Steamed Artichokes with a Lemon Pepper Mayonnaise   219

Pauline's Homemade Applesauce   220

Fresh Green Beans with Herbs.   220

Broccoli Soufflé   221

Luau Baked Beans   222

My Favorite Picnic Beans   223

Roasted Corn on the Cob   224

Polenta Pie   225

Roasted Garlic   225

Grilled Garlic Bread   226

Grilled Portobello Mushrooms.   226

Stuffed Portobello Mushrooms   227

Grilled Vegetables   228

Rotini in an Artichoke Butter Sauce   229

Herb Roasted New Potatoes.   230

Perfect Garlic Mashed Potatoes   230

Golden Potato Brulèe   231

Mashed Potatoes with Jalapeños and Cheddar Cheese   232

Smashed New Red Potatoes.   233

Grilled Tomatoes   234

Baked Acorn Squash   234

Carol Ann's Rice Pilaf   235

Old-Fashioned Candied Yams   236

Herbed Yorkshire Pudding   237

There are dynamite recipes for side dishes in this chapter.

Steamed Artichokes
with a Lemon Pepper Mayonnaise
SERVES 4

FOR THE LEMON PEPPER SAUCE

½ cup sour cream
½ cup mayonnaise
¾ teaspoon bon appétit
½ teaspoon lemon pepper
¼ teaspoon onion powder

In a small bowl, combine sour cream, mayonnaise, bon appétit, lemon pepper, and onion powder and whisk to blend. Cover with plastic wrap and refrigerate until ready to serve.

4 artichokes
2 tablespoons lemon juice
2 tablespoons olive oil
2 teaspoons minced garlic

Place artichokes on a cutting board. Using a sharp knife, cut off the stem so that artichokes will stand upright and slice an inch off its top. Remove any tough, outer leaves around the stem. Using cooking shears, snip off the sharp tips of the leaves. Hold artichokes upright and place under a solid stream of running water to wash out any debris.

Fill a large kettle with water, lemon juice, olive oil, and garlic and place over high heat. Bring water to a solid rolling boil, add artichokes, and cook 20 to 45 minutes, depending upon size. Artichokes are done when a fork can be easily inserted into the base and the outside leaves pull out easily.

 I've found the best way to serve artichokes is on a saucer. Serve lemon pepper mayonnaise at each place setting in individual serving cups. Kitchen stores sell artichoke steamer racks. These racks support the artichokes upright in a steaming kettle so that the tough stems remain immersed in boiling water.

 For tips on buying artichokes, see Page 315.

In the 1920s, Ciro "Whitey" Terranova a member of the mafia, monopolized the artichoke market in New York City by purchasing all artichokes shipped to New York from California for $6 a crate. Terranova formed a produce company and resold the artichokes for a 40 percent profit. Dubbed the "Artichoke King," Terranova terrorized produce distributors, food markets, and even the farmers in California creating a full-fledged "artichoke war."

This war created such havoc for the city that the Mayor of New York, Fiorello La Gaurdia, declared it illegal to sell, display, or possess artichokes. Because Mayor La Gaurdia loved artichokes so much, the ban lasted only one week.

Pauline's Homemade Applesauce

MAKES ABOUT 7 CUPS

When I was a little girl, my mother made homemade applesauce. It was my favorite after-school snack on crisp, fall afternoons. This is a great accompaniment to Baked Pork Chops in a Tomato Chutney Sauce or Potato Pancakes.

20 Granny Smith apples, peeled, cored, and cut into chunks
2 cups apple cider
½ cup sugar
2 teaspoons ground cinnamon
½ teaspoon ground nutmeg

In a large saucepan, combine apples and apple cider. Bring to a boil over medium-high heat. Reduce to low heat and simmer uncovered for 40 minutes, stirring occasionally to prevent sticking. Add sugar, cinnamon, and nutmeg and stir, blending well. When apples are soft, mash with a potato masher to desired consistency.

Fresh Green Beans with Herbs

SERVES 6

1 pound fresh green beans
4 tablespoons butter
⅓ cup white onion, chopped
¼ cup celery, finely chopped
¼ cup fresh parsley, minced
¼ cup fresh basil, slivered
1 teaspoon minced garlic
½ teaspoon salt

Trim and clean beans. Fill a large kettle half full with water and bring to a boil over high heat. Add beans and cook until tender but not limp, about 5 to 6 minutes. Fill a large bowl with ice water. When beans are tender, immediately immerse in ice water to retard cooking and set color. Cool beans, drain thoroughly, and set aside.

In a large skillet, melt butter over medium heat. Add onion and celery and sauté until soft but not browned, about 5 minutes. Add parsley, basil, garlic, and salt and stir, cooking 3 more minutes. Add beans and toss to combine. Cook uncovered, until beans are heated through, stirring frequently. Serve immediately.

Sometimes it's hard to forget the meals our mothers made that were unpalatable. For me, it's my mother's fresh green beans that were cooked into a bacon-like stew. I disliked my mother's beans and bacon so much, I wrote these words to the tune of "Oh, Suzanna" expressing my distaste.

Oh, my mother spoils bacon by cooking it with beans. It is the awfulest stuff that I have ever seen. You may talk about your burned delights and sing of Chef-Boy-Ar-Dee.

But my mother's beans and bacon taste the awfulest to me. Beans and bacon, oh, I can wait for you. Cuz when I get home I'll have to eat that awful bacon stew.

I much prefer this recipe.

To sliver basil, roll 3 to 4 leaves in a tight cylinder and cut into thin strips with cooking scissors. To sliver basil, roll 3 to 4 leaves in a tight cylinder and cut into thin strips with cooking scissors.

Broccoli Soufflé

SERVES 4

In the days of Thomas Jefferson, broccoli was a vegetable eaten only by the rich. In 1923, the D'Arrigo Bros. Co. planted trial crops of Italian sprouting broccoli in the Santa Clara Valley near San Jose, California. The brothers began shipping broccoli in ice-packed crates to eastern markets in 1924. D'Arrigo began advertising this little known vegetable in 1929 on an Italian-speaking radio program and in Italian language newspapers. Its popularity spread, allowing the working man to savor what the British called "Italian asparagus."

FOR THE BROCCOLI

½ pound fresh broccoli
1 teaspoon minced garlic
2 tablespoons butter
2 tablespoons flour
1 cup milk
⅔ cup large grated Parmesan cheese
¼ teaspoon salt
¼ teaspoon large grind black pepper
4 egg yolks, slightly beaten
5 egg whites, stiffly beaten

Preheat the oven to 350 degrees. Wash broccoli and cut into stems. In a medium saucepan, place broccoli and garlic with just enough water to cover. Bring to a boil over medium-high heat and boil broccoli about 7 minutes. Drain broccoli in a large colander, chop into bite-size pieces, and set aside. This should yield about 2 cups chopped broccoli.

In a small saucepan, melt butter over low heat. Add flour and blend well. Cook for 2 to 3 minutes over low heat, stirring constantly to prevent lumps. Gradually add milk to the butter mixture, stirring constantly to prevent lumps. When well blended, add Parmesan cheese and stir until sauce thickens. Season with salt and pepper. Put egg yolks in a large bowl and egg whites in a bowl for the electric mixer. Slightly beat egg yolks. Add one-third of the cheese sauce to the egg yolks, stirring constantly. Then add the remainder of the cheese sauce slowly to the egg mixture, stirring constantly. Add broccoli and blend.

Using an electric mixer, beat egg whites until stiff and batter forms a peak. Gently fold one-third of the stiffly beaten egg whites into the sauce and then fold in the remainder. Pour ingredients into a greased and floured soufflé dish. Place the dish in a pan of hot water and bake at 350 degrees for 30 to 40 minutes, or until set and lightly browned on top.

It is a good idea not to open the oven door until at least half way through the baking process. Doing so can cause the soufflé not to rise.

Luau Baked Beans

SERVES 10 TO 12

The pineapple in this recipe makes this a real hit with kids.

½ pound sliced bacon
2 tablespoons pan drippings
2 white onions, thinly sliced
2 cans (28-ounces) Bush's® Baked Beans
1 can (9-ounces) crushed pineapple
¼ cup chili sauce
2 tablespoons molasses
1 ½ teaspoons dry mustard
½ teaspoon salt

Preheat the oven to 325 degrees. In a large skillet, fry bacon over medium heat, turning occasionally, until browned and crisp, about 10 minutes. Remove bacon slices from the skillet and transfer to paper towels to dry. Drain off excess pan drippings, reserving about 2 tablespoons. Add onions to the skillet and sauté in pan drippings until onions are soft, about 5 minutes. Remove onions and place in a colander to drain. Crumble bacon into bite-size pieces. In a large ovenproof casserole dish, combine bacon, onions, baked beans, pineapple, chili sauce, molasses, mustard, and salt and mix thoroughly. Cover and bake at 325 degrees for 1 ½ hours.

In 1969, the same year as Woodstock and U.S. astronauts set foot on the moon, the Bush family shared the delicious flavor of their secret family recipe by launching Bush's® Original Baked Beans.

There are three grades of canned, frozen, and dried fruits and vegetables: U.S. Grade A (fancy), U.S. Grade B (choice or extra standard), and U.S. Grade C (standard). Grades B and C are just as nutritious but have more blemishes.

My Favorite Picnic Beans

MAKES 12 TO 15 SERVINGS

½ pound bacon
2 tablespoons pan drippings
1 ½ cups yellow onion, diced
1 tablespoon minced garlic
½ cup ketchup
¼ cup dark molasses
¼ cup yellow mustard
¼ cup bourbon
2 tablespoons brown sugar
2 tablespoons Worcestershire® sauce
3 to 4 dashes Tabasco® sauce
2 cans (28-ounces) Bush's® baked beans

Preheat the oven to 350 degrees. In a large skillet, fry bacon over medium heat, turning occasionally, until browned and crisp, about 10 minutes. Remove bacon slices and transfer to paper towels to drain.

Drain off excess pan drippings, reserving about 2 tablespoons. Add onion and garlic and sauté until soft, about 5 minutes. Add ketchup, molasses, yellow mustard, bourbon, brown sugar, Worcestershire® sauce, and Tabasco® sauce and mix well.

Bring to a boil, reduce heat, and simmer sauce for 5 minutes. Rinse and drain baked beans and put them into a 2-quart ovenproof casserole. Add the sauce from the skillet to the casserole. Stir to combine thoroughly. Bake beans for 1 ½ to 2 hours. Serve warm.

During the early years of the market before my parents married, one lady customer became quite smitten with my father. She preferred to have Merrill wait on her, and this suited his employees to a tee because as my father so politely phrased it, "She would make these odors." Not only would she randomly break wind, this woman possessed a somewhat repugnant body odor. Sadly, she became the customer no grocer in town wanted. Perplexed by this dilemma, my father took the bull by the horns in a diplomatic although somewhat defensive fashion. When the stinky customer patronized his establishment, my father would discreetly slip a complimentary bar of soap into her grocery bags. In addition, he charged her ten cents every time she broke wind. He considered this hazardous duty pay and assumed once she realized he had overcharged her, she would shop somewhere else. Her odor never improved, nor did she ever complain about the random ten cent charges appearing on her bill. The Stinky Customer remained a loyal Steele's shopper. Still today, I am fascinated by this concept. Imagine the millions Wal-Mart® could add to their bottom line if they charged each and every shopper who broke wind in their establishment ten cents.

Roasted Corn on the Cob

SERVES 6

Leaving the husks on makes corn on the cob more festive.

½ cup butter, softened
1 teaspoon salt
2 tablespoons green onions, minced
¼ teaspoon ground cumin
½ teaspoon dried oregano, crushed
Freshly ground black pepper to taste
6 ears corn

In a small bowl, cream together butter and salt until fluffy. Add green onions, cumin, oregano, and pepper and mix thoroughly. Keep mixture at room temperature for 1 hour to blend flavors. Turn back husks of corn, leave husks attached at the bottom of cob, and remove silks with stiff brush. Place each ear of corn on two pieces of heavy-duty foil. Spread corn with 1 tablespoon of the butter mixture. Lay husks back into position, covering cob. Wrap corn securely with foil. Repeat until all 6 ears have been spread with butter and wrapped with foil.

Prepare grill. Place ears on an elevated rack over medium coals and roast until corn is tender, turning frequently with tongs, about 30 minutes.

 The season for fresh corn is May through September. As soon as it is picked, sugar in corn starts converting to starch, decreasing its natural sweetness. It's important to buy corn as soon after it's picked as possible. Fresh corn should be cooked and served the day it's purchased.

 Corn can be refrigerated for 1 to 2 days.

 *The secret to preparing good roasted corn is to be diligent in turning it while roasting. Frequent turning roasts the corn evenly and prevents one side from getting overdone.*

The word picnic comes from the French words piquer, to pick, and nique, an obsolete word meaning trifle. Originally, the word referred to a party where everyone brought along a dish to share. It wasn't until the 19th century that the word picnic was associated with an outdoor meal.

To judge the quality of an ear of corn, peel back enough of the husks to see the kernels. See Page 320.

CAROL ANN'S DAD

224

Polenta Pie

SERVES 4 TO 6

An Italian cornbread that's fun to serve at barbecues.

4 cups water
1 ½ cups polenta or coarse-grained yellow cornmeal
Dash salt
2 tablespoons butter
¾ cup grated Asiago cheese
1 cup shredded Cheddar cheese

Preheat the oven to 350 degrees. Fill a large saucepan with 4 cups of cold salted water and whisk in polenta. Bring to a boil over medium heat, stirring constantly. Reduce heat to low and continue cooking until polenta is the consistency of cereal, about 30 to 40 minutes, stirring frequently. Add butter and Asiago cheese to polenta. Mix well, until butter melts, then pour mixture into a cast iron skillet or ovenproof pan, spreading polenta evenly. Spread Cheddar cheese evenly over the top and bake for 25 minutes, or until cheese is bubbling and brown. Remove from the oven and allow polenta to cool to room temperature before slicing into wedges and serving.

*I*n 1958, Sargento becomes the first company to market shredded cheese.

When stored in an airtight plastic bag and refrigerated, shredded cheese should keep 2 weeks.

Roasted Garlic

SERVES 8

This is the perfect dip and spread for Italian or French bread.

8 whole garlic heads
4 tablespoons butter
¼ cup olive oil
1 ½ cups canned chicken broth
½ cup white wine
1 tablespoon fresh rosemary, chopped
1 loaf Italian or French bread, sliced

Preheat the oven to 350 degrees. Cut ½-inch off the top end (the end opposite the root) of each garlic head, exposing the cloves. Carefully remove the outer papery skin from garlic heads, leaving whole garlic intact. Arrange garlic heads in a small ceramic baking dish so that they fit comfortably. Dot with butter and top with olive oil. Pour chicken broth and white wine into the pan. Sprinkle rosemary over heads. Cover the dish with aluminum foil and bake, basting frequently, for 1 hour. Uncover and bake 15 minutes longer. Serve garlic heads in the baking dish with pan juices. To eat, remove cloves of garlic from heads with a knife and spread on Italian or French bread. The broth is great for dipping. Serve heads of garlic in baking dish with pan juices.

*C*erts®, the first candy advertised as a breath mint entered the market place in 1956. Five decades later, Certs® dominates the field. You might want to put Certs® on your shopping list when serving roasted garlic. Especially, if company is coming!

Grilled Garlic Bread

MAKES 16 SERVINGS

Garlic bread on the grill is perfect for cookouts.

½ cup butter, room temperature
⅛ cup fresh basil, chopped
⅛ cup fresh oregano, chopped
½ cup olive oil
2¼ cups large grated Parmesan cheese
8 teaspoons minced garlic
2 sourdough baguettes, halved crosswise, then lengthwise

In a food processor, blend butter, basil, and oregano on a slow speed. Gradually add olive oil and continue processing on a low speed until thoroughly mixed. Remove the butter mixture to a medium-sized bowl and add Parmesan cheese and garlic. Blend until thoroughly combined. Spread the cheese mixture over bread slices. Wrap each section of bread loosely in double layers of foil. Grill, cheese side up, by placing bread on an elevated rack over medium coals until bread is crusty and golden, about 8 minutes. If baking in the oven, place bread, cheese side up and wrapped in foil, on a baking sheet and bake at 400 degrees for about 10 minutes. Cut each section of bread into 4 pieces and serve warm.

Henry Ford, with the help of Thomas Edison, invented the charcoal briquette in 1920 from wood scraps and sawdust from his car factory. E. G. Kingsford bought the invention from Ford and put charcoal briquettes into commercial production.

Whole, vacuum-sealed portobellos will keep 14 days refrigerated.

Grilled Portobello Mushrooms

SERVES 2 TO 4

3 tablespoons olive oil
3 tablespoons balsamic vinegar
3 teaspoons minced garlic
2 portabello mushrooms, 6 to 7 inches in diameter, stemmed and washed
1 teaspoon fresh rosemary, minced
Salt to taste
Large grind black pepper to taste

In a large non-stick skillet, heat olive oil and balsamic vinegar over medium-high heat. Add garlic and stir. Add mushrooms and sauté until browned, about 4 minutes per side. Add rosemary the last 30 to 60 seconds and cook until fragrant. Remove from heat and season with salt and pepper.

A brilliant marketing ploy during the 1980s renamed an unpopular mushroom that growers couldn't sell, and the "portobello" mushroom was born. The portobello is actually an extremely large, dark brown, fully mature form of the crimino, a variation of the white mushroom.

Stuffed Portobello Mushrooms

SERVES 5 TO 10

A great accompaniment for a steak.

2 tablespoons olive oil
1 large yellow onion, sliced
3 teaspoons minced garlic
1 tablespoon fresh thyme, minced
½ teaspoon salt
¼ teaspoon large grind black pepper
1 cup red wine
4 ounces spinach leaves, washed and coarsely chopped

FOR THE STUFFING

In a heavy large skillet, heat 2 tablespoons olive oil over medium heat. Add onion and sauté until soft and lightly browned, about 10 minutes. Add garlic, thyme, salt, and pepper and cook for another 5 minutes. Add red wine and cook until the liquid is reduced by two-thirds, another 10 minutes. Add spinach and cook until wilted. Set aside in a mixing bowl, saving juices. Wipe the skillet clean.

2 tablespoons olive oil
5 medium portobello mushrooms,
    stems removed and wiped clean
Salt to taste
Large grind pepper to taste
1 tablespoon water
2 ounces blue cheese, crumbled

TO PREPARE MUSHROOMS

Gently rub a spoon on the underside of mushroom caps, scraping out the gills. This is best done when mushrooms are dry. Heat 2 tablespoons olive oil in the same skillet over medium-high heat. When hot, add mushrooms, gill side up, and cook for 2 minutes. Turn and cook for another 2 minutes. Turn again so the gill side is up. Season with salt and pepper. Fill each mushroom with the spinach mixture, pouring juices over mushrooms. Add 1 tablespoon water to the pan and simmer, covered, until mushrooms are barely tender, an additional 5 minutes. Top with blue cheese, cover, and cook until cheese is melted, about 5 minutes.

For a main course salad, toss some spinach with a little olive oil and balsamic vinegar, pour the hot pan juices over the spinach leaves to wilt them, and mound a stuffed mushroom in the center.

To clean: Brush with a mushroom brush or wipe off any unsightly flesh with a paper towel.

Grilled Vegetables

SERVES 4

3 tablespoons olive oil

1 red bell pepper, cored, seeded,
and cut into ¼-inch wide strips

1 yellow bell pepper, cored, seeded,
and cut into ¼-inch wide strips

1 small onion, thinly sliced

2 zucchini, trimmed and cut crosswise into ½-inch thick
rounds

2 yellow summer squash, trimmed and
cut crosswise into ½-inch thick rounds

3 tablespoons balsamic vinegar

Salt to taste

Large grind black pepper to taste

Remember the commercials with the green giant? In 1935, a Chicago advertising copywriter named Leo Burnett turned the giant symbol of the Minnesota Valley Canning Company into the valley of the Jolly Ho, Ho, Ho, Green Giant.

In a large non-stick skillet, heat olive oil over medium-high heat. When hot, add red and yellow peppers and onion and sauté until vegetables begin to soften, about 4 minutes. Add zucchini and yellow squash and sauté until tender, about 8 minutes. Add balsamic vinegar to the skillet and boil until liquid is reduced to a glaze and coats the vegetables, about 2 minutes. Season with salt and pepper.

For tips on selecting the freshest produce, refer to Selecting Superior Produce Section.

When asparagus is good or on sale, I like to add it to this dish. I cut it into 2-inch pieces.

Don't wash vegetables when you bring them home from the market. They should be washed just before you use them.

Rotini in an Artichoke and Butter Sauce

SERVES 4 TO 6

In the summer, this makes a nice accompaniment with barbecued meats. In the winter, it's a great side dish. This recipe is perfect for specialty pastas—like pumpkin-shaped pasta for Thanksgiving—we receive for the holidays.

FOR THE SAUCE

¼ cup olive oil
¼ cup butter
1 teaspoon flour
1 cup canned chicken broth
1 teaspoon minced garlic
2 teaspoons lemon juice
1 teaspoon parsley, minced
½ teaspoon salt
¼ teaspoon large grind black pepper
1 can (14-ounces) water-packed artichoke hearts, drained and quartered
4 tablespoons large grated Parmesan cheese

In a large heavy skillet, heat olive oil and butter over medium-low heat. Add flour and cook mixture for 3 minutes, stirring constantly. Increase heat to medium-high. Add chicken broth and cook 1 minute. Add garlic, lemon juice, parsley, salt, and pepper. Reduce heat to medium-low and cook for 5 minutes, stirring occasionally. Add artichoke hearts and Parmesan cheese and simmer, covered, for 8 minutes.

16 ounces garden variety rotini, cooked al dente and drained

Cook rotini al dente according to package directions or see Tips for Cooking Pasta on Page 241.

2 tablespoons olive oil
2 tablespoons large grated Parmesan cheese
1 tablespoon softened butter
¼ teaspoon salt

In a large ovenproof casserole, combine olive oil, Parmesan cheese, butter, and salt. Add cooked rotini to the casserole and toss with the cheese mixture until pasta is evenly coated. Pour the sauce over pasta and mix gently. Garnish the top of the casserole with additional Parmesan cheese. Keep pasta warm in a 250-degree oven until ready to serve. Holds nicely for 30 minutes.

*W*hen my dad began plans to build the Foothills location, he approached First National Bank to discuss financing. The bank, naturally, wanted to see the store's financial statement before they would consider giving him a loan. Merrill returned to the market, prepared a hand-written profit-and-loss statement on a paper bag, and was back at the bank within the hour, financial statement in hand. Rumor has it that the bank still has this brown bag in their archives.

For some time, supermarkets sold only pre-grated Parmesan in cans. Now you can purchase both pre-grated or chunk, and domestic or imported Although pre-grated cheese is available in 1-pint containers in the deli department, it doesn't compare to freshly grated.

Herb Roasted New Potatoes

SERVES 6

16 small red new potatoes, scrubbed
and cut into bite-size pieces

2 teaspoons Creole or Cajun seasoning

¼ cup olive oil

1 tablespoon Worcestershire® sauce

1 teaspoon minced garlic

½ teaspoon paprika

1 tablespoon fresh rosemary, minced

1 tablespoon fresh thyme, minced

1 tablespoon fresh parsley, minced

½ teaspoon salt

¼ teaspoon large grind black pepper

Preheat the oven to 375 degrees. Place potatoes on a non-stick baking sheet, skin side down. Sprinkle potatoes with Creole or Cajun seasoning and set aside. In a small bowl, combine olive oil, Worcestershire® sauce, garlic, paprika, rosemary, thyme, parsley, salt, and pepper and mix thoroughly. Drizzle the olive oil mixture over potatoes and toss gently until potatoes are evenly coated. Spread potatoes out on the baking sheet so they lay comfortably and bake for 50 to 60 minutes, or until potatoes are browned and tender.

You can find several different kinds of Cajun seasonings blends in the supermarket. Most Cajun seasonings include garlic, onion, chiles, black pepper, mustard, and celery. Each brand has its own distinct blend.

Perfect Garlic Mashed Potatoes

SERVES 6 TO 8

2 pounds russet potatoes, peeled and cut into chunks

Dash salt

4 tablespoons unsalted butter

½ cup half-and-half

8 teaspoons minced garlic

1 teaspoon salt

½ teaspoon large grind black pepper

In a heavy saucepan, place potatoes and salt with just enough cold water to cover. Bring to a boil over medium-high heat, reduce heat to medium-low, cover, and simmer until tender, about 20 to 30 minutes. To test potatoes, pierce with a fork. Potatoes should be soft when ready to mash. Drain. Return potatoes to the saucepan and mash with a potato masher. Add butter. In a small bowl, combine half-and-half, garlic, salt, and pepper. Add half-and-half mixture to the potatoes and beat constantly with a wooden spoon until potatoes are smooth.

For perfect mashed potatoes use only russet potatoes and mash them by hand. Grandma Gladys says elbow grease is the secret ingredient. The longer and harder you beat potatoes by hand, the fluffier and smoother the results.

Golden Potato Brulèe

SERVES 6

2 pounds Yukon Gold potatoes, peeled and quartered
1 head garlic

*M*ilk was first homogenized in 1927. By 1949, a year after I was born, 70 percent of all milk produced in the United States was homogenized, compared to only 33 percent in 1940.

In a large heavy saucepan, place potatoes with just enough water to cover. Cut ½ inch off top end of garlic head exposing cloves. With a paring knife, remove cloves and dispose of outer papery skin. Add cloves to the saucepan. Bring potatoes and garlic to a boil over medium-high heat and cook until tender, about 20 to 30 minutes. Drain into a large colander. Return potatoes and garlic to the same saucepan and mash with a potato masher. Cover to keep warm and set aside.

½ cup whipping cream
¼ cup milk
¼ cup unsalted butter
¼ cup crumbled goat cheese
¼ cup shredded Cheddar cheese
¼ cup shredded Swiss cheese
½ cup green onions, thinly sliced
1 ¼ teaspoons salt
1 teaspoon large grind black pepper
Grated Parmesan cheese for topping

In a heavy medium saucepan, bring cream, milk, and butter to a boil over medium heat, stirring frequently. Add goat, Cheddar, and Swiss cheeses and whisk until cheeses melt. Add green onions, salt, and pepper to the cheese mixture and blend gently. Pour the cheese mixture over potatoes and stir to blend thoroughly. Spoon potatoes into an 11-inch circular ceramic baking dish with 1-inch high sides. Sprinkle with Parmesan cheese to cover. Preheat the broiler. Broil the potato mixture until the top is golden brown and potatoes are heated through, about 5 minutes.

The most flavorful potatoes in the world are Yukon Gold. What better potato to use in this elegant presentation of the everyday mashed potato.

Garlic Mashed Potatoes
with Jalapeños and Cheddar Cheese
SERVES 8 TO 10

Special occasion mashed potatoes.

3 pounds russet potatoes, peeled and cut into chunks
Dash salt
2 tablespoons canola oil
6 teaspoons minced garlic
1 cup green onions, thinly sliced
2 jalapeño peppers, stemmed, seeded, and minced
1 cup half-and-half
4 tablespoons butter
1 cup grated Cheddar cheese
1 teaspoon salt
½ teaspoon large grind black pepper

Preheat the oven to 375 degrees. In a heavy saucepan, place potatoes and salt with just enough water to cover. Bring to a boil over medium-high heat, then reduce heat to medium-low, cover, and simmer until tender about 20 to 30 minutes.

While potatoes are cooking, in a medium-sized skillet, heat canola oil over medium-low heat. Add garlic and green onions and sauté for 5 minutes. Stir in jalapeños peppers and sauté for another 3 minutes. Remove from heat, cover to keep warm, and set aside.

To test potatoes, pierce with a fork. Potatoes should be soft when ready to mash. Drain. Return potatoes to the saucepan and mash with a potato masher. Add half-and-half and butter and beat constantly with a wooden spoon until potatoes are light and fluffy. Add the garlic mixture to mashed potatoes. Blend well. Add Cheddar cheese, salt, and pepper and blend thoroughly until cheese melts. If mixture seems dry, add a bit more half-and-half. Transfer to a large ceramic ovenproof baking dish. Bake until hot, about 15 minutes.

While some cookbooks recommend using a potato ricer for a smooth purèe, I like a few lumps in mine. Also, food processors or mixers only beat the potatoes into tasteless submission. I prefer the wooden spoon method. The longer and harder you beat potatoes by hand, the fluffier and smoother the results. This is the perfect job for teenage boys. They love showing off their prowess by giving the potatoes a good whipping.

It's best to serve mashed potatoes right away. To keep mashed potatoes warm on holidays when there are lots of last minute preparations, I put mine into my slow cooker on low for no more than 30 minutes.

Smashed New Red Potatoes

SERVES 8

I ate smashed new potatoes in a Denver restaurant. This is my version of that delicious side dish. Smashed potatoes are chunky, not whipped and creamy.

1 whole garlic head, roasted
Salt to taste
Large grind black pepper to taste
1 tablespoon olive oil
3 pounds new red potatoes, scrubbed, cut in half, skins left on
Dash salt
4 tablespoons butter
½ cup half-and-half
2 ounces blue cheese
1 package (½-ounce) fresh chives, thinly sliced
Salt to taste
Large grind black pepper to taste

Preheat the oven to 375 degrees. Cut one-third inch off top end of garlic head, exposing cloves. Place garlic on a 6-inch square piece of aluminum foil, season with salt and pepper, and douse with olive oil. Wrap garlic with foil and bake in the oven for 45 minutes. When garlic is roasted, remove cloves from head and set aside.

In a heavy saucepan, place potatoes and salt with just enough water to cover. Bring potatoes to a boil over medium-high heat, reduce heat to medium-low, cover, and simmer until tender, about 20 to 30 minutes. To test potatoes for doneness, pierce with a fork. Potatoes should be soft when ready to smash. Drain potatoes and return to the saucepan. Add butter, half-and-half, blue cheese, and garlic to potatoes. With a potato masher, smash, with skins on, until potatoes are chunky and ingredients are thoroughly blended. Season with chives, salt, and pepper and mix thoroughly. Serve immediately.

The first chore I took seriously in my father's market was sacking potatoes —my salary for this important position—25 cents for every 100 pounds of potatoes sacked. My brother hadn't developed his fine motor skills, so the job of pricing was mine alone. I'd proudly scrawl on brown paper bags in elementary first grade handwriting— "Red Potatoes, 10 lbs. for 39 cents." White potatoes were 59 cents.

My brother's job was to open the plain, brown receptacles for these treasures and place them on a produce scale. The bags teetered precariously as he filled them with potatoes until they weighed as close to ten pounds as possible. He was only a toddler at the time and, thus, a bit short for this task. Only occasionally did the contents spill onto the floor. Because the bags were a bit heavy for youngsters, we both lifted them off the scale and then took turns stapling the top closed. I remember how proud I'd feel when I'd gaze upon the sacks we'd filled for sale in the produce department.

New potatoes are simply young potatoes that haven't had time to convert their sugar completely into starch. Their season is late winter through mid-summer.

Grilled Tomatoes

MAKES 6 SERVINGS

Here's a fun way to prepare tomatoes in the summer that will really spice up your next barbecue.

- 6 small to medium red or yellow tomatoes,
  cored and halved crosswise
- 3 tablespoons prepared pesto
- 1 Vidalia onion, thinly sliced
- 1 cup shredded Gruyere cheese
- 3 tablespoons fresh parsley, minced

Using a spoon, hollow out the top ¼-inch of each tomato half. Spread each tomato half with ¼ tablespoon pesto and then fill with onion slices. Place stuffed tomatoes in a foil dish or construct your own foil baking dish with aluminum foil. Grill tomatoes in foil dish over medium coals for 10 minutes, or until tomatoes are heated through. In a small bowl, mix Gruyere cheese and parsley. Sprinkle the cheese mixture over tomatoes. Grill 5 more minutes, or until cheese is melted.

Baked Acorn Squash

SERVES 4

Acorn squash is in season in the fall. This goes nicely with pork entreés.

- 2 whole acorn squash
- 4 tablespoons butter
- 4 to 8 tablespoons brown sugar

Preheat the oven to 350 degrees. Wash acorn squash thoroughly and cut in half lengthwise. With a spoon, scrape out pulp and seeds. Place acorn squash on a baking sheet cut side down and bake for 30 minutes. Turn cut side up and place 1 tablespoon butter in each acorn squash. Place acorn squash back in the oven for a few minutes. When butter melts, add 1 to 2 tablespoons brown sugar to each acorn squash. Mix butter and brown sugar gently. Continue to bake 30 minutes for smaller acorn squash or 60 minutes for larger acorn squash, or until squash is done.

When shopping, look for smaller acorn squash.
They are usually more flavorful.

*L*egend has it that in the early 1800s, a crowd gathered in Salem County, New Jersey, to watch Colonel Robert Gibbon Johnson consume an entire basket of tomatoes. According to popular beliefs of the time, the tomato was considered poisonous. Believing the tomato to be the food of the future, Colonel Johnson wanted to publicly dispel any concerns about its safety, announcing he would publicly down a lethal dose. A throng of spectators gathered to watch Johnson expire from eating the deadly food, and you know the rest of the story.

Carol Ann's Rice Pilaf

SERVES 4 TO 6

Many supermarkets and most specialty food stores sell already-assembled shish kabobs. This dish adds a home-made touch to a chef-prepared entrée or is a great accompaniment to any meat or fish entrée you make at home.

4 tablespoons butter
2 tomatoes, peeled, seeded, and chopped
1 cup zucchini, diced
1 cup yellow summer squash, diced
½ cup mushrooms, thinly sliced
1 teaspoon minced garlic
3 tablespoons jarred roasted red peppers, diced
1 teaspoon salt
½ teaspoon large grind black pepper
1 cup uncooked white rice
2 cups canned chicken broth

In a large saucepan, melt butter over medium heat. Add tomatoes, zucchini, squash, mushrooms, garlic, roasted red peppers, salt, and pepper and sauté for 5 minutes, stirring frequently. Add rice and stir. Add chicken broth and heat to boiling. Cover and reduce heat to low. Cook for 25 to 30 minutes, or until liquid is absorbed and rice is tender.

s American consumers wanted more convenience, Minute Rice® was introduced in 1950.

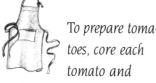

To prepare tomatoes, core each tomato and make an X in the top for easy peeling. Drop each tomato into boiling water for 10 seconds. Immediately peel off the skin and then plunge tomatoes into ice water to retard cooking. Seed and chop tomatoes.

Pilaf is a rice or bulghur dish that originated in the Near East. The process always begins by first browning the rice in butter or oil before cooking it in stock. Pilafs normally contain other ingredients like chopped vegetables, meats, etc.

Old-Fashioned Candied Yams

SERVES 6

I watched my mother, aunt, and grandmother make this every Thanksgiving and Easter. I only serve it on holidays.

    4 whole yams
    ½ teaspoon salt
    1 ½ sticks butter
    1 cup lightly-packed brown sugar

Scrub yams thoroughly with a vegetable brush, cut off woody ends, and leave skins on. In a large heavy kettle, place yams with just enough salted water to cover and bring to a boil over high heat. Reduce heat to medium and cook yams for 30 to 40 minutes at a gentle boil, or until yams are done. Test for doneness by piercing with a fork. Yams will be soft yet still firm. Drain yams and cool. Peel skin from cooled yams with a paring knife and cut yams into halves both lengthwise and crosswise. In a large electric skillet, melt butter over medium-low heat. Add brown sugar and bring to a boil until brown sugar and butter start to candy, stirring constantly. Add yam pieces to candied butter and simmer slowly, basting yams often. Turn occasionally and continue basting. Yams should be simmered and basted in the candied butter sauce for 15 to 20 minutes.

Select yams that are free of bruises and cracks.

As a young girl, I got my start in the kitchen basting yams as the women in the family fluttered about mashing potatoes, making gravy, and all the last minute preparations a holiday meal requires. This is a great job for kids. In fact, that's how my kids started in the kitchen. It gives a youngster a real sense of contributing to holiday meals.

236

Herbed Yorkshire Pudding

SERVES 10

I traditionally serve Standing Prime Rib Roast for Christmas dinner. Sometimes I like an English feel for that meal. I make sure I have Christmas crackers at each place setting, serve Yorkshire Pudding with my roast, and, of course, a Christmas Trifle for dessert.

2 cups flour
1 teaspoon salt
1 cup milk
1 cup water
4 large eggs
3 tablespoons green onions, minced
1 tablespoon fresh chives, minced
1 teaspoon fresh rosemary, minced
1/2 teaspoon large grind black pepper

In a medium bowl, combine flour and salt. In a 2-cup glass measuring cup, combine milk and water. Stir until blended. Gradually add the milk mixture to flour, beating until smooth. Add eggs one at a time, beating well after each egg is added. Stir in green onions, chives, rosemary, and pepper. Cover and refrigerate mixture at least 2 hours.

10 tablespoons pan drippings from a standing rib roast

Heat the oven to 450 degrees. Remove pan drippings from prime rib. Measure 1 tablespoon pan drippings into ten 1 1/3-cup ovenproof custard dishes. Place dishes on a baking sheet, put the baking sheet into the oven, and heat just until drippings begin to smoke. Remove from the oven. Divide batter equally among the custard dishes, allotting about 1/3 cup batter per dish. Bake puddings 15 minutes. Reduce the oven temperature to 350 degrees and bake until edges are golden and centers are puffed, about 25 additional minutes. Puddings will sink when removed from the oven.

The rotary egg beater eliminated the laborious task of beating eggs by hand. In the 1897 Sears catalog, a "Dover" egg beater sold for 9 cents.

The traditional way to make Yorkshire pudding is using pan drippings in the bottom of a muffin pan. If you won't want to follow this practice, substitute butter.

Muffin pans with some age will make a better pudding than custard dishes. They don't make as nice a presentation.

November 8, 1979

Tips for Cooking Pasta. 241

Lasagna. 242

Penne Pasta with Four Cheeses. 243

Spaghetti Alfredo. 244

Three-Cheese Tortellini in a Tomato Basil Sauce. 245

Spaghetti and Chicken in a Scampi Sauce 246

Chicken Piccata in a Lemon Basil Sauce. 247

Penne Pasta and Chicken in a Ricotta Cream Sauce . . . 248

Chicken Risotto with Snow Peas 249

Chicken and Artichoke Risotto. 250

Bow-Tie Pasta with Sun-Dried Tomatoes and Arugula . . 251

Spinach Pasta with Italian Sausage. 252

Penne Pasta with Italian Sausage and Roma Tomatoes 253

A Fancy Feast for Fishermen. 254

Angel Hair Pasta with Shrimp and Feta Cheese. 255

Shrimp and Scallops in a Tomato Garlic Sauce 256

Spinach Fettuccine and Scallops. 257

Swordfish and Snow Peas over Fettuccine 258

Lobster in a Light Pink Cream Garlic Sauce 259

When you want to put pasta on your plate, pick up the fixings for one of these.

Pasta

Tips for Cooking Pasta

I usually fill a kettle with 4 to 6 quarts of water to cook 1 pound of dried pasta and place it over high heat. If you don't cook pasta in enough water, it ends up a sticky clump. The water should be at a solid rolling boil before the pasta is added. I prefer to add 1 to 2 tablespoons of olive oil and 1 tablespoon of salt to the water. Stirring often helps prevent the pasta from sticking together. Adding the oil makes the pasta easier to separate if it cools too long before it's covered with sauce. Some pastas take longer to cook than others. I generally follow the cooking times specified on the package, but a general rule of thumb is about 10 minutes.

A few minutes before the end of cooking time, test a small section of the noodle by removing it from the boiling water and biting into it. If it remains firm, yet slightly tender to the bite, it's cooked al dente and ready to serve. If it's not done, it will have a white streak through the middle and taste raw. When pasta is done, drain it into a large colander — If using the pasta immediately, there is no need to rinse it. Just serve. The only time you should rinse pasta after draining it is when you plan to use it in a cold dish or salad or when you are not going to add sauce and serve it immediately. In these cases, rinse the pasta under cold water to retard the cooking process and drain well. Then toss it a bit to help remove the water.

If you want to use the pasta at a later time, then it should be rinsed to retard the cooking process. Pasta will keep up to 3 days in the refrigerator. If storing it for later use, toss it with 1 to 2 tablespoons of olive oil to help prevent the noodles from sticking together. To reheat the pasta, place it in a colander and dip the colander into boiling salted water for 1 minute, or until heated through. Pasta cookers work nicely for this purpose. Then toss it a bit to help remove the water.

Lasagna

SERVES 8 TO 10

FOR THE MEAT SAUCE

> 2 pounds Italian sausage
> 1 teaspoon minced garlic
> 1 tablespoon whole dried basil
> 1 ½ teaspoons salt
> 1 can (16-ounces) peeled tomatoes, chopped
> 2 cans (6-ounces) tomato paste

In a large heavy skillet, brown Italian sausage slowly, crumbling it with a fork until it is the size of peas. Spoon off excess fat. Add garlic, basil, salt, tomatoes, and tomato paste and mix thoroughly. Simmer uncovered 30 minutes, stirring occasionally.

> 10 ounces Lasagna noodles, cooked al dente and drained

Cook Lasagna al dente according to package directions or see Tips for Cooking Pasta found on Page 241.

FOR THE RICOTTA MIXTURE

> 2 eggs
> 3 cups fresh ricotta or cream-style cottage cheese
> ½ cup large grated Parmesan cheese
> 2 tablespoons dried parsley flakes
> 1 teaspoon salt
> ½ teaspoon large grind black pepper

In a medium bowl, beat eggs. Add ricotta cheese, Parmesan cheese, parsley, salt, and pepper and blend thoroughly.

> 1 pound mozzarella cheese, thinly sliced

Preheat the oven to 375 degrees. In a 13 X 9 X 2-inch baking dish, layer half the noodles. Spread half the ricotta mixture on top of noodles, cover with half the mozzarella cheese slices, and top with half the meat sauce. Repeat the layers. Bake at 375 degrees for 30 minutes, or until bubbly. (If assembled early and refrigerated, bake 45 minutes at 375 degrees.) Let Lasagna rest 10 minutes before serving.

Pasta shapes that are best for freezing are those used in baked recipes, like lasagna, jumbo shells, ziti, and manicotti. Prepare the recipe, then freeze it before baking. To bake, thaw the dish to room temperature, then bake according to recipe directions.

The secret to outstanding Lasagna is using Italian sausage not ground beef. Be sure to pick some up.

Penne Pasta with Four Cheeses

SERVES 6 TO 8

An upscale version of macaroni and cheese. This recipe is my granddaughter's favorite. She says, "ReRe, you're the best cooker I ever saw." She's only three. She hasn't known that many cookers. But my heart melts every time she calls me the best. I'd make this for her in the middle of the night.

16 ounces penne pasta, cooked al dente and drained

Cook penne pasta according to package directions or see Tips for Cooking Pasta found on Page 241.

4 tablespoons butter
½ cup all-purpose flour
1 ½ cups skim milk
1 ½ cups half-and-half
1 cup shredded sharp Cheddar cheese
1 ½ cups shredded Asiago cheese
1 ½ cups shredded Swiss cheese
1 teaspoon salt
½ teaspoon large grind black pepper
Large grated Parmesan cheese for garnish

In a large heavy saucepan, melt butter over medium heat. Add flour all at once and cook 5 minutes, stirring frequently to blend. Slowly add milk and half-and-half, whisking until sauce is thick and creamy. Simmer about 15 minutes. Stir in Cheddar, Asiago, and Swiss cheeses. Season with salt and pepper. Reduce heat and stir until smooth and thick. Do not overcook sauce as it may separate. Add drained pasta to the sauce and stir until completely blended and heated through. Spoon into heated serving bowls and sprinkle with Parmesan cheese.

*S*pam® hit the grocery shelves in 1937. I remember as a young girl having Spam® for dinner. My mother would slice it in ½ inch strips and then sear it in a frying pan. The same year Kraft Foods® introduced the first boxed meal that sold for only 19 cents. The advertising slogan for the first macaroni and cheese dinner was simple: "A Meal for Four in Nine Minutes." By the end of the twentieth century, Kraft® was selling a million boxes a day of Kraft® Macaroni and Cheese.

Penne means "pens" or "quills." This type of pasta has diagonally-cut smooth tubes. Penne rigate have rippled edges.

When stored in airtight containers, in a cool, dry place in its uncooked form, dry pasta will last almost indefinitely.

Spaghetti Alfredo

SERVES 6

This is an extremely easy meal to prepare. I always make this on evenings that follow a busy afternoon. You know the kind—soccer practice, dancing lessons, and parent-teacher conferences. Serve with a Caesar salad and warmed French or sourdough bread. My oldest daughter, Jenny, called this the perfect meal.

24 ounces spaghetti noodles, cooked al dente

Cook spaghetti according to package directions or see Tips for Cooking Pasta found on Page 241.

FOR THE ALFREDO SAUCE

1 ½ sticks butter, softened (12 tablespoons)
2 egg yolks
½ cup heavy cream
1 cup large grated Parmesan cheese
½ teaspoon salt
¼ teaspoon large grind black pepper
½ cup Parmesan cheese (optional)

In a medium bowl, cream butter until fluffy. Beat constantly while adding egg yolks, heavy cream, and Parmesan cheese, 1 tablespoon at a time. Season with salt and pepper and blend thoroughly. Place cooked spaghetti in a large heated serving bowl. Add the cheese mixture and toss thoroughly. For a cheesier taste, add an additional ½ cup Parmesan cheese as you blend the spaghetti with the Alfredo sauce.

Alfredo di Lelio is credited with originating the Alfredo sauce in 1914. A Rome restaurateur, di Lelio created this dish for his wife who lost her appetite during pregnancy. A rather extravagant character, di Lelio served his paper-thin fettuccine with golden forks given to him by Mary Pickford and Douglas Fairbanks. His restaurant, still in operation, is run by his grandson who still serves this dish with golden forks.

For tips on cooking with eggs, see Page 348.
Milk was not always pasteurized. Currently, egg producers are beginning to pasteurize eggs. The American Egg Board advises that eggs that have been pasteurized in their shells are safe to use without cooking in recipes. Pasteurization kills salmonella bacteria that may be present inside the shell. Look for the letter "P" on egg cartons. This designates that the eggs have been pasteurized and are safe to use raw.

Three-Cheese Tortellini
in a Tomato Basil Sauce

SERVES 6

A gourmet meal in minutes. Serve with a green salad and a sourdough baguette.

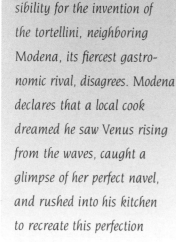

While the
City of
Bologna, Italy, claim respon
sibility for the invention of
the tortellini, neighboring
Modena, its fiercest gastro-
nomic rival, disagrees. Modena
declares that a local cook
dreamed he saw Venus rising
from the waves, caught a
glimpse of her perfect navel,
and rushed into his kitchen
to recreate this perfection
in pasta.

> 18 ounces DiGiorno® three-cheese tortellini,
>   cooked al dente and drained

Cook tortellini al dente according to package directions or see Tips for Cooking Pasta found on Page 241.

> 3 cups canned tomato sauce

In a large saucepan, heat tomato sauce over medium heat.

> 2 tablespoons olive oil
> ½ cup half-and-half
> ½ cup fresh basil, slivered
> ½ teaspoon salt
> ¼ teaspoon large grind black pepper
> 1 cup shredded Asiago cheese, divided

In a large sauté pan, place olive oil and half-and-half over medium-low heat. Add cooked tortellini and basil, stir, and simmer for 2 minutes, or until tortellini is heated through. Season with salt and pepper.

TO SERVE

Spoon ½ cup tomato sauce onto 6 warm plates. Toss ½ cup Asiago cheese into tortellini mixture and mound in center of each plate. Sprinkle each serving with the remaining Asiago cheese.

Tortellini means "little twists". They are small and stuffed.

Two ounces of dry pasta yields about 1 cup of cooked pasta or two servings. According to the Food Guide Pyramid ½ cup of cooked pasta is equivalent to one serving of carbohydrates. A plate of pasta is most likely equivalent to three to four servings of low-fat carbohydrates, half the recommended daily amount of grain foods.

Spaghetti and Chicken
in a Scampi Sauce

SERVES 4 TO 6

16 ounces spaghetti, cooked al dente

Cook spaghetti al dente according to package directions or see Tips for Cooking Pasta found on Page 241.

FOR THE CHICKEN

½ cup butter
¼ cup olive oil
½ cup green onions, thinly sliced
1 tablespoon minced garlic
3 tablespoons lemon juice
2 pounds boneless, skinless chicken breasts, cut into ½-inch strips
1 teaspoon salt
½ teaspoon large grind black pepper
½ cup fresh parsley, snipped
½ cup grated Parmesan cheese

While spaghetti is cooking, in a large skillet, heat butter and olive oil over medium heat. Add green onions and garlic and sauté for 2 minutes. Add lemon juice and chicken breasts and continue to sauté 7 to 10 minutes, or until chicken is cooked through. Season with salt, pepper, and parsley.

Transfer cooked spaghetti to a large serving bowl. Pour chicken over spaghetti and toss gently to coat spaghetti evenly with the sauce. Sprinkle with Parmesan cheese and toss again or serve Parmesan cheese separately on the side.

The word "scampi" means large shrimp in Italian. Over the years, the term scampi has come to mean anything cooked in a butter and garlic sauce.

If time is limited, purchase presliced chicken strips.

How much pasta should I make for dinner? Eight (8) ounces uncooked long pasta—spaghetti, angel hair, linguine, vermicelli, or fettuccine— yields 4 cups of cooked pasta, or 8 servings.

Chicken Piccata
in a Lemon Basil Sauce

SERVES 4

FOR THE PASTA

> 1 pound penne pasta, cooked al dente and drained

Cook penne pasta al dente according to package directions or see Tips for Cooking Pasta on Page 241.

FOR THE CHICKEN

> 4 boneless, skinless chicken breasts
> Salt to taste
> Large grind black pepper to taste
> 3 tablespoons olive oil
> 3 teaspoons minced garlic
> 2 shallots, finely chopped
> 2 teaspoons lemon rind
> 3 tablespoons lemon juice
> 1 cup white wine
> 2 tablespoons capers
> 2 tablespoons fresh basil, slivered
> 1 cup large grated Parmesan cheese, plus additional for garnish
> 1 lemon, sliced

Piccata is a classic Italian dish made from veal scaloppini, an Italian term that means a thin "scallop" of meat—usually veal. The veal is seasoned and dredged in flour, then quickly sautéed. To serve it piccata means it has a sauce made from pan drippings, lemon juice, and chopped parsley. Often veal is expensive, so I like to substitute chicken.

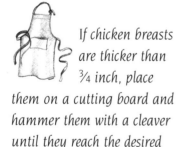

If chicken breasts are thicker than ¾ inch, place them on a cutting board and hammer them with a cleaver until they reach the desired thickness.

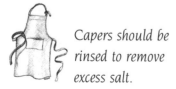

Capers should be rinsed to remove excess salt.

While pasta is cooking, season chicken breasts with salt and pepper. Lightly pound chicken breasts so they are no thicker than ¾-inch. This ensures they will cook through. In a large heavy sauté pan, heat olive oil over medium-high heat. Place chicken breasts in the hot sauté pan and sear on one side for 3 minutes. Turn and sear the second side for another 3 minutes. Add garlic and shallots to the sauté pan and cook until slightly browned. Add lemon rind, lemon juice, wine, capers, and basil. Continue to cook chicken breasts for another 5 minutes, or until chicken breasts are cooked through and liquid in the sauté pan has been reduced by half. Remove chicken breasts from the sauce.

Transfer cooked pasta to a large serving bowl. Pour the sauce over penne and toss gently to coat evenly. Add Parmesan cheese and toss again. Divide pasta among 4 dinner plates. Place cooked chicken breasts on top of penne. Sprinkle with additional Parmesan cheese and garnish with lemon slices.

Penne Pasta and Chicken
in a Ricotta Cream Sauce

SERVES 4 TO 6

This is one of my favorites. It's easy to make and soothing to the soul. A loaf of bread, a bottle of wine, and this recipe—the perfect ending to a long day.

16 ounces penne pasta, cooked al dente and drained

Cook penne pasta al dente according to package directions or see Tips for Cooking Pasta on Page 241.

2 tablespoons butter
2 tablespoons olive oil
2 teaspoons minced garlic
2 pounds boneless, skinless chicken breasts, cut into 1-inch cubes
1 cup ricotta or cottage cheese
1 teaspoon salt
1 teaspoon large grind black pepper
1 cup chardonnay wine
1 package (½-ounce) chives, chopped
½ cup sour cream

While pasta is cooking, in a large skillet, melt butter over medium-high heat. Add olive oil, garlic, and chicken cubes and sauté until chicken cubes are lightly browned on all sides, about 10 minutes. Stir in ricotta or cottage cheese, salt, pepper, chardonnay wine, and chives and blend thoroughly. Simmer for 5 minutes. Add sour cream and heat through. Remove from the heat. Place cooked pasta in a large serving bowl, mound the chicken mixture in the center, and toss.

Thomas Jefferson is credited with bringing the first "macaroni" machine to America in 1789 when he returned from France after serving as its ambassador.

When buying fresh chives, look for ones with a uniform green color and no signs of wilting or yellowing.

 I prefer to snip fresh chives with cooking shears to the desired length.

Chicken Risotto with Snow Peas

MAKES 4 ENTREÉ SERVINGS

FOR THE CHICKEN

> 2 tablespoons brown sugar
> 2 tablespoons salt
> 1 teaspoon large grind black pepper
> 4 boneless, skinless chicken breasts

In a small bowl, mix brown sugar, salt, and pepper. Coat chicken breasts evenly with the brown sugar mixture. Place chicken breasts in a medium-sized bowl, cover, and refrigerate for at least 2 hours, or as long as 6 hours. Grill chicken breasts over medium heat, turning once, until meat is opaque throughout and juices run clear, about 10 to 12 minutes. Remove from the grill and slice thinly. Set aside.

FOR THE SNOW PEAS

> 6 ounces snow peas

Fill a medium saucepan ¾ full with salted water and bring to a boil over medium-high heat. Add snow peas and parboil until barely tender, about 2 minutes. Drain and blanch under cold, running water. Drain again and cut into ½-inch pieces. Set aside.

FOR THE RISOTTO

> 1 can (14½-ounces) chicken broth
> 1 cup water
> 4 tablespoons butter
> 1 teaspoon minced garlic
> 1 medium yellow onion, chopped
> 2 cups arborio rice
> 1 can (14½-ounces) chicken broth
> 2 bay leaves
> 3 tablespoons fresh parsley, snipped
> ½ cup grated Parmesan cheese
> 4 tablespoons butter
> Salt to taste
> Large grind black pepper to taste

In a large saucepan, bring 1 can chicken broth plus 1 cup water to a simmer over medium heat. Add 4 tablespoons butter, garlic, and onion and cook, stirring occasionally, until onion is soft, about 5 minutes. Add arborio rice and stir until the grains are coated with butter. As liquid cooks down, add the second can chicken broth ½ cup at a time, and bay leaves and cook, stirring occasionally, until arborio rice absorbs all the liquid, about 25 minutes. Adjust the heat as necessary so that the mixture maintains a gentle boil. Remove bay leaves and add parsley, Parmesan cheese, 4 tablespoons butter, chicken, and snow peas. Mix and cook only long enough to heat through. Season with salt and pepper to taste. Sprinkle with additional Parmesan cheese if desired. Serve immediately.

My father proudly donned the traditional garb of grocers every day of his life; attire I fondly refer to as the "uniform." It consisted of a starched, long-sleeved white shirt, sleeves rolled up, pocket a must. Gray dress slacks, a necktie, and a white apron completed his attire. The shirt pocket served as storage compartment for important documents—bits of paper scribbled with telephone numbers, financial statements scrawled on pieces of brown paper bags, and post-dated checks he'd received as makeshift promissory notes from customers down on their luck. Most of these checks were never cashed. Pocket width at the time of his death—two inches.

His grocer's fingers, tattooed with small cuts from repeated contact with razor-sharp knives received while trimming lettuce, smelled of discarded produce. Perspiration from prolonged hours of grueling labor permanently stewed the aromas of freshly cut cardboard, sawdust, and ink into his pores.

Chicken and Artichoke Risotto

SERVES 4

6 slices bacon

¼ cup pan drippings

1 cup white onion, chopped

1 pound boneless, skinless chicken breasts,
  cut into 1-inch pieces

2 cups arborio rice

1 cup white wine

2 cans (14½-ounces) chicken broth, divided

1 can (14½-ounces) water-packed artichoke hearts,
  drained and quartered

½ cup sour cream

1 package (½ ounce) fresh chives, chopped

¾ cup large grated Parmesan cheese

Marilyn Monroe was the first official California Artichoke Queen in 1949.

In a heavy large skillet, cook bacon over medium heat until crisp, about 5 minutes. Transfer bacon to paper towels to drain. When dry, crumble bacon into bite-size pieces and set aside. Using ¼ cup pan drippings, add onion and chicken cubes and sauté until onions are soft and chicken is cooked through. Add arborio rice and stir until well coated. Add ½ cup white wine, stirring constantly, until Arborio rice has completely absorbed the liquid. Add remaining ½ cup wine and continue stirring until rice has absorbed all the liquid. Follow this same process with chicken broth, adding ½ cup at a time until all liquid has been absorbed. Reduce heat to low, stirring frequently. Adjust heat as necessary so that the mixture maintains a gentle boil. Continue to ladle in ½ cup broth at a time, stirring continually, and cook until liquid has been absorbed, all chicken broth has been added, and arborio rice is tender. Add bacon pieces, artichoke hearts, sour cream, chives, and grated Parmesan cheese. Mix well. Serve immediately.

Although labor intensive, it is important to add the liquid ½ cup at a time. Stir continually until all the liquid is absorbed. Then add another ½ cup. This technique results in rice that is delectably creamy while the grains remain separate and firm.

Bow-Tie Pasta
with Sun-Dried Tomatoes and Arugula

SERVES 6

Arugula is perishable and should be wrapped in damp paper towels, placed in a plastic bag, and refrigerated for no more than 3 days.

16 ounces bow-tie shaped pasta, cooked al dente and drained

Cook bow-tie pasta al dente according to package directions or see Tips for Cooking Pasta on Page 241.

1 jar (8 ½-ounces) sun-dried tomatoes, drained and chopped
Reserved oil from sun-dried tomatoes
1 teaspoon minced garlic
¼ cup olive oil
1 cup dry white wine
3 cups arugula, coarsely chopped
½ cup grated Romano cheese

There are several varieties of Romano cheese that all take their name from the city of Rome. The best known is the sharp, tangy Pecorino Romano, made from sheep's milk. For this recipe, buy a hard, dry cheese. I prefer the Pecorino Romano.

While pasta is cooking, in a medium skillet, heat reserved oil from sun-dried tomatoes over medium-high heat. Add garlic and sauté about 1 minute. Add olive oil, sun-dried tomatoes, and white wine and stir. Simmer about 5 minutes. Add arugula and sauté, stirring constantly, until wilted, about 1 minute. Place cooked pasta on a serving platter. Cover pasta with the sauce and sprinkle with Romano cheese. Toss until blended. Serve immediately.

Arugula leaves should be washed thoroughly before using. See page 316.

1 pound of dried pasta makes 6 to 8 servings.

spinach Pasta with Italian Sausage

SERVES 4 TO 6

12 ounces spinach Fettuccine, cooked al dente and drained

Cook Fettuccine al dente according to package directions or see Tips for Cooking Tips on Pasta on Page 241.

½ pound sweet Italian sausage
½ pound hot Italian sausage
½ cup olive oil
½ cup butter
12 large mushrooms, sliced
1 teaspoon minced garlic
1 large green bell pepper, cored, seeded, and chopped
1 cup green onions, thinly sliced
2 teaspoons dried parsley
2 teaspoons dried basil
1 cup large grated Parmesan cheese
1 cup sour cream

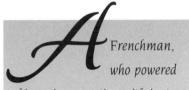

A Frenchman, who powered his entire operation with just one horse, built the first pasta factory in America in Brooklyn in 1848. He spread strands of spaghetti out on the roof to dry in the sunshine.

While fettuccine is cooking, in a heavy large skillet, cook sausages over medium heat until brown, crumbling with a fork until the sausage is the size of peas. Remove sausage from the skillet, drain grease from sausage using a wire colander, and set aside. Drain grease from the skillet and wipe clean with a paper towel. Heat olive oil and butter in the same skillet, add mushrooms, garlic, green bell pepper, green onions, parsley, and basil and sauté until tender. Add sausage and mix well. Place cooked Fettuccine in a heated serving dish and add the sausage mixture, Parmesan cheese, and sour cream. Toss until Fettuccine is evenly coated. Serve immediately.

Usually sold in links, Italian sausage is flavored with either fennel or anise seeds and garlic. The 'hot' variety is spiced with hot, red peppers; the 'sweet' is not.

Italian sausage is perishable. It will only keep in the refrigerator 1 to 2 days. I prefer to buy it either the day or day before I plan to use it.

Penne Pasta
with Italian Sausage and Roma Tomatoes

SERVES 4 TO 6

16 ounces penne pasta, cooked al dente and drained

Cook penne pasta al dente according to package directions or see Tips for Cooking Pasta on Page 241.

2 pounds Italian link sausage, casings removed
  and cut into ½-inch pieces
¼ cup olive oil
2 tablespoons butter
1 teaspoon minced garlic
1½ pounds ripe, fresh Roma tomatoes, chopped
6 fresh basil leaves, slivered
1½ tablespoons fresh rosemary, chopped
Salt to taste
Large grind black pepper to taste
½ cup heavy cream

I like to have my tomatoes chopped and the fresh herbs prepped before I start the pasta. This makes assembling this recipe much smoother.

FOR THE SAUCE

While pasta is cooking, in a large heavy skillet, heat olive oil and butter over medium heat. When butter is melted, add sausage pieces and garlic. Sauté for 10 minutes, stirring frequently, until sausage pieces are browned and cooked through. Add tomatoes to the skillet and simmer for 30 minutes, stirring occasionally. Add basil, rosemary, salt, and large grind black pepper to taste and simmer 1 minute.

When pasta is done, drain and add it to the skillet. While stirring continuously, sauté pasta directly in the sauce. Pasta will continue to cook. Add heavy cream, ¼ cup at a time. Sauté until the liquid is completely absorbed by pasta, about 4 minutes. Remove from the skillet, transfer pasta to a warmed platter, and serve immediately.

A Fancy Feast for Fishermen

SERVES 4 TO 6

FOR THE TROUT

1 tablespoon butter	Salt to taste
5 trout fillets, deboned	Large grind black pepper to taste
½ cup milk	3 bay leaves
½ cup water	

In a large non-stick electric skillet, melt butter over medium heat. Place boned trout fillets in the pan side-by-side and add milk and water to almost cover fish. Sprinkle with salt and pepper and add bay leaves. Cover the skillet and heat liquid to boiling. Reduce heat and cook for 15 minutes, or until fish flakes easily when pierced with a fork but is still firm. Remove fish from the skillet and discard skin. Discard bay leaves. Transfer to a plate and cover with aluminum foil to keep warm.

FOR THE SAUCE

½ cup butter
¾ pound mushrooms, stems removed and sliced
2 teaspoons minced garlic
5 green onions, thinly sliced
½ pound cooked shrimp, peeled and de-veined
2 tablespoons flour
½ cup milk
1 cup heavy cream
Large grated Parmesan cheese
Salt to taste
Large grind black pepper to taste

In a medium skillet, melt butter, add mushrooms and garlic, and sauté for 5 minutes over medium heat, stirring occasionally. Add green onions and cook for another 2 minutes. Add shrimp and heat through. While stirring constantly, sprinkle with flour and cook for 2 minutes. Reduce heat to low. Gradually add milk and heavy cream and simmer for 10 minutes until smooth and thickened. Season with salt and pepper to taste.

16 ounces angel hair pasta, cooked al dente and drained
2 tablespoons butter
Salt to taste
Large grind black pepper to taste

Cook angel hair pasta al dente, according to package directions or see Tips for Cooking Pasta on Page 241. Drain pasta, add butter, and toss. Season with salt and pepper to taste. Place cooked angel hair pasta on a large serving platter and mound trout on top. Pour the sauce over trout and sprinkle with Parmesan cheese. Toss gently.

*S*paghetti is the best selling pasta in the American supermarket.

Fillet means to cut the bones out. Before filleting trout, you must descale. Under a slow stream of running water, take a sharp knife and scrape from the tail to the head, removing any scales. Rinse fish well so all scales are removed. To fillet fish: Start at the base of the head. Using a sharp, thin-bladed knife, cut down behind the gill cover until you find the bone. Then cut down the back to the tail, following the backbone. On one side of the fish, cut with a sliding motion along the backbone until you release the fillet. Repeat the same process on the other side. The fillet should be in one piece. Lift out bones. Then, using needle-nose pliers or tweezers, remove any remaining bones or pin bones which might remain in the center of the fillet. Cut off tail and cut the fish into two halves.

Angel Hair Pasta
with Shrimp and Feta Cheese

SERVES 4 TO 6

H ave you ever wondered why you see numbers on packages of pasta, like Thin Spaghetti #9? In the early days, Irish, German, Italian, and Asian immigrants worked in pasta factories. They spoke so many different languages it was difficult for the factory managers to give instructions. In order to convey the distinctions between the various noodles, pastas were given numbers so that the employees understood which pasta they would make that day. "Today, we are making #9."

24 ounces angel hair pasta, cooked al dente and drained

Cook angel hair pasta al dente according to package directions or see Tips for Cooking Pasta on Page 241.

5 teaspoons minced garlic
4 tablespoons olive oil
1 pound small shrimp, peeled and de-veined, tails intact
¼ cup white wine
4 vine ripe tomatoes, chopped
1 package (½-ounce) fresh basil, slivered
8 ounces feta cheese, crumbled
Salt to taste
Large grind pepper to taste

While pasta is cooking, in a heavy large skillet, sauté garlic in olive oil over medium-high heat until fragrant. Add shrimp and sauté until pink and cooked through. Add white wine, stir, and reduce slightly. Add tomatoes and lower heat. Add basil and feta cheese and stir to blend. Season with salt and pepper to taste. Do not overcook shrimp or they become rubbery. Set shrimp mixture aside until pasta is done. Drain pasta and add to the sauce. Mix thoroughly and heat until warmed.

Purchase shrimp with a count of 41–60 per pound.

Angel hair pasta is also called capelli d'angelo.

Once your water starts to boil, add pasta all at once. As the pasta softens, give it a stir so that all the pasta sinks into the boiling water. Angel hair pasta is very thin. It cooks quickly — 2 to 4 minutes.

shrimp and scallops
in a Tomato Garlic Sauce over Spaghetti

SERVES 4

12 ounces spaghetti, cooked al dente and drained

Cook spaghetti al dente according to package directions or see Tips for Cooking Pasta on Page 241.

¼ cup olive oil

6 teaspoons minced garlic

¾ teaspoon dried crushed red pepper

4 cups plum tomatoes, chopped (4 to 6 tomatoes)

12 large sea scallops, rinsed and drained

12 large uncooked shrimp, peeled and de-veined

3 tablespoons fresh parsley, chopped

While pasta is cooking, in a heavy large skillet, heat olive oil over medium heat. Add garlic and red pepper and stir. Add tomatoes, sea scallops, and shrimp and cook until scallops and shrimp are cooked through, turning once with tongs, about 5 minutes. Shrimp will be pink in color when done, scallops opaque. Add cooked pasta to the skillet and toss to coat evenly with the sauce. Transfer to a warm platter and garnish with parsley. Serve immediately.

Sea scallops often leak. Ask the sacker to bag them separately in plastic.

To de-vein shrimp, *hold them under a slow stream of water and run the tip of an ice pick or sharp knife down their back, scraping out the intestine, yet leaving the shrimp intact. Rinse gently to remove any black from the shrimp.* **Scallops** *can be cooked so that their interior remains cool, creamy, and almost raw or cooked through. If you cook them longer, don't cook them to the point they become rubbery. Smaller scallops will usually cook in about 2 minutes. Larger bay and sea scallops will usually cook in 3 to 4 minutes.*

*S*ometimes we love people because of their faults. My father had a gruff demeanor, causing many people to be afraid of him. He could be softened instantaneously, however, with a kiss on the cheek and a simple question—"How's my crotchety old goat today?"

During my teenage years I worked in the office—entering accounts payable and receivable, doing the deposit, figuring payroll. One afternoon while I was busy punching numbers into the calculator, my father came into the office in a huff—his face red, his breathing quick. By my calculations it was time for the kiss and the question. My attempts at softening his mood were met with: "Don't kiss me in the office. What will people think? You're fired!" He sent me packing. That was the third and last time he fired me. He did rehire me that evening.

I learned a valuable lesson that day—no kissing in the office. And as time went by and I became involved in the business, I came to understand his reasons for that tough exterior.

Spinach Fettuccine and Scallops
in a Boursin Cheese Sauce

In 1993, the nation's first 24-hour food channel, the Food Network, went on the air.

SERVES 4 TO 6

Boursin cheese adds a savory flavor to tender scallops.

12 ounces spinach Fettuccine, cooked al dente and drained

Cook pasta al dente according to package directions or see Tips for Cooking Pasta on Page 241.

Boursin is a triple-cream cheese with a white, smooth consistency and a buttery texture. It is often flavored with herbs, garlic, or cracked pepper. For this recipe, select the variety with garlic.

2 tablespoons butter
2 tablespoons olive oil
¾ pound bay scallops, rinsed and drained
½ green bell pepper, cored, seeded, and diced
1 large tomato, seeded and diced
4 green onions, sliced
10 mushrooms, stems removed and sliced
2 cups heavy cream
¼ cup large grated Parmesan cheese
5 ounces Boursin garlic cheese
Salt to taste
Large grind black pepper to taste

Sea scallops are quite perishable. Buy them the same day you prepare them.

While pasta is cooking, in a heavy large skillet, melt butter over medium heat. Add olive oil and scallops and sauté 2 to 3 minutes, or until scallops are opaque and cooked through. Remove scallops and transfer to a plate. Cover with foil to keep warm and set aside. Add green bell pepper, tomato, green onions, and mushrooms to the skillet and sauté for 4 minutes. Add heavy cream and Parmesan cheese and stir until well blended. Reduce heat and simmer until sauce thickens, about 8 to 10 minutes. Add Boursin cheese and scallops and blend well, cooking until scallops are warmed through. Place cooked pasta on a heated serving platter. Pour the scallop mixture over Fettuccine and toss gently. Season to taste with salt and pepper. Serve immediately.

Pasta is best served hot. It will stay hotter if you serve it in bowls rather than flat plates.

Swordfish and Snow Peas over Fettuccine

SERVES 4 TO 6

12 ounces frozen snow pea pods, thawed
2 medium carrots, peeled and julienned

Fill a large saucepan three quarters full with water and bring to a boil over medium-high heat. Blanch peas and carrots in boiling water for 1 minute. Remove, drain, and set aside.

16 ounces fettuccine, cooked al dente and drained.

Cook Fettuccine al dente according to package directions or see Tips for Cooking Pasta on Page 241.

2 teaspoons olive oil
1 pound skinless swordfish steaks
Salt to taste
Large grind pepper to taste

While pasta is cooking, in a large non-stick skillet, heat olive oil over medium-high heat. Sprinkle fish with salt and pepper and place fish in the skillet. Sauté until golden brown and cooked through, turning once with tongs, between 2 to 5 minutes depending on the thickness of fish. If fish is thick and takes longer to cook, add a small amount of water to the skillet to prevent fish from becoming too brown. Transfer fish to a plate and cut into ¾-inch cubes. Cover the plate with foil to keep fish warm and set aside.

1 tablespoon flour
½ cup bottled clam juice
½ cup canned chicken broth
½ cup white wine
1 tablespoon fresh lemon juice
2 tablespoons fresh parsley, chopped
Salt to taste
Large grind black pepper to taste
Paprika to taste
4 green onions, thinly sliced
Lemon wedges

Add flour to the skillet and blend well with pan juices. Add clam juice, chicken broth, white wine, lemon juice, and parsley and blend well. Simmer until the sauce thickens, stirring frequently, about 5 minutes. Add peas and carrots and stir 1 minute. Add fish, stirring gently until heated through. Season with salt, pepper, and paprika to taste.

Place cooked pasta on a large warm serving platter. Spoon the fish sauce over pasta and garnish with green onions and lemon wedges. Serve immediately.

Lobster in a Light Pink Cream Garlic Sauce
over Mostaccioli Rigati

SERVES 6

When my son was a sophomore in high school, he and five friends decided they wanted to cook dinner for their homecoming dates. Under my supervision, six teenage boys prepared this dish in my kitchen. Their menu also included crab cakes with a pineapple salsa, focaccia bread, Caesar salad, and crème brulee. We had a blast, and it warmed my heart watching them serve their dates with pride.

16 ounces mostaccioli rigati pasta, cooked al dente and drained

Cook mostaccioli rigati al dente according to package directions or see Tips for Cooking Pasta on Page 241.

1 pound lobster tails
¼ cup butter
4 teaspoons minced garlic
½ cup Marsala wine
2 cups white wine
1 ½ cups whipping cream
4 teaspoons tomato paste
2 teaspoons fresh parsley, chopped
½ teaspoon salt
½ teaspoon large grind black pepper

Remove shells from lobster tails and cut into bite-size pieces. In a large heavy skillet, melt butter over medium heat. When butter foams, add lobster pieces and garlic. Sauté 2 minutes, or until lobster is lightly colored. While sautéing lobster, continue to cut meat into smaller pieces if it was difficult to cut in the raw state. When lobster meat is cooked through, remove from the skillet and transfer to a plate. Cover with foil to keep warm and set aside.

To the same skillet, add Marsala and white wines and cook until liquid is reduced by half. Stir in whipping cream, tomato paste, parsley, salt, and pepper. Cook 1 minute, or until sauce begins to thicken. When thickened, reduce heat to simmer. Transfer cooked pasta and lobster meat to the skillet. Toss gently until pasta is evenly coated with the sauce and lobster meat is warmed through. Serve immediately.

The October 1973 issue of New York magazine ran an article entitled "Eating Well Is the Best Revenge," signaling Americans were beginning to develop an interest in international cuisine.

This recipe is so good you'll want to eat any leftovers. If you want to reheat leftover pasta, add a bit of olive oil or butter to the skillet to prevent sticking. Heat over medium heat.

Mostaccioli means "little moustaches." This pasta is a two-inch long smooth or ridged tube. When rigati is included in the name, the tubes are ridged.

Looking back . . .

Steeles Cash Market Window 1940

After working for 12 years in several department stores in Northern Colorado, Merrill Steele opened Steele's Cash Market with his brother, Al. The store opened, in June 1940 and was located at 113 E. Oak Street. Merrill and Al were later joined by their brother George, who operated the Steele's Brothers Store in Eaton until 1972.

Old Franklin School Site West Mountain

On the site of the old Franklin School at 309 W. Mountain, another store was opened in October 1963. Shortly after that, the store at 113 E. Oak closed.

1964 was the year Kenney Walsh of the former Palace Grocery joined the firm to manage the meat departments. Larry Jordan, an employee since 1955 manages the produce departments.

Steeles Market

200 W. Foothills Parkway was the site of a second store which opened in May 1974. Robert M. Steele, Merrill's son, now manages both stores.

We appreciate the services of our employees and thank our customers for their loyal patronage for the last 41 years.

Smothered Beef and Bean Burritos   263

Lobster Tacos with an Avocado Salsa   264

Chicken Enchiladas with a Green Chile Sauce   265

Carol Ann's Homemade Guacamole   266

Chicken Enchiladas with a Tomatillo Sauce   267

Chile Relleños   268

Pork Carnitas with Red Chile Sauce.   269

Chili Marinated Pork Fajitas   270

Tequila Marinated Chicken Fajitas.   271

Carol Ann's Salsa   272

Shrimp Fajitas   273

Tomatillo Salsa.   274

My family loves Mexican food. They think the recipes in this chapter are to die for.

DELI

Mexican

Smothered Beef and Bean Burritos

MAKES 6 BURRITOS. SERVES 6

FOR THE GREEN CHILE

2 tablespoons vegetable oil
2 pounds boneless pork chops, cut into bite-size pieces
4 tablespoons flour
1 can (28 ounces) peeled tomatoes
1 can (28-ounces) water
¾ cup white onion, chopped
1 can (4-ounces) chopped green chiles
1 teaspoon minced garlic
½ teaspoon cumin
Salt to taste
Large grind black pepper to taste

To shed fewer tears when slicing onions, cut the root off last, refrigerate before slicing, and peel the onion under cold water.

In a large kettle, heat vegetable oil over medium-high heat. Add bite-size pieces of pork and sauté until brown. Add flour, one tablespoon at a time, and continue to brown pork, stirring constantly, for 3 to 4 minutes. Add peeled tomatoes by squeezing each tomato into the kettle, then add juices. Fill the peeled tomato can (28-ounces) with water and add water to the kettle, along with onion, green chiles, garlic, and cumin. Season with salt and pepper to taste. Cover and simmer for at least 1 hour. The longer this chile cooks, the better the flavor.

Tear lettuce by hand into bite-size pieces. Chopping it with a knife causes it to turn brown.

FOR THE BURRITOS

1 pound ground beef
½ cup white onion, chopped
1 can (16-ounces) refried beans
⅓ cup picante sauce
1 cup green chile
6 burrito-size flour tortillas
3 cups shredded Cheddar cheese

FOR THE GARNISH

Chopped tomato
Lettuce, shredded, see tip
Sour cream
Guacamole
(for recipe see Page 266)

This green chile is better when made a day ahead and stored in the refrigerator overnight.

Preheat the oven to broil. For burrito filling: In a large skillet, cook ground beef and onion over medium heat until ground beef is brown, crumbling meat with a fork until it is the size of peas. Drain. Add refried beans, picante sauce, and green chile and mix. To prepare burritos, place tortillas on an oven-proof dinner plate and place one-sixth of the filling down the center of each tortilla and roll. Position rolled burrito so that the edges are down on the dinner plate. Smother the burrito with 1 cup green chile, or to taste, and top with ½ cup shredded Cheddar cheese. Place the plate under the broiler of your oven until cheese melts. Garnish as desired.

Lobster Tacos with an Avocado Salsa

MAKES 12 TACOS. SERVES 6

This dish can be prepared in about 25 minutes.

FOR AVOCADO SALSA

    2 large ripe avocados, skinned, seeded, and mashed
    3 Roma tomatoes, peeled and diced
    4 tablespoons red onion, diced
    ½ cup cilantro, finely chopped
    Minced garlic to taste
    Minced jalapeño peppers to taste
    2 tablespoons lemon juice
    Dash Tabasco® sauce

In a medium bowl, combine avocados, tomatoes, red onion, and cilantro. Add garlic and jalapeño to taste. Toss gently. Season with lemon juice and Tabasco® sauce. Cover and refrigerate until ready to serve.

FOR THE TACOS

    Vegetable oil for frying
    12 (6-inch) yellow corn tortillas
    6 green leaf lettuce leaves, washed, dried,
        and torn into 2 pieces
    2 pounds fresh lobster, cooked
    2 cups frozen sweet peas, thawed and blanched
    Avocado salsa
    ½ cup cilantro, coarsely chopped
    2 fresh limes
    6 tablespoons olive oil

In a large frying pan, heat vegetable oil over medium-high heat. Fry tortillas quickly in hot oil until soft and pliable. Lay tortillas on a paper towel and pat dry. Build each taco by layering the ingredients in this order: a piece of lettuce, approximately 4 tablespoons lobster, 1 tablespoon sweet peas, approximately one-twelfth of avocado salsa, and a pinch of chopped cilantro. Finish each taco by squeezing fresh lime juice over the lobster and drizzling with ½ tablespoon of olive oil. Fold tacos in half to serve.

Ensenada, Mexico, claims to be the home of the first fish taco, its origination corresponding to the opening of the Ensenada Mercado in 1958.

While vacationing in Baja, Mexico, during spring break in 1983, Ralph Rubio tried a fish taco at a hole-in-the-wall taco stand operated by a Baja vendor named Carlos. Rubio tried to persuade Carlos to move to San Diego and partner with him in a fish taco restaurant, but Carlos refused. He did agree to share his recipe with Rubio, which he scribbled on a piece of paper yanked from his wallet. Ralph Rubio later established "Rubio's—Home of the Fish Taco," introducing the fish taco to the American palate.

Chicken Enchiladas with a Green Chile Sauce

SERVES 6

Some historians credit Christopher Columbus with discovering the chile pepper in the Bahamas, a place he mistakenly thought was the Orient. By the time he set foot in the New World, chile peppers flourished in South America, the Caribbean, Mexico, and South America. Some sources believe Columbus christened the plant pimentito or "pepper", believing he had actually discovered black pepper.

FOR THE CHICKEN FILLING

  2 whole (4 halves) chicken breasts, bones and skin on
  3 cups water
  1 teaspoon salt
  1 small carrot, quartered
  1 small onion, quartered
  1 tablespoon parsley
  1 stalk celery, quartered
  1 cup shredded Monterey Jack cheese
  2 cups sour cream

In a small saucepan, place chicken breasts with just enough water to cover. Bring to a boil over medium-high heat and add salt, carrot, onion, parsley, and celery. Cover the saucepan, reduce heat, and simmer for 45 minutes. Let chicken cool in the broth. Remove chicken and discard skin and bones. Strain broth, discarding vegetables and reserving 1 cup broth. Preheat the oven to 350 degrees. Shred chicken meat into a bowl. Add 1 cup Monterey Jack cheese and sour cream to chicken and mix thoroughly.

FOR GREEN CHILE SAUCE

  4 tablespoons olive oil
  1 teaspoon minced garlic
  1 can (16-ounces) chopped green chiles
  4 medium tomatoes, peeled and chopped
  1 medium onion, finely chopped
  ½ teaspoon dried oregano
  ½ teaspoon salt
  1 cup reserved chicken broth

In a sauté pan, heat olive oil over medium heat. Add garlic and sauté until golden. Add green chiles, tomatoes, onion, oregano, and salt and stir. Add reserved chicken broth and cook over low heat until liquid is reduced by half.

To shred chicken: Use two forks and insert the prongs, back sides facing each other, into the center of the breast. Pull the forks gently away from each other causing the meat to break into thin strips. Continue the process until the entire breast has been pulled apart.

TO ASSEMBLE ENCHILADAS

Chicken filling
Green chile sauce
12 (7-inch) flour tortillas
Vegetable spray for coating pans
1 cup shredded Monterey Jack cheese

FOR THE GARNISH

Chopped lettuce
Guacamole (see recipe below)

Place one-twelfth of chicken filling in each tortilla. Top with 2 tablespoons green chile sauce and then roll. Place rolled tortillas in a 9 X 13-inch baking pan that has been lightly coated with vegetable spray (I usually need 2 pans) and cover with remaining sauce and remaining 1 cup Monterey Jack cheese. Bake uncovered until heated through, about 15 to 20 minutes. Garnish with lettuce and guacamole. Makes 12 enchiladas.

Carol Ann's Homemade Guacamole

4 large ripe avocados
¾ cup red onion, chopped
1 tomato, chopped
¾ cup diced green chiles
1 teaspoon minced garlic
1 teaspoon salt
2 tablespoons fresh lemon juice

Remove skins and seeds from avocados. With a spoon, scoop out avocado meat into a medium bowl and mash with a fork, leaving some small chunks. Add onion, tomato, green chiles, garlic, salt, and lemon juice. Blend gently.

If your supermarket only has rock-hard avocados, see Page 317 for tips on ripening.

CAROL ANN'S DAD

To help retard browning, place avocado pits in guacamole until ready to serve. Also, guacamole will keep overnight if placed in a covered container with pits and refrigerated.

Chicken Enchiladas with a Tomatillo Sauce

SERVES 6

FOR THE TOMATILLO SAUCE

2 dozen tomatillos, husked
8 jalapeño peppers, stems removed and seeded
3 cups canned chicken broth
2 tablespoons cornstarch
1 to 2 tablespoons water
1 teaspoon salt
2 tablespoons fresh cilantro, chopped

We've all heard the expression, "Oil and water don't mix." This saying explains why drinking water doesn't take the edge off when hot, spicy peppers leave your mouth on fire. Spices are oily, so water merely rolls off the spices. The Chinese eat rice to dilute the heat. Beer or milk will also diminish the effects.

In a large saucepan, boil tomatillos and jalapeño peppers in chicken broth over medium-high heat for 7 to 10 minutes. Dissolve cornstarch in 1 to 2 tablespoons of cold water to form a smooth paste. Add cornstarch paste to boiling mixture along with salt and cilantro. Boil sauce for 5 minutes, stirring frequently. Remove sauce from heat, cool slightly, and pureé in blender until smooth. Makes enough sauce for 6 enchiladas.

FOR THE FILLING

½ cup half-and-half
8 ounces cream cheese, softened
4 boneless, skinless chicken breasts, cooked and shredded
¾ cup finely chopped onion
½ teaspoon salt

Beat half-and-half and cream cheese until smooth. Add chicken, onion, and salt to mixture and blend well.

The secret ingredient in this recipe is tomatillos. When picking up this vegetable, don't just grab a handful. Select ones that are firm and fit tightly in their husks. The husks should be dry to the touch. Underneath the husk, the tomatillo should be green. This is its preferred state. Do not buy sticky or yellow tomatillos.

FOR THE ENCHILADAS

6 burrito-size flour tortillas
1 cup shredded Cheddar cheese
1 cup shredded Monterey Jack cheese

FOR THE GARNISH

Shredded lettuce
Chopped tomatoes
Sour cream
Guacamole (for recipe see Page 266)

Preheat the oven to 350 degrees. Spoon a thin layer of tomatillo sauce into a greased 9 X 13-inch baking dish. Spread each tortilla with a thin layer of tomatillo sauce. Put one-sixth chicken mixture down center of tortilla, roll tortilla, and place seam side down in the baking dish. Spoon remaining tomatillo sauce over tortillas. Cover with foil and bake for 20 minutes, or until hot. Remove the foil, sprinkle with Cheddar and Monterey Jack cheeses, and continue to bake until cheese is melted. Serve with garnishes and any remaining tomatillo sauce.

Chile Relleños

MAKES 8. SERVES 4

Farmers' markets and specialty foods stores often roast chile peppers. I love this aroma—it charms the air with the fragrance of Old Mexico. Try this recipe when you can't resist the smell of fresh, roasting peppers.

8 fresh long green chiles, roasted and peeled
8 ounces Monterey Jack cheese, shredded
8 eggs, separated
1 cup flour
Salt to taste
Pepper to taste
Vegetable oil for frying

SMOTHER WITH

Green Chile (see recipe on Page 263)
2 cups shredded Cheddar cheese

GARNISH WITH

Diced tomatoes
Shredded lettuce
Sliced, pickled jalapeño peppers
Sour cream
Guacamole (see recipe on Page 266)

Slit roasted chiles down one side, being careful to make only one slit. Make the slit large enough to only allow room to fill roasted chiles with cheese. Beat egg whites until stiff. Beat egg yolks until very light. Add yolks to whites, beating constantly. Season flour with salt and pepper to taste. Dredge chiles in flour, then dip into the egg mixture. In a large skillet, fry two at a time over medium-high heat in ½-inch hot vegetable oil until golden. Turn once, browning both sides.

TO ROAST YOUR OWN PEPPERS

Grilling gives peppers a mellow, smoky flavor. They can be roasted by broiling them in the oven or browning them on a grill. The skin must be blackened before it can be peeled off. After grilling, place peppers in a brown bag to steam; this helps loosen the skin.

Contrary to popular opinion, the people of Thailand consume more hot peppers a day than any other nationality, averaging five grams of hot peppers per person, per day.

It's best to wear plastic gloves when handling red chiles and jalapeño pepper.

After the grilled peppers cool, peel the outer skin off under running water.

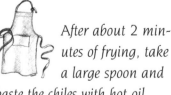

After about 2 minutes of frying, take a large spoon and baste the chiles with hot oil. When they are golden brown underneath, turn them with the same spoon.

Pork Carnitas with Red Chile Sauce

SERVES 6

*C*hile peppers are ranked according to their heat by the Scoville scale. This scale measures capsaicinoid content in parts per million. These parts are converted into heat units. Bell peppers register zero, whereas the habanero, the hottest pepper, registers 200,000 to 300,000 on the Scoville scale.

FOR THE PORK FILLING

> 3 pounds pork butt
> 3 cups water
> 2 teaspoons minced garlic
> 1 teaspoon chili powder
> 1 teaspoon ground cumin
> 1 teaspoon salt
> 1 teaspoon large grind black pepper

In a large kettle, place pork, water, garlic, chili powder, cumin, salt, and pepper. Bring to a boil over medium-high heat. Reduce heat, cover, and simmer pork for at least 2 hours, or until it is tender enough to be easily shredded with a fork. Remove pork from the kettle and drain. Shred the pork and place in a medium bowl. Set aside.

FOR THE RED CHILE SAUCE

> 2 ounces dried New Mexico red chile peppers
> 1 jalapeño pepper, seeded
> 2 cups water
> 2 teaspoons minced garlic
> ¾ teaspoon ground cumin
> ¾ teaspoon salt

Preheat the oven to 350 degrees. On a cookie sheet, place dried New Mexico chile peppers and bake for 10 minutes. Remove chiles from the oven and discard the stems and seeds.

In a medium saucepan over medium-high heat, place red and jalapeño peppers and water. Bring to a boil, then reduce heat, and simmer for 20 minutes. Remove chiles and place in a blender. Pour in some of the water and purée peppers. Add remaining water, garlic, cumin, and salt. Blend well.

See Page 265 for tips on shredding chicken.

> 1 tablespoon vegetable oil
> 1 tablespoon flour
> ½ cup canned beef broth
> 2 tablespoons sour cream

In a large saucepan, heat vegetable oil over medium heat until hot. Add flour and stir. Add red chile sauce to the saucepan, stirring constantly. Blend in beef broth and sour cream. Simmer sauce for 5 minutes, stirring constantly. Add shredded pork to the sauce and mix thoroughly.

Pork Carnitas with Red Chile Sauce (continued)

TO ASSEMBLE

3 cups shredded Cheddar cheese
6 burrito-size flour tortillas

FOR THE GARNISH

Sour Cream
Guacamole (see recipe on Page 266)
Salsa (see recipe on Page 272)

Preheat the oven to broil. Place the shredded pork and red chili sauce in a flour tortilla and roll up like a burrito. Place the rolled carnitas in an ovenproof dish, rolled side down, and sprinkle with ½ cup shredded Cheddar cheese. Place 4 to 5 inches under the heat and broil until cheese melts. Garnish with sour cream, guacamole, and salsa.

Chili Marinated Pork Fajitas

SERVES 6

FOR THE FAJITAS

½ cup distilled white vinegar
¼ cup chili powder
3 teaspoons minced garlic
1 teaspoon dried oregano
1 teaspoon salt
1 teaspoon large grind black pepper
1½ pounds pork chops, boned and butterflied
12 (7-inch) flour tortillas

FOR THE GARNISH

Guacamole (see recipe on Page 266)
Salsa (see recipe on Page 272)

In a blender, combine white vinegar, chili powder, garlic, oregano, salt, pepper and process to a smooth, wet paste. Butterfly and de-bone pork chops into ¼-inch sheets. Spread chili mixture over pork slices and place in a ceramic baking dish. Cover and refrigerate for a minimum of 4 hours. Arrange pork slices on a hot grate and grill over high heat, turning with tongs, until nicely browned and cooked through, 2 to 3 minutes per side. Slice pork into ¼ to ½-inch strips. Serve immediately by wrapping pork in a flour tortilla and garnishing with guacamole and salsa.

If you are not skilled in meat cutting, ask a butcher to butterfly the pork chops for you or purchase them already butterflied.

To butterfly the chops yourself: Lay the pork chop on a cutting board. Using a very sharp knife, make a parallel cut ¼ inch from the bottom of the chop all the way through its center to the other side. Continue in this manner, until you have sliced the chop into ¼-inch pieces. Remove any bones.

Tequila Marinated Chicken Fajitas

MAKES 12 FAJITAS. SERVES 6

Sirloin steak makes a nice substitute if you're hungry for beef fajitas.

FOR THE CHICKEN

½ cup tequila
¼ cup lime juice
¼ cup soy sauce
3 dashes Tabasco® sauce
½ teaspoon large grind black pepper
3 pounds boneless, skinless chicken breasts

In a large bowl, combine tequila, lime juice, soy sauce, Tabasco® sauce, and black pepper. Add chicken breasts, cover with plastic wrap, and marinate 4 hours in the refrigerator, turning occasionally. Remove chicken from the marinade and reserve marinade. Grill breasts over hot coals until they're almost done. Cut breasts into ¼ to ½-inch strips.

12 (7-inch) flour tortillas, warmed

If you don't have a tortilla warmer, preheat the oven to 250 degrees. Wrap 3 to 4 tortillas per package in aluminum foil and place in the oven for about 10 minutes.

FOR THE CHICKEN AND VEGETABLE FAJITA MIXTURE

12 tablespoons vegetable oil for sautéing
Reserved marinade
3 cups green bell pepper, cored, seeded, and
   cut into ¼ to ½-inch strips
3 cups onion, peeled and sliced into ¼ to ½-inch strips
3 cups tomato, cored and cut into wedges
Grilled chicken breasts, cut into ¼ to ½-inch strips

For each serving, place 2 tablespoons of vegetable oil and 2 tablespoons reserved marinade in a large skillet. Sauté ½ cup each of green pepper, onion, and tomato over medium-high heat for 2 to 3 minutes. Add one-sixth chicken breasts and sauté for 2 to 3 minutes. It's nice to serve this in a fajita skillet if you have one.

continued next page

The fajita is a blending of Texas cowboy and Mexican panchero foods, a truly Tex-Mex cuisine. When steers were butchered on Texas cattle ranches in the late 1930s, Mexican ranch workers were given the least desirable parts of the steer as partial payment for their labor. The workers learned to make tasty dishes from this tough cut of beef, the skirt steak. In Spanish, fajita comes from the word 'faja' which means belt or girdle in English.

The secret ingredient in the marinade is tequila. Don't forget to pick some up.

FOR THE GARNISH

    Shredded Cheddar cheese
    Sour cream
    Carol Ann's Guacamole (see recipe on Page 266)
    Carol Ann's Salsa

You can serve the garnish in separate bowls or mound them in sections on a plate of shredded lettuce. Fill warmed tortillas with cooked chicken and vegetable mixture and garnish with shredded Cheddar cheese, sour cream, guacamole, and salsa.

Roll the tortillas like you would a burrito. You can eat fajitas with your hands; or, if you're like the men in my family and make them too big, use a knife and fork.

Carol Ann's Salsa

    2 ripe tomatoes, chopped
    ½ cup white onion, chopped
    2 jalapeño peppers, seeded and chopped
    2 Anaheim peppers, seeded and chopped
    1 teaspoon minced garlic
    ¼ cup fresh cilantro, chopped
    3 tablespoons lime juice
    ½ teaspoon salt

In a small bowl, combine tomatoes, onion, jalapeño and Anaheim peppers, garlic, cilantro, lime juice, and salt and toss gently. Cover with plastic wrap and refrigerate until ready to serve.

To speed the ripening process for tomatoes to make them perfect for this recipe, place them in a paper bag and keep at room temperature. Check daily. When the stem end smells like a tomato, it's ripe.

CAROL ANN'S DAD

Shrimp Fajitas

MAKES 12 FAJITAS. SERVES 6

FOR THE SHRIMP

½ cup tequila
¼ cup fresh lime juice
¼ cup soy sauce
1 teaspoon minced garlic
½ teaspoon large grind black pepper
3+ dashes Tabasco® sauce
2 pounds shrimp, peeled and de-veined
1 large onion, peeled and sliced into ¼ to ½-inch strips

I purchase medium shrimp for this recipe – 36-42 count per pound.

In a large bowl, combine tequila, lime juice, soy sauce, garlic, black pepper, and Tabasco® sauce and blend thoroughly. Add shrimp and onion to marinade and toss to coat. Cover and chill for 2 hours. Drain shrimp and onion, reserving marinade.

12 (7-inch) flour tortillas, warmed

If you don't have a tortilla warmer, preheat the oven to 250 degrees. Wrap 3 to 4 tortillas per package in aluminum foil and place in the oven for about 10 minutes.

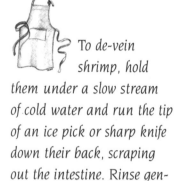

To de-vein shrimp, hold them under a slow stream of cold water and run the tip of an ice pick or sharp knife down their back, scraping out the intestine. Rinse gently to remove any black.

FOR THE SHRIMP AND VEGETABLE FAJITAS MIXTURE

6 tablespoons olive oil
Reserved marinade
1 large green bell pepper, cored, seeded, and cut into ¼ to ½-inch strips
1 large red bell pepper, cored, seeded, and cut into ¼ to ½-inch strips

In large a skillet, heat 2 tablespoon olive oil and 2 tablespoons reserved marinade. Add one-third of green and red bell peppers and cook 5 minutes, stirring frequently. Add one-third of shrimp and onion mixture and cook, stirring constantly, until shrimp are pink. Remove and transfer to a plate and cover with aluminum foil to keep warm. Cook each one-third of the ingredients as indicated above, adding 2 tablespoons olive oil and 2 tablespoons reserved marinade to the skillet before adding the peppers, shrimp, and onions.

Shrimp Fajitas (continued)

FOR THE GARNISH

Guacamole (see recipe on Page 266)
Sour cream
Shredded Cheddar cheese
Tomatillo salsa

Fill warmed tortillas with cooked shrimp and vegetable mixture and garnish with guacamole, sour cream, shredded Cheddar cheese, and salsa. You can serve the garnish in separate bowls or mound them in sections on a plate of shredded lettuce.

Although the tomatillo is a recent edition to the American supermarket, historical references date this vegetable, which was domesticated by the Aztecs, back to at least 800 B.C.

Tomatillo Salsa

2 tablespoons olive oil
1 pound tomatillos, husked, cored, and quartered
1 tablespoon olive oil
¾ cup red onion, diced
2 to 3 canned jalapeño peppers, seeded and finely minced
½ cup fresh cilantro, chopped

In a large skillet, heat 2 tablespoons olive oil over medium-high heat. Add tomatillos and cook about 5 minutes. Remove, chop, and set aside. Add the remaining 1 tablespoon olive oil to the skillet and sauté onion over medium heat until browned. Return tomatillos to the skillet and stir in jalapeño peppers. Remove from heat and stir in cilantro. Serve warm or at room temperature.

Cilantro will keep 1 week in a plastic bag when refrigerated. To keep cilantro fresher a bit longer, place it in a glass of water, cover with a plastic bag, and secure the bag to the glass with a rubber band. Change the water every 2 to 3 days.

Jazzed-Up Jambalaya 277

Red Beans and Rice. 278

New Year's Day Lucky Black-Eyed Peas 279

Carol Ann's Cassoulet 280

Poor Man's Paella 281

Corned Beef, Cabbage, and Sauerkraut. 283

A Light New England Boiled Dinner 284

Braised Corned Beef in Beer. 284

From New Orleans to New England, Ireland to Spain, these meals all cook up in one pot.

DELI

One Dish Meals

Jazzed-Up Jambalaya

SERVES 4 TO 6

I ate Jambalaya for the first time in New Orleans. I loved it and had to make it when I got home.

1 pound mild Italian sausage
2 tablespoons olive oil
⅔ cup green bell pepper, cored, seeded, and chopped
1 teaspoon minced garlic
1 tablespoon dried parsley
1 cup celery, chopped
2 cans (14½-ounces) peeled tomatoes, chopped
5 cups canned chicken broth
1 cup green onions, sliced
1 teaspoon dried thyme
1 bay leaf
1 teaspoon dried oregano
¼ teaspoon cayenne pepper
¼ teaspoon large grind black pepper
1 teaspoon chili powder

*J*ambalaya is a Southern dish most often associated with the cooking of New Orleans. Some believe the name was derived from the French word for ham, jambon—the main ingredient in many of the first jambalayas. This dish is often made from leftovers or ingredients on hand, so let yourself get creative when you prepare it.

In a large heavy 5-quart kettle, brown sausage over medium heat, crumbling with a fork. Remove sausage from the kettle with a slotted spoon and set aside. In a large skillet, heat olive oil over medium heat. Add green bell pepper, garlic, parsley, and celery and sauté until soft, about 5 minutes. Transfer sautéed vegetables to the kettle. Add tomatoes, along with their juices, chicken broth, green onions, thyme, bay leaf, oregano, cayenne pepper, black pepper, and chili powder.

TO COOK RICE

3⅓ cups water
1 tablespoon butter
¾ teaspoon salt
1½ cups uncooked rice

Fresh Italian sausage is quite perishable. It will keep for only 1 or 2 days in the refrigerator.

In a large saucepan, bring 3⅓ cups water to a boil over high heat. Add butter and salt. Stir in rice. Reduce heat, cover, and simmer 20 minutes. Remove from heat. Let stand covered 5 minutes, or until water is absorbed. Add cooked rice to the kettle of vegetables, stir, and cover, simmering for 30 minutes.

2 pounds cooked small shrimp, peeled and tails removed

Browned sausage
1 cup canned chicken broth

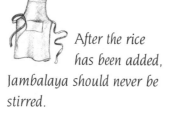

After the rice has been added, Jambalaya should never be stirred.

Just before serving, add shrimp, browned sausage, and the remaining 1 cup chicken broth and simmer gently until shrimp are pink and warm.

Red Beans and Rice

SERVES 6

I met a woman from the South named Louise who shared her recipe for Red Beans and Rice. Following is my take on Louise's recipe combining some ideas from a cookbook given to me by my friend, Pamela Wyman, entitled "The Cotton Country Collection."

1 pound dried red beans

1 ½ cups yellow onion, chopped

1 ½ cups celery, chopped

3 tablespoons fresh parsley, snipped

3 teaspoons minced garlic

1 teaspoon crushed red pepper

½ cup roasted red bell pepper

½ cup green onions, sliced

2 teaspoons salt

8 cups water

1 pound Boulder® Cajun-Style Sausage

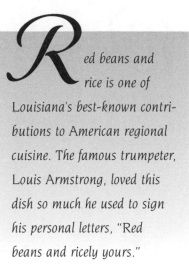

Red beans and rice is one of Louisiana's best-known contributions to American regional cuisine. The famous trumpeter, Louis Armstrong, loved this dish so much he used to sign his personal letters, "Red beans and ricely yours."

THE NIGHT BEFORE

Rinse and sort beans. Soak beans overnight in just enough water to cover.

FOR THE BEANS

Wash beans, rinse well until water is clear, and drain. Put beans into a large kettle along with onion, celery, parsley, garlic, crushed red pepper, roasted red bell pepper, green onions, and salt. Add 8 cups of water, or enough water to cover all ingredients. Bring to a boil over high heat. Reduce the heat to low and simmer until beans are soft, about 2 hours, stirring occasionally. If the liquid disappears during the cooking process, add additional water so that beans do not dry out. Remove 1 cup of beans and transfer to a medium-size bowl. Mash beans with a potato masher and return to the kettle. The last 45 minutes of cooking time for the beans, brown sausage in a large skillet over medium heat. Turn sausages frequently, until cooked through, about 10 minutes. Slice sausage into bite-size pieces and add the slices to the kettle so that they simmer 30 minutes with the vegetables.

FOR THE RICE

3 ⅓ cups water

1 tablespoon butter

¾ teaspoon salt

1 ½ cups uncooked rice

Be sure to pick up roasted red bell peppers. It's my special touch and the secret ingredient.

In a large saucepan, bring 3 ⅓ cups water to a boil. Add butter and salt. Stir in rice. Reduce heat, cover, and simmer 20 minutes. Remove from heat. Let stand covered 5 minutes, or until water is absorbed. Fluff with a fork. Serve red beans over rice.

New Year's Day Lucky Black-Eyed Peas

SERVES 6 TO 8

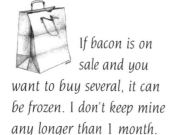

My friend, Martha Cranor, introduced our family to black-eyed peas a few years ago. The traditional Southern New Year's Day meal consists of ham eaten to bring wealth, collard greens for good health, and black-eyed peas for good luck. And, in keeping with this tradition, you must eat one black-eyed pea for every year lived. For some of us, that's quite a few peas. I enjoy beginning the new year with meaningful traditions shared by good friends.

If bacon is on sale and you want to buy several, it can be frozen. I don't keep mine any longer than 1 month.

1 pound fresh or dried black-eyes peas
3 slices bacon
2 cups canned chicken broth
1 cup water
1 can (16-ounces) peeled tomatoes, diced
1 large onion, chopped
3 teaspoons minced garlic
½ teaspoon red pepper flakes
½ teaspoon salt
¼ teaspoon large grind black pepper

If dried, wash peas, cover with water, and soak overnight. In a large kettle, fry bacon until browned and crisp. Remove bacon with a slotted spoon and transfer to paper towels to drain. Cool and crumble into bite-size pieces. To the same kettle, add black-eyed peas, crumbled bacon, chicken broth, water, tomatoes, onion, garlic, and red pepper flakes. Cook slowly, about 2 hours, over low heat. Season with salt and pepper. Serve hot.

I've had enough bad luck. I start the New Year off right by making black-eyed peas.

Most upscale supermarkets carry fresh black-eyed peas in their produce departments at the end of December. They package black-eyed peas in 1-pint containers. If you want to make this recipe, fresh black-eyed peas are superior. My friend, Martha, imports hers from Texas.

My mother taught me to never cook bacon over high heat. Low to medium heat works best.

Carol Ann's Cassoulet

SERVES 4 TO 6

1 pound white beans

8 cups water

2 pounds mild Italian sausage

1 tablespoon reserved pan drippings from Italian sausage

2 pounds beef chuck, cut into 1-inch cubes

1 tablespoon reserved pan drippings from Italian sausage

1 large onion, sliced

½ teaspoon minced garlic

2 green bell peppers, cored, seeded, and cut into eighths

1 tablespoon dried parsley

1 teaspoon dried basil

1 teaspoon paprika

½ teaspoon salt

¼ teaspoon large grind black pepper

2 beef bouillon cubes, dissolved in 1 cup boiling water

Rinse and sort beans. In a large kettle, place beans with 8 cups of water and bring to a boil over high heat. Reduce heat to low and simmer until beans are soft, about 2 hours, stirring occasionally. If liquid disappears during the cooking process, add additional water so that beans do not dry out.

In a large skillet, brown sausage over medium heat, turning occasionally. Remove, cut into thirds, and place in a 3-quart casserole. Drain grease from the skillet, reserving 2 tablespoons. In the same skillet, brown beef cubes in 1 tablespoon of reserved pan drippings, stirring frequently to brown sides evenly. Add to the casserole. Add remaining 1 tablespoon reserved pan drippings to the skillet and sauté onion and garlic until tender, about 5 minutes. Add green bell peppers and cook 1 minute, stirring constantly. Add onion, garlic, and green bell peppers to the casserole along with cooked beans. Add parsley, basil, paprika, salt, and black pepper and mix lightly. Add bouillon, cover, and bake for 1 hour and 15 minutes, or until beef is tender.

*C*assoulet is a classic dish from the Languedoc region of France. It is made of white beans and a combination of meats, like sausage, pork and duck or goose confit. It is covered and cooked slowly. Legend has it a group of cassoulet connoisseurs became so enamored with the dish that they gathered regularly to enjoy it. They dressed in funny hats and robes, told jokes, and had "passing wind" contests.

Chuck is a good cut to use in cassoulet as it must be cooked slowly. Shopping in a meat market can sometimes be confusing because the names on packages don't correspond with the cuts referred to in your cookbook. Chuck roast might be called chuck top blade roast, top chuck roast, chuck shoulder pot roast, or chuck mock tender roast.

Poor Man's Paella

SERVES 6

Paella is a dish that can be quite costly to prepare. Here is a version that won't bankrupt your pocketbook and is just as tasty as the rich man's recipe, which includes lobster tails, mussels, and asparagus. When you want to impress company, this is elegant, delicious, and well worth the time.

The name paella comes from the Spanish word "la paella" and refers to a cooking utensil traditionally made of iron. This pan is circular and shallow with two round handles on opposite sides and a thick, flat base. Following the establishment of rice in Spain, the peasants of Valencia would use the paella pan to cook rice with easily accessible ingredients from the countryside, like tomatoes, onions, and snails. On special occasions, the peasants added rabbit, duck, or chicken. By the end of the 19th century, the dish known as "paella valenciana" had spread throughout the region.

FOR THE CHORIZO AND CHICKEN

½ pound chorizo sausage links
2 tablespoons olive oil
6 chicken thighs
Salt
Large grind black pepper

Slice chorizo sausage into ½-inch pieces. In a large heavy skillet that has a cover, heat olive oil over medium-high heat. Add sausage slices and sauté until browned and cooked through. Remove chorizo to a plate lined with paper towels. Season chicken thighs with salt and pepper. Place chicken in the same skillet, skin side down, searing until skin is golden brown, but chicken meat is still rare. Turn and sear the other side, cooking about 5 minutes per side. Remove and set aside.

FOR THE RICE

2 tablespoons olive oil
1 medium white onion, finely diced
1 large green bell pepper, cored, seeded, and finely diced
2 teaspoons minced garlic
2 medium Roma tomatoes, diced
2 cups raw white rice
4 cups canned chicken broth
1 pinch saffron
½ teaspoon salt
¼ teaspoon large grind black pepper

Add 2 tablespoons olive oil to the same large skillet. Stir in onion and green bell pepper and sauté until onion becomes translucent, stirring frequently. Add garlic, stir, and sauté another minute. Add tomatoes, stir, and sauté another minute. Cook for several more minutes, until pan juices evaporate. Add rice, chicken broth, saffron, salt, and pepper. Mix well. Cover the skillet and simmer rice for 20 minutes, or until cooked through.

continued next page

ADDING THE PEAS

> 1 package (10-ounces) frozen green peas, thawed

Preheat the oven to 400 degrees. When rice is cooked, add green peas, blending gently, and remove from heat. Transfer to a large ovenproof casserole. Arrange chicken thighs and chorizo sausage slices on top of the casserole. Place the casserole in the oven and bake for 20 minutes.

FOR THE CLAMS

> 12 littleneck clams, scrubbed

While casserole is baking, scrub clams thoroughly with a brush. In a steamer pan, bring water to a boil. Steam clams just until shells open. Transfer to a plate and cover with foil to keep warm. Set aside.

FOR THE SCALLOPS, SHRIMP, AND LANGOSTINOS

> 2 tablespoons olive oil
> 6 large scallops, rinsed and drained
> 6 large shrimp
> 12 langostinos
> Salt to taste
> Large grind black pepper to taste

While casserole continues to bake, use the same skillet as before to heat 2 tablespoons olive oil over medium-high heat. Season scallops, shrimp, and langostinos with salt and pepper and place in the skillet. Sauté until shrimp and langostinos are pink and tails curl. Sauté scallops until cooked through and golden brown. Remove the shells from shrimp and langostinos and veins from shrimp. Transfer to a plate and cover with foil to keep warm.

When casserole is done, arrange clams, scallops, shrimp, and langostinos on top of rice and serve.

Never buy clams with gaping shells. This means the animal is dead.

Before cooking clams, fill a large bowl with cold water and soak for 20 minutes. Once the ingredients for paella have been mixed, it should not be stirred.

When you bring clams home from the market, place them in a bowl, cover with a damp towel, and refrigerate.

Corned Beef, Cabbage, and Sauerkraut

SERVES 6 TO 8

Fun to serve on St. Patrick's Day.

2 quarts boiling water
1 (4-pound) corned beef brisket
4 bay leaves
1 tablespoon peppercorns
1 jar (32-ounces) sauerkraut
12 new potatoes, scrubbed, with thin strips peeled
   around the middle
8 medium carrots, peeled and cut into 2-inch slices
1 medium onion, peeled and cut into eighths
1 head cabbage, cut into eighths

At breakfast, in a large saucepan, bring 2 quarts of water to a boil over high heat. In a large heavy kettle, place brisket over low heat and add enough boiling water to cover brisket. Simmer for about 4 hours. At lunchtime, strain out the water and discard. In the same kettle, add bay leaves, peppercorns, and sauerkraut. Add more boiling water to just cover brisket. Simmer for an additional 4 hours, or until brisket is tender. Remove brisket and transfer to a plate. Cover with foil to keep warm and set aside. To the same kettle, add new potatoes, carrots, onion, and cabbage. Simmer vegetables for 30 minutes, or until all vegetables are tender. Slice brisket across the grain and place in the middle of a large serving platter. Arrange vegetables around the slices of corned beef.

Never buy cabbage that has a strong odor. For more tips on selecting the perfect head, see Page 319.

CAROL ANN'S DAD

Corned beef is made from brisket or a round that has been cured in a seasoned brine. The term "corned" comes from the English term "corn"—meaning any small particle. Depending upon where you live, there are two types of corned beefs available in butcher shops. The old-fashioned version is grayish pink in color and quite salty. The trendier version has less salt and a bright rosy red color. I much prefer a rosy red corned beef.

A Light New England Boiled Dinner

SERVES 4

This is a light version of an all time favorite that calls for chicken. Serve with horseradish.

Vegetable cooking spray
4 chicken breasts, bone in with skins removed
2 teaspoons minced garlic
4 slices white onion
½ cup dry white wine
10 new potatoes, scrubbed
12 peeled mini carrots
½ to ¾ head green cabbage, cut into thin wedges
2 tomatoes, peeled, seeded, and coarsely chopped
1 teaspoon caraway seeds
1 teaspoon dried tarragon
1 bay leaf
6 cups low-sodium canned chicken broth

Spray a 4-quart Dutch oven with vegetable cooking spray and place over moderate heat. Add chicken and sauté until lightly browned on both sides, about 5 to 7 minutes in all. Add garlic, onion slices, and white wine and cook 5 more minutes. Add new potatoes, carrots, cabbage, tomatoes, caraway seeds, tarragon, bay leaf, and chicken broth. Bring to a boil over high heat, then reduce heat to moderately low. Cook, covered, until vegetables are tender, about 30 minutes. Remove bay leaf. Serve the chicken and vegetables with broth in large soup bowls.

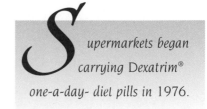

Supermarkets began carrying Dexatrim® one-a-day- diet pills in 1976.

To remove skin from chicken breasts, simply peel it off using your hands.

To add a touch of class to new potatoes, use a potato peeler to remove a strip of the peel around the center of each new potato.

Braised Corned Beef in Beer

SERVES 6 TO 8

1 (3 to 4-pound) corned beef brisket
½ cup Dijon mustard
⅔ cup brown sugar
4 whole cloves
2 tablespoon vegetable oil
2 cans (12-ounces) Coors® Light Beer
1 large onion, quartered
½ cup celery leaves
10 peppercorns

Preheat the oven to 375 degrees. Rub brisket with mustard and roll in brown sugar. Press cloves into meat. In a large ovenproof pan or Dutch oven, heat vegetable oil over medium heat. Brown brisket, taking care not to burn sugar. Add beer, onion, celery leaves, and peppercorns. Cover the pot with foil. Roast in an oven for 2½ to 3 hours.

Carol Ann's Christmas Trifle 287

Carol Ann's Crème Brulèc 288

Angel Food Cake with Mixed Berries and Crème Anglaise 289

White Chocolate Chip Cookies 290

Cream Cheese and Macadamia Nut Cookies 291

Pauline's Peach Pie 292

Kiwifruit and Banana Sorbets with a Raspberry Sauce . 293

Rich Vanilla Peach Ice Cream 294

Auntie Beryl's Pumpkin Pie 295

A little something for the sweet tooth.

Desserts

Carol Ann's Christmas Trifle

SERVES

Absolutely delicious and very elegant. The perfect ending to a Christmas Dinner.

FOR THE PEARS AND SYRUP

- 1 lemon
- 5 cups water
- ¾ cup sugar
- 3 tablespoons fresh lemon juice
- 5 ripe but firm pears, peeled, halved, and cored

Remove peel from lemon with a vegetable peeler and set aside. Squeeze juice from lemon into a small bowl. In a large saucepan, combine water, sugar, lemon juice, and lemon peel. Cook over medium heat, stirring frequently, until sugar dissolves. Increase heat and boil 5 minutes. Reduce heat and add pears. Simmer until pears are tender, turning occasionally, about 8 to 10 minutes. Using a slotted spoon, transfer pears to a bowl. Boil pear liquid until reduced to 1 cup, about 20 minutes. Strain the reduced syrup through a sieve and pour over pears. Cool to room temperature.

FOR THE CUSTARD

- 4½ cups whole milk
- 9 egg yolks
- 1 cup sugar
- 3 tablespoons cornstarch
- ⅓ cup minced crystallized ginger

In a large saucepan, scald milk over medium-high heat. In a large bowl, combine egg yolks, sugar, and cornstarch and whisk until smooth. Gradually whisk hot milk the into egg yolk mixture. Return the custard mixture to the same saucepan. Cook over medium heat until custard boils and thickens, stirring constantly, about 8 minutes. Transfer to a bowl and add ginger, mixing gently until thoroughly blended. Cover and refrigerate until custard is cold.

FOR THE CAKE

- 1 angel food cake
- 2 cans (16-ounces) prepared whole berry cranberry sauce
- 5 tablespoons pear syrup
- 5 tablespoons apricot brandy

Cut cake horizontally in half. Spread the cut sides with 1 cup cranberry sauce. Reassemble cake. Cut cake crosswise into ½-inch wide cranberry cake sandwiches. Arrange half of the sandwiches in a single layer cut-side up over the bottom of 12-cup clear glass bowl. Spread cake sandwiches with ⅓-cup cranberry sauce.

continued next page

A good cranberry will bounce.

You can buy crystallized ginger in the spice section of your supermarket. Crystallized ginger is cooked in sugar syrup, then coated with coarse sugar.

Using a slotted spoon, transfer pears to a work surface. Cut pears into ½-inch pieces. Arrange ⅓ of pears over cranberry sauce. In a small bowl, place 5 tablespoons of pear syrup. Add brandy and stir to mix. Brush pears with ¼ cup of the brandy mixture. Spread with 1 ½ cups custard. Place the remaining cake sandwiches in a single layer over custard. Spread with ⅔ cup cranberry sauce. Top with the remaining pears. Brush pears with the remaining brandy mixture. Spread with the remaining custard. Smooth the top. Cover and refrigerate, chilling overnight.

> 1 cup whipped cream
> 3 tablespoons slivered almonds, toasted

Before serving, spread 1 ½ cups cranberry sauce over custard. Decorate with whipped cream and garnish with slivered almonds.

To toast nuts, place on a baking sheet in a 350-degree preheated oven for 5 to 10 minutes, or until golden brown. Watch closely as nuts turn from golden brown to black very quickly. I personally prefer to toast nuts by sautéing them in a small skillet that has been lightly coated with butter. For this method, stir frequently over medium heat for 5 to 7 minutes

Carol Ann's Crème Brulèe

SERVES 8

Raspberries and fresh mint leaves make a nice garnish for this creamy dessert.

> 1 quart heavy cream
> 1 large vanilla bean, cut lengthwise with insides scraped out
> 1 pinch salt
> 8 egg yolks
> ¾ cup sifted white sugar
> ½ cup brown sugar

In a medium heavy saucepan, heat heavy cream, vanilla bean (both husk and insides), and salt over medium heat until cream almost reaches a boil. Remove the pan from heat. Combine egg yolks and sifted white sugar in a medium bowl. Whisk them together until a ribbon is formed. Remove vanilla bean from the cream. Strain the cream mixture slowly through a mesh strainer into the egg yolk mixture. Skim off any foam that appears on the surface. Preheat the oven to 300 degrees.

Divide the custard into 8 ramekin dishes. Set the dishes in a large baking dish. Pour hot water into the baking dish, until the water comes halfway up the sides of the ramekins. Place the baking dish in the oven and bake for 1 ¼ hours, or until the custard is set. Let the custard cool on the kitchen counter. Sprinkle each ramekin with brown sugar. Place the ramekins on a baking sheet and broil for about 1 ½ minutes, or until sugar is melted, bubbly, and caramelized. Watch carefully. Remove and serve immediately or chill until served.

The rack of your oven should be about 2 inches from the heating element. Try to cover the ramekins as evenly as possible with the brown sugar. Once in the oven, the brown sugar in some ramekins may melt and bubble sooner than others. You can rotate your pan for more uniform results.

If you want to make this ahead, cover it tightly with plastic wrap. It can be refrigerated up to 2 days.

Angel Food Cake
with Mixed Berries and Crème Anglaise

SERVES 8

Adds a new twist to Strawberry Shortcake.

FOR THE CRÈME ANGLAISE

2 ½ cups half-and-half

1 vanilla bean, cut lengthwise with insides scraped out

6 egg yolks

¾ cup sugar

2 teaspoons cornstarch

1 tablespoon Cognac

In a heavy medium saucepan, place half-and-half and the insides of vanilla bean. (Husk is discarded.) Bring to a simmer over medium-low heat. Whisk yolks, sugar, and cornstarch in a medium bowl to blend. Gradually whisk in the hot half-and-half mixture. Return the mixture to the saucepan over medium heat until custard thickens, about 6 minutes, stirring constantly with a wooden spoon. Strain through a sieve into a bowl. Add Cognac and blend gently to mix. Refrigerate until well chilled then cover.

TO SERVE

1 angel food cake

8 cups mixed assorted berries in season
  strawberries
  blueberries
  raspberries
  blackberries

Fresh mint sprigs

Cut angel food cake into slices. Ladle cremé anglaise over slices of angel food cake. Mound berries in the center of each cake slice. Garnish with mint sprigs.

The Washburn Crosby Co. created the fictitious Betty Crocker® in 1921 after running a promotion for a pincushion shaped like a flour sack. The company wanted to respond personally to customer inquiries regarding their product. Betty Crocker® became this faceless icon. Washburn Crosby gave her the first name, Betty, because it seemed friendly and the surname, Crocker, to honor retiring director, William G. Crocker. The company's female employees submitted handwriting signatures, and the most unique signature was chosen as Betty's own.

To store vanilla beans, wrap them tightly in plastic wrap, place in an airtight jar, and refrigerate. When stored this way, they will keep nicely for 6 months.

White Chocolate Chip Cookies
with Coconut and Macadamia Nuts

MAKES ABOUT 3 DOZEN COOKIES

My family's favorite cookie, bar none.

2 ½ cups all-purpose flour
1 teaspoon baking soda
½ teaspoon salt
1 cup butter, softened
⅔ cup sugar
⅔ cup firmly-packed light brown sugar
1 large egg, lightly beaten
3 tablespoons milk
1 ½ teaspoons vanilla extract
1 ½ cups Nestle® white chocolate chips
1 cup sweetened coconut, shredded
1 cup macadamia nuts, coarsely chopped

Preheat the oven to 350 degrees. In a large bowl, combine flour, baking soda, and salt and set aside. In a another large bowl, cream butter and sugars until smooth using an electric mixer. Add egg, milk, and vanilla extract and mix well. Add dry ingredients to the sugar mixture and beat thoroughly, until a smooth cookie dough is formed. Stir in white chocolate chips, coconut, and macadamia nuts by hand.

Drop by rounded teaspoons onto an ungreased cookie sheet, leaving 2 inches between cookies for expansion. Bake for 10 to 12 minutes, or until lightly golden. Allow the cookies to sit 1 minute on the sheet and then remove to a rack to cool completely.

 Vanilla extract *will keep indefinitely if sealed airtight and kept in a cool, dark place. Flour should be stored in an airtight container. It will keep up to 6 months at room temperature.*

White chocolate *should not be stored more than 9 months.*

Grated fresh coconut *should be tightly covered and can be refrigerated 4 days. It can be frozen up to 6 months.*

The chocolate chip cookie was created by Ruth Wakefield in 1937 at the Toll House, an inn near Whitman, Massachusetts. One evening her creative juices erupted, inspiring her to concoct a chocolate butter cookie for her guests. She broke up semi-sweet chocolate bars given to her by Andrew Nestle into morsels and added them to her dough. Unfortunately, the chocolate morsels didn't melt into the dough as she'd anticipated, but she served the chip-laden butter cookies to her guests anyway. Needless to say, they were a smashing success, and the Chocolate Crunch Cookie became standard fare at the Toll House®.

Like any penny-pinching business owner, Ruth made a deal with Nestle® allowing them to place her recipe on the label of their chocolate bar if they supplied her with free chocolate for her cookies. Originally, Nestle® included a small chopper with every chocolate bar, but convenience for the consumer sparked the introduction of Nestle® Tollhouse Morsels in 1939.

Today, the chocolate chip cookie is the most popular cookie in America with over seven billion of these Ruth Wakefield wonders eaten annually.

Cream Cheese and Macadamia Nut Cookies

MAKES ABOUT 4 DOZEN COOKIES

½ cup butter, softened
1 package (8-ounces) cream cheese, softened
¾ cup lightly packed brown sugar
1 teaspoon orange zest
2 teaspoons vanilla extract
1 ½ cups all-purpose flour
2 teaspoons baking powder
1 cup macadamia nuts, coarsely chopped

In a large mixing bowl and using an electric mixer, beat butter and cream cheese until light and fluffy. Beat in brown sugar, orange zest, and vanilla extract. In a medium bowl, sift flour and baking powder together, add to the butter mixture, and beat thoroughly until a smooth cookie dough is formed. Stir in macadamia nuts by hand. Cover with plastic wrap and refrigerate dough for at least 1 hour or overnight.

Preheat the oven to 400 degrees. Lightly butter cookie sheets. Drop by rounded teaspoons onto a cookie sheet, leaving 2 inches between cookies. Flatten dough by pressing on the cookies gently with the back of a spoon. Bake for 8 to 10 minutes, or until lightly golden. Allow the cookies to sit 1 minute on the sheet and then transfer to a wire rack to cool.

*F*rank Epperson, an eleven year old boy, invented the popsicle. One afternoon, Frank mixed soda water powder with water. He left the mixture on his back porch with the stirring stick still in the glass. Temperatures dropped to a record low that night. When he awoke the next morning, he found the stick frozen in the soda water. In 1923, at age 29, Epperson began manufacturing Epsicles in seven fruit flavors. He applied for a patent in 1924 and eventually changed the name to Popsicle.

To soften butter quickly, try grating it.

Macadamia nuts have a high fat content and should be stored in the refrigerator to prevent rancidity.

If brown sugar becomes hard, it can be softened by sealing it tightly in a plastic bag with an apple wedge for 1 to 2 days.

Pauline's Peach Pie

This is my mother's recipe for peach pie. Her cooking style was like her personality—simple, down-to-earth, and practical. She was a bit of a perfectionist and it showed in the meals she prepared. They were flawless.

FOR THE FILLING

> 5 cups fresh peaches, skinned and sliced
> 1 cup sugar
> 3 tablespoons flour
> ⅛ teaspoon ground nutmeg
> ⅛ teaspoon ground cinnamon
> Dash salt
> 2 tablespoons butter

In a large bowl, place peach slices. In a small bowl, combine sugar, flour, nutmeg, cinnamon, and salt. Mix dry ingredients and toss gently with peaches.

FOR THE CRUST

> 2 cups all-purpose flour, sifted
> 1 teaspoon salt
> ⅔ cup Crisco® shortening
> 5 to 7 tablespoons cold water
> Flour for flouring work surface

In a large bowl, sift flour and salt together. Add shortening and cut in with a pastry blender or a fork until the mixture is the size of small peas. The smaller the pieces, the more tender the pastry. Sprinkle 1 tablespoon water over the mixture and gently toss with a fork. Repeat this process until the mixture is moist. The less water that is added, the more tender the pastry. It is not necessary to add all of the water. Form the mixture into a ball. Divide dough into two equal parts. Flatten each part on a lightly floured surface by pressing the ball with the edges of hand 3 times across in both directions. Using a rolling pin, roll dough from the center out to the edges until dough is ⅛-inch thick. Line the bottom of a pie plate with one rolled pastry section. Trim the dough around the outside edges of the pie plate leaving 1 inch of dough.

TO ASSEMBLE PIE

> 2 tablespoons butter

Fill the bottom of the pie plate with peach filling. Dot the filling with butter. Using a pastry wheel or knife, cut strips of the second rolled pastry section into ½-inch strips. Lay strips on filled pie at 1-inch intervals. Fold back alternating strips so that the strips weave in and out. Trim the lattice strips even with the outer rim of the pie plate. Fold the bottom crust over the strips. Seal and flute the edge of the pie crust. Bake for 45 to 50 minutes at 400 degrees, or until the crust is golden brown.

Girl Scouts began commercially baking cookies in 1936. The only flavor, shortbread, sold for 25 cents a box. Pauline was a strong supporter of the Girl Scouts and instrumental in forming our local council.

Vegetable shortening can be stored up to 1 year at room temperature.

Granulated sugar will keep indefinitely when sealed in an airtight container and stored in a cool, dark place.

Kiwifruit and Banana Sorbets
with a Raspberry Sauce

SERVES 8

KIWIFRUIT SORBET

1 cup sugar
½ cup water
2 pounds kiwifruit, skinned and diced
1 tablespoon Cointreau (optional)

In a heavy saucepan, bring sugar and water to a boil over medium heat, stirring until sugar dissolves. Cool. In a food processor, purée diced kiwifruit. Add Cointreau and set aside 1 cup puréed kiwifruit. Strain remaining purée through a sieve. Place purée and strained purée in an ice cream maker and freeze according to manufacturer's directions. Once frozen, transfer sorbet to covered containers and freeze.

BANANA SORBET

1 ½ pounds ripe bananas
⅔ cup sugar
½ cup water
2 egg yolks, slightly beaten
1 tablespoon lemon juice
Pinch salt
Pinch ginger

Place bananas in the freezer to chill for 10 minutes. In a heavy saucepan, bring sugar and water to a boil over medium heat, stirring until sugar dissolves. Gradually add hot syrup to egg yolks. Reduce heat to low, return the syrup mixture to the same saucepan, and stir constantly until bubbles appear at the edge of the pan and the syrup mixture thickens slightly, about 2 minutes. Pour the syrup mixture into a food processor. Add lemon juice, salt, and ginger. Peel cold bananas, slice, and add to the food processor. Purée all ingredients until smooth. Immediately transfer the custard to an ice cream maker and freeze according to the manufacturer's directions. Once frozen, transfer to covered containers and freeze.

FOR THE RASPBERRY SAUCE

1 package (14-ounces) frozen raspberries, thawed
½ cup sugar
¼ cup raspberry jam

In a food processor, place raspberries, sugar, and raspberry jam and purée until smooth. Strain sauce through a fine sieve, place in a covered container, and refrigerate until ready to use.

To reduce the chance of foods susceptible to discoloration turning color, slice bananas, apples, pears, plums, and peaches with a stainless steel knife. Then combine them with any citrus fruit, sprinkle them with lemon or pineapple juice, and refrigerate as soon as possible.

One easy way to test fruits for ripeness is to stick a toothpick into the fruit at the stem end. If the toothpick goes in and comes out clean with ease, the fruit is ripe and ready to eat.

continued next page

POSSIBLE GARNISHES

    Kiwifruit slices
    Banana slices
    Fresh berries

Sorbets can be served individually or together as a light dessert. To serve as a light dessert, spread raspberry sauce in the center of dessert plates. Arrange 1 scoop kiwifruit sorbet and 1 scoop of banana sorbet on top. Garnish with fresh fruit.

Rich Vanilla Peach Ice Cream

SERVES 8

This recipe is very rich. A little goes a long way.

    3 cups heavy or whipping cream
    1 vanilla beans

THE NIGHT BEFORE

In a small metal bowl, place cream and add 1 vanilla bean. Cover and refrigerate overnight.

    1 vanilla bean
    ½ cup sugar
    6 egg yolks
    1½ cups fresh peaches, skinned and diced

THE NEXT DAY

In a food processor, place the second vanilla bean and blend until finely pulverized. Add sugar and continue to process until sugar is finely pulverized. Transfer the sugar mixture to a medium bowl, add egg yolks, and whisk until blended. In a medium saucepan, heat cream and vanilla bean over medium heat until almost boiling. Discard the first vanilla bean and pour cream in a thin stream into the egg yolk mixture, whisking constantly. Return the mixture to the saucepan and cook over medium-low heat to make a light custard, about 5 to 7 minutes. Do not allow to boil. Remove from heat, cool, cover, and refrigerate until cold. Pour the mixture into an ice cream freezer and fold in peaches. Freeze in an ice cream maker following manufacturer's directions.

During the 1904 World's Fair in St. Louis, Charles Menches sold ice cream at the Louisiana Purchase Exposition. Menches sold his ice cream in dishes. But as fate would have it, one day he sold so much ice cream he ran out of dishes by noon. Like any entrepeneur, Menches had to react quickly. The stand next to his, operated by a man named Ernest Hamwi, a Syrian, sold zalabia—a crisp, wafer-like pastry. Menches purchased Hamwi's zalabia, rolled them into cone shapes, scooped his ice cream on top, and created the ice cream cone.

If you don't like the effect whole vanilla beans give to your ice cream (tiny brown dots), try substituting about 2 teaspoons vanilla extract for the whole vanilla beans.

Auntie Beryl's Pumpkin Pie

My Auntie Beryl thought Libby's® makes the very best canned pumpkin. I have never used any other brand.

FOR THE FILLING

1 ½ cups canned Libby's® pumpkin

2 eggs, slightly beaten

1 ⅓ cups milk

¾ cup sugar

½ teaspoon ground cinnamon

¾ teaspoon ground allspice

¼ teaspoon ground ginger

½ teaspoon salt

In a large bowl, combine pumpkin, eggs, milk, sugar, cinnamon, allspice, ginger, and salt. Whisk to combine.

FOR THE PASTRY

1 ½ cups all purpose flour, sifted

½ teaspoon salt

½ cup Crisco® shortening

4 to 5 tablespoons cold water

Flour for flouring the work surface

In a large bowl, sift flour and salt together. Add shortening and cut it in with a pastry blender or a fork until the mixture is the size of small peas. The smaller the pieces, the more tender the pastry. Sprinkle 1 tablespoon water over the mixture and gently toss with a fork. Repeat this process until the mixture is moist. The less water that is added, the more tender the pastry. It is not necessary to add all of the water. Form the mixture into a ball. Flatten the dough on a lightly floured surface by pressing the ball with the edge of your hand 3 times across in both directions. Using a rolling pin, roll dough from the center out to the edges until the dough is ⅛-inch thick. Line the bottom of a pie plate with the pastry. Trim the dough around the outside edges of the pie plate leaving 1 inch of dough. Fold the dough under so that the pastry is double around the outside edge. Flute the edges by pressing the dough with the forefinger of one hand against a wedge made by the finger and thumb of your other hand, forming scallops. Fill the bottom of the pie plate with the pumpkin filling. Preheat the oven to 400 degrees and bake for 50 minutes, or until a knife inserted halfway between the center and the edge comes out clean. Cool.

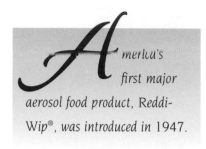

America's first major aerosol food product, Reddi-Wip®, was introduced in 1947.

Pick up Libby's® pumpkin. It's the secret ingredient.

Labor Day With Savings We're Proud Of

Finest Meats

Aged To Perfection, Boneless
Rib Eye Steak lb. **$3.99**

Holly Farms
Mixed Fryer Parts lb. **49¢**

Not Less Than 73% Lean
Fresh Ground Beef lb. **$1.09**

All Meat Or All Beef, 1 Pound Package
Sigman Hot Dogs lb. **99¢**

Loveland, 8 Ounce Package, 10 Varieties
Old Timer Lunch Meat pkg. **89¢**

Loveland, Fully Cooked, Water Added
Old Timer Boneless Ham lb. **$1.89**

Steele's, Fresh Ground
Homemade Italian Sausage lb. **$1.59**

1 Pound, Regular Or Thick Sliced
Bar-S Bacon lb. **$1.49**

Dairy and Frozen Foods

Cache Valley Natural Cheese 9 oz. **$1.07**
Longhorn Style, Cheddar Or Colby

Dannon Yogurt 8 oz. **39¢**

Totino's Party Pizza 10 oz. **89¢**

Welch's Orchard Fruit Juices 12 oz. **68¢**

Fleener's Bakery

Sprouted Wheat Bread 1 lb. loaf **98¢**

French Bread 1 lb. loaf **79¢**

Almond Butter Loaf Cake each **$1.89**

Chocolate Rum Loaf Cake each **$1.89**

Nice n' Fresh Produce

Russet Potatoes Colorado 10 lb. bag **$1.19**

Bartlett Pears Colorado lb. **29¢**

California
Castleman Plums lb. **29¢**

California
Fresh Mushrooms lb. **$1.35**

Colorado
Yellow Onions lb. **13¢**

Home Grown
Colorado Cabbage lb. **10¢**

California
Broccoli lb. **47¢**

The ABC's of Shopping September has been proclaimed Always Buy Colorado At Steele's we more much more. Stop in soon and Always Buy Colorado.

Shasta Soft Drinks Assorted flavors. 2 liters **59¢**

Nabisco Nilla Wafers 40% free. 12 oz. **95¢**

Nabisco Ritz Crackers 1 lb. **$1.27**

Dry Roasted Peanuts Evons — Regular or Unsalted 16 oz. **$1.39**

Vita Crunch Granola Banana, Hawaiian, Almond 2 lb. **$2.10**

Vlasic Kosher Dill Spears 32 oz. **97¢**

Capri Sun Natural Drinks 10 pack **$2.05**

Van Camps Pork & Beans 31 oz. **69¢**

Gold Medal Flour Regular or Unbleached 5 lb. **85¢**
Gold Medal Flour 25 lb. **$4.39**

Carnation Evaporated Milk 13 oz. **47¢**

Hershey's Chocolate Syrup 16 oz. **69¢**

Hidden Valley Ranch Dressing 16 oz. **$1.47**

Old Dutch Cleanser 17 oz. **28¢**

Gaylord Medium Diapers 36 count **$4.19**

Ivory Dish Liquid 2 pack, $1.00 off. 32 oz. **$2.69**

Charmin Bathroom Tissue White, Yellow, Blue, 4 rolls **99¢**

Hi-Dri Towels roll **48¢**

August 30, 1984

Fruits 300

Vegetables 315

When Your Kitchen Caters 338

Fruit Platters 340

Vegetable Platters 341

Herbs and Spices 342

Examining Eggs 346

Cooking is an art that requires careful shopping and fresh ingredients. Inside these pages I share everything I learned from my father about selecting superior produce. Remember, the quality of the fruits and vegetables you use in the meals you prepare is just as important as the recipe. Or, as my father would put it, "Garbage in; garbage out."

selecting
Superior
Produce

Selecting Superior Produce

Buying fresh produce is not like shopping for a can of beans, where the contents differ very little from one another. Each and every day most supermarkets will sell some fruits and vegetables that are fresh and delicious and some that can be classified as "garbage". My father was a taskmaster about fresh produce. His department stood tall every day. He trained me to select only the best and to love fresh fruits and vegetables. And, I learned my most valuable lesson about cooking from a grocer —"Garbage in. Garbage out." The quality of the produce you buy and use will effect the quality of the meal you prepare. Using fresh ingredients is just as important as the recipe you follow.

Since produce has a limited shelf life, it's best to shop often for fruits and vegetables. If you are concerned about your budget, buy only what you will use within the next few days. This eliminates waste. Your supermarket brings in fresh produce every few days. Why should it be any different at home?

Shop with your eyes and your nose. Look for produce with good shape, texture, and color and an appetizing aroma. If it smells like garbage, it probably is. Avoid produce that is moldy, bruised, or injured or has signs of insect damage.

Since produce is perishable, it should be handled gently to avoid bruising. Bruises or cuts can allow bacteria to enter causing it to spoil sooner.

When buying precut or prepacked items, make sure they are cold to the touch and are either refrigerated or surrounded by ice. Do not buy damaged, opened, or torn packages. Some prepackaged products, like lettuce, will have "Best if Used By" dates. Always check dates when shopping and use items by the recommended date.

CAROL ANN'S DAD

Selecting a Produce Market

When selecting a market to patronize, you might want to consider certain factors. Chain supermarkets decide at the corporate level what produce to purchase, giving the individual departments little control over what they sell. They are price oriented, so their quality will be hit-or-miss. Gourmet produce markets or small specialty food stores often personally select their produce. Their quality is normally good, but prices can sometimes be high. Farmers' markets normally have exceptional produce, but their prices can, also, be more expensive.

When selecting a market, I prefer a high-volume market that sells product before it overstays its welcome and begins to spoil. I avoid markets that smell or ones where flies hover over displays. The presence of flies is a good indication that some produce has begun to rot.

Most supermarkets claim to have superior produce, but there are few brand names on fruits and vegetables that guarantee consistency. In addition, produce does not carry any quality assurance labeling like meat or pork, so it's important to learn to distinguish the good, the bad, and the ugly.

Following are some tips on what to look for when buying produce and general guidelines on shelf life once you bring it home. I have included preparation tips only for the more unusual varieties of produce.

Fruits

About 2,500 varieties of apples are grown in the United States, and more than 7,500 are grown worldwide. Apples can be grouped into four categories based upon their usage: eating (or dessert), cooking (or baking), crab, and apples used for cider.

The most common apples found in supermarkets are:

Braeburn— This New Zealand apple has a mottled red and yellow skin. It is aromatic, crisp, and juicy and is good for eating or baking.

Crabapples – Apples are considered crab apples if they are 2 inches or less in diameter. Native to America, crabapples are tart and excellent for making jellies. These apples remain green even when ripe, although some hybrid varieties turn red, yellow, or purple as they ripen.

I always polished the apples I sold.

CAROL ANN'S DAD

Fuji– The Fuji apple came to the United States from Japan. It has a tart-edged sweetness, a green to yellow under color blushed with reds and, a firm, crisp texture, with outstanding flavor. The Fuji apple holds its texture well when baked.

Gala – This apple is red mottled over a yellow background. It is sweet and slightly spicy, and good for eating or using in salads.

Golden Delicious – The Golden Delicious apple, with its sweet, mellow flavor, is a versatile apple. It holds its shape well when baked yet is the perfect eating apple with a tart, crisp, and juicy taste.

Granny Smith– The Granny Smith apple is the number one choice for pies. It is also my favorite apple for snacking and salads. It has a freckled green skin.

Jonagold – This juicy, apple has a tangy, sweet flavor and is perfect for eating, cooking, or using in pies. It has a mottled red and yellow skin.

Jonathan – This is a crimson apple. It has a spicy tang and is often used in making cider.

McIntosh Red— The McIntosh Red has juicy, white flesh, and its skin is a mixture of both red and green coloring. It is a mainstay in making cider but is also great for eating or using in salads. It doesn't hold up well to lengthy cooking.

Red Delicious – This is the number one eating apple in the United States. This heart-shaped apple is bright red with a crunchy, mildly sweet flavor.

Rome Beauty– This apple was discovered in Rome, Ohio (not Italy), in 1816. The Rome Beauty is a nearly, solid red apple with firm flesh and a tough, smooth skin. It is best suited for baking as it keeps its shape along with its sweet flavor.

Winesap– The Winesap apple has a deep red skin, against a slightly yellow background, and is somewhat oblong in shape. It is used for both eating and cooking, as it has a firm, crisp flesh and a sweet aromatic flavor. The Winesap is also used in making cider.

SHOPPING: Apples should have a smooth, clean, shiny skin and possess a color that is consistent with their variety. Overripe apples will be soft and lack a firm crunch. Do not purchase apples with dull skin, bruises, or punctures.

STORING: Apples can be stored safely in the refrigerator for up to 2 weeks. Apples left at room temperature for more than 48 hours will turn soft.

AVAILABILITY: Most varieties of apples are available year-round. The Crab and Jonathan are usually available only in the fall and winter. Winesaps are available September through April or May, and Rome Beauties are available October through June or July.

Apricots

SHOPPING: Buy plump apricots with a golden, orange color and velvety skin. Unless they break the skin, blemishes will not affect the quality of apricots. When ripe, apricots will give to gentle pressure and smell fragrant. Soft, ripe fruit has the best flavor but needs to be eaten immediately. Avoid buying apricots that are pale-yellow or greenish-yellow in color or ones that are hard, shriveled, or bruised.

STORING: Ripe apricots should be stored in paper or plastic bags and refrigerated for 3 to 5 days. To ripen apricots, place them in a closed paper bag at room temperature. Allow them to soften for a few days.

AVAILABILITY: Apricots are harvested in the spring and summer, best in June and July.

Asian Pear

The Asian pear is firm, crunchy, and very juicy, with a lightly sweet, yet tart, taste. This fruit resembles a cross between an apple and a pear. Grown mostly in Japan, there are over 100 varieties of Asian pears. Skin colors range from greenish-russet brown, greenish yellow, to golden bronze.

SHOPPING: Asian pears have a mild pear fragrance and are best hard. Do not buy this fruit if it is wrinkled or soft.

STORAGE: When placed in a plastic bag and refrigerated, Asian pears will keep up to 4 weeks. They will keep up to 2 weeks at room temperature.

AVAILABILITY: The season for Asian pears varies according to variety, but they are generally available from July through late October.

Bananas and Plantains

There are two kinds of bananas — the sweet banana, which we eat, and the cooking banana, also known as plantains.

SHOPPING: Select plump bananas that do not feel mushy or show signs of damage. Avoid bananas with green tips, but select fruit with yellow skin that is flecked with tiny brown spots. When buying plantains, select plump fruit. Colors may range from green to black at any stage in the ripening process. When ripe, plantains will be soft with a dark-brown or black color and will have transparent, rather than opaque, skin.

STORING: Bananas should not be refrigerated. This will cause them to turn black. Store them at room temperature. Once home, this fruit will continue to ripen, turning brown when overripe. Bananas should last 4 to 5 days at home. If bananas are too green to eat, you can place them in a brown paper bag to accelerate the ripening process.

AVAILABILITY: Both bananas and plantains can be purchased year-round.

Cooking tip: Once cut, dipping bananas in a mixture of lemon juice and water will retard browning.

Blackberries

SHOPPING: Select berries that are plump with a blue to purplish-black color and bright, clean appearance. Blackberries should have a firm, but not hard, texture. Always check the bottom of the container for mold. Overripe berries are soft. If the hulls are still attached, this indicates they were picked too early; and they will have a tart flavor.

STORING: Blackberries should be refrigerated and used within 1 to 2 days. Do not wash berries until right before using.

AVAILABILITY: The peak season for blackberries is May through August; therefore, you'll find more competitive pricing during this time period. Due to the increased importation of fruit, blackberries can usually be purchased year-round.

Blueberries

SHOPPING: Look for deep, purple-blue to blue-black berries with a slight silver frost. Blueberries should be plump and free of moisture. The best indicator of maturity is color. Reddish berries are not ripe and, therefore, not as palatable; but they can still be used in cooking. Avoid green, dull, lifeless, or mushy berries. Always check for mold, especially on the bottom of the container.

STORING: Blueberries are the least fragile berry and can be stored in the refrigerator for 5 to 6 days. For best results, keep the berries dry during storage.

AVAILABILITY: Blueberries grown in North America are in season spring and summer. Imported fruit is available year-round.

Cactus Pears

This pear comes from the prickly pear cactus, native to the Americas. It has a stiff, spine-covered rind and is normally eaten raw. Its flavor and color vary according to the plant's blossom. The cactus pear can taste like a strawberry, watermelon, honeydew melon, fig, or banana.

SHOPPING: Cactus pears should be firm, not hard. Do not purchase shriveled, soggy, or overly hard fruit.

STORING: When placed in a plastic bag and refrigerated, this fruit will keep 1 week.

AVAILABILITY: Early spring through late fall.

To eat this spiny creature: It is important to wear gloves when prepping cactus pears. Pass the pears through an open flame, then pull out the spines, or simply cut them out with a knife. Once the spines are removed, slice off both ends, cut the pear in half lengthwise, and peel back the skin. Try sprinkling the fruit with lemon or lime juice before eating.

Cherries

There are three types of cherries: sweet, sour, and sweet-sour, a cross between the sweet and sour varieties. Sweet varieties are best for eating. The *Bing* cherry, a sweet variety, is most typically found in supermarkets. *Rainier* cherries, another sweet variety, are my husband's favorite. They are delicious, although they can be a bit expensive. This cherry has a golden skin with a pinkish-red blush and a very delicate, sweet flavor. Occasionally, markets run specials on Rainier cherries. Sour cherries are normally used for pies, preserves, and cooking.

SHOPPING: When purchasing sweet red cherries, select fruit that is plump, bright, and glossy with a deep-red to purple color. Cherries have passed their prime if they are soft, dull, or shriveled. Avoid buying fruit that has brown bruised spots. Rainier cherries are best when they are firm and lack blemishes. Sour cherries should be firm, not hard, and have even color.

STORING: Cherries are perishable and should be refrigerated immediately upon arriving home from the market. This fruit is best when eaten within 1 to 2 days of purchase. Always wash your cherries just before eating.

AVAILABILITY: Cherry season runs May through August.

Coconuts

SHOPPING: Coconuts are normally shipped by boat. Although they have a 2-month shelf life, it can take that long for them to reach the supermarket. Therefore, they should be inspected carefully before purchase. Coconuts sold in markets have their outer shell removed, exposing the inner nut, a woody-brown shell, covered with coarse brown fibers. Don't buy nuts with a gray color or ones that have moldy or wet spots.

When selecting a coconut, pick one that feels heavy. Shop with your ears. When you shake a ripe coconut, you can hear the juice splash inside. Shop with your nose. If the coconut has a fermented odor, pick one that doesn't smell. Patchy stains on the surface of the coconut indicate it may have a fractured shell that has allowed some of its liquid to escape.

STORING: Coconuts will keep up to 1 month when refrigerated. If you cut the coconut open, fresh coconut chunks or grated coconut should be stored in airtight containers in the refrigerator for no more than 2 weeks or frozen and kept up to 6 months.

AVAILABILITY: The peak season for coconuts is September through April, although they are available year-round in markets.

To open up this odd nut: The shell of the coconut has three eyes. Find the softest eye and poke it open with an ice pick or other sharp instrument. Drain out the coconut liquid and discard it. Bake the coconut in an oven for 25 minutes at 350 degrees. Remove the coconut from the oven and tap it with a hammer several times, until it cracks open. The shell should pop away, exposing a thin layer of dark skin over the flesh. Using a flexible spatula, separate the white flesh from the shell. You can peel off the dark skin if you prefer. Do this when the coconut is still warm, as it comes off easier then. Cut the coconut meat into desired sizes with a sharp knife.

Cranberries

SHOPPING: Look for brightly colored cranberries—the deeper the color, the less bitter the berry. Supermarkets normally sell cranberries in plastic bags, but avoid packages that contain mushy, wet cranberries or bags that are ripped or damaged.

STORING: Cranberries can be stored up to 1 month when refrigerated.

AVAILABILITY: Peak season for cranberries is November, but they season in the fall.

Currants and Gooseberries

Currants are small fresh berries that are red, white, gold, or black in color. Red currants are used in making jelly and glazes. White currants have a low acidity and are both eaten and used in cooking. Black currants have a harsh taste and are normally cooked prior to eating. Gooseberries are quite tart and resemble small, elongated green grapes covered with stripes. They are popular in Europe.

SHOPPING: This fruit should be firm and brightly colored with green stems. Avoid shriveled or leaky currants with brown stems.

STORING: Currants will only keep 1 or 2 days in the refrigerator.

AVAILABILITY: Currants are available in the summer. New Zealand gooseberries are in season from October through December. Oregon gooseberries season from July to August.

Dates

Dates are soft, semi-dry, or dry. Soft dates are moist, low in sugar, and have a soft flesh. Semi-dry dates are high in sugar, contain a moderate amount of moisture, and have firm flesh. Dry dates are high in sugar and have a hard, dry flesh.

SHOPPING: Do not buy shriveled dates or ones with mold or sugar crystals on their skin. Look for plump, soft fruit with smooth, shiny skin.

STORING: When placed in a plastic bag and refrigerated, fresh dates will keep up to 2 weeks. Store dried dates in an airtight container in a cool, dry place. They should keep about 6 months.

AVAILABILITY: Year-round, but peak season is late fall.

Figs

Figs are a very delicate fruit with protruding stems. This fruit must be harvested at its peak because it will not ripen after it is picked. Figs bruise and damage easily, have a short season, and are difficult to transport, making them a bit pricey.

SHOPPING: Buy only firm fruit whose stems are intact. The quality of this fruit will not be compromised if the skin around the stem is slightly shriveled or if its base is slightly torn or moist. Do not buy bruised figs. Overly green figs are not ripe.

STORING: This fruit will keep in the refrigerator for 2 days. Figs should be brought to room temperature before eating.

AVAILABILITY: *Black Mission*– May through November, *Brown Turkey*– May through December, *Calimyrna*– July and August, *Katdota*– May through October.

Grapes

Grapes are green, red, or blue-black in color and can either contain seeds or be seedless. Supermarkets normally carry the *Thompson seedless* green grapes. This grape has a delicate, sweet flavor with tart undertones. Red grapes are sweet, with a spicy edge. Varieties include the *Flame seedless, Cardinal, Emperor, Red Globe,* and *Tokay.* Blue-black grapes have a richer flavor and a sweet tartness.

SHOPPING: Color is the best measure of flavor. Select full-colored fruit. Grapes should be plump, fragrant, and firmly attached to their stems. Avoid packages with shriveled grapes that have fallen off their stems. Check the area where the grape attaches to its stem, and avoid grapes that are soft or brown around the stem.

STORING: Supermarkets normally package grapes in vented plastic bags. Grapes will keep up to 1 week when refrigerated in this type of packaging.

AVAILABILITY: Your market will carry grapes year-round, although different varieties of grapes peak at different times.

Grapefruit

Grapefruits either have a thick or thin peel. This variation is caused by differences in the climate where the fruit is produced and is a measure of taste. A low-humidity climate will produce grapefruits with a thick peel, a blemish-free skin, and a more acidic flavor. Grapefruits grown in a tropical climate will have a thin peel, a slightly blemished skin, and a sweeter taste.

SHOPPING: Select grapefruit that are shiny and seem heavy for their size—the heavier the fruit, the juicier it will be. This fruit should be firm. Rough skin or skin that does not "give" when pressed is an indication of dry fruit. Skin color is a gauge of flesh color—the more blush of pink or red to the skin, the deeper the color of the fruit.

STORING: Grapefruits can be stored for up to 2 weeks in the refrigerator.

AVAILABILITY: Year-round.

Guava

Guavas vary in appearance. This fruit can be round or pear-shaped and will have either rough or smooth greenish-white, yellow, or red skin. Its flesh is yellow, bright-pink, or red. Pear-shaped, white fruits are considered superior.

SHOPPING: Do not buy spotted, mushy, or very green guavas. This fruit should feel tender and "give" to gentle pressure when pressed. Look for skins that have some yellow color but are spot free. Shop with your nose. Guavas should smell sweet and flowery, yet slightly musky.

STORAGE: Store at room temperature until soft, then place in a plastic or paper bag and refrigerate. Guavas will last 2 days once ripe.

AVAILABILITY: June to August and November to March.

To eat: Cut guavas in half crosswise and scoop the flesh with a spoon.

Kiwifruit

The kiwifruit is a small, oblong fruit with thin, hairy brown skin. Its flesh is emerald-green and dotted with tiny black seeds. The taste of kiwifruit is a mixture of strawberries and melon. Gold kiwifruit has thin, smooth-brown skin and bright yellow flesh. Although the hairy, brown skin of a kiwifruit is edible, it is normally peeled before eating.

SHOPPING: Kiwifruit should feel firm to the touch, not soft or mushy. Avoid fruit with soft spots or bruises. Test for ripeness by pressing gently on the skin. This fruit will yield slightly to pressure when ripe.

STORING: Kiwifruit can be stored in the refrigerator for a few days. To ripen this fruit, place it in a paper bag and leave it at room temperature.

AVAILABILITY: If imported, kiwifruit is available year-round.

To eat: Peel the hairy skin off with a paring knife and cut into slices, wedges, or cubes.

Kumquats

Kumquats are a tiny orange citrus fruit with an oblong or round shape. Because of its thin skin, kumquats are normally eaten whole, rind and all.

SHOPPING: Buy firm, glossy fruit, with leaves still attached to the stem. Pass up fruit that is bruised, wet, or shriveled.

STORING: Kumquats will last a few days when stored at room temperature. If placed in a plastic bag, they will keep 2 weeks in the refrigerator.

AVAILABILITY: December through June.

H*int for Eating*: Gently squeeze and massage the skin to blend the flavors of the rind and the flesh before eating.

Lemons

SHOPPING: Lemons should be plump and feel heavy for their size. Select bright, shiny fruit. If the rind is an orange-yellow color, it means the lemon was picked when fully ripe. Pass up shriveled, hard-skinned, soft, or spongy fruit. Lemons with a greenish rind are not as juicy.

STORING: Placed in a plastic bag, lemons will keep up to 2 weeks in the refrigerator.

AVAILABILITY: Year-round. The peak season is April through July.

Limes

There are three varieties of limes—the *Key lime,* the *Persian lime,* and the *sweet lime.* The Key lime is small and full of seeds with a thin, splotchy, yellow-green rind. It is aromatic and juicy, with a strong acidic taste. The Persian lime is larger and almost always seedless. It has a thicker "lime-green" rind. The sweet lime has little acidity and is popular in the Middle East and India.

SHOPPING: Persian limes should feel heavy for their size but not hard when squeezed. Select smooth-skinned, brightly colored fruit that is not shriveled. Brown spots on the rind of Persian limes will not effect the flavor. Key limes should be light yellow with a fine-grained skin. Pass up fruit that is moldy or blotchy. Brown spots on the rind of Key limes will effect their quality.

STORING: Place limes in a plastic bag. Persian limes will keep in the refrigerator for 10 days, Key limes for 5 days.

AVAILABILITY: Persian limes – year-round, Key limes — June through August.

Lychee Nuts

The lychee nut is a most interesting creature. It is a small, round fruit with a tough, knobby shell and a perfume-like fragrance of roses and musk. It is a deep-red color when picked, but turns rosy brown within a few days. This fruit has clear or white pulp, and its jelly-like flesh will pop out of its shell much like a hard-boiled egg.

SHOPPING: Do not buy lychee nuts that are dried out. Look for nuts with a deep rose color and a thin skin.

STORING: Unshelled, this fruit will keep for several weeks in the refrigerator.

AVAILABILITY: June to August.

To eat this interesting creature: Slice open the shell with a paring knife. Gently squeeze the skin until it opens, slide the inner flesh out, and remove its hard seed by cutting the fruit open.

Mangoes

SHOPPING: Mangoes should feel heavy for their size and have firm, unblemished skin. Shop with your sense of smell. Hold the mango to your nose, stem end up, and smell the fruit. If it smells sweet and feels slightly soft to the touch, it is ready to eat. If it smells sour or a bit like alcohol, it has fermented and is not palatable. Also, check the area surrounding the stem. It should be plump and round. A few brown speckles are normal, but avoid spotted or shriveled fruit.

STORING: Most supermarkets sell hard mangoes, and you must ripen them before eating. Therefore, it is a good idea to plan ahead when buying mangoes to allow the fruit time to properly ripen. Leave the fruit at room temperature until the skin yields to pressure but does not feel mushy. Once ripened, mangoes will keep in the refrigerator for 4 days.

AVAILABILITY: In season, May to September, but available year-round.

To eat: The mango is a pitted fruit. Slice off the top and bottom of the mango, exposing the pit. Place the mango upright on a cutting board and slice the skin off in a downward motion, parallel with the pit. Remove sections of the flesh by cutting the fruit into desired sizes. The pit is a real draw back in this fruit and must be carefully carved out with a sharp knife.

Melons

SHOPPING: Melons with lumps or soft spots are passed their prime. Shop with your ears. Knock melons with your knuckle. Hard melons should sound hollow. Do not buy melons that are rock-hard or lopsided.

When selecting a cantaloupe, look for one that is completely covered with a thick straw-colored netting. There should no trace of the stem. Use your sense of smell. When ripe, cantaloupes will emit a slight cantaloupe fragrance. They will, also, yield to slight pressure on the blossom end, which is the end opposite the stem.

A good honeydew melon should weigh at least 5 pounds and have a waxy, cream-colored rind. Honeydew melons smell like honey. This fruit should yield to pressure when pressed gently around its stem.

My father taught me to thump a watermelon with my knuckle. If it sounds hollow, it's ripe. Characteristics to look for are a symmetrical, dull-colored body and a slightly flat, yellowish underbelly. It should not have flat sides.

Crenshaw melons should have a golden-yellow rind. When ripe, they give off a spicy fragrance and have springy, but not mushy skin. A Crenshaw melon is softer than other melons, and, therefore requires gentler handling.

STORING: Melons should be stored at room temperature until fully ripe. Once the fruit has matured, it can be stored in the refrigerator up to 5 days. Once you cut your melon, it should be wrapped tightly with plastic, as it can absorb odors from other foods. Cut melon will keep 3 days in the refrigerator.

AVAILABILITY: North American canataloupes – June through November, Crenshaws – July through October, Watermelons – May through September.

> Thump a watermelon with your knuckle. If it sounds hollow, it's ripe.

CAROL ANN'S DAD

Papayas

There are two types of papayas, Hawaiian and Mexican. The Hawaiian variety weighs about one pound, is shaped like a pear, and has yellow skin when ripe. Its fruit is bright orange or pink, and its center is filled with black, edible seeds. The Mexican variety can weigh up to 10 pounds, has green skin, and salmon-red to bright-orange flesh.

SHOPPING: Hawaiian papayas should have a warm, yellow color with smooth, unblemished skin. Shop with your nose. Papayas will have little aroma. When ripe, the neck of the fruit will be somewhat green. Mexican papayas stay green even when ripe. Select fruit that has "give" when pressed. Do not buy hard or shriveled papayas or ones that are overly soft or smell fermented. Dark spots on the skin of papayas often penetrate the fruit and spoil the flavor.

If your supermarket sells already cut papayas, choose one with a deep-salmon or red flesh. Pale red or pinkish pulp indicates under-ripe fruit.

STORING: To ripen a papaya quickly, place it in a paper bag with a banana and let it sit at room temperature. Once ripe, this fruit should be placed in either a paper or plastic bag before refrigerating. It will keep 3 days.

AVAILABILITY: Year-round.

To eat: Cut the papaya in half, lengthwise, scoop out the small black seeds, and eat the flesh with a spoon. Papaya can be peeled with a vegetable peeler. Although the seeds are edible, they are usually discarded.

Passion Fruit

Similar in size to an egg, passion fruit has a hard shell that is smooth and waxy. It is either purple or yellow in color and has a yellowish, jelly-like pulp. Its flavor is slightly musky with a sweet-tart to very tart taste.

SHOPPING: Look for fruit that is large, plump, fragrant, and feels heavy for its size. Ripe passion fruit will have a deep purple, dimpled shell. If you find mold on the shell, simply wipe it off. Mold will not effect the quality of this fruit. Very hard passion fruit is not ripe.

STORING: If your passion fruit has smooth skin, it needs to ripen at room temperature. Turn the fruit over occasionally as it ripens. Once ripe, it will keep 5 days in the refrigerator.

AVAILABILITY: Florida fruit – year-round, New Zealand fruit – February to July, California fruit – July to March.

To eat: Slice the fruit in half and spoon out the pulp.

Peaches and Nectarines

Peaches and nectarines are very similar. Peaches have a fuzzy skin, and the skin of nectarines is smooth. Both peaches and nectarines are classified as either Clingstone or Freestone. Clingstone varieties have flesh that is firmly attached to the stone or pit. The flesh of Freestone varieties separates easily from the stone.

SHOPPING: Peaches should have a well-defined crease, a sweet fragrance, and be soft to the touch, not mushy. Do not buy peaches that have "green shoulders" around the stem end. This is an indication the peach was picked prematurely. Peaches with large, flattened bruises will not ripen well. If the skin of the fruit is shriveled at the stem end or has turned a red-brown color, the peach is over-ripe. Nectarines should be plump, have a smooth, unblemished skin, and a slight softening along the crease. Do not buy hard, dull, or shriveled nectarines

STORING: To ripen peaches, place them in a cool place, with their stem end down. If the peaches give slightly when pressed and begin to smell, they are ready to eat. If you place nectarines in a paper bag, they will ripen in about a day. Handle peaches and nectarines gently as any bruising will show. Once ripe, these fruits will keep in the refrigerator 3 to 5 days.

AVAILABILITY: North American fruit is available spring and summer. Imported fruit is available year-round.

Pears

There are two types of pears—the granular, hard winter pears used for poaching and the buttery, soft pears that we eat. Pears come in nearly 1,000 varieties. This fruit does not ripen well on trees and is, therefore, picked in a fully mature state, but unripe condition.

Anjou: This pear is egg-shaped with pale-green or red skin. It has firm, juicy flesh and a sweet, mellow flavor. Anjou pears do not change colors as they ripen. This pear can be used for both cooking and eating.

Bartlett: The majority of pears grown in the United States are Bartlett pears. This pear is considered to be one of the better eating pears. It has a smooth texture and juicy flesh, and its green skin turns yellow as it ripens. A majority of the Bartlett harvest is canned.

Bosc: The Bosc pear has yellow-brown skin. It has crisp, creamy white flesh that tastes sweet, yet spicy. Bosc pears have long, tapering necks that come to a point and fat bottoms. They do not change colors as they ripen and are ideal for both baking and cooking.

Comice: Known as the "Queen of Pears", the Comice is considered the best eating pear. This French variety is a fat pear with yellowish-green skin and a russet to red blush. Its flesh has a buttery, sweet taste and a fruity fragrance.

SHOPPING: Pears should be firm and have good color for their variety. Do not buy pears that have bruises or blemishes. When purchased, the skin on pears should be bright, shiny, and tight.

STORING: To ripen, place them on their bottom in a cool place. To speed the ripening process, place pears, along with an apple or banana, in a paper bag that has a few punctures. Pears will be fragrant when ripe, and the flesh near the stem will yield to gentle pressure. Also, as a pear ripens, its flesh will become matte and may contain a few brown spots. Once ripe, pears can be stored for 2 to 3 days in the refrigerator.

AVAILABILITY: Anjou and Bosc – fall, winter, and spring, Bartlett and Comice – fall and winter.

Persimmons

The persimmon is grown in America, Japan, and Israel. All varieties have an orangish skin and four papery leaves called the calyx that sit on its top. As the national fruit of Japan, persimmons are traditionally eaten on Japanese New Year. Its name in Latin means "food of the gods".

Common Japanese varieties are the *Hachiya* and the *Fuyu.* Hachiya persimmons are heart-shaped with a creamy, sweet flavor and apricot-like flesh. They have a sharper taste than other varieties. Because it is quite fragile, Hachiya fruit is wrapped in tissue and packed in wooden boxes when shipped. The Fuyu fruit is shaped like a tomato and eaten like an apple. It has a sweet, slightly spicy taste. The persimmon fruit grown in Israel is called the *Sharon fruit.* It has a square shape and an orange-tan color. The Sharon fruit is both seedless and coreless with sweet flesh.

SHOPPING: Look for bright red-orange fruit that is plump and glossy. Yellow patches on persimmons are an indication they are not ripe. Because Hachiya persimmons are so delicate, they are shipped hard and should be ripened at home. Fuyu persimmons should be purchased firm and may need only a bit of ripening.

STORING: Hachiya fruit can be stored up to 1 month at home before ripening. To ripen, place at room temperature until soft. This could take up to 1 week. Fuyu fruit may need only a bit of ripening or may be ready to eat when purchased. Once ripe, persimmons have a short shelf life, so eat immediately. To ripen Sharon fruit, place at room temperature for 48 hours. Once ripe, the Sharon fruit may last up to 10 days refrigerated.

AVAILABILITY: California fruit – October to December, with peak season in mid-October, Sharon fruit – late November to mid-February.

To eat: Wash the fruit and cut it in half with a knife. Remove the core and discard the seeds and the calyx. The skin is edible.

Pineapples

The pineapple is a large fruit with a crown of spiny leaves. It has a tough, waxy rind that is either dark-green, yellow, orange-yellow, or reddish when the fruit ripens. The flesh of pineapples ranges from white to yellow depending upon their variety. Pineapples are picked ripe because once they are off the tree their starch will not turn to sugar.

SHOPPING: Select pineapples that are plump. This fruit should seem heavy for its size, and its outer skin should feel slightly soft to the touch. Leaves on the crown should be fresh, with a deep green color. Pineapples with dry, brown leaves or a dull, yellow appearance will be more acidic to the palate. My father taught me to pull gently on the leaves. If the leaves can be removed easily with gentle pressure, the pineapple is ripe. Shop with your nose. The stem end of fresh pineapples will have a sweet aroma. Highly colored pineapples will have a sweeter taste because they were picked ripe. Avoid bruised, discolored pineapples with soft spots, an unpleasant odor, or dark, watery eyes. The eyes of a pineapple should be flat and almost hollow.

STORING: If you buy your pineapple chilled, keep it refrigerated. If it was room temperature at the time of purchase, keep it at room temperature. Pineapples ferment quickly, so they should be kept in a cool place out of direct sunlight. Once you cut your pineapple, wrap the pieces tightly in plastic wrap or place them in an airtight container. Cut pineapple wrapped tightly in plastic will keep 3 days in the refrigerator.

AVAILABILITY: Year-round. Peak season is March to June.

To eat: Cut off the top and bottom with a large, sharp knife. Slice off the skin from the top downward. I prefer to remove the eyes of the pineapple with a small paring knife. Cut in a circular motion around the eye and pry it out. Cut the fruit into four wedges and remove the core.

Pull gently on the leaves of a pineapple. If they can be removed easily, the pineapple is ripe.

CAROL ANN'S DAD

Plums

Plums can be as small as a cherry or as large as a baseball with either a round, elongated, or heart shape. A good, ripe plum has a sweet-tart taste. The skin of this fruit can be green, yellow, red, blue, purple, or almost black depending upon its variety. Most varieties of plums have a yellow, golden, or amber flesh, although a few have a red tone.

SHOPPING: Plums should have good color and feel firm to the touch. Do not buy fruit that is too soft or too hard, and avoid plums with cracks or blemishes.

STORING: Ripen at room temperature. The skin of a plum will lose its shine when it is ready to eat. Once ripened, plums will keep 4 to 5 days in the refrigerator.

AVAILABILITY: California plums – June through September, Chilean plums – January through March.

Pomegranates

A pomegranate is a round fruit, 2 ½ to 5 inches in diameter. It has a hard, pink or crimson skin and is topped with a calyx. Just inside this unusual fruit is a white, spongy pith that surrounds a thin membrane. Inside the membrane are pods of ruby-red kernels that contain translucent, edible, crimson seeds. The pomegranate's many tiny seeds have made it the symbol of fertility legends all around the world.

SHOPPING: Pomegranates should be firm to the touch and feel heavy for their size. Shop with your ears. To determine ripeness, tap the fruit. If it makes a metallic sound, it is ripe. Fruit that is overripe will have cracks in its skin. Do not buy bruised, shriveled, dull, or overly hard pomegranates. Plan to buy this fruit ahead as pomegranates become juicier and have more flavor over time.

STORING: This fruit will keep at room temperature 2 to 3 weeks or up to 1 month in the refrigerator.

AVAILABILITY: August to December.

To eat: Cut off the crown and scoop out some of the white core with a spoon. With a knife, cut the outer rind, dividing the fruit into quarters. Place your thumb down the center of the core and pull the four sections apart. Remove the white pith and discard. Turn the skin of the pomegranate inside out and pop the seeds out. To remove any remaining white pith from the seeds, place the quartered sections into a bowl of cold water. The pith will float to the top, and the seeds will sink to the bottom.

Raspberries

A raspberry consists of a cluster of cells called drupelets that look like tiny beads. There are three main types of raspberries: red, golden, and black. Red raspberries thrive in cool, marine climates. Golden raspberries taste a bit like an apricot. Black raspberries are purplish-black in color and have small seeds and a hollow core.

SHOPPING: Select berries that are full and round with a soft, hazy gloss. Always look at the bottom of the container when buying raspberries. A stained, moldy bottom is a sign of decay. Avoid raspberries that have dents or bruises or ones that have broken apart. Raspberries will turn quickly, so it is best to use them the day of purchase.

STORING: Raspberries are very delicate and must be refrigerated. Wash raspberries just before serving, as water speeds their decay. This fruit will keep 1 to 2 days refrigerated.

AVAILABILITY: Red raspberries – Year-round, peaking June to early September, golden raspberries – June to October, black raspberries – season in July.

Star Fruit

The star fruit is an oval fruit with five prominent ribs. It has a yellow, waxy skin and yellow, translucent flesh. It gets its name from the five-pointed star that is exposed when it is cut open. This greenish-yellow fruit, about 2½ to 5 inches in length, turns a dark-yellow color when ripe, and its ribs will have brownish edges. There are two types of star fruit: sweet and tart. The tart fruit is smaller and has a lemony taste. It is mainly used in cooking. The sweet fruit is larger with thicker, fleshier ribs. Star fruit may or may not contain seeds.

SHOPPING: Star fruit should be large, plump, and firm with shiny skin. A general rule of thumb to follow when selecting this fruit is the more yellow its color, the sweeter its flesh. Avoid fruits with green skin or brown spots.

STORING: Place star fruit in a covered container and keep at room temperature for 2 days to ripen. When the fruit is a solid golden yellow, it will be ready to eat. Star fruit will keep 1 week in the refrigerator.

AVAILABILITY: Sweet star fruits – summer to late winter, tart star fruits – late summer to midwinter.

To eat: Slice off the ends of the fruit and discard. If the outer edges of the ribs are too brown, they will be tough and bitter. Cut any overly brown edges off the ribs. Slice the star fruit crosswise and pick out any seeds.

Strawberries

SHOPPING: Strawberries should be plump with a bright red color. Their caps should be green and look fresh. Avoid fruit with limp or spoiled caps. The size of a strawberry is not an indication of flavor. Small or large strawberries can be sweet and juicy. Do not buy strawberries with white or green splotches or mold. Moisture speeds decay, so don't buy fruit with excess moisture. Always check the quality of the fruit from the bottom of the container as well.

STORING: When you bring this fruit home, it is a good idea to pick through the strawberries and discard any bruised or damaged berries. Cover and refrigerate the strawberries by lightly wrapping them in plastic. Do not wash them until just before eating.

AVAILABILITY: Year-round. Peak season for strawberries is spring through summer.

Tangerines and Tangelos

Tangerines are orange-colored citrus fruits with a loose skin that can be easily separated from the fruit. Tangerines contain more water and less sugar than oranges and are less acidic and darker in color. Tangelos are a hybrid of grapefruits and tangerines and are known for their juiciness and mildly sweet flavor. Clementines, a member of the tangerine family, are small with thin peels and usually seedless.

SHOPPING: Tangerines should fill their skin. You can count on a high-quality fruit when tangerines are sold with their stems and leaves on. When buying a clementine, check the top and stem end to make sure it has not softened. Do not buy fruit with soft or dented spots or fruit that feels hollow.

STORING: Tangerines, placed in a plastic bag and stored in the refrigerator, will keep 1 week. Clementines should be eaten within 4 to 5 days.

AVAILABILITY: Tangerines – winter through early spring, tangelos – winter, clementines – late October to February.

Vegetables
Artichokes

SHOPPING: A good artichoke will have tightly packed, crisp leaves. As artichokes age, their leaves spread apart. Look on the cut end. A black end means the artichoke has been stored too long. Do not buy this vegetable if it is wilting, dried out, or moldy. Fall and winter artichokes may have bronze tips or a whitish, blistered appearance. This is caused by exposure to a light frost. Some artichoke connoisseurs believe this vegetable is more tender and intensely flavored after a frost.

STORING: If refrigerated in a plastic bag, an artichoke will keep up to 1 week.

AVAILABILITY: Year-round, with a peak season March through May and again in October. Fresh artichokes cannot be imported into the United States.

To prepare for boiling: Place the artichoke on a cutting board. Using a sharp knife, cut off the stem so that the artichoke will stand upright and then slice an inch off its top. Remove any tough, outer leaves around the stem. Using your cooking shears, snip off the sharp tips of the leaves. Hold the artichoke upright and place it under a solid stream of running water to wash out any debris.

To remove the heart when eating: Gently open up the leaves to expose the hairy choke inside. The inside of an artichoke has three parts—the stem, the heart, and the hairy choke. Put your hand over the stem end and gently separate the heart from the body of the artichoke. Using a spoon, separate the hairy choke from the artichoke heart. The hairy choke is not edible. Cut off the stem end and discard the hairy choke, which starts at the heart and ends at the stem.

Arugula

Arugula that is grown in hothouses has a milder taste. It is often added to mesclun or spring mix prepackaged salads. When grown in fields with a lot of exposure to sunlight, arugula will have a peppery taste and can be extremely sandy.

SHOPPING: Arugula should have crisp, emerald green colored leaves. Do not buy this vegetable if it is yellow or if its leaves are limp or its stems are withered or slimy. If your supermarket sells arugula in bunches, check the area where the stems have been rubber-banded together. This is the first place rot may develop.

STORING: If you buy arugula in bunches, loosely wrap it in damp paper towels and place it in a plastic bag before refrigerating it. This vegetable will keep up to 3 days when refrigerated.

AVAILABILITY: Year-round, but it is more plentiful in late summer.

Cleaning: If you buy bunches of fresh arugula, it is important to clean it thoroughly to remove any sandy grit. Place the leaves in a large bowl of cold water and gently swirl them about to release the sand. Remove them from the water and transfer to paper towels to dry or spin them in a salad spinner.

Asparagus

SHOPPING: The skin of asparagus is a medium green color with purple highlights. The cut ends are white or light colored. Take note of the ends. Spears with large, white-woody stalks and only a few inches of green at the tips were harvested late and will be tough. The white, woody bottoms of asparagus should be less than 15 percent of the total length of the spear. Look for firm, plump, round spears. The tips of asparagus should be tight and compact. Do not buy asparagus that has wet, slimy, or smelly tips. Shop with your ears when buying asparagus. If you give the bunch a squeeze and it squeaks, it is fresh. Also, its spears should snap easily when bent.

STORING: Asparagus will keep 2 to 3 days if refrigerated. When shopping in your supermarket, you may find asparagus standing upright with its cut ends in ice or water. This procedure prolongs its shelf life. You can do this at home as well, but it's important to change the ice or water several times a day. To pamper asparagus for a special dinner party, cut an inch off the bottoms, wrap the ends with wet paper towels, place the spears in a plastic bag, and store them in the vegetable crisper of your refrigerator.

AVAILABILITY: Year-round, with a peak season March through June. Prices on asparagus will be better between November and early July.

Avocado

Eighty percent of the avocados grown in California are *Hass.* This vegetable has a green, pebbly skin that turns black as it ripens. The skin is pliable and peels off easily.

SHOPPING: If you want to use your avocado immediately, select one that yields to gentle pressure. If you are shopping ahead and plan to use the avocado in a few days, pick one that is firm to the touch. Pass up avocados that are bright green and feel rock-hard. They are difficult to ripen. Also, don't buy this vegetable if it is sunken, shriveled, or feels mushy.

STORING: Avocados should be stored at room temperature until they are ready to eat. To speed the ripening process, place them in a paper bag with an apple. Once ripe, avocados will keep up to 2 days in the refrigerator. If you only use half of an avocado, leave the pit in, brush the flesh with lemon juice, wrap tightly with plastic wrap, and refrigerate.

AVAILABILITY: Year-round.

Beans

A bean by any other name is still a bean, and beans have many names. Among them are the flat green bean, French green bean, haricot vert, Pole bean, string bean, wax bean, and yellow bean. My mother always referred to them as string beans. They got this name because older varieties had fibrous side strings. Beans can be purple, yellow, creamy white, or deep-green in color and can have a round or flat shape.

SHOPPING: Don't just grab a handful of beans. Pick through them and select tender, crisp, well-formed beans. If freshly picked, green beans will have a smooth, velvety skin. Do not buy beans that have white mold on their tips or beans that are dried or shriveled. If the beans inside the pods are visible, the beans were overgrown.

STORING: When you get home from the supermarket, wash the beans before storing them in a plastic bag. This extra moisture helps them stay fresh and crisp. Beans will keep 4 to 5 days in the refrigerator.

AVAILABILITY: Year-round, with a peak in summer months. Yellow wax beans are not generally available during the hot summer months.

To use: Cut off the stem ends but leave the curved tips if they are in good condition. If the beans have side strings, pull these off.

Black-eyed Peas

Black-eyed peas are cream colored with a kidney shape. Their name reflects the distinctive black eye on their curved, inner side.

SHOPPING: Black-eyed peas should be firm and plump. Most supermarkets sell fresh, shelled black-eyed peas in 1-pint containers.

STORING: Refrigerate and keep no more than 1 week.

AVAILABILITY: Year-round, but most supermarkets stock fresh black-eyed peas around the holidays for New Years.

Beets

While beets are normally red in color, many varieties are now available including the golden beet, white beet, and the *Chioggia* beet, which has red and white candy-cane like stripes.

SHOPPING: The greens on beets should be bright, dark green, and fresh. Select smooth, hard, round beets with deep color. Beets with a diameter of 3 inches are fine for cooking, but small, younger beets with a diameter of approximately 1 ½ inches cook faster. Avoid large beets with unpalatable, woody cores, as they take the longest time to cook. Do not buy beets that have soft, moist spots or shriveled, flabby skin. Beets with wilted greens may be acceptable to purchase because the leaves deteriorate faster than the roots.

STORING: Cut the greens off the beets, leaving at least 1 inch of the stem attached, before refrigerating. Pick through the leaves, discarding the ones that are damaged. Greens stored in perforated plastic bags will keep 2 days in the refrigerator. Unwashed roots will keep up to 3 weeks in the refrigerator.

AVAILABILITY: Year-round, with a peak season June through October.

Bok Choy

SHOPPING: Good quality bok choy should be thick, firm, and fleshy. Its leaves should be crisp and green, and its stalks should be plump and firm. Poor quality bok choy will have wilted or spotted leaves with limp, discolored stalks.

STORING: Bok choy will wilt in a few days. Refrigerate it in perforated plastic bags.

AVAILABILITY: Year-round.

Broccoli and Broccoli Rabe

Broccoli rabe is a broccoli-like vegetable that resembles broccoli florets on long, thin stems. It has a bitter, but zesty flavor.

SHOPPING: When buying broccoli, look for buds that are tightly closed and crisp leaves. The buds should be an even, deep green color, and the stems should be a lighter green than the buds. Avoid broccoli with large, thick, whitish stalks. Select broccoli rabe with small, firm, green stems, tightly closed buds, and an abundance of florets. Shop with your nose. Smell the stalks of broccoli rabe where they are tied together and avoid any with a mustard-like smell. Pass up broccoli rabe that has yellowed flowers or stalks that are split at the bottom. This is a sign of age.

STORING: Broccoli will keep in the refrigerator up to 4 days. Broccoli rabe should be wrapped in a wet paper towel and placed in a plastic bag before refrigerating.

AVAILABILITY: Broccoli – Year-round, with a peak season from October through April. Broccoli rabe – Year-round, but best in late fall to early spring.

Cabbage

Members of the cabbage family include common green cabbage, red cabbage, white cabbage, Savoy cabbage, and Brussels sprouts. The Savoy cabbage is not readily available but is considered to have better flavor. Brussels sprouts are miniature heads of cabbage that grow around a central stem.

SHOPPING: Cabbage will normally feel very heavy for its size. When buying green or Savoy cabbage, select heads with dark green leaves. As cabbage ages, its outer leaves wilt and are removed, exposing the lighter colored underneath leaves. The leaves on cabbage should be thick and crisp, not limp. A fresh cabbage will show no signs of browning. Do not buy cabbage that has a strong odor. If it smells like garbage, it probably is. Avoid purchasing this vegetable if its core is woody or split.

Brussels sprouts should be firm with a good green color, have compact leaves, and clean ends. Do not buy puffy, yellow, or wilted Brussels sprouts.

STORING: This vegetable keeps up to 1 week in the refrigerator when tightly wrapped in plastic.

AVAILABILITY: Red, green, and white cabbage – Year-round, Savoy cabbage – fall, Brussels sprouts – Year-round, peaking in November and December.

Carrots

Carrots have evolved over the years, resulting in purple, white, gold, and round varieties. Most of us only find the typical orange carrots in our supermarkets. "Mini-peeled carrots" are also now available in most markets.

SHOPPING: Select well shaped carrots with smooth exteriors and closely trimmed tops. My father taught me the brighter the color, the sweeter the flavor. Do not buy soft, wilted, or split carrots. Dark, slimy, yellowed tops that are beginning to sprout are an indication of decay. Mini-peeled carrots should be plump, not slimy, broken, or whitish. For the freshest carrots, buy bunches with bright green, leafy tops. The tops deteriorate quickly once the carrots are harvested, so if the tops are green, it means they were recently picked.

STORING: Carrots should be stored in plastic and will keep in the refrigerator up to 10 days. If you buy carrots with green tops, remove the leaves before storing. Do not store carrots with fruit, like apples or pears. These fruits emit ethylene gas, which causes carrots to turn bitter.

AVAILABILITY: Year-round. Fresh, young bunch carrots that have their tops are found in the spring.

The brighter the color, the sweeter the flavor.

CAROL ANN'S DAD

Cauliflower

SHOPPING: A good quality head of cauliflower will have creamy white, compact curls with bright green leaves that are firmly attached to its core. Pass up this vegetable when it has tiny, black mold spots or yellow, wilted leaves. This is an indication of an old cauliflower.

STORING: Cauliflower will keep up to 1 week in the refrigerator when placed in a plastic bag.

AVAILABILITY: Year-round, though you'll find the best quality during colder months.

Tips on prepping: I have found it more and more difficult to purchase cauliflower that is free of black spots. If this is the only product available, cut the black mold spots off with a sharp paring knife.

Celery

Most supermarkets sell *Pascal* celery.

SHOPPING: Good quality celery will have straight stalks and rigid ribs that snap crisply when bent. The leafy tops should look fresh with good green color. Do not buy celery with slimy leaves. When celery is overly large with dark green stalks, it may be bitter or stringy.

STORING: Keep celery in a perforated bag in the vegetable crisper of your refrigerator. It will keep up to 1 week.

AVAILABILITY: Year-round.

Tips on prepping: My mother taught me to remove the strings from celery by snapping the rib at the point where the stalk changes in color from green to white. This exposes the strings. Using a small paring knife, gently pull the strings from the stalk.

Chestnuts

SHOPPING: It is a difficult task to select good chestnuts because it is hard to judge their inner quality by their outer shells. Your best bet is to buy chestnuts at a high-volume market that moves product quickly. Once the shells are cracked open, a good quality chestnut will be light-tan in color and plump and meaty. Chestnuts that have greenish mold between the nut and its outer skin or hard, darkened areas should be discarded.

STORING: Chestnuts will keep up to 1 week in the refrigerator.

AVAILABILITY: October through March, peaking in December.

To remove the shell: Using a sharp paring knife, make an X on the domed side of the chestnut. Roast in an oven at 400 degrees for 20 minutes. It is easier to remove the shells when the chestnuts are warm, so remove only a few at a time from the oven. Cool slightly and break away the shell. Remove the brown inner skin.

Corn

SHOPPING: Examine the husks first. Husks should be bright green and fit snugly. My father taught me to pull back enough of the husk to expose the kernels. To judge the

Peel back enough of the husk to see the kernels.

CAROL ANN'S DAD

quality of corn by its kernels, look for evenly spaced rows that are plump and milky all the way to the ear. The silks should be dry and deep gold in color. Avoid corn with soggy silks. Occasionally, you will find your supermarket sells corn packed in trays. Examine these ears carefully as they may be old. Corn with flattened, tightly packed kernels will be starchy.

STORING: Place the ears in plastic bags before refrigerating. They will keep 1 to 2 days.

AVAILABILITY: Florida corn – October to June, peaking in April to June, California corn – May to October, peaking in June and July, Ohio corn – peaking from August to October, Colorado Olathe corn – peaking late July and early August.

Cucumber

This vegetable has a crisp texture and mild flavor. The Common American cucumber is about 8 inches in length with smooth, dark green skin that is often waxed. Pickling cucumbers, known as gherkins, American dills, and French cornichons, are small. Gherkins and cornichons are about 2 inches in length, while American dills are about 4 inches. American pickling cucumbers have knobby warts and pale stripes, and their skin ranges in color from dark to light. Supermarkets often carry the English cucumber, which is narrow and thin-skinned. It has a mild flavor, fewer seeds, and firmer flesh.

SHOPPING: Look for cucumbers that are firm and well shaped with deep green color. Do not buy yellowing, puffy, or shriveled cucumbers. Check for soft spots or soft ends, which is an indication of spoilage. The flesh of cucumbers should be pale green. Yellow flesh indicates they have started to decay.

STORING: Wrapped in plastic, cucumbers should keep 1 week in the refrigerator.

AVAILABILITY: American Common cucumbers – year-round, Pickling cucumbers – summer.

Edamame

Edamame are fresh soybeans. They are as bright in color and as sweet to the taste as green peas. Inside their small, flattened pods are smooth-skinned, plump beans that resemble lima beans.

SHOPPING: Select brightly colored, even-sized, plump pods. Avoid shriveled or discolored edamame.

STORING: This vegetable should be placed in an open container and will keep 1 week in the refrigerator.

AVAILABILITY: Year-round.

To prepare: Place the pods in a bowl and sprinkle them with salt. Rub the salt over their skin, coating evenly. Allow the beans to sit for 15 minutes, then boil 1 pound of edamame in 1 gallon of water over high heat for 7 to 10 minutes. To remove the beans inside the pod, place the pod to your lips and squeeze the beans out into your mouth.

Eggplant

Although there are several varieties of eggplants, the most common type found in supermarkets is the deep purple *Black Beauty.*

SHOPPING: Eggplants should be firm and hard and feel heavy for their size. Choose eggplants with a smooth, glossy, dark purple skin with no signs of green. Pass up soft or spotted eggplants or ones that have wrinkly skin. Shriveling is a sign of aging. Eggplants become bitter with age.

STORING: Eggplants keep about 4 days in the refrigerator.

AVAILABILITY: Year-round.

Endive and Escarole

The most common endive found in supermarkets is curly endive. It is tough with a bitter taste and is best cooked in soup or vegetable ragouts. Endive grows in bunches of long, deep green, curly-edged leaves with thin white ribs. Escarole has broad, lightly ruffled leaves that form an open, flattened head. Escarole is light-yellow to deep-green in color.

SHOPPING: Curly endive or escarole should be brightly colored and have perky leaves. Do not buy endive that has brown discoloration, excessive dirt, or dry, yellowing leaves.

STORING: When placed in plastic bags and refrigerated, endive and escarole will keep up to 5 days.

AVAILABILITY: Year-round, peaking in December through April.

Fennel

This odd-looking vegetable has become a popular ingredient in recipes. It can be eaten raw or cooked. Its enlarged bulb bottom, composed of onion-like layers, culminates in stringy, celery-like stalks. The bulb bottom and stalks enclose a sweet-tasting, dense heart. Fennel tastes like licorice or anise and has the crisp, crunchy texture of an apple.

SHOPPING: Pick fennel that has large, squatty, white bulbs, a pale green color, and fluffy green fronds. Do not buy split, shriveled, dried-out bulbs with brown or soft spots. If the stalks have been cut away, it means the fennel has been on the shelf too long.

STORING: If wrapped in plastic and stored in your vegetable crisper, fennel will last up to 3 days.

AVAILABILITY: Year-round.

Cut off the stalks at the top of the bulb and trim a thin slice off the darkened end of the bulb. Gently pull away the outer layer and discard it. This part of the fennel tends to be stringy and tough. Separate and discard the dark green, outer stalks from the light colored, tender inner portions. Immediately place the bulb into a bowl filled with cold water and 1 tablespoon lemon juice until ready to use.

Garlic

There are two main types of garlic—softneck and hardneck. The softneck garlic has a fibrous stem that dries into a grass-like top. Hardneck garlic has an intense flavor and a long, hard stem, surrounded by firm cloves that are easy to peel. Elephant garlic looks like a large garlic bulb but is more closely related to the leek. It has a mild flavor and a potato-like flesh.

SHOPPING: Look for large, plump, and firm bulbs with a tight, unbroken covering. As it ages, garlic shrivels, looses its plumpness, and begins to sprout. Age turns the flavor bitter. Do not buy soft or spongy bulbs. Some specialty food stores sell peeled garlic. If you are buying garlic that has already been peeled, look for pearly white, firm cloves with no shriveling, mold, or soft stickiness.

STORING: Garlic bulbs will keep up to 3 weeks in the refrigerator. Moisture will make garlic spoil, so be sure to keep it dry. Peeled garlic will keep in the refrigerator up to 2 weeks. You'll be sorry if you don't store it in a covered container.

AVAILABILITY: Year-round.

To extract the cloves: Rub or cut off the loose outer skin to expose the cloves. Gently pull the cloves away from the core of the bulb. Using the side of a large knife, smash each individual clove to break its skin. Peel the skin from each clove.

Ginger

SHOPPING: The skin of this root should be firm and smooth, with a light sheen. Shop with your nose. Fresh ginger will have a spicy fragrance. Do not buy knobby, shriveled, or moldy ginger.

STORING: To store ginger in your refrigerator, wrap it in dry paper towels and place it in a plastic bag. Ginger will keep up to 2 weeks.

AVAILABILITY: Year-round, peaking March through September.

To use: Cut off only as much ginger as you need. Using a vegetable peeler, remove the outer skin. Grate, slice across the grain, or chop as needed.

Greens

Collard greens: These greens are popular in the American South. They resemble flat cabbage leaves.

Dandelion greens: When young, these leaves add a bitter, tangy flavor to salads. When old, they should be cooked.

Kale: Kale has a lacey appearance and tough texture. It has deep green, long, thin leaves with ruffled edges and is most often used as a garnish.

Mustard greens/turnip greens: Mustard greens are dark-green in color and have a sharp mustard flavor. Turnip greens are similar to mustard greens but have a purplish tint and a mellow, turnip flavor.

SHOPPING: Look for fresh plump, crisp leaves. Do not buy greens with yellow or pitted leaves or thick fibrous stems. Shop with your nose. Greens with a strong odor have deteriorating leaves.

STORING: Place in a plastic bag and refrigerate. Greens will keep up to 5 days.

AVAILABILITY: Collard greens – Year-round, peaking December through April, Dandelion greens – Year-round, peaking in April and May, Kale – Year-round, peaking in December through February, Mustard greens – Year-round, peaking December through April, Turnip greens – Year-round, peaking in October through March.

Horseradish

SHOPPING: Buy horseradish that is hard and free of spongy or soft spots. Overly large horseradish may be fibrous. Sprouting, green-tinged roots may be bitter.

STORING: Upon arriving home, wrap horseradish in a slightly dampened dishtowel, then a dry one, and refrigerate. This root will keep up to 2 weeks in the refrigerator.

AVAILABILITY: Harvested early spring and late fall.

To use: Cut off only as much as you need. Using a vegetable peeler, remove the outer skin. It is best to wear gloves when handling horseradish and to use a blender or food processor to grind it.

Jicama

Raw jicama is crunchy with an apple-like, nutty flavor similar to a water chestnut. It is sometimes referred to as a Mexican potato because when cooked it has a potato-like texture.

SHOPPING: Select medium-sized jicamas with smooth, unblemished skin. Scratch the skin with your nail. It should be thin, and the flesh underneath should be juicy. Do not buy jicamas with cracks or bruises or ones that are shriveled or sticky.

STORING: When stored uncovered in a cool, dry place, jicama will keep up to 3 weeks. Once you cut into it, it will keep 1 week, refrigerated and wrapped in plastic.

AVAILABILITY: Year-round, imported from Mexico and South America.

To use: Peel like you would a potato using a vegetable peeler.

Kohlrabi

Kohlrabi has two parts—a root and leaves. The root is spicy like a radish and somewhat sweet like a turnip. Its leaves are similar to turnip greens.

SHOPPING: Do not buy extremely large kohlrabi. They are tough and have a strong taste. Choose small to medium specimens with small, smooth bulb-stems and firm, green leaves.

STORING: The leaves will only keep for a few days. Remove the leaves and store them separately. The root, however, will keep for several weeks in the refrigerator.

AVAILABILITY: Year-round, peaking in early summer.

To use: The leaves should be removed. Discard the stems and any tough center ribs. The leaves can be cooked like greens. Steam the bulb to loosen its skin. Then pare away the tough outer skin before cooking.

Leeks

SHOPPING: Good quality leeks are firm and smooth with crisp, brightly colored leaves and flexible stems. Do not buy leeks with blemishes or ones that have withered, yellowed, or slimy leaves. Leeks with a rounded rather than a flat bottom are old.

STORING: Remove and discard the tough, dark green tops. To refrigerate, wrap leeks in damp paper towels and place them in a plastic bag. They should last up to 1 week. Do not store leeks with soft fruit because they produce odors that will be absorbed by soft fruits.

AVAILABILITY: Year-round, peaking in October through May.

To use: Place cut pieces of leek into a large bowl filled with warm water. Using your fingers, whirl the pieces of leek vigorously to remove any sandy grit. The sand should sink to the bottom of the bowl. Scoop out the leeks and transfer them to a colander. Rinse and drain thoroughly. If the bottom of the bowl has a lot of grit, repeat the process.

Lettuce

Butterhead lettuce (Boston, Bibb): This type of lettuce has small, round, loosely formed heads with soft, buttery-textured leaves. Its outer leaves are pale-green in color, and its inner leaves are pale, yellow-green. It has a sweet and succulent flavor.

Iceberg: This lettuce, also known as crisphead, was dubbed iceberg during the 1920s when California growers shipped it covered with crushed ice. This lettuce has a solid head of tightly wrapped leaves. It is crisp, succulent, and wilt-resistant with a neutral, watery flavor.

Looseleaf: Supermarkets typically carry green and red leaf lettuce. This variety is crisper and more fully flavored than iceberg lettuce, although more perishable. Its leaves branch from a single stalk rather than forming a tight head.

Romaine: Romaine has an elongated head of dark green, narrow, stiff leaves with a distinctive rib that reaches almost to the tip of the leaf.

SHOPPING: Any type of lettuce should be free of blemishes. Its leaves should be an even green in color with little browning on the outside edges. When buying looseleaf lettuce, look for whole, unbroken leaves with no wilting or spoilage at either the tip or base of the leaves. Do not buy iceberg lettuce that lacks green color or is irregular in shape. Romaine with rust, oversized butts, or large, strong, milky ribs is not good quality. Select romaine that is cut close to the leaf stems and is free of browning. Good romaine lettuce will have deep green leaves all the way down to its center.

STORING: Do not wash lettuce until ready to use. Store whole heads in plastic bags. This helps them retain their natural moisture and stay crisp. Romaine and iceberg lettuce will keep up to 1 week in the refrigerator. Butterhead varieties and leaf lettuce will keep 3 to 4 days. Do not store lettuce with apples, bananas, or pears, as these fruits emit ethylene gas that will turn lettuce brown.

AVAILABILITY: Year-round.

To prepare: Lettuce must be washed thoroughly, particularly bibb lettuce which can be quite sandy. Do not soak lettuce in water. This only softens the leaves. One of the greatest conveniences invented for the kitchen is the salad spinner. It gives freshly washed leaves a little spin and dries them in no time. If you don't have one, consider purchasing one. It's a real time saver.

Mushrooms

Mushrooms are most mysterious. They can be delicious, deadly poisonous, or have hallucinogenic properties. There are over 300 types of cultivated mushrooms, not including the many edible varieties that grow in the wild. Every year, more varieties of mushrooms are introduced. Following are the varieties most commonly found in supermarkets:

Chanterelle: Depending upon the variety, the cap of a chanterelle can be yellow, orange, white, brown-gray, or black. Its caps are cup-shaped, wavy, and firm. Its underside has wrinkles, not gills. This mushroom has soft flesh and an apricot-like fragrance. It grows in the wild and is also cultivated.

Cremini: The cremini is quite similar to the common white mushroom; however, they have a deeper flavor. Cremini mushrooms have naturally light tan to rich brown caps, are firm, and reasonably priced with a good shelf life.

Enoki: This variety is a cultivated Japanese mushroom that grows in small, fragile clusters. It has white stems topped by tiny caps. Enoki mushrooms have a mild, light flavor with a slight crunch. This mushroom is normally eaten raw in salads or used as a garnish.

Lobster: This mushroom gets its name from its brightly colored, pimply surface and knobby appearance. Lobster mushrooms have a fishy aroma and crisp, white flesh.

Morels: This mushroom may be tan, yellow, or black. It has short, thick, hollow stems topped with honeycomb-like, pointed caps. Morels have a rich, nutty flavor and a woodsy fragrance.

Porcini: This mushroom has fat, firm, curved, white stalks and broad, dark brown caps. Porcini mushrooms have a spongy layer of long, tiny tubes underneath the caps. With a rich, meaty flavor, porcini are delicate enough for sauces yet perfect with grilled steaks.

Portobello: Portobello mushrooms are large, fully mature cremini mushrooms with caps that span 6 inches in diameter. This mushroom has a long growing cycle, which gives them a solid, meat-like texture and flavor. Supermarkets sell these whole, caps only, or already sliced.

Shitakes: This mushroom originated in Japan and is the most widely used mushroom in Japanese and Chinese cuisine. Shitakes have wide, umbrella-shaped caps with open veils and tan gills. They range in color from tan to dark brown. The caps of shitake mushrooms are soft and spongy with a meaty, chewy texture. Shitakes have a smoky aroma. Their stems are too woody to eat.

White: This is the most common mushroom found in American supermarkets. White mushrooms range in color from creamy white to beige and can be eaten raw or cooked. The caps of freshly picked white mushrooms fit closely to the stem. Mature white mushrooms have open veils and darkened caps. Fresh whites have a delicate flavor and are good in salads. Mature whites have a richer, deep flavor and are more suitable for cooking.

SHOPPING: Mushrooms should have spongy, firm, and fleshy caps. Do not buy mushrooms if they have black spots or worms. Avoid mushrooms with a discolored, shriveled appearance. Wet or slimy mushrooms are passed their prime.

STORING: Most mushrooms will remain fresh for 3 to 5 days. Slicing mushrooms decreases their shelf life. Store them whole. If your supermarket sells mushrooms pre-packed in 1-pint containers, remove the plastic wrap when you get home and put the mushrooms in a paper bag or wrap them in paper towels. Vacuum-sealed mushrooms should keep for 7 days if refrigerated.

AVAILABILITY: Year-round, Chanterelles – season in the spring, summer, and fall, Lobster mushrooms – peak in August through October, Porcini mushrooms – peak in May and June and again in October, Wild morels – season in the spring.

To clean mushrooms: Either brush them with a mushroom brush or rub off any unsightly flesh. Rinse under cold, running water. While some people peel mushrooms, this is not necessary. Before using chanterelles, rinse them carefully, especially inside the wrinkles and dry them with paper towels. Before using fresh porcini, scrape any dirt off the stalks and wipe them clean with damp paper towels. Porcini mushrooms should be used as soon as possible. If you keep them for a few days, it is a good idea to stand them on their caps to prevent the tiny worms that sometimes inhabit their stalks from traveling into the caps.

Napa cabbage

This Chinese cabbage has crinkly, thick-veined, fibrous leaves. Its thin, crisp, delicate leaves are cream-colored, and it has celadon green tips. Napa cabbage has a mild, sweet taste.

SHOPPING: Select napa cabbage that has a compact head and tightly closed, crisp, green-tipped leaves. Do not buy heads with wilted, yellowed, or brown leaves.

STORING: Place napa cabbage in a plastic bag and refrigerate. It should keep 1 week. Do not store with ethylene-producing fruits like apples.

AVAILABILITY: Year-round.

Okra

Okra pods are fuzzy, deeply ridged, and usually olive-green in color. Some specialty food markets will sell red, white, and purple varieties.

SHOPPING: This vegetable is highly perishable, so it is important to select the freshest possible specimens. Choose pods that are free of bruises, uniform in color, tender but not soft, and no more than 4 inches long. Okra that is soft, shriveled, or large will be tough and fibrous. Avoid dried-out or stringy okra.

STORING: To store okra, place it in a paper bag or wrap it in paper towels, then place it in a plastic bag before refrigerating. It should keep 2 to 3 days.

AVAILABILITY: Year-round in the South. May to October in other areas. Peak season is June through August.

Onion

Onions can be classified into two different categories: spring/summer fresh bulb onions and storage onions. Fresh onions are yellow, white, or red with varied shapes—flat, top-shaped, round, or long. They have a mild, juicy taste, a thin, light-colored skin, and are often used raw. Storage onions are always round.

Bermuda: This onion is mild and red, white, or yellow in color.

Boiling: These are small, thin-skinned onions meant for cooking whole.

Green onions (scallions): These onions are pulled while their tops are still green and before a large bulb has formed.

Italian red: This onion is flat with thick layers. Its inner skin layers are deep purple. The Italian red has a sweeter flavor and a crunchier texture than other red onions.

Maui: This sweet, mild onion grows in Maui, Hawaii.

Pearl onions: These onions are small because they are planted close together and picked early. Pearl onions are as pungent as storage onions and have just as good a shelf life.

Spanish: This is the most common onion found in supermarkets. It is a mild, globe onion.

Vidalia: These onions are grown in Georgia and known for their sweet, mild flavor.

Walla Walla: This sweet, jumbo, round variety is a French onion that is grown in Walla Walla, Washington.

White: White onions have a mild flavor and papery, white skin. They are good either raw or cooked.

SHOPPING: Onions should be dry, firm, and shiny with a thin outer skin. Do not buy onions that have sprouts. They will taste bitter. The neck of an onion should be tightly closed. Do not buy onions that have dark patches, soft spots, or black mold. Examine the sprout end of Italian red onions. It often times is sunken. This is the first place spoilage will begin. Do not buy the Italian red onion if it has a soft, deeply sunken, yellow top. Good quality pearl onions will be uniform in size and have firm, clear skin. Do not buy pearl onions that have bruises or blemishes, soft or moldy spots, or that are too big. Look for scallions with medium-sized necks and white blanching that extends 2 to 3 inches above the root.

STORING: Onions should be stored in a cool, dark, dry, well ventilated place. Do not store onions and potatoes together. Potatoes give off moisture that can cause onions to spoil. Fluorescent lighting will turn pearl onions green.

AVAILABILITY: Year-round, Italian red onions – in season April through August, Pearl onions – July through March, Vidalia onions — April through mid-July, Walla Walla onions – best in June and July.

Parsnip

I just recently started cooking with parsnips. They are amazingly sweet and tasty. If you haven't used them in soups or stews, you should really give them a try.

SHOPPING: Parsnips should be small to medium, well shaped, and free of pitting. It is the age rather than the size of parsnips that determines tenderness. Old specimens that have been stored too long may be tough and woody. Do not buy shriveled or spotted parsnips. When thin and long, this vegetable tends to be stringy.

STORING: To store parsnips, wrap them in dry paper towels, place them inside a plastic bag, and refrigerate in the coldest part of the refrigerator. When stored in this manner, parsnips will keep up to 1 month.

AVAILABILITY: Parsnips are harvested after the first frost.

Peas

Garden or English: This is the name given to the familiar "peas in a pod." Peas are removed from the pod before eating since the pod is too stringy to eat. This type of pea is best when it's as small as possible.

Sugar snap or snow peas: These peas are tender and have edible pods. Sugar snap peas resemble English peas, but have smaller, smooth, curved pods, and are eaten whole.

SHOPPING: Select garden peas with bright green, velvety pods. Discernible pearl-shaped peas should barely fill the pod. Avoid overgrown peas that are flattened against each other like teeth. Do not buy immature peas that are flat, dark green, and wilted or overgrown peas that are swollen and freckled with gray spots. A yellow color indicates age or damage.

When buying snow pea pods, the miniature peas should be barely visible. Snow peas are light-green in color. Snap peas are a brilliant green. When selecting snow peas, inspect them for small circles of rot. Avoid overgrown sugar snap peas where the visible peas bulge. Do not buy pods that are broken or have white patches or soft or moldy tips.

STORING: Peas are best eaten immediately after they are picked. When stored in plastic bags and refrigerated, garden peas will last 3 to 4 days. Sugar snap or snow peas are more perishable. When stored in the same manner, they will last up to 2 days.

AVAILABILITY: Sweet young peas are available February through September, but are at peak in May. Sugar snap and snow peas – year-round.

Pepper, Chile

There are hundreds of varieties of chile peppers. Each type of chile has a unique subtle flavor in addition to its heat. As a general rule, the smaller the chile, the hotter it will be. Individual chiles from the same plant can vary in hotness, which in the U. S. is measured by the Scoville scale. Bell peppers have a value of zero and habaneros rank 200,000 to 300,000.

Anaheims: This red or green pepper is mild with long, rounded tips. Anaheims rank 1,000 on the Scoville scale.

Cherry hots: These peppers are shaped like a cherry. They are bright-red in color, very meaty, and medium hot.

Habaneros: This pepper is known for its intense heat and its sweet apple-tomato flavor. It ranks 200,000 to 300,000 on the Scoville scale. Habaneros are squat, 1 to 2 inches in length, orange in color, and shaped like a lantern.

Hungarian wax: This pepper is mild to medium hot. It is waxy-yellow in color, with small, elongated, pointed tips. When mature, Hungarian wax peppers turn light red.

Jalapeños: Jalapeños are about 2 inches long with green, blunt, oval pods. They are the most common hot pepper sold in the United States, rated medium-hot to hot, and registering 2,500 to 4,000 on the Scoville scale. Most jalapeños are green, although occasionally markets carry red ones. When smoke-dried, red jalapeños are called chipotles.

New Mexico: This pepper is fairly mild, long, and tapered and may be brown, green, red, orange, or yellow. When fresh, they are often stuffed. When dried, they are used for chili powder.

Pasillas: This is a mild, dried Mexican chile often used to make mole sauce. In Mexico, it is called chilaca. However, in California the term pasilla is incorrectly given to poblano chiles. Pasillas rank 1,000 to 2,000 on the Scoville scale.

Poblanos: This is a large chile shaped like a long, pointed heart. It is deep-green in color and is moderately hot. It is often used in chile relleños. When smoke-dried, it's called an ancho chile.

Serranos: This chile has a small, bullet-shaped pod. Serranos are commonly used in salsa and guacamole and are twice as hot as jalapeños. Serranos rank 5,000 to 15,000 on the Scoville scale.

SHOPPING: Select firm, plump chiles with shiny skin and a fresh smell. Do not buy wrinkled or soft chiles. Also, if the skin is mushy toward the stem end, or if the skin is soft, or brown, the chile will be inferior.

STORING: Refrigerate in plastic bags for up to 1 week.

AVAILABILITY: Normally year-round.

To use: It is a good idea to wear gloves when handling chile peppers. Once your hands have been in touch with hot peppers, do not touch delicate parts of your body, like lips, eye, or face.

Pepper, Sweet Bell

The most common bell pepper is green. Bell peppers are also red, yellow, orange, purple, white, and even brown. Many supermarkets now carry red, orange, and yellow bell peppers. They are sweeter than green but also more expensive.

SHOPPING: Look for fresh, firm peppers that are bright and thick-fleshed with a firm green calyx and stem. Bell peppers should feel heavy for their size. Immature green bell peppers are soft, pliable, thin-fleshed, and pale-green in color. Do not buy bell peppers with wrinkled skin or any soft or brown spots.

STORING: Sweet bell peppers will keep in the refrigerator 3 to 4 days. It is best not to wash bell peppers until you are ready to use them.

AVAILABILITY: Year-round, with peak season May through August.

Potato

There are numerous varieties of potatoes. New potatoes are immature, freshly dug potatoes that have never been kept in storage. They have thin skins and fine textured flesh.

Starchy potatoes, like russets, are high in starch. The cells in starchy potatoes separate easily during the cooking process. When cooked, they have a glistening appearance and a dry, fluffy texture. They make good baked or mashed potatoes. Starchy potatoes also have a low-sugar content, so they do not brown excessively if deep-fried.

Waxy potatoes, like red-skinned potatoes, are low in starch. They are smooth, creamy, and moist when cooked. The cells in these potatoes adhere during the cooking process, helping them hold their shape. They make good boiling or steaming potatoes.

Blue and purple: These potatoes originated in South America and have only recently been available in the United States. They have a nutty flavor, and their flesh colors range from dark blue to lavender to white.

Creamers: Also known as baby potatoes, these marble-sized potatoes are less than 1 ½ inches in diameter.

Fingerlings: Fingerlings are small, thin-skinned potatoes that are shaped like a fat finger. Normally, these potatoes have a rich, buttery texture and are excellent for baking, roasting, grilling, and steaming.

Long whites: This potato has thin, light tan skin and a firm creamy texture. When exposed to light, they have a tendency to turn green.

Round reds: Also know as the new potato, red bliss, or boiling potato, this variety has rosy red skin with dense, waxy white flesh.

Round whites: This variety has smooth, light tan skin with white flesh. An all-purpose potato, they are creamy in texture and hold their shape well after cooking.

Russet potatoes: This is the most widely used potato in the United States. Russets grown in Idaho are called the Idaho potato. Russets grown outside of Idaho are called russets. This variety has thick, netted, brown skin and white flesh. Their low-moisture, high-starch content makes them light and fluffy when cooked. Russets are good for baking, French fries, and mashing.

Yukon gold: This potato has golden flesh with a dense, creamy texture and a buttery flavor. They are the best mashing potato.

SHOPPING: Select firm, smooth, clean potatoes that have few eyes and good color. Potatoes should be blemish-free. Russets should have a net-like textured skin, oval shape, and brown color. Irregular-shaped potatoes produce more waste when peeling. Do not buy potatoes with wrinkled or wilted skin, sprouts, or cut surfaces. Avoid potatoes with soft, dark spots.

STORING: Potatoes will keep up to 2 weeks when stored in a cool, dark, well ventilated place. Prolonged exposure to light will turn potatoes green. Green potatoes contain solanine, which has a bitter flavor and can be toxic if eaten in large quantities. When stored at temperatures below 40 degrees F, potatoes become sweeter.

AVAILABILITY: Blue and purple potatoes are more available in the fall, Fingerlings – October through April, Long whites – spring through summer, New potatoes – late winter through midsummer, Round red potatoes – late summer and early fall, Russets – year-round.

Cooking tip: Peeled, uncooked potatoes will discolor. To prevent this, immerse peeled potatoes in cold water for no more than 2 hours until ready to use.

Radicchio

Radicchio looks like a small head of red lettuce. It has a distinctive, bitter flavor. Radicchio is often used in cooking, although its color turns rich brown when cooked.

SHOPPING: Select heads that have crisp, full-colored leaves. This product is expensive and, therefore, is a slow mover. Buy from a high-volume store. Do not buy radicchio if the leaves are brown or wilted.

AVAILABILITY: Year-round, with a peak season from midwinter to early spring.

Radish

Although normally eaten raw, radishes can be steamed, sautéed, or stir-fried. Their green tops are edible and add a peppery taste to salads. There are several varieties of radishes. However, most supermarkets carry only *red globes.* This radish is small, round or oval in shape with solid, crisp flesh. Red globe radishes are sold in bunches with their greens still attached or in bags with their tops removed.

SHOPPING: Select fresh, bright radishes that are firm, well formed, tender, and crisp. Skin should be smooth and unblemished. If the tops are attached, the greens should be firm and perky. When gently squeezed, radishes should feel firm. Do not buy radishes with cracks, cuts, or yellowing. If you are buying prepackaged radishes, check the bag to be sure the radishes are free of mold and excessive cracking.

STORING: If you buy radishes with their leaves attached, remove the greens before storing. The tops deteriorate first and can hasten spoilage. If not already packaged in plastic, put in a plastic bag before storing. They will keep up to 2 weeks in the refrigerator.

AVAILABILITY: Year-round, peaking during the spring.

Rhubarb

There are two types of rhubarb—*strawberry* rhubarb grown in hothouses and *cherry* rhubarb grown in fields. Rhubarb grown in fields has deeper color and more juice but is, also, more acidic. The stalks of rhubarb are edible, but the leaves are toxic if eaten in large quantity, because they contain oxalic acid. The leaves are normally removed before sale.

SHOPPING: Select firm, crisp rhubarb with brightly colored stalks. Look at the ends of the stalks. Do not buy rhubarb with bruises or blemishes.

STORING: Place in a plastic bag and refrigerate for up to 1 week.

AVAILABILITY: Seasons in spring and summer. Hothouse rhubarb is available mid-January through mid-April.

Shallots

Shallots have a garlic-like head that is composed of many cloves. Their skin color varies from golden brown to gray to rose-red, and their off-white flesh is tinted with magenta. Shallots have a firm texture and a sweet, aromatic, yet pungent, flavor.

SHOPPING: Look for large, plump, firm, well shaped shallots. Do not buy this vegetable if it is wrinkled, or sprouting, or shows any signs of black mold.

STORING: Shallots, when stored in a cool, dry, well ventilated place, will keep up to 1 month.

AVAILABILITY: Fresh green shallots are available in the spring. Dry shallots are available year-round.

Spinach

There are two main types of spinach—flat-leafed and curly. Flat-leafed spinach has a milder flavor, especially in the baby variety. The leaves of curly spinach are firm and dark. It is normally sold in bunches and has a strong iron flavor with a slightly bitter aftertaste.

SHOPPING: Spinach should be deep-green in color with crisp, perky leaves. Do not buy spinach if it has yellow or broken leaves. Shop with your nose. If you smell an unpleasant odor, pass. If you are buying bagged spinach, inspect the bag carefully. Spinach deteriorates quickly. Also, check the "Best if Used by Date" to be sure it hasn't passed its freshness date.

STORING: Place in plastic and store for 2 to 3 days in the refrigerator.

AVAILABILITY: Year-round.

Sprouts

Sprouts can grow from the seeds of vegetables like broccoli and radishes, from grains like alfalfa, or from beans like soybeans. Sprouts vary in taste and texture. Radish and onion sprouts are spicy. Soybean and mung sprouts are hardy and will hold up nicely when cooked. Alfalfa and pea sprouts are delicate and used in salads and sandwiches.

One of the most common sprouts found in a grocery store is the alfalfa sprout. They are thread-thin and white with tiny green tops, a subtle nutty flavor, and crisp texture. Another common variety is mung. These bean sprouts are 2 inches long with small, light yellow leaves and silvery white shoots. They have a high-water content and a subtle nutty flavor.

Other sprouts that are occasionally available are clover, dill, lentil, onion, pea, pumpkin, radish, soybean, sunflower, and wheat.

SHOPPING: Look for crisp sprouts with firm, moist, white roots. Do not buy slimy, dark, or musty-smelling sprouts.

STORING: Hardy sprouts will keep in the vegetable crisper up to 3 days. Delicate sprouts generally last about 2 days.

AVAILABILITY: Year-round.

Sweet potato

There are three common varieties of sweet potato, also called the yam, the *Beauregard, Garnets,* and *Jewels.* The most popular variety, the Beauregard, is uniform in size and shape with smooth skin and deep-orange flesh. Garnets, more popular with organic farmers, have a garnet-colored skin, orange-yellow flesh, and excellent flavor. Jewels have a more orangey skin and deep-orange flesh.

SHOPPING: Look for firm sweet potatoes, with smooth skins that are free of bruises and cracks. Avoid wrinkled or sticky sweet potatoes or ones that have sprouts.

STORING: Do not refrigerate sweet potatoes, but keep them in a cool, dark place. This vegetable will keep 1 to 2 weeks.

AVAILABILITY: Year-round.

Swiss Chard

The leaves of Swiss chard are similar to beet greens but are larger, flatter, and wider with a mild flavor and texture similar to spinach.

SHOPPING: Select Swiss chard that has fresh, green leaves that are moist and crisp. Do not buy this vegetable if its leaves are yellowed, wilted, or browned. If the leaves have tiny holes, this is an indication of insect damage.

STORING: Do not wash Swiss chard until ready to use. Wrap it in damp paper towels, place it in a plastic bag, and store it in the refrigerator. It will keep 3 to 5 days.

AVAILABILITY: April through November.

Tomatillo

The tomatillo is native to Mexico. It is greenish-yellow in color, 1 to 2 inches in diameter, and encased in papery husks.

SHOPPING: Choose firm, dry tomatillos that fit tightly into their husks. Check to be sure the husks are dry to the touch. Underneath the husk, a tomatillo should be green, which is an indication it is not totally ripe—its preferred state. Do not buy sticky or yellow tomatillos.

STORING: If kept in their husks, placed in a paper bag, and refrigerated, tomatillos will keep up to 1 month.

AVAILABILITY: Year-round.

Tomato

Hothouse tomatoes represent one-fourth of the tomatoes sold in supermarkets.

SHOPPING: Select firm and plump tomatoes. Do not buy pale, spotted, or mushy specimens. Avoid tomatoes with blemishes or cracks. Color is a good indicator of freshness. Pick brightly colored tomatoes. My father taught me to shop with my nose. Smell the stem end of the tomato. If it's ripe, it will smell like a tomato. Ripe tomatoes should give slightly when pressed.

STORING: Tomatoes must be treated gently. Place only ripened tomatoes in the refrigerator. Cool temperatures slow the ripening process. To ripen, place tomatoes at room temperature stem side down. To hasten the ripening process, place tomatoes in a paper bag and keep at room temperature.

AVAILABILITY: Year-round.

Smell the stem end of the tomato. If it's ripe, it will smell like a tomato.

CAROL ANN'S DAD

Turnip and Rutabaga

Turnips have a smooth, white, purple-tinged skin with several circles of ridges at the base of their leaves. Their flesh is normally white. Young turnips have a delicate, slightly sweet flavor. As they age, their taste becomes stronger and their texture becomes woody. Rutabagas are larger and rounder than turnips and their flavor is sweeter.

SHOPPING: Turnips should feel heavy for their size. Look for smooth, firm, unblemished skin and fresh green leaves. Do not buy turnips that are larger than 3 inches in diameter because they may be woody. When buying rutabaga, select specimens with smooth skin that feel heavy for their size. When a rutabaga is bruised or cut, it means it has been in storage too long.

STORING: Place turnips in a plastic bag and refrigerate for 1 week. Place rutabaga in a plastic bag and refrigerate for 2 weeks.

AVAILABILITY: Turnips – year-round, peaking in October through March, Rutabaga – in season September through June.

Wasabi

Wasabi roots are grated to make a smooth, green paste, which is used as a condiment for sashimi and sushi.

SHOPPING: Look for whole firm roots. Avoid roots that are slimy or deteriorating.

STORING: Place in water and store in the refrigerator. Wasabi lasts only a few days.

AVAILABILITY: Only occasionally available in specialty food markets.

To use: Wash wasabi and scrub it with a brush. Carefully peel and grate.

Watercress

SHOPPING: Buy watercress that has deep green, whole leaves. Shop with your nose. Smell the watercress. If it has an unpleasant odor, do not buy it.

STORING: Remove the rubber band that holds the stems together. Wash, spin dry in a salad spinner, place in a plastic bag, and refrigerate. Keeps up to 3 to 4 days.

AVAILABILITY: Year-round.

Winter Squash

Acorn squash: The skin of an acorn squash is buff-colored, orange, or dark green. Its flesh is sweet and a bit stringy.

Buttercup squash: This squash has a stocky shape and a turban-like top that enlarges as the squash matures. When baked, it tastes like roasted chestnuts and sweet potatoes.

Butternut squash: This squash has smooth skin and a thick neck that attaches to a bulbous bottom. Its flesh is a blazing orange, and it has a creamy texture when cooked.

Hubbard: Found in a variety of colors ranging from bluish, gray, orange, dark green, and light green, the Hubbard squash has a teardrop shape.

Pumpkin: This is a name given to hard-skinned squash. In the United States, it refers to a large, rounded, orange squash that is used for jack-o'-lanterns. Miniature pumpkins can be cream or orange in color.

Spaghetti squash: This squash has a golden yellow color with a thin, hard shell. Its flesh has a lightly sweet, mild flavor and, once steamed or cooked, resembles pasta.

SHOPPING: Buy rock-hard squash. When you press hard on squash, it should not give to pressure. Its skin should be matte, not shiny. Select squash with firm, full, cork-like stems. Avoid specimens that have skinny or green stems. When buying butternut squash, look for small bottoms and a long neck. Do not buy squash with soft spots or bruises.

STORING: Store squash in a cool, dry place. Thick-skinned squash can last for months. Squash with soft, moist flesh surrounding the seedpod deteriorate more quickly.

AVAILABILITY: Year-round, but September and October are prime months.

Zucchini, Summer Squash, and Squash Blossoms

Zucchini have a deep green color. *Yellow crooknecks* have thick warty skin, curved necks, sweet flavor, and crunchy texture. Some newer varieties of the crookneck are straight with thin, soft skin. *Squash blossoms* are extremely perishable. They are sometimes found in specialty food markets.

SHOPPING: Select small to medium squash with shiny, taut skin. If the skin is lightly scratched or bruised, it will not compromise the quality of the squash. Do not buy overly large squash or ones with pitted skin or a spongy texture.

STORING: Place in plastic bags and store for 2 to 3 days in the refrigerator.

AVAILABILITY: Year-round, but peak season is spring to summer.

When your Kitchen Caters
a large gathering

Entertaining a crowd is manageable with proper planning. One of the hardest parts about entertaining is knowing how much food to prepare. Following are guidelines we used in our delis to calculate the amounts necessary to feed a crowd of 50.

FOOD	AMOUNT PER SERVING	APPROXIMATE AMOUNT FOR 50
Coffee	one (6-ounce) serving	1 pound makes 50 servings
Punch	one (6-ounce) serving	9 to 10 quarts
Rolls	1 ½ per person	6 dozen
Butter		1 to 1 ½ pounds
Finger Sandwiches	4 per person	16 dozen
Soup	one (6 to 8-ounce) serving	2 ½ to 3 gallons
Palate Refresher	⅓ cup per person	17 cups
Ham (boneless-cooked)		
Meal	one (4-ounce) serving	12 pounds
Reception	2 to 3 ounces per serving	7 to 9 pounds
Beef (boneless top round for roasting and slicing)		
Meal	about 6 ounces per serving	20 pounds
Reception	3 to 4 ounces per serving	10 to 13 pounds
Meat and cheese trays		
Meat	2 ounces per serving	6 pounds
Cheese	1 ounce per serving	3 pounds
Main Course Entrée (boneless meat or fish, depending upon richness or units or parts of units)		
	4 to 8 ounces per serving	12 to 25 pounds
Sauce for Entrée	1 to 2 ounces per serving	½ to 1 gallon
Pasta as a Small Course (dry pasta)		
	6 to 8 servings per pound	6 to 8 pounds
Chicken Salad		
Meal	1 cup serving	3 gallons
Reception	½ cup serving	1½ to 2 gallons
Tossed Green Salad	1 cup serving	10 heads (25-ounces) iceberg 10 bags (10-ounces) spinach
Salad Dressing	2 ounces per serving	1 gallon
Side Dishes—Potato Salad, Cole Slaw, Baked Beans		
	½ cup per serving	1½ to 2 gallons
Cooked starch	2 ounces per serving	6 pounds
Vegetable	½ cup per serving	1½ to 2 gallons or 12½ pounds

FOOD	AMOUNT PER SERVING	APPROXIMATE AMOUNT FOR 50
Cheese Course (one cheese or a selection of cheeses)		
	3 ounces per serving	9 ½ pounds
Crackers	4 per serving	2 to 2 ½ pounds
Potato Chips	1 ounce per serving	3 pounds
Olives or Pickles		2 quarts
Mixed Nuts		1 ½ pounds
Mints		
Pillow		1 pound
Wafer		1 ½ pounds

For Desserts:

Ice Cream	½ cup	2 gallons
8 to 10-inch cake		
White or lemon (serves 8 to 12 people)		6 cakes
Rich cakes, like cheesecakes or dense		
chocolate cakes (serves 14 people)		4 cakes
Fruit tart (serves 6 people)		8 to 9 cakes
Cookies, petit fours,		
or dessert truffles	2 per person	8 to 9 dozen

The above suggestions work well if you are plating your meals and are in charge of portion control. If you plan to serve buffet style, increase portions about 10 percent to ensure you'll have adequate amounts.

Fruit Platters

It's easier than you might imagine to assemble attractive fruit platters. And it's lots of fun. When I first started, I was uptight about the finishing touches. An experienced deli professional advised, "Just relax and have fun. When it's time to add the garnish, let your creative juices flow. Do something funky." You can purchase deli platters with fitted covers at good party stores.

FRUIT	APPROXIMATE YIELD
1 pineapple (3 to 4-pounds)	40 chunks
1 cantaloupe (4-pounds)	36 chunks
1 honeydew (2-pounds)	36 chunks
1 seedless watermelon (4 to 5-pounds)	48 chunks
1 pound seedless green grapes	12 to 15 clusters
1 pound seedless red grapes	12 to 15 clusters
1 pound strawberries	20 berries

SHOPPING: The most important part of serving a fruit platter is fresh fruit. For Tips on Selecting Superior Fruits see Page 300.

SERVING PINEAPPLE IN SHELL: Place the pineapple on a cutting board and with a large knife cut it into fourths from the base through the green top. Remove the core and loosen the pineapple from its shell using a sharp paring knife. Slice each quarter into 5 triangular-shaped wedges. Cut each wedge in half by slicing the wedges down the center. Place frilly picks in each pineapple piece. If making a large tray, pineapple prepared in this manner makes an attractive centerpiece.

PREPPING FRUIT: Cut cantaloupe and honeydew melon in half with a large utility knife and scrape out the seeds with a spoon. Remove the peel and cut the fruit into bite-size chunks or use a melon baller to make nice round balls. Cut the watermelon in half with a large utility knife and remove the peel. Cut into bite-size chunks. If the watermelon is not seedless, use a paring knife to remove the seeds. Wash grapes thoroughly. Remove any shriveled or dried grapes. Using cooking scissors, snip grapes into small clusters. Wash strawberries, leaving the stems on.

ARRANGING FRUIT ON TRAY: Delis typically line platters with leaf lettuce or romaine before arranging the fruit on top. I like using kale leaves to separate the different fruits into sections. Kale helps prevent the juices from running into other sections. Kiwifruit, star fruit, and berries are fun to use as garnish. When cutting your cantaloupe for the tray, try cutting it in half using a zigzag pattern, then scoop out the rind, making a bowl. This zigzag bowl makes an attractive centerpiece for serving dip. Serves 25. See recipes for fruit dips on Page 368.

Vegetable Platters

VEGETABLE	WEIGHT	APPROXIMATE NUMBER OF PREPARED PIECES
Asparagus	1 pound	30 spears, ends and scales removed
Broccoli	2¾ pounds	45 (1¼-inch) florets
Carrots	1 pound	65 (3 X ½-inch) sticks, peeled
Cauliflower	4¾ pounds	75 (1¼-inch) florets
Celery	1¾ pounds	100 (4 X ½-inch) sticks
Cherry Tomatoes	1 pint (¾ pound)	25 (1-inch) tomatoes
Cucumber	1¾ pounds	45 (4 X ¾-inch) spears, unpeeled and unseeded
Green Bell Pepper	7 ounces	24 (3½ X ½-inch) sticks
Jicama	1¼ pounds	40 (4 X ½-inch) sticks, peeled
Mushrooms	1 pound	20 whole (1 to 1½-inch) caps
Pea Pods	¼ pound	30 pods
Jerusalem artichokes	1 pound	50 (¼-inch) slices, unpeeled
Zucchini	1¼ pounds (three 6-inch)	35 (½-inch) slices, unpeeled
Yellow Squash	1¼ pounds (three 6-inch)	35 (½-inch) slices, unpeeled

SHOPPING: Use any combination of vegetables you prefer. When shopping, select firm, unblemished vegetables; i.e., avoid cauliflower that has black spots. Mushrooms should have closed caps and not be wrinkled, spongy, or spotted. For Tips on Selecting Superior Vegetables see Page 315.

PREPPING VEGETABLES: What is most important when serving crudités is clean, crisp vegetables. Wash and cut the vegetables into the desired shapes and sizes. Blanch asparagus, broccoli, and pea pods for a brighter color. To blanch, plunge vegetables into a saucepan of boiling water for no more than 2 minutes. Remove the vegetables and immediately plunge them into ice water to retard cooking. Drain and pat the vegetables dry with paper towels. A hint for celery: My mother taught me to de-string celery by using a small paring knife and lifting the strings from the celery ends by pulling them up and off. Soak celery and carrot sticks in ice water for 30 minutes to make them extra crispy. Soak Jerusalem artichokes in a solution of 1 tablespoon lemon juice and 1 quart water for about 10 minutes to prevent darkening. Drain and pat dry with paper towels.

SERVING: Allow 4 to 8 pieces per person. If you are using the crudités as a relish, plan on 4 pieces per person. If it's used as a salad, increase that number to 8 per person. Delis typically line platters with leaf lettuce or romaine before arranging the vegetables on top. I like using kale to separate the different vegetables into sections. Cherry tomatoes, olives, and cherry peppers make fun garnishes. Try hollowing out a green, red, or yellow bell pepper to use as containers for serving dip. Using both a green and a red bell pepper makes a nice color contrast. Use ranch dressing or Carol Ann's Blue Cheese Dressing (recipe on Page 11) for dip.

Buying and Storing Herbs and Spices

Herbs are the fragrant leaves of annuals or perennial plants that grow in temperate zones and are used to flavor foods. They are sold dried or fresh. Dried herbs are available all year-round in the spice aisle of your supermarket. They possess a stronger, more concentrated flavor than fresh, but lose their spiciness quickly. When ground or crushed, their zest diminishes even more quickly. When substituting dried for fresh, follow these guidelines: ¼ teaspoon powdered herb = 1 teaspoon dried = 1 tablespoon fresh. Dried herbs give off more flavor when heated, so add them at the beginning of cooking. When you buy dried herbs, keep them in tightly sealed containers in a cool, dark place. Mark the date you open the jar with a black marker and keep up to 6 months.

When shopping for fresh herbs, select ones with even green color and no signs of wilting, yellowing, or insect damage. Fresh herbs should be washed before using. After washing, pat dry with paper towels. To help prolong the life of some herbs, place them in a glass of water, stems down, cover with a plastic bag, secure the glass with a rubber band, and refrigerate. Change the water every 2 days. This works nicely with basil, cilantro, mint, and parsley. Fresh herbs lose their flavor if you cook them too long, so they should be added towards the end of cooking.

Allspice: Known as Jamaica pepper, allspice comes from the pea-size berries of evergreen pimiento trees. The dried berries are dark brown and can be purchased whole or ground. This spice tastes of cloves, cinnamon, and nutmeg.

Basil: A member of the mint family, the taste of basil is a cross between licorice and cloves. Although it is a summer herb, it is available year-round in supermarkets in both a fresh and dried form. When buying fresh basil, choose evenly colored leaves that show no sign of wilting or yellowing. To store, wrap the leaves in damp paper towels, place in a plastic bag, and refrigerate.

Bay leaves: Most often used to flavor soups, stews, vegetables, and meats, bay leaves, also known as bay laurel, have a complex flavor—a combination of eucalyptus, mint, lemon, and fresh-cut grass. There are two varieties— *Turkish* and *Californian.* The

Turkish variety has a more subtle flavor. Bay leaves are always available dried, although fresh leaves can sometimes be found in the produce department.

Caraway seeds: Most often used in German cuisine, these seeds have a warm, nutty flavor with a delicate touch of anise. A member of the parsley family, these tiny brown seeds are hard, ridged, tapered, and slightly curved.

Cardamom seeds: Native to India, cardamom has a warm, spicy sweet flavor and pungent aroma. A member of the ginger family, cardamom can be purchased in the pod or ground. While ground is more convenient, it is not as flavorful. You can grind the entire pod or remove the seeds from the pod and grind them separately. A mortar and pestle works nicely for this purpose.

Chervil: A member of the parsley family, chervil can be used like parsley. This aromatic herb has curly, dark green leaves that resemble ferns and an elusive anise flavor.

Chili powder: Most often used in Southwestern cuisine, chili powder is a blending of many spices—dried chiles, garlic, oregano, cumin, coriander, and cloves.

Chives: Related to the onion and leek, this herb has slender, vivid green hollow stems and a mild onion flavor. It is available fresh year-round, and when stored in plastic, will keep 1 week in the refrigerator. Select ones with a uniform, green color and no signs of wilting or yellowing. Chives are, also, sold freeze dried.

Cilantro: These leaves have a lively, pungent fragrance, which some describe as a mix of orange and sage. Cilantro is the name given to the lacy, green leaves of the coriander plant and are best purchased fresh. Select leaves with a bright, even color with no sign of wilting or yellowing. Cilantro will keep 1 week in a plastic bag when refrigerated. For hint on storing, see Page 342.

Cinnamon: This spice has a pungent, slightly bittersweet flavor. When dried, it curls into long quills, sold as cinnamon sticks, or it is ground into powder or sold as oil.

Cloves: One of the world's most important spices, cloves are the dried, unopened flower bud of the tropical evergreen clove tree. Reddish brown and nail-shaped, they are sold whole or ground.

Coriander: Related to the parsley family, coriander is known both for its seeds and its leaves, which are called cilantro. The tiny, yellow-tan coriander seeds are lightly ridged and have the aroma of lemon, sage, and caraway. It is sold ground or whole. When whole, it is used for pickling.

Cumin: Cumin is the dried fruit of a plant from the parsley family. Its aromatic, nutty-flavored seeds can be white, black or amber. The white and amber seeds are similar in flavor, but black cumin seeds have a more complex, peppery flavor. It is also sold ground.

Curry powder: Curry is actually a powdered blend of up to 20 different spices, herbs, and seeds. Among those are cardamom, chiles, cinnamon, cloves, coriander, cumin, fennel seed, fenugreek, mace, nutmeg, red and black pepper, poppy and sesame seeds, saffron, tamarind, and turmeric. It comes in two varieties—standard and *Madras*, which is the hotter of the two. Curry powder should only be stored up to 2 months.

Dill: Dill weed is sold fresh, dried, and as seeds. When fresh, dill will not look crisp. Select bunches with deep green leaves with no sign of rot or yellowing. When dried, it is sold as dill weed. Dill seed is the dried fruit of this plant. When heated, it has a stronger, more pungent flavor than the leaves.

Fennel: Fennel seeds come from the common fennel plant. The seeds can be purchased whole or ground and taste like licorice. To use fennel in its fresh form, see Page 322.

Ginger: Ground ginger sold in the spice section of your supermarket is quite different from fresh ginger and is not a good substitute. It is the spice used in gingerbread cookies and ginger ale. For tips on using fresh ginger, see Page 323.

Lemon grass: One of the most important flavorings in Thai and Vietnamese cooking, lemon grass has long, thin, gray-green leaves and a woody scallion-like base. Avoid ones with blemishes. Store fresh lemon grass in the refrigerator, tightly wrapped in a plastic bag, for up to 2 weeks.

Mace: Mace is the bright red membrane that covers the nutmeg seed. After it is removed from the seed, it is dried and ground. This turns it a yellow-orange color. It is sold ground or whole. Mace tastes and smells like a strong version of nutmeg.

Marjoram: The most common type of marjoram sold in supermarkets is **sweet marjoram,** a member of the mint family. It is a summer herb with oval, inch-long, pale green leaves. It is spicy, sweet, and intense yet light.

Mint: The two most popular varieties of mint are **peppermint** and **spearmint**. It is sold dried, fresh, or as an extract. Peppermint has bright green leaves, purple-tinged stems and a peppery taste. Spearmint has true green leaves and a milder flavor and aroma. It is sold year-round but is more readily available in the summer. Choose leaves with even coloring that show no signs of wilting.

Mustard: Mustard greens are a member of the same family as broccoli. Its seeds are white (or yellow), brown, or black. The white seed is the main ingredient in American style mustard, while the brown are used for pickling, as a seasoning, and in European and Chinese mustards. The seeds are sold whole or ground into powder.

Nutmeg: This herb comes from the nutmeg tree. When picked, its fruit is split to expose the seed. The membrane surrounding the seed is removed and becomes the spice mace. The seed is sold ground or whole. Nutmeg has a warm, spicy, sweet flavor and aroma.

Oregano: This herb belongs to the mint family and is related to marjoram and thyme. Oregano is sold either fresh or dried. It has a similar taste to marjoram but is not as sweet and has a stronger, more pungent flavor and aroma. When buying this fresh, select bright green bunches with no sign of wilting or yellowing. It can be refrigerated when placed in a plastic bag for 3 days.

Paprika: Paprika is a powder made from sweet red pepper pods. Its color can vary from bright orange-red to deep blood-red and its flavor from mild to hot. Most supermarkets carry a mild paprika. More pungent varieties can be found at gourmet or ethnic shops.

Parsley: Sold fresh or dried, the most popular varieties are the *curly-leaf* parsley and *Italian* or *flat leaf* parsley. Curly-leaf is in most supermarkets; Italian is harder to find. Select bunches with bright green leaves and no sign of wilting. Wash parsley, shake off excess moisture, wrap in paper towels, then in plastic, and refrigerate up to 1 week.

Pepper: The world's most popular spice comes from berries found in grape-like clusters on the pepper plant. Peppercorns are black, white, or green. When picked before fully ripe and dried, it shrivels and turns dark. This black peppercorn is the strongest—slightly hot with a hint of sweetness. The white peppercorn is ripened, then the skin is removed before drying, resulting in a milder flavor and a light tan color. Black or white peppercorns are available whole, cracked, or coarsely or finely ground. Whole peppercorns will keep for 1 year, while ground pepper is best used within 4 months. Information on the green peppercorn is found on Page 179.

Rosemary: Part of the mint family, rosemary has silver-green, needle-shaped leaves and the flavor of lemon and pine. It is available fresh, dried (whole leaf), or powdered.

Saffron: The world's most expensive spice, saffron comes from the yellow-orange stigmas of the purple crocus. Each flower has only three stigmas, which are hand-picked and then dried. It is sold in threads or powdered. When powdered, it loses its flavor quickly. The threads should be crushed just before using.

Sage: Sage has narrow, oval, gray-green leaves and a musty mint taste and smell. It is sold fresh or dried. When buying fresh, choose sage that looks fresh and has a musty mint smell. When dried, sage comes whole, rubbed (crumbled), and ground.

Sesame seed: These tiny, flat seeds can be brown, red, or black. A pale grayish ivory color is the most common. Possessing a slightly sweet, nutty flavor, they can be stored airtight in a cool, dark place for up to 3 months or refrigerated up to 6 months.

Tarragon: This herb has narrow, pointed, dark green leaves and an anise-like flavor. It is sold either fresh, dried, or powdered.

Thyme: The most common variety of thyme is *garden*. It has gray-green leaves that give off a minty, light-lemon aroma. It is sold fresh, dried, or powdered.

Turmeric: This herb comes from the root of a tropical plant related to ginger. It tastes, musky, peppery, gingery, and warm and has an intense yellow-orange color. It is available in supermarkets in a powdered form.

Vanilla: The vanilla bean is a pod from an orchid flower. It is cured for several months—a labor intensive, expensive process—making the vanilla bean quite pricey. You can purchase it whole, powdered, or as an extract. Vanilla extract comes pure or imitation—pure being the most expensive. Vanilla beans should be wrapped tightly in plastic wrap, placed in an airtight jar and refrigerated up to 6 months. Extracts can be stored indefinitely if sealed airtight and kept in a cool, dark place.

Examining Eggs

Shopping

Only purchase eggs that are in a refrigerated case. Open the carton to make sure the shells are clean and not cracked. Select the appropriate size for your intended use.

If you are purchasing egg products or substitutes, be sure the containers are tightly sealed.

Check the expiration date to avoid buying out-of-date eggs. Always purchase eggs that have at least two weeks before their "Sell-By" date expires. Eggs cartons with a USDA shield must bear a "pack date" (the day the eggs were washed, graded, and placed in their carton). This date is a three-digit code which represents the consecutive day of the year—so January 1 is 001, January 31 is 031, February 1 is 032, December 31 is 365.

Grading

USDA grading of eggs is voluntary. Egg packers must pay to be inspected by the USDA. If your egg carton has a USDA shield it means the eggs were checked for quality standards, grades, and size under the supervision of a trained USDA grader. State agencies also monitor quality standards for egg packers. These cartons will bear terms like "Grade A" on their cartons and will not have a USDA shield.

Eggs have three grades: U. S. Grade AA, A, or B. The grade is established by the interior quality of the egg and the condition of its shell.

GRADE AA eggs have thick, firm whites. Their yolks are high, round, and nearly free of defects. Their shells are clean and unbroken. Grade AA eggs are best for poaching or frying when appearance is important.

GRADE A eggs are similar to Grade AA eggs, but their whites are "reasonably" firm. Grade A eggs are the grade most commonly sold in supermarkets.

GRADE B eggs have thinner whites, and their yolks may be wider and flatter. Shells on Grade B eggs must be unbroken, but they may have slight stains. Grade B eggs are normally made into liquid, frozen, or dried egg products.

Sizing

Sizing on eggs is determined by its weight not its size; therefore, some eggs in the same carton may look larger or smaller than the rest.

continued next page

SIZE	MINIMUM NET WEIGHT PER DOZEN
Jumbo	30 ounces
Extra Large	27 ounces
Large	24 ounces
Medium	21 ounces
Small	18 ounces
Peewee	15 ounces

Storing and Using Eggs at Home

Refrigerate eggs immediately upon arriving home. Store them in the coldest part of your refrigerator, not in the door. Eggs should not be left out of the refrigerator for more than 2 hours.

If eggs crack on the way home from the store, break them into a clean container, cover tightly, refrigerate, and use them within 2 days.

It is not necessary to wash eggs. Washing eggs can remove their protective mineral oil coating and increase the possibility of bacteria on the shell entering the egg.

When combining eggs with other ingredients according to recipe directions, cook immediately or refrigerate and cook within 24 hours.

Questions About Appearance

Blood spots are the result of small blood vessels rupturing in the yolk at the time of ovulation. The presence of blood spots does not mean the egg is unsafe.

A clear white is the sign of a fresh egg; a cloudy white is the sign of aging.

A pink, fluorescent, or greenish egg white indicates spoilage.

The color of the yolk varies depending upon the hen's diet. If she eats more yellow-orange plant pigment, the yolk will be a darker yellow than if she eats a diet of white cornmeal.

A green ring around the yolk of a hard-boiled egg is a sign of overcooking. Scrambled eggs cooked at too high a temperature may also develop a greenish cast. The discoloration does not effect the safety of the egg.

Why are hard-boiled eggs sometimes hard to peel?

The fresher the egg, the harder it is to peel. When first laid, an egg has no air cell. This air cell, found at the larger end of the egg between the shell membranes, develops and increases in size the longer the egg is stored. Therefore, fresher eggs once hard-boiled are harder to peel, as the air cell is smaller. Older eggs have a larger air cell, making them better candidates for peeling.

Safe Cooking

If eggs crack during the hard-boiling process, they are still safe for consumption. Hard-boiled eggs should be refrigerated within 2 hours of cooking and used within 7 days.

To cook eggs safely, whether poaching, frying, baking, or hard-boiling, yolks should be firm. Scrambled eggs should not be runny.

To make a recipe safe that calls for using eggs that aren't cooked, heat the eggs along with all the liquid from the recipe over low heat, stirring constantly, until the mixture reaches 160 degrees F. Then cool, if necessary, before combining it with the other ingredients in the recipe.

Currently, egg producers are beginning to pasteurize eggs. The American Egg Board advises that eggs that have been pasteurized in their shells are safe to use without cooking in recipes. Pasteurization kills salmonella bacteria that may be present inside the shell. Look for the letter "P" on egg cartons. This designates that the eggs have been pasteurized and are safe to use raw.

To determine if egg dishes like quiche are done, test the center of the mixture with a food thermometer. When the center reaches 160 degrees F, the dish is done.

Safe Refrigeration Times

Raw eggs in shell	3 to 5 weeks
Raw egg whites	2 to 4 days
Raw egg yolks	2 to 4 days
Hard-boiled eggs	1 week
Egg substitutes, unopened	10 days
Egg substitutes, opened	3 days
Casseroles made with eggs	3 to 4 days
Eggnog, commercial	3 to 5 days
Pies, custard, and chiffon	3 to 4 days
Quiche	3 to 4 days

Pauline's Potato Salad 351

Creamy Potato Salad with Chives 352

Secret Recipe Potato Salad 353

The Original Steele's Pasta Salad . . . 354

The Best Macaroni Salad Ever 355

Asian Pasta Primavera 356

Deli Style Greek Salad 357

Three Bean Salad 358

Fiesta Black Bean, Corn,
 and Bell Pepper Salad 359

Broccoli Salad 360

Cucumber Slices in Sour Cream 360

Carol Ann's Coleslaw 361

Greek Slaw 361

Pea Salad with Ham and Cheese 362

Vegetable Medley Salad 363

Crunchy Cottage Cheese 364

Carol Ann's Deli Ham Salad 364

Antipasto Salad 365

Crab Louis 366

Chunky Turkey Salad 366

Bean Dip 367

Jalapeño Cheese Dip 367

Dill Dip 368

Honey Yogurt Dip 368

Strawberry Cream Cheese Dip 368

Carol Ann's Cheese Ball 369

Fiesta Cheese Ball 369

Holiday Cheese Ball 370

Heavenly Hash 370

Cranberry Salad 371

Waldorf Fruit Salad 371

Acapulco Salad 372

Couscous Salad 373

Oriental Chicken Salad 374

Deviled Eggs 375

Steele's Hit the Road Breakfast Burrito 376

Quiche Lorraine 377

Ham and Mushroom Quiche 378

Vegetable Quiche 379

Tomato Quiche 380

Twice Baked Potatoes 381

Dauphinois 382

Potato Pancakes (Latkes) 383

Ratatouille 384

Chicken Pot Pie 385

Old-Fashioned Krautburgers 387

Mince Pie Filling 388

Ollie's Old-Fashioned Rice Pudding . . 389

Bread Pudding with a
 Vanilla Bourbon Sauce 390

From Carol Ann's Deli

Pauline's Potato Salad

SERVES 8

This is my mother's recipe for the perfect picnic potato salad. Her mother, Gladys, passed it down to her; and she, in turn, shared it with me. My family thinks it's the best ever.

6 medium potatoes, peeled and quartered
8 hard-boiled eggs, cubed in ¼-inch pieces
6 green onions, thinly sliced
1 cup mayonnaise
1 tablespoon Dijon mustard
¾ cup pickle relish
1 ½ teaspoons salt
¾ teaspoon large grind black pepper
1 ½ teaspoons celery seed

In a large saucepan, place potatoes with just enough water to cover. Bring to a boil over medium-high heat. Reduce heat and simmer gently until pieces are tender yet remain firm when pierced with a fork, about 20 to 25 minutes. Drain, cool, and cut into bite-size pieces.

In a large bowl, combine potatoes, eggs, and green onions. In a separate bowl, combine mayonnaise, Dijon mustard, pickle relish, salt, pepper, and celery seed. Blending the spices into the mayonnaise mixture provides an even distribution of the seasonings. Fold the mayonnaise mixture into the potato mixture and mix gently. Chill for at least 4 hours, but best when chilled overnight.

*I*n 1894, Asa Candler, a druggist, bought the formula for CocaCola® for $2,300. To encourage his customers to sample his new fountain drink, he distributed handwritten tickets for free samples, originating the concept of "the coupon." The next entrepeneur to use this marketing approach was C. W. Post, who distributed the first coupon used in a grocery store in 1895. The coupon was redeemed for one cent when purchasing a box of his new healthy cereal, Grape Nuts®. Coupons caught on like wildfire during the 1930s when the Depression left Americans desparate, hungry, and pinching pennies just to survive.

Don't forget to pick up celery seed. Grandma Gladys claims its the secret ingredient.

The secret to making great potato salad is neither overcooking nor undercooking the potatoes. When preparing potatoes for boiling, keep portions as similar in size as possible. I prefer to quarter the potatoes. If quartered, boil between 20 to 25 minutes. Potatoes are done when they are tender yet remain firm when pierced with a fork. Soft, soggy potatoes make a mushy salad. Cool potatoes completely before proceeding.

Creamy Potato Salad with Chives

SERVES 8

I always liked having homemade salads in our delis. It set us apart from our competitors. We occasionally added this version to our selections because it provided a nice alternative to the traditional mustard-style potato salads. Now I find a creamy chive potato salad in almost every supermarket deli.

3 pounds new red potatoes, washed and
    cut into bite-size pieces, leave skins on
2 teaspoons Dijon mustard
2 tablespoons red wine vinegar
4 tablespoons olive oil
2 teaspoons salt
2 teaspoons large grind black pepper
1 package (8-ounces) cream cheese, softened
1 cup sour cream
4 celery sticks, finely diced
4 green onions, thinly sliced
2 packages (1-ounce) fresh chives, snipped

In a large saucepan, place potatoes with just enough water to cover. Bring to a boil over medium-high heat. Reduce heat to low and simmer gently until pieces are tender yet remain firm when pierced with a fork, about 10 to 15 minutes. Drain.

In a large bowl, mix Dijon mustard, red wine vinegar, olive oil, salt, and pepper until smooth. Add hot potatoes and toss gently to coat each potato piece. Set aside for 30 minutes to allow flavors to combine.

Beat cream cheese and sour cream until smooth. Stir in celery, green onions, and chives. Mix gently with potatoes to coat evenly. Refrigerate for at least 6 hours before serving. Best when chilled overnight.

To hard boil eggs: Place them in a saucepan and add just enough cold water to cover. Adding a dash of salt and one teaspoon of vinegar to the water helps prevent the shells from cracking. Place the saucepan over a high heat and bring the water to a boil. Cook them for at least 10 minutes once the water reaches a rolling boil.

Chives need to be refrigerated and used within 3 to 4 days of purchase for the best flavor.

When did the market become a supermarket? At the beginning of the 20th century, customers purchased their dry goods at one shop and their perishables at different specialty markets—meat at the butcher shop, bread at the bakery, produce at produce stands, and milk, of course, was delivered to their doors by the "milk man." In those days, proprietors displayed merchandise behind the counter or stocked it in back rooms, creating a "full-service environment" where clerks individually retrieved each and every item on the shopper's list. These dry goods markets carried only one brand, so consumers had no choices. A can of beans was a can of beans.

In 1916, Clarence Saunder opened the first self-service grocery store in Memphis, Tennessee. He patented his concept "self-serving store" in 1917 under the name Piggly Wiggly and issued franchises to other progressive-thinking retailers. Customers entered this self-service market through turnstiles and walked a narrow maze of shelves containing groceries. Saunder was the first to provide American shoppers with the privilege of selecting their own products. As the American shopper got up close and personal with the products she purchased, brand name and packaging recognition became important.

During the 1930's, a large number of independent groceries and chains stores switched to this concept. Seeking to gain a bigger piece of the pie, dry good operators began offering perishable products in these self-service establishments. One-stop shopping in the 1930s meant American consumers could purchase meat, dairy, fruit and vegetables, and bread all under one roof. Thus, the entrepeneurial spirit conceived the "supermarket" format, which became entrenched in America during the 1940s.

Secret Recipe Potato Salad

SERVES 8

This recipe was created by one of our in-house chefs and sold in our delis. One culinary lesson I learned the hard way is that most chefs will not share recipes. In fact, several got so possessive of their secrets, I often wondered if I needed FBI clearance just to have a peek. I feel fortunate to have latched on to this one.

The American supermarket is the product of the vision "that there should be universal access to the finest goods and services available." Ryan Mathews, The Progressive Grocer. This became painfully obvious when a group of Russian children visited our markets. They were particularly impressed with our large assortment of crayons.

3 pounds red potatoes, washed and
  cut into bite-size pieces, leave skins on
5 green onions, thinly sliced
2 celery stalks, chopped
6 slices bacon, fried crisp and crumbled
⅔ cup mayonnaise
⅔ cup sour cream
2 teaspoons Dijon mustard
2 tablespoons fresh dill, chopped
½ teaspoon salt
¼ teaspoon white pepper

In a large saucepan, place potatoes with just enough water to cover. Bring to a boil over medium-high heat. Reduce heat and simmer gently until pieces are tender yet remain firm when pierced with a fork, about 10 to 15 minutes. Drain. In a large bowl, combine potatoes, green onions, celery, and bacon.

In a medium bowl, blend mayonnaise, sour cream, Dijon mustard, dill, salt, and pepper. Fold the mayonnaise mixture into the potato mixture and toss gently to coat evenly. Best when chilled overnight.

Allow potatoes to cool slightly before adding the dressing; however, do not refrigerate them until the dressing has been added. This causes potatoes to lose some of their savor.

Be sure to pick up dill. It's the secret ingredient.

The Original Steele's Pasta Salad
with a Balsamic Vinaigrette Dressing

SERVES 12

During the 1980s, the American palate was surprised by the taste of pasta eaten cold. Pasta salads hit our country like a tidal wave. These salads were simple at first. Sparked by American ingenuity, they noodled their way into Heinz 57® varieties. This is the recipe for the first pasta salad we created and served in Carol Ann's Delis.

FOR THE DRESSING

⅛ cup fresh parsley, chopped

1 teaspoon minced garlic

¼ medium red bell pepper, cored, seeded, and chopped

1 teaspoon dried thyme

½ cup balsamic vinegar

2 teaspoons Dijon mustard

½ cup olive oil

1 cup vegetable oil

½ teaspoon salt

½ teaspoon pepper

In 1925, the average American homemaker prepared all her food at home. Just forty years later, 75 to 90 percent of the food she put on her family's table had undergone some sort of factory processing.

In a blender, combine parsley, garlic, red bell pepper, thyme, balsamic vinegar, and Dijon mustard. Process at a slow speed until red bell pepper is liquefied. Gradually add olive and vegetable oils until desired consistency is achieved. Pour into a covered container, add salt and pepper, and whisk to combine. Cover and refrigerate 1 hour.

Rotelle means "little wheels." They have a small, spoked-wheel shape. You can also use rotini, which are short spiral-shaped pasta.

FOR THE SALAD

12 ounces tri-colored rotelle pasta, cooked al dente and drained

1 package (3½-ounces) sliced pepperoni

4 ounces mozzarella cheese, cubed

1 can (12-ounces) large ripe olives, halved

5 green onions, thinly sliced

16 cherry tomatoes, halved

½ large green bell pepper, cored, seeded, and chopped

Once a pepperoni has been cut or a package of presliced pepperoni has been opened, it should be tightly wrapped in plastic and refrigerated for no more than 2 weeks.

Cook pasta according to package directions or See Tips for Cooking Pasta on Page 241. Drain, rinse with cool water, and drain again. In a large bowl, combine pasta, pepperoni, mozzarella cheese, black olives, green onions, tomatoes, and green bell pepper and mix gently. Add dressing to taste and toss gently to coat evenly.

The Best Macaroni Salad Ever

SERVES 8

I'm not fond of macaroni salads that swim in mayonnaise. This recipe is light and refreshing and stays beautifully in the refrigerator for 3 days.

In 1927, the refrigerator was introduced by General Mills. This modern convenience revolutionized the way the American housewife shopped. Before refrigeration, she shopped every day. She kept her food cold in iceboxes, which had to be regularly reloaded with ice. The refrigerator allowed her to keep foods cold and fresh for days.

FOR THE DRESSING

4 egg yolks
4 tablespoons fresh lemon juice
½ teaspoon salt
¼ teaspoon freshly ground black pepper
1 ½ cups extra light olive oil

In a blender, place egg yolks, lemon juice, salt, and pepper. While blending on a low speed, slowly add olive oil and process until mixture thickens. Transfer to a bowl, cover, and chill. Dressing stays fresh for 3 days in the refrigerator.

FOR THE SALAD

16 ounces elbow macaroni, cooked al dente and drained

Cook macaroni al dente according to the package directions or see Tips for Cooking Pasta on Page 241. Drain, rinse with cool water, and drain again.

1 ½ cups celery, diced
½ cup red bell pepper, cored, seeded, and finely diced
½ cup green bell pepper, cored, seeded, and finely diced
⅔ cup green onions, thinly sliced
6 tablespoons fresh parsley, finely minced
1 teaspoon salt
½ teaspoon white pepper

Milk was not always pasteurized. Currently, egg producers are beginning to pasteurize eggs. The American Egg Board advises that eggs that have been pasteurized in their shells are safe to use without cooking in recipes. Pasteurization kills salmonella bacteria that may be present inside the shell. Look for the letter "P" on egg cartons. This designates that the eggs have been pasteurized and are safe to use raw.

In a large bowl, combine macaroni with 1 cup dressing. Cover with plastic wrap and refrigerate for 1 hour. Add celery, red and green bell peppers, green onions, parsley, and the remaining 1 cup dressing. Stir ingredients, mixing thoroughly. Season with salt and white pepper. Refrigerate until ready to serve.

When using raw egg yolks, see Safe Cooking Tips for eggs found on Page 348.

Asian Pasta Primavera

SERVES 4 TO 6

FOR THE DRESSING

¼ cup red wine vinegar
1 tablespoon sesame oil
1 tablespoon peanut oil
1 tablespoon soy sauce
1 teaspoon hoisin sauce
2 tablespoons green onions, minced
½ teaspoon Chinese chili hot sauce
½ teaspoon minced ginger
½ teaspoon minced garlic
½ teaspoon salt

In a small bowl, combine red wine vinegar, sesame and peanut oils, soy and hoisin sauces, green onions, Chinese chili hot sauce, ginger, garlic, and salt and whisk to blend. Cover with plastic wrap and refrigerate until ready to use.

1 pound linguine, cooked al dente and drained

Cook linguine al dente according to package directions or see Tips for Cooking Pasta on Page 241. Drain, rinse with cool water, and drain again.

FOR THE SALAD

2 chicken breast halves, cooked and cubed with skin and bones removed
½ cup fresh snow peas, julienned
8 ounces bean sprouts
½ cup red cabbage, shredded
½ cup red onion, quartered and thinly sliced
½ cup chopped cashews, toasted
Sesame seeds for garnish

In a large bowl, combine linguine, cooked chicken, snow peas, bean sprouts, red cabbage, red onion, and cashews and toss gently. Add just enough dressing to moisten and toss again, evenly coating pasta. Sprinkle with sesame seeds before serving.

Independent grocers first began running weekly specials in the late 1920s in an attempt to lure shoppers away from chain stores.

Sesame oil is either light in color or dark. The lighter variety has a delicious, nutty flavor. The darker has a stronger flavor and fragrance. This recipe uses the lighter.

To toast nuts, place on a baking sheet in a 350-degree preheated oven for 5 to 10 minutes, or until golden brown. Watch closely as nuts turn from golden brown to black very quickly. I personally prefer to toast nuts by sautéing them in a small skillet that has been lightly coated with butter. For this method, stir frequently over medium heat for 5 to 7 minutes.

Deli-Style Greek Salad
in a Light Vinaigrette

SERVES 4

This is a fun and different way to use fresh vegetables from the garden. We sold this salad in our deli, and it was always a big hit. I'm quite fond of this homemade vinaigrette. Try it with a Cobb salad, potato salad, or tossed with your favorite greens.

In the late 1920s, Michael S. Cullen, a former Kroger store manager, conceived the notion of "monstrous grocery stores away from high rent districts" that would attract customers with low price. And look where that notion led.

FOR THE DRESSING

1 ½ cups safflower oil
⅔ cup lemon juice
4 teaspoons Dijon mustard
4 teaspoons sugar
1 teaspoon paprika
1 teaspoon dried basil
1 teaspoon dried tarragon
2 teaspoons minced garlic
1 teaspoon salt
½ teaspoon large grind black

In a blender, combine safflower oil, lemon juice, Dijon mustard, sugar, paprika, basil, tarragon, garlic, salt, and pepper. Cover tightly and process on a slow speed until well blended. Place dressing in a covered container and refrigerate until ready to toss salad.

Unopened olives can be stored at room temperature for up to 2 years. Once opened, they can be refrigerated in their own liquid for several weeks.

FOR THE SALAD

4 tomatoes, cut into wedges
1 large cucumber, peeled, halved lengthwise, and sliced
½ large red onion, quartered and thinly sliced
1 medium red bell pepper, cored, seeded, and cut into 1-inch strips
1 medium green bell pepper, cored, seeded, and cut into 1-inch strips
¾ cup pitted kalamata olives
1½ teaspoons minced garlic
4 ounces crumbled feta cheese

In a large bowl, combine tomatoes, cucumber, onion, red and green bell peppers, kalamata olives, garlic, and feta cheese and toss gently. When ready to serve, add just enough dressing to moisten and toss gently coating evenly.

This dressing will keep up to one week in the refrigerator.

Three Bean Salad

SERVES 6 TO 8

FOR THE DRESSING

⅓ cup canola oil
½ cup + 2 tablespoons cider vinegar
1 teaspoon minced ginger
1 teaspoon minced garlic
¾ cup sugar
1½ teaspoons salt
½ teaspoon white pepper

In a small bowl, combine canola oil, cider vinegar, ginger, garlic, sugar, salt, and pepper and whisk to combine. Cover with plastic wrap and refrigerate until ready to toss salad.

FOR THE SALAD

1 package (16-ounces) frozen wax beans, thawed
1 package (16-ounces) frozen green beans, thawed
1 can (15-ounces) red kidney beans, rinsed and drained
1 large red onion, quartered and thinly sliced

In a large bowl, combine wax, green, and kidney beans and red onion. Toss gently. Pour dressing over salad and toss to coat evenly. Cover and refrigerate until ready to serve.

Many independent grocers purchase their groceries from co-ops, an affiliation of independents that form a buying unit to buy collectively. J. Frank Grimes, a Chicago accountant, conceived the idea for a co-op in 1926. The first affiliation of small groceries began in New York when 60 grocers banded together to battle the chains.

If you want to make this with fresh green and yellow wax beans, boil in just enough salted water to cover until tender but slightly crunchy, about 2 minutes.

Be sure to pick up ginger. It's the secret ingredient.

Fresh yellow wax beans are not generally available during the hot summer months.

Fiesta Black Bean, Corn, and Bell Pepper Salad

SERVES 12

This is a colorful salad to serve as a side dish with your favorite Mexican entrées. I like to make servings for 12 so I have leftovers for lunch, or you can easily halve this recipe. We offered this salad in our delis, and it was always a smashing success.

FOR THE DRESSING

4 tablespoons olive oil
6 tablespoons lime juice
1 teaspoon salt
2 teaspoons large grind black pepper

In a small bowl, combine olive oil, lime juice, salt, and pepper and whisk to blend. Cover with plastic wrap and refrigerate until ready to toss salad.

FOR THE SALAD

1 pound black beans, soaked overnight
1 package (10-ounces) frozen corn, thawed
2 green bell peppers, cored, seeded, and chopped
2 red bell peppers, cored, seeded, and chopped
2 jalapeño peppers, seeded and chopped
8 green onions, thinly sliced
5 tablespoons fresh parsley, snipped

Drain beans. In a large kettle, place beans with just enough water to cover. Bring to a boil over high heat. Reduce heat to medium and simmer for 1 hour, or until tender. Cool beans, drain, and rinse. In a large bowl, combine beans, corn, green and red bell peppers, jalapeño peppers, green onions, and parsley. Pour dressing over salad and toss gently. Chill.

Dried beans that are labeled "quick-cooking" have been presoaked and redried before packaging. They require no presoaking and take less time to prepare. Their texture is not as firm to the bite as regular dried beans.

Dried beans can be stored in an airtight container for up to 1 year.

Kroger Grocery & Bakery Co. opened in 1932 in Indianapolis and was the first supermarket to have a parking lot. This freestanding market, completely surrounded on all four sides by a parking lot, had 75 spaces for cars. Customer surveys indicated that 80 percent of customers arrived by automobile.

Broccoli Salad

SERVES 6

FOR THE DRESSING

1 ⅓ cups mayonnaise

4 tablespoons white wine vinegar

1 teaspoon salt

½ teaspoon large grind black pepper

In a small bowl, combine mayonnaise, white wine vinegar, salt, and pepper and whisk to combine. Cover with plastic wrap and refrigerate until ready to toss salad.

FOR THE SALAD

6 cups broccoli florets

¼ cup yellow onion, chopped

7 slices bacon, fried crisp and crumbled

¾ cup shredded Cheddar cheese

In a large bowl, combine broccoli florets, onion, bacon, and Cheddar cheese. Add dressing to the broccoli mixture and toss gently.

As early as 1933, Americans found "ready-to-heat-and-eat" sections in the grocery store.

Trying to recoup lost revenue from an ever-growing trend to eat more meals in restaurants, grocers began stocking cans of clam chowder, baked beans, corned beef hash, beef stew, prepared spaghetti, chop suey, chili con carne, brown bread, and plum pudding.

Cucumber Slices in Sour Cream

SERVES 4

FOR THE SALAD

1 cucumber, thinly sliced

1 teaspoon salt

Lay cucumber slices on a plate and sprinkle with salt. Let stand at room temperature 30 minutes, transfer to a colander, and drain.

FOR THE DRESSING

½ cup sour cream

4 teaspoons white wine vinegar

1 to 2 drops Tabasco® sauce

2 tablespoons fresh chives, snipped

2 tablespoons fresh dill, snipped

Large grind black pepper to taste

If you want a more decorative look to cucumbers, leave them unpeeled and score them with a fork.

In a large bowl, combine sour cream, white vinegar, Tabasco® sauce, chives, and dill. Season to taste with pepper. Blend thoroughly. Add cucumber slices and toss gently. Cover and refrigerate at least 30 minutes before serving.

The shopping cart first appeared in a grocery store in 1937. Sylvan Goldman, owner of Standard Food Markets and the Humpty Dumpty Stores in Oklahoma City, thought like a typical grocer. If his customers could carry more, they'd buy more. He devised the first shopping cart by utilizing parts of lawn chairs to build a frame that held two hand baskets. Unfortunately, his customers didn't catch on to the idea. He had to pay "shills" to trek around his stores pretending to use the carts until eventually, his patrons got the hang of it.

Cabbage breaks down and coleslaw becomes creamier after sitting for at least 1 hour in the refrigerator.

Soaking shredded cabbage in ice-cold water for 1 hour makes it crisper. Drain thoroughly before adding dressing.

Carol Ann's Coleslaw

SERVES 4 TO 6

FOR THE DRESSING

⅔ cup mayonnaise
2 tablespoons white vinegar
2 tablespoons milk
1 teaspoon sugar
¼ teaspoon celery salt

In a small bowl, combine mayonnaise, white vinegar, milk, sugar, and celery salt and whisk to blend. Cover with plastic wrap and refrigerate until ready to toss salad.

1 package (16-ounces) coleslaw mix

In a large bowl, place coleslaw mix, pour dressing over top, and toss to combine. Cover coleslaw with plastic wrap and refrigerate for 45 minutes to 1 hour before serving.

Greek Slaw

SERVES 8

FOR THE DRESSING

¾ cup mayonnaise
⅛ cup distilled white vinegar
2 tablespoons dried oregano

In a small bowl, combine mayonnaise, white vinegar, and oregano and blend gently. Cover with plastic wrap and refrigerate until ready to toss salad.

FOR THE SALAD

1 pound green cabbage, thinly sliced
2 medium Roma tomatoes, seeded and chopped
¼ cup green bell pepper, cored, seeded, and diced
¼ cup green onions, thinly sliced
1 cup whole black olives
4 ounces feta cheese

In a large bowl, combine cabbage, Roma tomatoes, green bell pepper, green onions, black olives, and feta cheese. Add the mayonnaise mixture to the slaw mixture and toss to coat evenly.

Pea Salad with Ham and Cheese

SERVES 6

I used to make this salad for my children when they were small. It brings back fond memories of their childhoods when my days were spent flying kites and bandaging bruised knees.

FOR THE DRESSING

    1 cup mayonnaise
    1 tablespoon + ½ teaspoon white vinegar
    ½ teaspoon salt
    ½ teaspoon white pepper

In a small bowl, combine mayonnaise, white vinegar, salt, and pepper and whisk to blend. Cover with plastic wrap and refrigerate until ready to toss salad.

FOR THE SALAD

    2 packages (16-ounces) frozen peas, thawed and drained
    ½ pound Cheddar cheese, cubed the size of peas
    ½ pound honey ham, cubed the size of peas
    ¾ cup yellow onion, diced

In a large bowl, combine peas, Cheddar cheese, ham, and onion. Add dressing and toss to coat evenly.

The first precooked frozen meals were introduced at the 1939 World's Fair by General Foods® under the Birds Eye® label.

When making this recipe, I buy a ½-pound piece of honey ham from the deli. I buy the ham the day I'm going to make the salad.

Store deli ham in a zip-lock bag. It should be used within 3 days.

One of our chefs added white vinegar to mayonnaise. I like the flavor white vinegar gives to mayonnaise, so I followed her lead on this one.

Vegetable Medley Salad

SERVES 6 TO 8

FOR THE DRESSING

To cut broccoli florets: Cut the florets off at the base of their stalks. If some are larger than others, cut them so they are all about the same size.

⅜ cup mayonnaise

⅛ cup sour cream

1 teaspoon white wine vinegar

½ teaspoon dried basil

½ teaspoon minced garlic

1 teaspoon salt

¼ teaspoon black pepper

4 tablespoons Parmesan cheese

In a medium bowl, combine mayonnaise, sour cream, white wine vinegar, basil, garlic, salt, pepper, and Parmesan cheese. Whisk to blend, cover, and refrigerate until ready to toss salad.

FOR THE SALAD

To cut a cauliflower into florets: Cut the head into fourths, remove the core, then cut the florets into the desired size.

1 ½ cups broccoli florets

1 cup cauliflower florets

1 cup zucchini, cut in half lengthwise and then into half moons

1 cup yellow summer squash, cut in half lengthwise and then into half moons

1 cup carrots, peeled and thinly sliced

1 cup canned garbanzo beans, drained

4 green onions, thinly sliced

½ cup red bell pepper, cored, seeded, and chopped

½ cup yellow bell pepper, cored, seeded, and chopped

1 stalk celery, sliced

Sunflower seeds for garnish

In a large bowl, combine broccoli and cauliflower florets, zucchini, summer squash, carrots, garbanzo beans, green onions, red and yellow bell peppers, and celery. Add dressing and toss to coat evenly. Sprinkle with sunflower seeds and serve.

Curling carrots sticks makes a festive addition. Peel slices with a potato peeler and drop them in a bowl of ice water.

Crunchy Cottage Cheese

SERVES 4

½ cup carrots, peeled and finely chopped
½ cup green onions, thinly sliced
½ cup yellow bell pepper, cored, seeded, and finely chopped
½ cup tomato, seeded and finely chopped
½ teaspoon onion salt
⅛ teaspoon minced garlic
1 teaspoon lemon juice
Large grind black pepper to taste
2 cups large curd cottage cheese

In a medium bowl, combine carrots, green onions, yellow bell pepper, tomato, onion salt, garlic, and lemon juice. Add pepper to taste. Gently fold cottage cheese into the vegetable mixture.

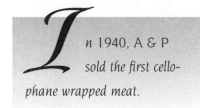

*I*n 1940, A & P sold the first cellophane wrapped meat.

Although cottage cheese will keep when opened for 10 to 30 days, when vegetables are added you should only keep it 3 days.

Carol Ann's Deli Ham Salad

MAKES 4 SANDWICHES

This is a 1-pound recipe for our ham salad. When breaking this recipe down for home use, I reduced the quantity of the mayonnaise. You can finely chop the ham if you don't have a food processor, but you get a better consistency when the ham is finely ground.

1 pound piece deli ham
3 tablespoons celery stalks, finely diced
3 tablespoons onion, finely diced
1 ½ tablespoons sweet pickle relish
½ teaspoon minced garlic
½ cup mayonnaise

Using a food processor, grind ham to the consistency of ground beef. Transfer to a large mixing bowl. Add celery, onion, pickle relish, and garlic. Mix well. Add mayonnaise and blend until thoroughly combined.

My mother used a meat grinder when she made ham salad. If you have one, this works the best.

Antipasto Salad

SERVES 6 TO 8

FOR THE DRESSING

½ cup olive oil
4 tablespoons red wine vinegar
2 teaspoons minced garlic
2 tablespoons fresh oregano, finely chopped
4 teaspoons fresh rosemary, finely chopped
2 teaspoons Dijon mustard
Salt to taste
Large grind black pepper to taste

In a large bowl, combine olive oil, red wine vinegar, garlic, oregano, rosemary, and Dijon mustard and whisk to blend. Season to taste with salt and pepper. Cover with plastic wrap and refrigerate until ready to toss salad.

FOR THE SALAD

½ pound Provolone cheese, cut into 2-inch long strips
½ pound salami, cut into 2-inch long strips
½ pound low-salt ham, cut into 2-inch long strips
½ pound prosciutto, cut into 2-inch long strips
½ cup red bell pepper, cored, seeded, and julienned
½ cup yellow bell pepper, cored, seeded, and julienned
½ cup green bell pepper, cored, seeded, and julienned
½ cup kalamata olives
½ cup canned garbanzo beans, drained
1 cup marinated artichoke hearts, drained and cut into quarters
1 cup grape tomatoes

In a large bowl, combine Provolone cheese, salami, ham, proscuitto, red, yellow, and green bell peppers, kalamata olives, garbanzo beans, artichoke hearts, and grape tomatoes. Add enough dressing to moisten and toss to coat evenly.

Many women entered the workforce during World War II when the men went to war. A 1943 edition of the Progressive Grocer, stated: "Most food merchants today who lose clerks to the draft or war jobs have two choices. Do without or employ women." The Progressive Grocer surveyed its readers and found that after the war began the number of women employed in food stores doubled to approximately 150,000. "Consensus of opinion," the magazine went on to state: "is that with proper training women can do all store work except heavy lifting."

Italian prosciuttos are labeled either "cotto", cooked, or "crudo", raw. Because the raw version has been cured, it is ready to eat. Some prosciutto connoisseurs believe prosciutto di Parma is the best.

Crab Louis

SERVES 4 TO 6

Serve in a bowl with slices of sourdough baguette or over a bed of greens.

1 ½ pounds imitation crab
⅔ cup green bell pepper, cored, seeded, and diced
1 cup mayonnaise
⅔ cup chili sauce
½ cup heavy cream
2 tablespoons lemon juice
1 teaspoon Worcestershire® sauce

In a large bowl, combine crab and green bell pepper. In a small bowl, combine mayonnaise, chili sauce, heavy cream, lemon juice, and Worcestershire® sauce. Add the mayonnaise mixture to the crab mixture and blend gently.

The August 1945 issue of the Progressive Grocer announced that July 1945 was the first month in history since 1857 when a grocery store did not fail.

Chunky Turkey Salad

SERVES 4 TO 5

I really enjoy making this salad at home. It has always been one of my favorite recipes.

FOR THE DRESSING

½ cup mayonnaise
½ cup low-fat plain yogurt
1 tablespoon Dijon mustard
¼ teaspoon salt
¼ teaspoon large grind black pepper

In a small bowl, combine mayonnaise, plain yogurt, Dijon mustard, salt, and pepper and whisk to blend. Cover with plastic wrap and refrigerate until ready to toss salad.

Imitation crab-meat is found in the seafood section of your supermarket. It's inexpensive, and I prefer using it instead of canned crab in this recipe. This recipe is best when made with fresh crab.

FOR THE SALAD

1 ⅓ pound piece oven-roasted deli turkey breast, cubed
2 cups celery, chopped
1 cup green onions, thinly sliced
¼ cup sliced almonds
¼ cup fresh parsley, minced

In a large bowl, combine turkey, celery, green onions, almonds, and parsley. Add dressing and toss to coat evenly.

Bean Dip

MAKES ABOUT 5 CUPS

The original deli recipe called for dried refried beans. Using canned refried beans simplifies the preparation.

rozen French fries were intro- duced in the American super- market in 1946.

2 cans (16-ounces) refried beans
1 ½ tablespoons jalapeño peppers, minced
¼ cup white onion, finely chopped
1 can (4-ounces) diced mild green chiles
½ cup shredded Cheddar cheese
4 teaspoons minced garlic
½ teaspoon sea salt
½ teaspoon dried oregano

In a large bowl, combine refried beans, jalapeño peppers, onion, green chiles, Cheddar cheese, garlic, salt, and oregano. Mix thoroughly. Cover with plastic wrap and refrigerate until ready to serve.

he first truly upscale supermarket, forerunner of today's gourmet and specialty food stores, Jim Jamail & Sons, opened in 1946 in Houston, Texas.

Jalapeño Cheese Dip

MAKES ABOUT 6 CUPS

This is a kitchen sink recipe—you can use whatever cheese you happen to have on hand, like Cheddar, Colby, Monterey Jack or a combination of Mexican cheeses. For a milder flavor, reduce the fresh jalapeño pepper.

Home-made dips should be eaten in 5 days.

4 cups shredded Cheddar cheese
1 ⅔ cups mayonnaise
1 to 2 ounces pickled jalapeño peppers, finely chopped
¼ fresh jalapeño pepper, minced (or to taste)
1 to 2 tablespoons red bell pepper, cored, seeded, and finely chopped
⅛ to ¼ can evaporated milk, for desired consistency

In a large bowl, combine Cheddar cheese, mayonnaise, pickled jalapeños, fresh jalapeño pepper, and red bell pepper. Mix thoroughly. Add evaporated milk according to desired consistency. Cover with plastic wrap and refrigerate until ready to serve.

Dill Dip

MAKES ABOUT 5 CUPS

2 ½ cups mayonnaise
2 ½ cups sour cream
½ cup dried dill
¼ cup Knorr® vegetable soup mix

In a medium bowl, combine mayonnaise, sour cream, dill, and vegetable soup mix and whisk to blend thoroughly. Cover with plastic wrap and refrigerate until ready to serve.

Honey Yogurt Dip
a Steele's HealthMark Recipe

MAKES ABOUT 2 CUPS

Carol Ann's Deli served this dip with fruit trays. The following makes enough dip to serve 25 people.

2 cups non-fat plain yogurt
½ cup honey
½ teaspoon cinnamon + ⅛ teaspoon cinnamon
Pinch nutmeg

In a small bowl, combine plain yogurt, honey, cinnamon, and nutmeg and whisk to blend. Cover and refrigerate until ready to serve.

HN *HealthMark selections are carefully prepared in accordance with the guidelines issued by HealthMark for a low-fat, low-cholesterol, deliciously healthy recipe.*

Strawberry Cream Cheese Dip

MAKES ABOUT 2 CUPS

1 package (8-ounces) cream cheese, softened
1 cup marshmallow cream
¼ cup strawberry preserves
¼ cup milk

In a medium bowl, combine cream cheese, marshmallow cream, strawberry preserves, and milk and whisk to blend. Cover with plastic wrap and refrigerate until time to serve. Makes enough dip for one large fruit tray.

Marshmallow cream originated in 1920 when two young entrepreneurs, H. Allen Durkee and Fred L. Mower, started Marshmallow Fluff®.

Carol Ann's Cheese Ball

MAKES 1 BALL

2 packages (8-ounces) cream cheese, softened
1 wedge (8-ounces) sharp Cheddar cheese, shredded
1 tablespoon pimiento, chopped
1 tablespoon green bell pepper, cored, seeded, and diced
1 tablespoon green onions, thinly sliced
2 teaspoons Worcestershire® sauce
1 teaspoon lemon juice
Dash cayenne pepper

In a medium bowl, combine cream and Cheddar cheeses and blend thoroughly. Add pimiento, green bell pepper, green onions, Worcestershire® sauce, and lemon juice. Season to taste with cayenne pepper. Mix thoroughly, cover, and refrigerate until well chilled.

1 cup pecans, finely chopped
or, 1 cup parsley, finely chopped

Form the cheese mixture into a ball and roll in chopped pecans or parsley, coating evenly. Refrigerate in a covered container until ready to serve.

Cheese balls will keep in the refrigerator for 5 days.

Fiesta Cheese Ball

MAKES 1 BALL

Shelled pecans should be refrigerated in an airtight container for no more than 3 months.

2 packages (8-ounces) cream cheese, softened
⅓ cup mild Pace® picante sauce (or your favorite salsa)
1 packet (1¼-ounces) taco seasoning mix
1 tablespoon green onions, thinly sliced

In a medium bowl, combine cream cheese, salsa, and taco seasoning mix and blend. Add green onions and mix thoroughly. Cover and refrigerate until well chilled.

1 cup pecans, finely chopped
1 cup sharp Cheddar cheese, shredded

Form the cheese mixture into a ball and roll in chopped pecans and Cheddar cheese, coating evenly. Refrigerate in a covered container until ready to serve.

Holiday Cheese Ball

MAKES 1 BALL

> 2 packages (8-ounces) cream cheese, softened
> ½ cup amaretto liqueur
> 2 tablespoons almonds, finely chopped

In a medium bowl, combine cream cheese, amaretto, and almonds and blend thoroughly. Cover and refrigerate until well chilled.

> 2 packages (3-ounces) almonds, chopped

Form the cream cheese mixture into a ball and roll in almonds, coating evenly. Refrigerate in a covered container until ready to serve.

Heavenly Hash

SERVES 6 TO 8

FOR THE DRESSING

> 1 cup sour cream
> 1 cup whipped cream or Cool Whip®
> ¼ cup sugar

In a small bowl, combine sour cream, whipped cream, and sugar and whisk to blend. Cover with plastic wrap and refrigerate until ready to toss salad.

FOR THE SALAD

> 1 ½ cups pineapple tidbits, drained
> 1 ½ cups mandarin oranges, drained
> ⅜ cup maraschino cherries, drained
> 3 cups miniature marshmallows
> 1 cup shredded coconut

Place pineapple tidbits in a colander to drain. Place the colander over the sink and shake gently, removing any extra moisture. Follow the same procedure for mandarin oranges and maraschino cherries. In a large bowl, combine pineapple tidbits, mandarin oranges, maraschino cherries, marshmallows, and coconut. Fold in dressing and mix gently. Cover and refrigerate until ready to serve.

Produce was first packaged in plastic in 1947. By the end of the century, innovation in packaging revolutionized the produce department. Convenience foods included a multitude of pre-washed, precut fresh fruits and vegetables, saving the American consumer countless hours of washing, chopping, and slicing. Cabbage, broccoli, cauliflower, carrots, onions, and stir-fry veggies made mealtime a snap. Prepackaged salads, coleslaw, and a rainbow assortment of fresh cut fruit in carry-home containers gave us salads in seconds.

If you purchase shredded or flaked coconut: Unopened canned coconut can be stored at room temperature up to 18 months; coconut in plastic bags up to 6 months. Once opened, both should be refrigerated in airtight containers.*

Cranberry Salad

SERVES 6

1 package (16-ounces) fresh cranberries
3 gala apples, cored
1 stalk celery
⅓ cup walnuts, finely chopped
½ cup water
1 package (3-ounces) cherry flavored Jell-O®
⅓ cup sugar + 1 tablespoon sugar

Place cranberries in a colander and rinse thoroughly. Pick out any damaged berries. Using a food processor, grind cranberries, apples, and celery to a very fine consistency. In a large bowl, place cranberries, apples, celery, and walnuts. Cover with plastic wrap to help retard discoloration. In a small saucepan, add water, Jell-O®, and sugar and bring to a boil over medium-high heat. Cook until gelatin and sugar are dissolved. Pour the Jell-O® mixture over the cranberry mixture and mix thoroughly. Cover, refrigerate, and chill until gelatin takes a solid shape.

Cranberries, apples, and celery should be finely ground, not mushy. If you don't have a food processor, a Good Grips® chopper works nicely. These are available at most kitchen stores.

Waldorf Fruit Salad
a HealthMark Salad

SERVES 10 TO 12

FOR THE DRESSING

3 cups non-fat plain yogurt
½ cup honey
1 teaspoon ground ginger
1 ½ teaspoons vanilla

In a large bowl, combine yogurt, honey, ginger, and vanilla and whisk to blend. Cover with plastic wrap and refrigerate until ready to toss salad.

FOR THE SALAD

7 apples, cored and diced
1 ¾ cups red seedless grapes
1 ¾ cups raisins
1 ¾ cups celery, thinly sliced
¼ cup + 2 tablespoons walnuts, chopped

As each apple is cored and diced, add immediately to dressing to prevent discoloration. Add grapes, raisins, celery, and walnuts and toss gently. Cover and refrigerate until ready to serve.

HN *HealthMark selections are carefully prepared in accordance with the guidelines issued by HealthMark for a low-fat, low-cholesterol, deliciously healthy recipe.*

Raisins can be stored at room temperature for several months if tightly wrapped. To keep raisins up to a year, refrigerate them in a tightly sealed plastic bag.

Acapulco Salad
a HealthMark Salad

SERVES 6

FOR THE DRESSING

    1 cup non-fat plain yogurt
    ½ cup lemon juice
    2 teaspoons olive oil
    2 teaspoons honey

In a blender, place plain yogurt, lemon juice, olive oil, and honey and purée until smooth. Transfer to a covered container and refrigerate until ready to toss salad.

HealthMark selections are carefully prepared in accordance with the guidelines issued by HealthMark for a low-fat, low-cholesterol, deliciously healthy recipe.

FOR THE SALAD

    1½ pounds jicama, peeled and julienned, (1 large)
    7 carrots, peeled and julienned
    1 large red bell pepper, cored, seeded, and sliced into thin strips
    1 large yellow bell pepper, cored, seeded, and sliced into thin strips
    ¼ cup cilantro, minced

In a large bowl, combine jicama, carrots, red and yellow bell peppers, and cilantro. Add dressing and toss to coat evenly. Cover and refrigerate until ready to serve.

Jicama has a white crunchy flesh and a sweet nutty flavor. It's available year-round in most supermarkets.

When stored in a cool, dry place, jicama will keep for up to 3 weeks. Once cut, tightly wrap it in plastic and refrigerate. It will keep 1 week.

Couscous Salad
a HealthMark Salad

SERVES 6 TO 8

FOR THE DRESSING

½ cup canola oil
½ cup lemon juice
2 teaspoons minced garlic
3 teaspoons ground cumin
2 tablespoons dried oregano
1 teaspoon salt

In a small bowl, combine canola oil, lemon juice, garlic, cumin, oregano, and salt and whisk to blend. Cover with plastic wrap and refrigerate until ready to toss salad.

FOR THE SALAD

3 cups fat-free and salt-free canned chicken broth
1 tablespoon olive oil
1 box (12-ounces) couscous
1 cup Roma tomatoes, chopped
1 cup zucchini, chopped
1 cup green onions, thinly sliced
2 tablespoons fresh cilantro, minced

In a medium saucepan, combine chicken broth and olive oil and bring to a boil. Stir in couscous and cover. Remove from heat and let stand 5 minutes. Fluff couscous with a fork and transfer to a large bowl. Add Roma tomatoes, zucchini, green onions, and cilantro and toss. Pour dressing over the salad and toss to coat evenly.

Pillsbury® launched the Pillsbury® "bake-off" in 1950 as a way of promoting its flour. This was the same year both General Mills and Pillsbury introduced prepared cake mixes and Chicago baker, Charles Lubin, debuted Sara Lee® cheesecake.

HealthMark selections are carefully prepared in accordance with the guidelines issued by HealthMark for a low-fat, low-cholesterol, deliciously healthy recipe.

Canola oil is the market name for rapeseed oil, which is expressed from rapeseeds. The name was changed to canola by the Canadian seed-oil industry. Canola is Canada's most widely used oil. Its popularity is growing in the United States because it is lower in saturated fat than any other oil. It also contains more cholesterol-balancing monounsaturated fat than other oils except for olive oil.

Oriental Chicken Salad
a HealthMark Salad

SERVES 4 TO 6

FOR THE DRESSING

¼ cup sesame oil

1 cup lemon juice

¼ cup + 2 tablespoons sugar

1 tablespoon + 1 teaspoon dry mustard

2 tablespoons minced ginger

1 teaspoon salt

In a small bowl, combine sesame oil, lemon juice, sugar, dry mustard, ginger, and salt and whisk to blend. Cover with plastic wrap and refrigerate until ready to toss salad.

FOR THE SALAD

1½ pounds boneless, skinless chicken breasts cubed, (about 3 breasts)

Salt to taste

Large grind black pepper to taste

¼ cup water

4 cups green cabbage, thinly sliced

1 cup red cabbage, thinly sliced

¾ cup green onions, thinly sliced

¾ cup carrots, shredded

1 medium red bell pepper, cored, seeded, and julienned

1 cup fresh bean sprouts

1 cup frozen pea pods, thawed

⅓ cup slivered almonds, toasted

Preheat the oven to 325 degrees. Place chicken breasts in a medium-sized baking dish, season with salt and pepper, and pour water over breasts. Place the baking dish in the oven and bake uncovered until chicken is cooked through, about 45 minutes. Remove from the oven and cool.

In a large bowl, combine green and red cabbages, green onions, carrots, red bell pepper, bean sprouts, pea pods, and almonds. When chicken has cooled, cut into bite-size pieces, and mix into the cabbage mixture. Drizzle dressing over salad and toss to coat evenly.

HN HealthMark selections are carefully prepared in accordance with the guidelines issued by HealthMark for a low-fat, low-cholesterol, deliciously healthy recipe.

To toast nuts, place on a baking sheet in a 350-degree preheated oven for 5 to 10 minutes, or until golden brown. Watch closely as nuts turn from golden brown to black very quickly. I personally prefer to toast nuts by sautéing them in a small skillet that has been lightly coated with vegetable oil. For this method, stir continually over medium heat for 5 to 7 minutes.

Deviled Eggs

SERVES 10

10 eggs, hard-boiled
2 tablespoons mayonnaise
3 tablespoons ranch dressing
Pinch paprika
Dash seasoned salt
Dash white pepper

With a knife, halve hard-boiled eggs lengthwise. Using a spoon, gently remove yolks and place in a medium bowl. Transfer whites to a tray and set aside. Using a fork, mash yolks. Add mayonnaise, ranch dressing, paprika, seasoned salt, and white pepper and blend thoroughly. Refill whites with the egg yolk mixture.

SUGGESTED GARNISHES

Chopped fresh chives
Chopped fresh parsley
Chopped green onions
Sliced stuffed green olives
Crumbled crisp bacon

Garnish deviled eggs with any of the above garnishes.

One of the original customer incentive programs, S & H Green Stamps, first appeared in 1951 at King Soopers, a Denver supermarket chain. The S & H program rewarded customers who shopped at participating grocery or other retail outlets by doling out bonus stamps to customers based upon their purchases. The more they spent, the more they got. Consumers pasted the green stickers into booklets, then redeemed them for premiums at Green Stamp stores or mail order catalogs. The competing program was Blue Chip Stamps.

Thoroughly chilling hard boiled eggs before peeling helps firm the white, making peeling easier.

If an egg cracks while being boiled in water, pour a generous amount of salt over the crack. This will seal it and contain the egg white.

Steele's "Hit the Road" Breakfast Burritos

SERVES 4

This is the perfect breakfast to prepare for a family fishing trip or anytime you need breakfast for the road. Wrap the burritos in aluminum foil to keep them warm until you reach your favorite fishing hole.

1 ½ cups frozen hash brown potatoes
Vegetable spray
Taco seasoning mix to taste

Preheat the oven to 350 degrees. Place hash browns on a cookie sheet and coat with vegetable spray to moisten. Sprinkle potatoes with taco seasoning to taste and toss gently to coat evenly. Using a spoon, spread hash browns evenly on the cookie sheet and bake until crisp, about 25 minutes. Remove from the oven and transfer to a bowl to cool.

¼ pound chorizo sausage

In a small skillet, brown chorizo sausage over medium heat until crisp and cooked through, about 5 to 7 minutes. Remove sausage from the skillet, place on paper towels to drain, and set aside.

1 tablespoon butter
8 eggs, lightly beaten
¼ pound piece deli ham, diced into ¼-inch cubes
½ cup shredded Cheddar cheese
¼ teaspoon large grind black pepper
Cooked hash browns
Cooked chorizo sausage
4 tablespoons 505 Southwestern® prepared green chile sauce

In a large skillet, melt butter over medium heat. Add eggs, stirring constantly, to scramble. When eggs begin to set, add ham and continue stirring, about 1 minute. Add Cheddar cheese and pepper and continue stirring. When eggs are set, add potatoes, chorizo sausage, and green chile sauce, and blend gently.

4 (10-inch) flour tortillas

Lay tortillas on a flat surface. Place ¼ of the burrito mixture down the center of tortilla and fold 2 sides of tortilla into the middle so the edges just meet. Holding the 2 sides in place, roll the loose end up from the bottom, developing a roll. Serve immediately or wrap in aluminum foil to transport or to store in the refrigerator.

In 1928, the average grocery store carried 870 items. By 1952, the number increased to 4,000.

Carol Ann's Deli used to make this burrito in batches of 140 to 560. For the sake of convenience and ease in preparation to make four servings, I substituted taco seasoning mix to season the potatoes and used prepared green chile sauce rather than complicating the recipe with additional steps. My family thinks this is a darn-close replica of the original. If you've recently made the burrito recipe in this cookbook, you will have some leftover green chile. Use it instead of prepared green chile sauce.

376

Quiche Lorraine

SERVES 8 TO 10 AS AN APPETIZER; 4 TO 6 AS AN ENTRÉE

1 unbaked (8-inch) pie shell

Preheat the oven to 425 degrees. Prick the bottom of pie shell with a fork and bake 5 to 7 minutes.

Pizza came of age in 1953. There were at least 15,000 pizzerias in America, and over 100,000 grocery stores sold either ready-made refrigerated or frozen pizzas.

6 slices bacon
2 tablespoons pan drippings
½ cup yellow onion, diced
1 cup shredded Swiss cheese
2 eggs, lightly beaten
1 cup heavy cream
¼ teaspoon nutmeg
¼ teaspoon salt
¼ teaspoon white pepper

Reduce heat in the oven to 375 degrees. In a large skillet, fry bacon over medium heat until crisp and transfer to paper towels to drain. Cool and crumble into ½-inch pieces. Drain skillet of all but 2 tablespoons pan drippings. Add onion to the skillet and sauté until translucent. In a medium bowl, combine bacon, onion, and Swiss cheese and toss gently. Place the bacon mixture in the bottom of the pie shell. In a small bowl, combine eggs, heavy cream, nutmeg, salt, and white pepper and whisk to blend. Pour the egg mixture over the bacon mixture. Bake for 35 to 40 minutes, or until a knife inserted in the center of quiche comes out clean. Cool on a rack before cutting into wedges.

Egglands Best® eggs ensure the safety of their product by vaccinating hens against Salmonella, by testing extensively to ensure Salmonella is not present, by eliminating animal by-products from feed, and by enforcing a strict sanitation program. It's the only egg product I purchase.

Ham and Mushroom Quiche

SERVES 8 TO 10 AS AN APPETIZER; 4 TO 6 AS AN ENTRÉE

1 unbaked (8-inch) pie shell

Preheat the oven to 425 degrees. Prick the bottom of pie shell with a fork and bake 5 to 7 minutes.

1 teaspoon butter
4 white button mushrooms, washed and thinly sliced
¼ pound piece deli ham, diced
½ cup green onions, thinly sliced
1 cup shredded Swiss cheese
2 eggs, lightly beaten
1 cup heavy cream
¼ teaspoon nutmeg
¼ teaspoon salt
¼ teaspoon white pepper

Reduce heat in the oven to 375 degrees. In a small skillet, melt butter over medium heat, add mushrooms and sauté until soft. In a medium bowl, combine mushrooms, ham, green onions, and Swiss cheese and toss gently. Place the mushroom mixture in the bottom of pie shell. In a small bowl, combine eggs, heavy cream, nutmeg, salt, and white pepper and whisk to blend. Pour the egg mixture over the mushroom mixture. Bake for 35 to 40 minutes, or until a knife inserted in the center of quiche comes out clean. Cool on a rack before cutting into wedges.

Nielsen Coupon Clearing House, the first clearing house devoted to coupon redemption, was established in 1957. By 1965, over half of American shoppers clipped coupons. In 1997, consumers saved over $2.9 billion by redeeming 4.8 billion coupons.

You can use milk instead of cream, but cream yields a richer, more custard-like quiche.

Vegetable Quiche

SERVES 8 TO 10 AS AN APPETIZER; 4 TO 6 AS AN ENTRÉE

1 unbaked (8-inch) pie shell

Preheat the oven to 425 degrees. Prick the bottom of pie shell with a fork and bake 5 to 7 minutes.

The year 1960 saw the advent of miniature "drive-in" convenience stores, ranging from 1,000 to 2,700 square feet.

1 cup fresh cauliflower florets
1 cup fresh broccoli florets
1 to 2 strips jarred roasted red bell pepper, diced
¼ cup green onions, thinly sliced
1 cup shredded Swiss cheese
2 eggs, lightly beaten
1 cup heavy cream
¼ teaspoon nutmeg
¼ teaspoon salt
¼ teaspoon white pepper

Reduce heat in the oven to 375 degrees. Fill a large saucepan half full with water. Place over high heat and bring to a boil. Add cauliflower and broccoli florets and blanch 2 minutes. Remove cauliflower and broccoli florets and plunge into ice water to retard cooking. Drain and cool. In a medium bowl, combine cauliflower and broccoli florets, roasted red bell pepper, green onions, and Swiss cheese and toss gently. Place the cauliflower mixture in the bottom of the pie shell. In a small bowl, combine eggs, heavy cream, nutmeg, salt, and white pepper and whisk to blend. Pour the egg mixture over the cauliflower mixture. Bake for 35 to 40 minutes, or until a knife inserted in the center of quiche comes out clean. Cool on a rack before cutting into wedges.

In 1961, the average supermarket was 21,300 square feet and the average sale per customer was $4.99.

You can bake quiche in individual tart shells, or forego the crust and cook them in well-buttered ramekins. If you make quiche without a crust, you must bake it in a water bath. Set the ramekins in a large baking dish. Pour hot water into the baking dish until it comes halfway up the sides of the ramekins, then follow cooking directions.

Tomato Quiche

SERVES 8 TO 10 AS AN APPETIZER; 4 TO 6 AS AN ENTRÉE

1 unbaked (8-inch) pie shell

Preheat the oven to 425 degrees. Prick the bottom of pie shell with a fork and bake 5 to 7 minutes.

2 ripe tomatoes, sliced ½-inch thick
Salt to taste
White pepper to taste
½ cup all-purpose flour
2 tablespoons vegetable oil
1 cup white onion, chopped
¼ cup shredded Provolone cheese
¼ cup shredded Swiss cheese
2 eggs, lightly beaten
1 cup heavy cream
¼ teaspoon salt
¼ teaspoon white pepper

Reduce heat in the oven to 375 degrees. Sprinkle tomato slices with salt and white pepper and dip in flour. In a large skillet, heat vegetable oil over medium heat. Add tomato slices and sauté 3 to 4 minutes per side. Remove with a spatula and transfer to paper towels to drain. Add onion to the same skillet and sauté until translucent. Place tomatoes and onion in the bottom of the pie shell. Sprinkle with Provolone and Swiss cheeses. In a small bowl, combine eggs, heavy cream, salt, and white pepper and whisk to blend. Pour the egg mixture over the cheeses. Bake for 35 to 40 minutes, or until a knife inserted in the center of quiche comes out clean. Cool on a rack before cutting into wedges.

New products introduced in 1964 included Pop Tarts®, Lucky Charms®, Chiffon® margarine, Seven Seas® salad dressings, Maxim®, Yoplait® yogurt, and Carnation® Instant Breakfast.

New products introduced in 1966 included Cool Whip®, Tang®, Apple Jacks®, Franco-American SpaghettiOs®, Diet Pepsi®, and Shake 'n Bake®.

For variety, try making this with green tomatoes when they are available.

Twice-Baked Potatoes

SERVES 4

Twice-baked potatoes were a popular item in the deli. This recipe can be divided in half to serve 2 or doubled to serve 8. This is a great side dish for steaks.

4 large baking potatoes, scrubbed
Olive oil
4 tablespoons butter
4 tablespoons sour cream
8 tablespoons shredded Cheddar cheese
4 tablespoons green onions, thinly sliced
2 teaspoons salt
1 teaspoon large grind black pepper
¼ cup milk, or as needed

The food industry has historically been a male-dominated business. But Carole Bitter broke the glass ceiling, becoming the first female store manager for Stop & Shop in 1972.

Preheat the oven to 400 degrees. Rub potatoes with olive oil to coat evenly. Bake potatoes for 1 hour, or until soft. Cool to the touch. Cut an oval shape in the top of each potato. Scoop out pulp, leaving potatoes hollow, and transfer pulp to a medium bowl. Mash potato pulp with a potato masher, keeping potatoes somewhat chunky. Add butter, sour cream, Cheddar cheese, green onions, salt, and pepper. Mix thoroughly. Add enough milk to the potato mixture to moisten and beat slightly. Spoon the potato mixture into the potato skins. Place on a cookie sheet and bake for 20 minutes, or until browned.

SUGGESTED GARNISHES

Chopped fresh chives
Chopped fresh parsley
Chopped green onions
Crumbled crisp bacon

Rubbing the potatoes with olive oil keeps them firm for stuffing. While some delis cut the potatoes in half, keeping them whole makes a nicer presentation. Twice-baked potatoes can be prepared the day before and baked just before serving at 400 degrees for 20 to 30 minutes.

For a good, quick snack for hungry kids who can't wait for dinner, save the oval potato tops. Sprinkle them with onion salt and Cheddar cheese and place under the broiler until cheese is melted and potato skins are heated through.

Dauphinois

SERVES 8

Dauphinois is the French term for potatoes au gratin. This was another really popular side dish we sold in our chef-prepared, home-meal replacement section. This is best when made with Gruyere cheese, but it is an expensive cheese. If you're pinching pennies, substitute Swiss cheese for the Gruyere.

    1 tablespoon butter
    2 pounds potatoes, peeled
    2 cups milk
    1 ½ cups heavy cream
    2 teaspoons minced garlic
    ¾ teaspoon salt
    ½ teaspoon ground white pepper
    4 ounces shredded Gruyere cheese
    3 tablespoons butter

Preheat the oven to 400 degrees. Coat a 3-quart baking dish with 1 tablespoon butter.

Using a food processor, slice potatoes ⅛-inch thick and place in a large saucepan. Add milk, heavy cream, garlic, salt, and white pepper and bring to a boil over medium heat, stirring frequently to prevent scorching. Remove the pan from heat. Pour the potato mixture into the prepared baking dish. Sprinkle cheese on top and dot with the remaining 3 tablespoons butter.

Set the baking dish on a rimmed cookie sheet, place in the oven, and bake uncovered for 30 minutes. Reduce heat to 350 degrees and continue baking for 30 more minutes. Potatoes are done when golden brown, or when the tip of a knife inserted in the center pierces the potatoes easily and comes out clean. Allow the dish to sit 15 minutes before serving.

The first Universal Product Code was introduced in 1973, paving the way for scanners in the check stands. In 1974, Marsh's Supermarket in Troy, Ohio, became the first supermarket to install scanners. Many Americans believed this new technology would destroy America. A price operator, Merrill Steele didn't install scanners in his markets because he wanted his customers to remain cognizant of pricing. The UPC eliminated individual pricing on grocery products. His concern, "If prices aren't clearly marked on products, our customers will lose sight of what they are paying."

Swiss Gruyere has a rich, sweet nutty flavor. Aged for 10 to 12 months, it has a golden brown rind and a firm, pale yellow consistency with well-spaced, medium-sized holes.

Potato Pancakes (Latkes)

SERVES 4 TO 6

Traditionally served at Hanukkah. Serve with warm applesauce found on Page 220.

1 ½ pounds red potatoes, scrubbed and dried, with skins left on
1 bunch green onions, thinly sliced
½ cup all-purpose flour
2 eggs, beaten
1 teaspoon salt
½ teaspoon white pepper

Using a food processor, shred potatoes. Drain shredded potatoes by squeezing excess moisture out with your hands. In a large bowl, combine potatoes, green onions, flour, eggs, salt, and white pepper and mix thoroughly. Cover the potato mixture with plastic wrap to help retard discoloration.

4 tablespoons olive oil

In a large non-stick skillet, heat 1 tablespoon olive oil over medium-high heat. Shape the potato mixture into pancakes that are approximately 2-inches in diameter and ¼-inch thick. Place pancakes in the hot skillet and cook for 2 to 3 minutes, or until pancakes are golden brown. Using a spatula, turn the pancakes and cook the other side until golden brown. Transfer pancakes to an ovenproof platter and hold in a warm oven until ready to serve. Repeat this process, adding 1 tablespoon olive oil at a time, until all pancakes are cooked.

*P*aper or Plastic? Always trying to save a penny, grocers began using plastic bags in 1977. Today, 4 out of 5 customers carry their groceries home in plastic bags. But for the environmental conscious shopper, answering this routine question can be a bit of a quandary. According to the Environmental Protection Agency, the production of the paper bag generates 70 percent more air and 50 percent more water pollutants than plastic. Paper bags are made from trees, a renewable resource; while plastic bags are made from polyethylene, a byproduct of crude oil and natural gas. It's really six of one, half a dozen of the other.

You can make this ahead and freeze it. Place the pancakes on a cookie sheet and then into the freezer. Once they are frozen, put them in a zip-lock freezer bag and then back into the freezer. To cook, partially thaw them, place on a cookie sheet, and reheat in a preheated 450 degrees F oven for about 5 minutes.

Ratatouille
a HealthMark Salad

SERVES 6 TO 8

2 tablespoons canola oil

1 medium eggplant, quartered and thinly sliced

1 large red onion, peeled, quartered, and thinly sliced

2 small green bell peppers, cored, seeded,
   and sliced into thin strips

2 small zucchini, thinly sliced

2 cans (14½-ounces) diced peeled tomatoes

2 teaspoons minced garlic

½ teaspoon dried red pepper flakes

1½ teaspoons dried basil

1½ teaspoons dried oregano

1 bay leaf

½ teaspoon salt

1 teaspoon large grind black pepper

1 tablespoon lemon juice

In a large skillet, heat canola oil over medium-high heat. Add eggplant and sauté 3 minutes. Add red onion, green bell peppers, zucchini, tomatoes, garlic, red pepper flakes, basil, oregano, bay leaf, salt, pepper, and lemon juice and sauté until vegetables are soft, another 10 minutes. Remove bay leaf and serve hot or cold.

Ratatouille can be prepared with any combination of vegetables. Serve it hot, cold, or at room temperature, either as a side dish or as an appetizer with bread or crackers.

HNE *HealthMark selections are carefully prepared in accordance with the guidelines issued by HealthMark for a low-fat, low-cholesterol, deliciously healthy recipe.*

Loblaws, a Canadian supermarket, under the leadership of David Nichol, introduced no-name products to the American continent. Jewel Food Stores introduced generics to the United States that same year, starting the private label craze. I, on the other hand, have always been a brand name kind of gal, and I'm not particularly fond of products that aren't proud enough of their contents to put a name on their label.

Merger mania began in 1979 when Pillsbury paid $148 million to acquire Green Giant. This started the trend where big food fish went in search of other big food fish to gobble up.

Chicken Pot Pie

SERVES 4

By the 1980s, the average size of supermarkets measured 35,000 to 50,000 square feet, and food manufacturers bombarded the market place with 25,000 new products each and every year, creating a myriad of choices for the American consumer. Keeping up with this continual blitz of new products put grocers in a persistent state of flux with the never-ending task of re-merchandising shelves to discontinue the old and make room for the new.

2 chicken breast halves, bones and skin on
Salt to taste
Pepper to taste
¼ cup water

Preheat the oven to 350 degrees. Place chicken breasts in a shallow baking dish. Season with salt and pepper and douse with water. Bake uncovered until chicken is cooked through, about 45 minutes. Remove chicken from the oven and cool. Remove skin and bones from chicken and cut meat into bite-size pieces.

4 tablespoons butter
½ cup white onion, finely chopped
5 tablespoons flour
2 cups canned chicken broth
½ cup celery, diced
1 cup carrots, diced
1 teaspoon salt
¼ teaspoon large grind black pepper
½ teaspoon dried sage
1 cup milk
1 cup frozen corn, thawed and drained
1 cup frozen petite peas, thawed and drained
2 cups cooked chicken, cut into bite-size pieces

In a large heavy skillet, melt butter over medium heat. Add onion and sauté for 2 minutes, or until onion is tender. Add flour and whisk until it bubbles. Gradually add chicken broth, stirring frequently, until the sauce is thick and smooth, about 3 minutes. Add celery, carrots, salt, pepper, and sage and reduce heat to low. Simmer for 5 minutes. Add milk, corn, petite peas, and cooked chicken, simmering for another 3 minutes. Pour the filling into a pie plate and cool. Can be made ahead and refrigerated, if covered, until ready to bake.

Be sure frozen vegetables are completely thawed before adding them to the sauce. Frozen peas will turn the sauce green.

continued next page

SUGGESTED CRUSTS

You can make your own crust following the pastry recipe on Page 294, or you can purchase Dufour's Puff Pastry Dough® found in the freezer section of your supermarket. I personally like topping mine with a biscuit crust.

2 cups all-purpose flour
1 tablespoon baking powder
½ teaspoon salt
2 tablespoons fresh chives, snipped
¼ cup Crisco® vegetable shortening
¾ cup milk

Preheat the oven to 375 degrees. Sift flour, baking powder, and salt together in a medium bowl. Add chives and mix thoroughly. Using a pastry blender or fork, cut in shortening until the mixture resembles small peas. Add milk, a few tablespoons at a time, until the mixture holds together. It is not necessary to add all the milk. Place dough on a floured surface, knead 4 to 5 times, and form into a ball. With a rolling pin, roll dough out so that it is ½-inch thick. Using a biscuit cutter, cut into biscuits and place on top of the pie.

Bake pie for 20 to 25 minutes, or until biscuits are browned and the pie is bubbling.

By end of the 1980s, supermarket operators began adding general merchandise and non-food items to their shelves, adopting the one-stop shopping concept to compete with their latest rivals--the European-style hypermarkets, deep-discount drug chains, warehouse club stores, mass merchandisers, and food-service operators.

In 1981, Americans spent 28 cents of every food dollar in restaurants, fast-food stores, and carry-home meals from supermarkets, compared to 26 cents in 1969.

 This is a good recipe to use up leftover turkey. One large chicken breast yields about 1 ½ cups meat. Substitute 3 cups chopped turkey.

Old-Fashioned Krautburgers

MAKES 16 KRAUTBURGERS

If you are really ambitious, you can make your own bread dough from scratch. This recipe takes the simpler approach and uses frozen.

2 loaves (1-pound) frozen bread dough

Thaw bread dough according to package directions.

2 ½ pounds lean ground beef
4 cups shredded cabbage
1 large yellow onion, chopped
1 teaspoon dry mustard
1 teaspoon garlic powder
1 ¼ teaspoons salt
½ teaspoon large grind black pepper

In a large skillet, brown ground beef over medium heat, crumbling with a fork. When meat is almost cooked, add cabbage and onion and continue cooking until vegetables are soft. Add mustard, garlic powder, salt, and pepper and mix thoroughly.

Vegetable cooking spray for coating cookie sheet
1 egg, beaten

Preheat the oven to 350 degrees. Roll each loaf of bread dough into a 16 X 8-inch rectangle, cut each one into eight 4-inch squares. Spoon the cabbage mixture into the center of each dough square, bring up the diagonal points, and pinch edges closed. Spray a cookie sheet with cooking spray, place krautburgers on the cookie sheet, and let rise for 10 minutes. Using a pastry brush, coat tops lightly with beaten egg. Bake for 20 minutes, or until golden brown.

*B*y 1986, the eating habits of Americans had changed dramatically. The average dinner took less than a half an hour to prepare as time-starved Americans learned there were a number of ways to find meals. Sit-down and fast-food restaurants began giving supermarkets a run for their money as Americans spent more of their food dollars eating out. Supermarkets fought back by developing chef-prepared entrees that could be carried home.

Mince Pie Filling

MAKES ENOUGH FOR 1 9-INCH PIE

At holiday time, Carol Ann's Deli sold a chef-prepared mince, an old-fashioned pie filling. Customers could purchase the already-prepared filling, making pie preparation more convenient at this very busy time of year. While some mincemeat pies actually contain meat, ours did not. This is my re-creation of that all-time customer favorite.

3 large Golden Delicious apples, cored, peeled, and cut into ¼-inch pieces
1 ½ cups raisins, coarsely chopped
½ cup walnuts, coarsely chopped
½ cup pecans, coarsely chopped
1 cup sugar
¼ cup apple cider
¼ cup brandy
4 tablespoons butter
Grated zest from ½ lemon
Juice of ½ lemon
1 tablespoon cider vinegar
1 teaspoon salt
1 teaspoon ground cinnamon
½ teaspoon ground nutmeg
½ teaspoon ground cloves

In a medium saucepan, place apples, raisins, walnuts, pecans, sugar, apple cider, brandy, butter, lemon zest, lemon juice, cider vinegar, salt, cinnamon, nutmeg, and cloves and bring to a boil over high heat. Reduce heat to low and simmer gently, stirring frequently, until the bottom of the saucepan is almost dry and fruit is glazed with a thick syrup, about 20 to 30 minutes.

1 (9-inch) pie shell
Butter for dotting mincemeat

Cool to room temperature before placing in an unbaked pie shell. To make your own crust, see recipe on Page 294. Preheat the oven to 400 degrees. Line 1 (9-inch) pie plate with pastry, fill with mincemeat, and dot with butter. Adjust top crust over filling, tucking edge under rim of bottom crust, seal, and crimp edge. Cut design in the top crust for steam to escape. Bake 30 to 35 minutes or until crust is golden brown.

General Mills introduced Pop Secret® microwave popcorn in 1986.

The health food craze began around 1993. To keep up with this growing trend, food manufacturers began producing healthy foods. Pet Inc. introduced Progresso® Healthy Classics, Lever Bros. introduced Promise® Ultra, and RJR Nabisco® introduced Snack-Well's® cookies and crackers.

In the 1990s, Americans spent 50 cents of every food dollar on prepared foods, citing time as the reason not to cook. The 1990s saw the growth of home-meal replacement departments in supermarkets, ready-to-reheat, freshly-made meals.

Ollie's Old-Fashioned Rice Pudding

SERVES 6

This is my Grandmother Steele's recipe. It should be eaten the same day it's prepared.

> When I was just a little girl, I spent a few days with my Grandmother Steele. On the first day of my visit, she took me to meet her sister, who lived a few blocks away. When we returned, she opened her refrigerator and retrieved homemade rice pudding. She told me she had made it from scratch—just for me. Needless to say, it impressed me she took the time to prepare a special treat just for me. I have attempted to follow in her footsteps and tuck unexpected goodies away to pamper the ones I love.

2 ½ cups water
1 cup uncooked white rice

In a large saucepan, bring water to a boil over high heat. Add rice, reduce heat to low, cover, and simmer until rice is cooked, about 20 to 25 minutes.

1 navel orange
½ cup raisins

Using a sharp paring knife, remove peel from orange in one long spiral. Squeeze orange juice into a small bowl and add raisins to plump. Set aside.

2 cups milk
Orange peel
⅓ cup sugar
2-inch piece stick cinnamon
½ teaspoon salt

When rice is cooked and liquid has been absorbed, add milk, orange peel, sugar, stick cinnamon, and salt. Simmer, covered, over low heat until creamy, about 30 minutes, stirring occasionally. Discard peel.

1 cup half-and-half
3 large egg yolks
1 teaspoon vanilla extract
Less than ⅛ teaspoon cinnamon, or to taste
Drained raisins

In a medium bowl, whisk together half-and-half and egg yolks. Add to the rice mixture in a thin stream, stirring constantly. Cover and simmer until thick, about 2 minutes. Discard stick cinnamon and stir in vanilla and cinnamon. Drain raisins and stir into pudding.

If it gets a bit dry on the second day, moisten by adding one tablespoon of milk at a time to achieve the desired consistency.

Bread Pudding
with a Vanilla-Bourbon Sauce

SERVES 8 TO 10

I like making bread pudding with leftover croissants, although you can use brioche, challah (egg bread), or any combination of white or wheat bread you happen to have on hand.

FOR THE VANILLA BOURBON SAUCE

3 egg yolks
⅓ cup sugar
⅓ cup milk
1 cup whipping cream
Pinch salt
⅛ cup bourbon
½ teaspoon vanilla extract

In a medium bowl, place egg yolks and sugar and whisk until well blended. Set aside. In a medium saucepan, combine milk, whipping cream, and salt and bring to a boil over medium heat, stirring frequently. Reduce heat to medium-low. Whisk ½ cup of the cream mixture into the egg yolk mixture. Slowly whisk the egg yolk mixture into the saucepan. Continue whisking over medium-low heat until the sauce begins to thicken. Do not boil. Remove from heat, add bourbon and vanilla, and blend gently. Strain through a fine strainer into a bowl. Cool, cover with plastic wrap, and chill.

FOR THE BREAD PUDDING

1 tablespoon unsalted butter, melted
1 pound leftover croissants
¼ cup golden raisins
¼ cup sugar mixed with 1 tablespoon cinnamon, divided
4 cups milk
1 cup sugar
7 eggs
1 teaspoon vanilla extract

Preheat the oven to 350 degrees. Brush an 8-inch square baking pan with butter. Slice croissants into 1-inch cubes and arrange in the buttered pan. Sprinkle with raisins and half the cinnamon-sugar mixture. In a large heavy saucepan, combine milk and sugar, bring to a boil, and stir until sugar dissolves. Cool. In a large bowl, beat eggs until light in color. Add 1 cup of milk mixture slowly to eggs. Then add the remaining milk mixture, beating well. Blend in vanilla. Pour half of the milk mixture over bread cubes, pressing gently on bread cubes with a large spoon to help croissants absorb the milk mixture. Add the remaining milk mixture and sprinkle with the remaining cinnamon-sugar mixture. Place the baking pan in a larger pan of hot water. Bake until a knife inserted in the center comes out moist (not wet), about 45 minutes. Cut into squares and drizzle with vanilla bourbon sauce.

How many of us got our entrepreneurial start collecting pop bottles and redeeming them at the corner market for cash? Returning pop bottles was such an important part of grocery shopping in the 1950s that cashiers asked each and every customer, "Do you have bottles?" Soft drinks found a new home in aluminum cans in 1957, slowly eroding the ability of young entrepreneurs to make a few extra quarters. But never fear, in the 1990s Steele's installed a can machine where pop cans could be deposited in exchange for cash and coupons.

Index

Appetizers

Asiago Cheese Bread 6
Brie, Baked 5

CHEESE BALLS
   Carol Ann's 369
   Fiesta Cheese 369
   Holiday Cheese 370
Crab Cakes with a Pineapple
   Salsa 13
Cream Cheese Holiday Wreath .. 5

DIPS
   Artichoke, Warmed 6
   Bean 367
   Dill 368
   Honey Yogurt 368
   Jalapeño Cheese 367
   Layered Mexican, Carol Ann's 9
   Spinach 15
   Strawberry Cream Cheese 368
   "Super Bowl" Dip 7
Eggs, Deviled 375
Focaccia Bread with Tomatoes
   and Mozzarella 16
Fondue, Four Cheese 14
Guacamole 266
Hot Wings, Russ' Fool-Proof 11
Nachos, "Super Bowl" Super 8
Quesadillas, Smoked Salmon 12

QUICHE
   Ham and Mushroom 378
   Lorraine 377
   Tomato 380
   Vegetable 379

SALSA
   Avocado 264
   Pineapple 13
   Shrimp and Scallops 10
   Spicy Salsa 171
   Tomato, Carol Ann's 272
   Tomatillo Salsa 274
Toasts, Three Cheese with Sun-
   Dried Tomatoes 15

Beef

Tips on Buying and Storing Beef. 153

BALL TIPS
   Grilled Steaks with a
     Horseradish Glaze 168
   Kates' Family Mother's Day
     Shish Kabobs 169
   Steak and Tomato Kabobs
     with Tomatillo and Avocado
     Sauce 170

Bottom Round Roast, Shredded
   Beef and Simmered Onion
   Hoagies 76
Brisket, Easy Barbecued 161

CHUCK ROAST
   Cassoulet, Carol Ann's 280
   Poor Man's Roast Feast 165
   Western Style Chili 63
Chuck Steak Green Chile Stew 67
Chuck Steak, Stew with
   Summer Vegetables 164

CORNED BEEF
   Corned Beef, Braised in Beer 284
   Corned Beef, Cabbage, and
     Sauerkraut 283
Cube Steaks, Spicy Skillet 157

GROUND BEEF
   Burritos, Smothered Beef and
     Bean 263
   Casserole, Old-Fashioned
     Beef and Rice 156
   Chili, Carol Ann's 62
   Chuck Wagon Chili 64
   Hamburgers, Fourth of July 73
   Krautburgers, Old-Fashioned .. 387
   Meatballs, Scandinavian Style 159
   Meat Loaf, Good Enough
     for Company 158
   Sloppy Joes, Carol Ann's
     Homemade 71
   Spaghetti Sauce, Hearty 160
   Taco Salad 33

FLANK STEAK
   Gyros in Pita Bread 77
   London Broil, Carol Ann's 162

NEW YORK STEAKS
   My Husband's Favorite
     Father's Day Steak 173
   Pepper 176
   Smothered with Mushrooms .. 174
   with Barbecued Vidalia
     Onions 175
Pastrami, Russ' Reuben
   Sandwich 83
Prime Rib, Uncle Eddie's
   Standing Rib Roast 181

RIB-EYE STEAKS
   Chili-Rubbed with Carol
     Ann's Salsa 180
Round Steak, Fiesta 163

SIRLOIN STEAK
   Beef Chop Suey 167
   Cheese Steak Sandwich 75
   Marinated Steak with Spicy

Salsa, Carol Ann's 171
   Steak Sandwich with a
     Horseradish Glaze 74
   Teriyaki, Russ' 172
   with Skewered Vegetables 177
Sirloin Tip Roast 178
Stew Meat, Thursday's Tutu
   Beef Stew 68
T-Bones, with Green
   Peppercorn Butter 179

TRI TIP
   Grilled Tri-Tip Roast 166
   Steak Sandwich with a
     Barbecue Sauce 79

Breads

Asiago Cheese 6
Focaccia Bread with Tomatoes
   and Mozzarella 16
Grilled Garlic 226
Toasts, Three Cheese with
   Sun-Dried Tomatoes 15

Catering for a Crowd 338

Cheese

Tips on Buying and Storing Dairy
   and Cheese 3
Blue Cheese, Carol Ann's
   Dressing 11

BRIE
   Baked 5
   Brie Lover's Picnic Sandwich . 84
Cottage Cheese, Crunchy 364

CREAM CHEESE
   Carol Ann's Cheese Ball 369
   Fiesta Cheese Ball 369
   Holiday Cheese Ball 370
   Holiday Wreath 5
   Strawberry Dip 368
Fondue, Four Cheese 14
Pizza, Four Cheese with
   Roma Tomatoes 86
Sandwich, Gourmet Grilled
   Cheese 78

Cheese Balls

Carol Ann's 369
Fiesta Cheese 369
Holiday Cheese 370

Chicken and Poultry

Tips on Buying and Storing
   Chicken and Poultry 91

APPETIZERS
Hot Wings, Russ' Fool Proof .. 11
ENTREES
BBQ, Finger Lickin' 109
Cacciatore 105
Cornish Game Hens, Stuffed . 115
Divine Chicken Divan 94
Enchiladas with a Green
   Chile Sauce 265
Enchiladas with a Tomatillo
   Sauce 267
Fajitas, Tequila Marinated 271
French Country Dinner 103
Fried, Perfect Picnic 110
German Style Baked 106
   GRILLED
   Chili-Rubbed 100
   Herbed 96
   Lemon Garlic 95
   Orange Tarragon 97
   with a Peach Salsa 111
   with Red Chili Sauce 98
Kabobs 114
New England Boiled Dinner,
   Light 284
Parisian Casserole 104
Poor Man's Paella 281
Pot Pie 385
Scampi, with Spaghetti 246
Sesame 107
Shrimp and Chicken, Sautéed 113
South-of-the-Border Chipotle. 99
Thai, in a Peanut Sauce 108
Vegetable Skillet Supper 112
PASTAS
Artichoke Risotto 250
Penne Pasta in a Ricotta
   Cream Sauce 248
Chicken Piccata in a Lemon
   Basil Sauce 247
Risotto with Snow Peas 249
SALADS
Chinese Chicken Salad 41
Chicken and Cantaloupe Salad 39
Cobb Salad a la Carol Ann 34
Grilled Chicken with Penne
   Pasta 28
Luau Chicken Salad 40
Oriental Chicken Salad 374
SANDWICHES
Barbecued Chicken on Onion
   Rolls 80
Chicken Salad Sandwiches 81

SOUPS
Chicken 'n Cheese Chowder .. 46
Jalapeño Chicken Chowder 45
Jewish Penicillin 53
White Bean Chili 65
WHOLE
Roasted Parsley Chicken 102
Roasted Lemon 101

Chutneys
Peach and Crab Apple 131

Cookies
Cream Cheese and
   Macadamia Nut 291
White Chocolate Chip 290

Desserts
Bread Pudding with a Vanilla
   Bourbon Sauce 390
COOKIES
Cream Cheese and
   Macadamia Nut 291
   White Chocolate Chip 290
Crème Anglaise, with Angel
   Food Cake and Mixed Berries .. 289
Crème Brulèe, Carol Ann's 288
Mince Pie Filling 388
Peach Ice Cream, Rich Vanilla 294
Peach Pie, Pauline's 292
Pumpkin Pie, Auntie Beryl's 295
Rice Pudding, Ollie's
   Old-Fashioned 389
Sorbets, Kiwifruit and Banana
   with a Raspberry Sauce 293
Trifle, Christmas 287

Dips
Artichoke 6
Bean 367
Dill 368
Honey Yogurt 368
Fondue, Four Cheese 14
Jalapeño Cheese 367
Layered Mexican, Carol Ann's 9
Spinach, Carol Ann's 15
Strawberry Cream Cheese 368
"Super Bowl," Carol Ann's 7

Eggs
Tips for Buying and
   Storing Eggs 346
Deviled Eggs 375

QUICHE
Ham and Mushroom 378
Lorriane 377
Tomato 380
Vegetable 379
Steele's Breakfast Burrito 376

Fish and Seafood
Tips about Buying and Storing
   Fish and Seafood 185
Bouillabaisse 215
Cape Capensis, Sesame Seed ... 213
CLAMS
Bouillabaisse 215
Hearty Chowder 50
Poor Man's Paella 281
COD
Blackened 197
Fish and Chips, English Style 198
CRAB
Alaskan King Crab Legs 212
Cakes with a Pineapple Salsa 13
Claws, Stone Crab 211
Dover Sole, Sautéed in a
   Chardonnay Sauce 193
Halibut, Teriyaki with an
   Asian Tartar Sauce 199
IMITATION CRAB
Crab Louis 366
Crab Salad Sandwiches with
   Gruyere Cheese 82
Piccadilly Circles with Crab
   Salad and Tomatoes 82
LANGOSTINOS
Bisque, with Arthichokes 60
Poor Man's Paella 281
LOBSTER
Bisque 61
Bouillabaisse 215
in a Light Pink Cream Garlic
   Sauce 259
Tacos, with an Avocado Salsa 264
Tails, Tarragon 204
Mahi-Mahi, with a Mushroom
   Dill Sauce 200
Mussels, Bouillabaisse 215
Orange Roughy, Kid-Friendly 195
Red Snapper, Puerto
   Vallarta Style 196
Rock Cod, Bouillabaisse 215
SALMON
Bisque 59
Blackened Salad 35

SALMON (CONTINUED)
Bourbon Basted 189
Grilled, with a Basil Cream
  Sauce 192
Herbed Grilled...................... 189
Honey Glazed with a Tomato
  Salsa 188
Smoked Salmon Quesadillas.. 12
Teriyaki, Grilled 191
Vermouth, Grilled 190

SCALLOPS
and Shrimp in a Tomato Garlic
  Sauce over Spaghetti 256
and Shrimp Salsa.................... 10
Caramelized Sea Scallops
  with a Chili Cream Sauce..... 209
Chowder, Company's Coming 47
Chowder, Easy Artichoke
  and Scallop 49
Hibachi Style Sautéed Bay..... 210
Pasta, Spinach Fettuccine with
  a Boursin Cheese Sauce 257
Poor Man's Paella 281

SHRIMP
and Chicken Sautéed.............. 113
and Crab Bake 205
and Scallops in a Tomato Garlic
  Sauce, over Spaghetti 256
and Scallop Salsa 10
Bouillabaisse........................ 215
Cajun 208
Fajitas, Tequila Marinated 273
Jazzed-Up Jambalaya.............. 277
Angel Hair Pasta with
  Feta Cheese 255
Pizza with Artichoke Hearts ... 88
Poor Man's Paella 281
Scampi a la Carol Ann 207
Szechuan................................ 206

SALADS
Blackened Salmon 35
Pasta, Angel Hair with
  Dilled Shrimp....................... 30
Warmed Shrimp in a Tarragon
  Cream Sauce 31

SOUPS
Clam Chowder, Hearty........... 50
Langostino and Artichoke
  Bisque................................. 60
Lobster Bisque 61
Salmon Bisque 59
Scallop Chowder, Company's
  Coming 47

Scallop and Artichoke
  Chowder......................... 49
SWORDFISH
Grilled with a Dijon Dill
  Sauce 202
Pan Grilled............................ 201
with Snow Peas over
  Fettucine 258
Tilapia in a Cremè Fraîche Sauce 203
Tuna, Grilled in a Sake Marinade 194
Trout, A Fancy Feast for
  Fishermen 254
Fondue, Four Cheese 14

Fruits
Applesauce, Pauline's 220
Cantaloupe and Chicken Salad .. 39
Chutney, Peach and Crab Apple.. 131
Cranberry Salad 371
Heavenly Hash 370
Pauline's 24-Hour Salad............. 42
PEACH
Ice Cream, Rich Vanilla 294
Pie, Pauline's 292
Pears, Christmas Trifle 287
Platters, Fruit 342
Raspberry Sauce 293
SORBET
Banana 293
Kiwifruit 293
Waldorf Salad............................ 371

HealthMark
Acapulco, Jicama Salad 372
Couscous Salad....................... 373
Honey Yogurt Dip 368
Oriental Chicken Salad.......... 374
Waldorf Salad......................... 371
Herbs and Spices...................... 342

Ice Cream
Rich Vanilla Peach 294

Lamb Chops
Grilled 182

Mexican
APPETIZERS
"Super Bowl" Super Nachos... 8
BURRITOS
Beef and Bean 263
Breakfast, Steele's
  Hit the Road....................... 376
Carnitas, Pork with
  Red Chile Sauce 269

DIPS
Bean 367
Guacamole............................. 266
Jalapeño Cheese 367
Layered Mexican 9
ENCHILADAS
Chicken with a
  Green Chile Sauce 265
Chicken with a Tomatillo
  Sauce 267
ENTREÉS
Chicken with Red Chili Sauce 98
Chicken, South-of-the-Border
  Chipotle............................... 99
Chili-Rubbed Chicken............. 100
Chile Rellenos 268
Red Snapper, Puerto Vallarta
  Style 196
FAJITAS
Chicken, Tequila Marinated ... 271
Pork, Chili Marinated 270
Shrimp, Tequila Marinated 273
Quesadillas, Smoked Salmon 12
SALADS
Black Bean, Corn, and Bell
  Pepper, Fiesta...................... 359
Taco, Back to the Seventies ... 33
SALSAS
Avocado 264
Shrimp and Scallop 10
Tomatillo................................ 274
Tomato, Carol Ann's 272
Soup, Green Chile 263
Stew, Green Chile 67
Tacos, Lobster with an
  Avocado Salsa.......................... 264

One Dish Meals
Beef and Rice Casserole 156
Black-Eyed Peas, New Year's
  Day Lucky 279
Braised Corned Beef in Beer 284
Cassoulet, Carol Ann's 280
Corned Beef, Cabbage, and
  Sauerkraut 283
Chuck Steak Stew 164
Jazzed-Up Jambalaya 277
Light New England Boiled
  Dinner 284
Poor Man's Paella 281
Red Beans and Rice.................... 278
Divine Chicken Divan 94

Pasta

Tips for Cooking Pasta 241

ANGEL HAIR
with Shrimp and Feta Cheese.. 255
with Trout, A Fancy Feast
for Fishermen 254

BOW-TIE
with Sun-Dried Tomatoes
and Arugula 251

FETTUCINE
Spinach, with Scallops in a
Boursin Cheese Sauce 257
with Swordfish and Snow
Peas 258
Lasagne, Carol Ann's 242

MOSTACCIOLI RIGATI
and Lobster in a Light Pink
Cream Garlic Sauce 259

PENNE
Chicken Piccata in a Lemon
Basil Sauce 247
with Chicken in a Ricotta
Cream Sauce 248
with Four Cheeses 243
with Italian Sausage and
Roma Tomatoes 253

RISOTTO
Chicken with Snow Peas 249
Chicken and Artichoke 250
Rotini in an Artichoke Butter
Sauce 229

SALADS
Asian Pasta Primavera............ 356
Dilled Shrimp and
Angel Hair Pasta 30
Grilled Chicken and
Penne Pasta.......................... 28
My Kids' Favorite Pasta Salad 26
Spaghetti in a Salad? 27
The Best Macaroni Salad Ever 355
The Original Steele's Pasta
Salad 354
Three-Cheese and Veggie
Salad 29

SPAGHETTI
Alfredo 244
and Chicken in a Scampi
Sauce 246
Asian Pasta Primavera............ 356
with Scallops and Shrimp in
a Tomato Garlic Sauce 256
Spinach Pasta with
Italian Sausage 252

TORTELLINI
Three-Cheese in a Tomato Basil
Sauce 245

Pies

Mince Pie Filling 388
Peach, Pauline's 292
Pumpkin, Auntie Beryl's............. 295

Pizza

Four Cheese with Roma
Tomatoes 86
Shrimp and Artichoke Pizza........ 88
Veggie Pita Pizzas 87
Polenta Pie 225

Pork

Tips about Buying and Storing
Pork 129
Baby Back Ribs, My Husband
Loves 144

CHOPS
with Artichokes in a Wine
Cream Sauce 136
with a Lemon Dill Sauce 138
with a Mango Sauce 135
with a Peach and
Crab Apple Chutney 131
with Spanish Rice,
Hand-Me-Down.................... 132
Baked in a Tomato
Chutney Sauce 134
Fajitas, Chile Marinated......... 270
Florentine 137
German Style Smoked........... 140
Green Chile............................ 263
Grilled Tequila, with an
Avocado Salsa 133
Rosemary............................... 139

ROAST
Carnitas with a Red Chile
Sauce 269
French Style............................ 143
Ribs, Baby Back, My Husband
Loves His................................ 144

RIBS, COUNTRY STYLE
Peachy Polynesian 146
Spicy 145

SAUSAGE

BRATWURST
Ball Park Sausages............. 72
Brats 'n Beer 72
Cajun-Style, Red Beans
and Rice................................ 278

Chorizo, Poor Man's Paella 281
Italian, Jazzed-Up Jambalaya.. 277
Italian, Cassoulet, Carol Ann's. 280
Italian, and Penne Pasta and
Roma Tomatoes.................... 253
Italian, and Spinach Pasta 252
Lasagna.................................... 242
Portuguese Style Vegetable
Soup 51

SPARERIBS
Barbecued with a Chutney
Sauce 147
Jamaican Jerk Barbecued........ 148

TENDERLOIN
Grilled Honey Sesame........... 142
with Wild Mushrooms 141

HAM
Carol Ann's Deli Ham Salad .. 364
French Bistro Ham and
Cheese Sandwich.................. 85
Smoked Holiday with a
Bourbon Mustard Glaze 149

Poultry, *see Chicken*

Puddings

Bread with a Vanilla Bourbon
Sauce 390
Rice, Ollie's Old-Fashioned 389
Yorkshire, Herbed 237
Quesadillas, Smoked Salmon 12

Quiche, *see Eggs*

Rice

ARBORIO
Chicken with Snow Peas 249
Chicken and Artichoke 250
Red Beans and Rice.................... 278
Jazzed-Up Jambalaya 277
Poor Man's Paella 281
Rice Pilaf, Carol Ann's 235
Rice Pudding, Ollie's 389
Salad, with a Medley of Veggies.. 37
Spanish Rice 132

Salad Dressings

Balsamic Vinaigrette 19
Blue Cheese, Carol Ann's........... 11
Caesar 20
Mustard Dressing 25
Raspberry Vinaigrette 23
Sweet-and-Sour 24
Tomato Vinaigrette 28

Salads

Acapulco, Jicama – HealthMark .. 372
Antipasto 365
BEAN
  Black Bean, Corn, and
    Bell Pepper 359
  Green Bean, Jazzed-Up 38
  Three Bean 358
Broccoli 360
Caesar, Carol Ann's 20
CHICKEN
  and Cantaloupe 39
  and Penne Pasta 28
  Chinese Chicken 41
  Luau 40
  Oriental Chicken 374
Cobb, a la Carol Ann 34
Coleslaw, Carol Ann's 361
Cottage Cheese, Crunchy 364
Couscous – HealthMark 373
Crab Louis 366
Cranberry 371
Cucumber Slices in Sour Cream 360
FRUIT
  Cranberry 371
  Heavenly Hash 370
  24-Hour, Pauline's 42
  Waldorf 371
GREEK
  Slaw 361
  Deli Style 357
  Toss It Greek Style 22
Ham, Carol Ann's Deli
  Ham Salad 364
Maui Onion and Tomato 19
PASTA
  Angel Hair and Shrimp 30
  Asian Pasta Primavera 356
  Best Macaroni Salad Ever, The 355
  Grilled Chicken and
    Penne Pasta 28
  My Kids' Favorite Pasta 26
  Shrimp and Angel Hair Pasta,
    Dilled 30
  Spaghetti in a Salad? 27
  The Steele's Original
    Pasta Salad 354
  Three-Cheese Tortellini and
    Veggie Salad 29
Pea Salad with Ham and Cheese. 362
POTATO
  Creamy Potato with Chives 352
  Pauline's 351
  Secret Recipe 353

Rice, with a Medley of Veggies ... 37
Romaine with a Twist 21
Salmon, Blackened 35
Shrimp Warmed in a Tarragon
  Cream Sauce 31
SPINACH
  Special Occasion 23
  with a Mustard Dressing 25
  with a Sweet-and-Sour
    Dressing 24
Taco, Back to the Seventies 33
Turkey, Chunky 366
Tomato, with Maui Onion 19
Vegetable Medley 363

Salsas

Avocado 264
Peach 111
Pineapple 13
Shrimp and Scallop 10
Tomato, Carol Ann's 272
Tomatillo 274

Sandwiches

BEEF
  Cheese Steak 75
  Flank Steak Gyros in
    Pita Bread 77
  Hamburgers, Fourth of July 73
  Homemade Sloppy Joes,
    Carol Ann's 71
  Krautburgers 387
  Shredded Beef and Simmered
    Onion Hoagies 76
  Sirloin Steak, with a
    Horseradish Sauce 74
  Tri-Tip Steak, with a Barbecue
    Sauce 79
BRATWURST
  Ball Park Sausages 72
  Brats 'n Beer 72
Brie, Lover's Picnic Sandwich 84
Cheese, Gourmet Grilled Cheese 78
CHICKEN
  Barbecued on Onion Rolls 80
  Chicken Salad Sandwiches 81
CRAB
  Crab Salad Sandwiches with
    Gruyere Cheese 82
  Picadilly Circles with Crab Salad
    and Tomatoes 82
Ham and Cheese, French Bistro 85
Pastrami, Russ' Reuben 83

Sauces

Crème Anglaise 289
Raspberry 293
Vanilla Bourbon Sauce 390

Selecting Superior Produce 299

Side Dishes

Applesauce, Pauline's
  Homemade 220
Artichokes, Steamed with a
  Lemon Pepper Mayonnaise 219
BEANS
  Baked, Luau 222
  Baked, My Favorite Picnic 223
  Fresh Green with Herbs 220
Bread, Grilled Garlic 226
Broccoli Soufflé 221
Corn on the Cob, Roasted 224
Garlic, Roasted 225
MUSHROOMS
  Grilled Portobello 226
  Stuffed Portobello 227
Pasta, Rotini in an Artichoke
  Butter Sauce 229
Polenta Pie 225
POTATOES
  Brulèe, Golden 231
  Dauphinois 382
  Garlic Mashed, Perfect 230
  Herb Roasted New 230
  Mashed with Jalapeño and
    Cheddar Cheese 232
  Pancakes (Latkes) 383
  Smashed New Red 233
  Twice-Baked 381
Pudding, Herbed Yorkshire 237
Ratatouille 384
Rice Pilaf 235
Squash, Baked Acorn 234
Tomatoes, Grilled 234
Vegetables, Grilled 228
Yams, Old-Fashioned Candied ... 236

Sorbets

Banana 293
Kiwifruit 293

Soups and Stews

BISQUE
  Artichoke Langostino 60
  Tomato with Basil 57
  Lobster 61
  Mushroom 58
  Salmon 59

Broccoli, Cream of 56
Chicken and Noodle,
  Jewish Penicillin 53
CHILI
  Carol Ann's 62
  Chuck Wagon........................... 64
  Vegetable................................. 66
  Western Style 63
  White Bean with Chicken 65
CHOWDER
  Artichoke and Scallop, Easy .. 49
  Chicken 'n Cheese.................. 46
  Clam, Hearty.......................... 50
  Corn, in Warmed Tortilla
    Bowls 48
  Jalapeño Chicken 45
  Scallop, Company's Coming .. 47
Green Chile 263
Onion, French 54
Potato Leek, Cream of............... 55
STEWS
  Beef, Thursdays Tutu 68
  Green Chile............................ 67
  Chuck Steak Stew................... 164
VEGETABLE
  Beef, Auntie Beryl's............... 52
  Portuguese Style 51

Stuffing
Corn Bread with Sausage
  and Jalapeños 125
Oyster, Pauline's Old-Fashioned .. 122
My Favorite Thanksgiving
  Stuffing 123

Turkey
Tips on Buying and Storing
  Turkey........................... 119
Entrée, Thanksgiving Turkey
  Carol Ann's............................. 121
Salad, Chunky Turkey Salad........ 366

Vegetables
ARTICHOKES
  Bisque, Artichoke Langostino 60

Chowder, Easy Artichoke and
  Scallop 49
Pizza, Artichoke and Shrimp .. 88
Pork Chops and Artichokes
  in a Cream Wine Sauce........ 136
Steamed with a Lemon
  Pepper Mayonnaise.............. 219
Arugula, Bow-Tie Pasta with
  Sun-Dried Tomatoes 251
AVOCADO
  Guacamole.............................. 266
  Salsa....................................... 264
BEANS
  Baked, Luau............................. 222
  Baked, My Favorite Picnic 223
  Fresh Green with Herbs 220
  Bean and Beef Burritos 263
Black-Eyed Peas, New Year's
  Day Lucky 279
Red Beans and Rice................... 278
White Beans, Cassoulet 280
White bean, Chili 65
  SALADS
    Black Bean 359
    Green Bean 38
    Three Bean......................... 358
BROCCOLI
  Cream Soup........................... 56
  Salad 360
  Soufflé 221
CABBAGE
  Coleslaw................................. 361
  Greek Slaw 361
Chile Peppers, Chile Rellenos 268
CORN
  Chowder in Warmed
    Tortilla Bowls 48
  on the Cob, Roasted.............. 224
Cucumber Salad 360
Garlic, Roasted.......................... 225
Grilled Vegetables...................... 228
Jicama, Acapulco Salad.............. 372
MUSHROOM
  Bisque 58
  Portobello, Grilled 226
  Portobello, Stuffed................. 227

ONION
  French Onion Soup................. 54
Pea Salad 362
Peppers, Chile Rellenos 268
Pizza, Veggie 87
Platters, Veggie 341
POTATOES
  Cream Soup........................... 55
  Creamy Potato Salad
    with Chives 352
  Dauphinois 382
  Golden Potato Brulèe 231
  Pancakes (Latkes) 383
  Pauline's Potato Salad 351
  Perfect Garlic Mashed 230
  Mashed with Jalapeños and
    Cheddar Cheese 232
  New Potatoes, Herb Roasted 230
  New Potatoes, Smashed 233
  Secret Recipe Potato Salad 353
  Twice-Baked.......................... 381
Ratatouille................................ 384
Skewers, Vegetable 177
SOUPS
  Portuguese Style Vegetable
    Soup 51
  Vegetable Beef, Auntie Beryl's 52
  Vegetable Chili 66
  White Bean Chili with Chicken 65
Squash, Acorn Baked 234
TOMATILLO
  Salsa...................................... 274
TOMATO
  Bisque with Basil 57
  Grilled 234
  Maui Onion and Tomato Salad 19
  Penne with Sausage
    and Tomatoes..................... 253
  Salsa...................................... 272

TOMATOES, SUN-DRIED
  Bow-Tie Pasta with Arugula ... 251
  Yams, Old-Fashioned Candied... 236

Bibliography

BOOKS
Bundy, Beverly. *The Century in Food*.
Portland: Collectors Press, Inc., 2002.

Green, Aliza. *Field Guide to Produce*.
Philadelphia: Quirk Books, 2004.

Herbst, Sharon Tyler. *Food Lover's Companion*. New York: Barron's Educational Series, Inc., 1995.

MAGAZINES
Mathews, Ryan. "Social Change & the Supermarket." *Progressive Grocer* Dec.1996: 29-96.

WEBSITES
www.fsis.usda.gov/oa/pubs

Order Form

CALL TO ORDER TODAY

1-970-223-8128

Penny Lane Press of Colorado
1518 Brentford Lane • Fort Collins, CO 80525-4703
PHONE: (970) 223-8128 • **FAX:** (303) 474-3590
E-MAIL: katescarol@aol.com

NAME: _____

ADDRESS: _____

CITY, STATE & ZIP CODE: _____ **PHONE: (** ____ **)** _____

BOOK TITLE	QUANTITY	PRICE	TOTAL
Secret Recipes from the Corner Market ISBN: 0-9773485-0-4	_____	$28.95 ea.	$ _____

SUBTOTAL	$_____
Colorado Res. Add 3.7% Sales Tax ($1.08 per book)	$_____
Fort Collins Res. Add 6.7% Sales Tax ($1.94 per book)	$_____
Shipping & Handling (see below)	$_____
TOTAL	$_____

CHECK OR MONEY ORDER PAYABLE TO: Penny Lane Press

CREDIT CARD: ☐ Visa ☐ Master Card Full name of card holder _____

CARD NUMBER _____ **EXP. DATE** _____

SIGNATURE _____

Canadian orders must be accompanied by a postal money order in U.S. funds.

SHIPPING AND HANDLING CHARGES ARE:
Priority $9.95 (allow 2 to 3 days)
Book Rate $4.95 (allow 3–5 days)

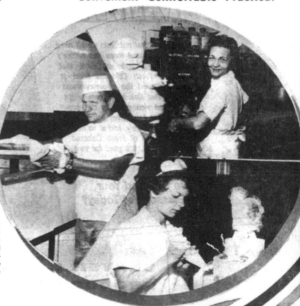